The Laird Rams

The Laird Rams
Britain's Ironclads Built for the Confederacy, 1862–1923

ANDREW R. ENGLISH

McFarland & Company, Inc., Publishers
Jefferson, North Carolina

This book has undergone peer review.

LIBRARY OF CONGRESS CATALOGUING-IN-PUBLICATION DATA

Names: English, Andrew R., author.
Title: The Laird rams : Britain's ironclads built for the Confederacy, 1862-1923 / Andrew R. English.
Other titles: Britain's ironclads built for the Confederacy, 1862-1923
Description: Jefferson, North Carolina : McFarland & Company, Inc., Publishers, 2021 | Includes bibliographical references and index.
Identifiers: LCCN 2021043153 | ISBN 9781476682761 (paperback : acid free paper) ∞
ISBN 9781476643670 (ebook)
Subjects: LCSH: Scorpion (Ironclad)—History. | Wivern (Ironclad)—History. | Armored vessels—Great Britain—History—19th century. | Armored vessels—Great Britain—Design and construction. | United States—History—Civil War, 1861-1865. | Warships—Confederate States of America. | BISAC: HISTORY / Military / Naval | HISTORY / United States / Civil War Period (1850-1877)
Classification: LCC V799 .E54 2021 | DDC 359.8/352—dc23
LC record available at https://lccn.loc.gov/2021043153

BRITISH LIBRARY CATALOGUING DATA ARE AVAILABLE

ISBN (print) 978-1-4766-8276-1
ISBN (ebook) 978-1-4766-4367-0

© 2021 Andrew R. English. All rights reserved

No part of this book may be reproduced or transmitted in any form or by any means, electronic or mechanical, including photocopying or recording, or by any information storage and retrieval system, without permission in writing from the publisher.

Front cover image: 294 and 295 in the Mersey, 1863 (author's collection); Title Font © 2021 Epifantsev/Shutterstock

Back cover image: HMS Scorpion, circa 1898 (author's collection)

Printed in the United States of America

McFarland & Company, Inc., Publishers
Box 611, Jefferson, North Carolina 28640
www.mcfarlandpub.com

Table of Contents

Introduction: The Laird Rams and the Evolution of the Ironclad Warship   1

One. Industry and Innovation: Building the Laird Rams 1862–1863   9

Two. Reluctant Actions: Seizure and Acquisition of the Laird Ironclads 1863–1864   43

Three. Technological Advances and Failings: The Laird Rams in Service 1865–1880   87

Four. Naval Weapons and Power Projection: The Laird Rams on Foreign Station 1874–1923   124

Conclusion. Exit the Ironclad: The Laird Rams in Perspective   157

Glossary of Terms/Abbreviations   159

Chapter Notes   161

Bibliography   189

Index   203

Introduction

The Laird Rams and the Evolution of the Ironclad Warship

The two ironclad sister ships built in England by Lairds shipbuilders of Birkenhead during the American Civil War have been largely overshadowed by another ship built by Lairds, the famous raider C.S.S. *Alabama*. Constructed after the equally famous H.M.S. *Warrior* and predating the ill-fated H.M.S. *Captain* (also a Lairds ship), the Confederate-intended Birkenhead ironclads were built in response to the combat-proven monitors of the Union fleet, yet were more capable of an oceangoing role (at least for coastal warfare) than the low-hulled Union turret warships. As they were nearing completion, the rams became the focus of intelligence gathering and diplomatic maneuver, which ended when the two Birkenhead-built turret ships were acquired by a reluctant government in London. They were quickly forgotten and regarded as failures, but that view is not accurate, and this book will attempt to show both their real worth and full histories.

Advances in naval gun manufacturing led one observer to note: "The ship may be cased with armor which today is shot-proof; but tomorrow it may be pierced with ease by shot or shell thrown by some new iron monster."[1] More than just the new guns, the British press warned that a new projectile would make ironclads like the celebrated *Warrior* and her sister the *Black Prince* obsolete, "and then our ironsides will take their place with Brown Bess among a class of antiquities which will be pronounced rusty."[2] With proper forging techniques, bigger guns could be crafted in the ironmakers' workshops capable of firing a larger powder charge, which could propel a larger projectile at increased velocity and range.[3] Jules Verne would write (in 1863) of the "absurd duel between armor and cannonballs, as to which would resist and which would penetrate." Verne predicted that eventually the projectile would emerge triumphant in this contest he called "a noble rivalry."[4]

Displayed at Woolwich Arsenal on the Thames, is an armored target from that era before steel when iron was supreme. Here was a testament to the transition from the primacy of iron plates to the heavy gun as the ultimate factor in naval warfare. The shield was some twelve inches thick, originally cast in two separate plates, and fitted one below and one above to create a single gunport at the center. The gunport was the obvious aim point for a range test circa 1868. The thick armor was not penetrated, but it was noticeably cracked and scalloped in appearance. The impact from shells and balls distorted the shield, giving the target an appearance more granular, not unlike wet clay. The armor was not dented much, but in some places, it looked as

Cammell Laird Shipyard, Birkenhead, England, 2015 (photograph by author).

though it had been scooped out, as if by hand. The iron was able to keep the shells out ... but, barely. This target, in a way, represents the dilemma faced by naval architects and navies of that era. The experts did not know when the continuous experimentation and exasperating drive to outdo the latest advance in armored construction and competing gunnery progress would end. Iron armor was made ever thicker, and consequently, guns became larger, massive beasts and were appropriately dubbed "monsters." As a result of this industrial race between enough iron to protect and sufficient power to overcome an armored belt, naval architects struggled to create the ultimate ironclad, which was usually superseded by another industrial advance before the ship had been completed by the builders.

The mid-nineteenth century return of the ram as a weapon was, at best, secondary to the heavy gun. The ram added shock power to compensate for the lack of accuracy and muzzle velocity typical of the heavy gun of the early 1860s. The heavy, rifled gun could achieve greater impact when ranges were decreased, and the ram offered a potential battle-winning advantage when contact was made. This combination was dramatically unveiled on 8 March 1862, when the Confederate ironclad *Virginia* drove her bows into the hapless wooden sloop U.S.S. *Cumberland* at Hampton Roads. The salvaged Confederate frigate, remade into an ironclad equipped with heavy guns and an underwater iron prow, threatened to upset the naval balance of power. In the press, the prototypical modern warship briefly became the mastless, steam-driven, iron-shielded, broadside frigate more associated with men-of-war built in the Confederacy. In Britain, *Punch* first depicted an American armorclad

Introduction 3

Woolwich Target, Image 1 (top) and Image 2 (above) (photographs by Sara J. English, 2015).

arriving in the Channel as a casemate ironclad ram, not the low-hulled, turret-equipped *Monitor*.[5]

The naval lessons of the Civil War were ambiguous. The ram, in Confederate service, usually proved to be a successful weapon when contact was made with the hull of a smaller and stationary Union warship. Those events were rare and Confederate armored vessels lacked the speed and maneuverability essential in a fight against superior numbers and in the shallow waters of the rivers and estuaries of the Southern States. Under wartime conditions, the Confederates could only produce a few dozen armored vessels of varying worth. The casemate ironclads, although innovative in design, suffered universal flaws in construction, especially the underpowered engines. One Confederate naval officer referred to these homemade ironclads as "miserable make-shift vessels."[6] Fitted with rams, these Confederate armored casemate warships were too heavy and too slow to drive off (and keep away) Federal steam-propelled frigates, sloops, light auxiliaries, and ironclads contesting their waters. Unlike the ever-changing armor and heavy guns, the ram was limited by the length and weight restrictions of its host. Although some Confederate ironclads were fitted with spar torpedoes, draft prevented their use against their more maneuverable Union adversaries. The Confederate home-built ironclads were both too heavy for effective use against a determined enemy in shallow waters and too unseaworthy for a deep-water role.

The ram was considered a potent weapon by commentators of that era. *Punch* had taken notice of the new naval weapons and, in a sketch, depicted John Bull fitted with a suit of armor. The breastplate was cast as the bow of an ironclad complete with a pointed iron cone, a clear threat to any potential opponent unwise enough to venture too near the determined-looking seafarer.[7] The iron spur was a weapon that reappeared from the annals of ancient warfare only to fade back into irrelevancy when heavy guns became more accurate, steam engines became more reliable, and higher speeds were achieved for these men-of-war. The locomotive torpedo was yet another weapon that doomed the ram. Only when the combination of speed, gunnery and the subsurface threat matured did the dead-end design feature of the ram fade away completely.

Until that time, the Lairds-built armorclads were cutting-edge weapons platforms built in a hurry for a country desperate for anything better than what they had available in home waters. The South needed purpose-built iron vessels of superior workmanship and engineering if it was going to overcome the lag in industrial output. Only the workshops of Britain could offer the capacity to make armored warships that could switch from defensive coastal roles to a more offensive capability.

Construction on the Laird rams began in secret, as the Confederate states urgently needed armored warships to lift the blockade. Early defeats on the battlefield and the incessant manpower demands of the army meant the South was unable to provide vital components for her navy from domestic resources. Stopgaps were attempted but, even with imported British components, the South could not achieve a suitable armored force to effectively defend all key harbors and coastal areas from an expanding Union Navy. The Confederacy needed British expertise and industrial capacity. By 1863, the South no longer had resources or time enough to build up the infrastructure needed to finish an adequate number of ironclads to hold back the Federal juggernaut and lift the blockade. Britain held the logical answer to the dilemma. Based on their reputation for quality workmanship with iron steamers and the expanding industrial capabilities along the Mersey, Lairds was the obvious choice. This firm was so known for its quality of work during this era that Jules Verne wrote that it was this yard (although he referred to them as "Leard") that built the steel hull plates for his mysterious submarine *Nautilus*, featured in his now-classic work of science fiction, *20,000 Leagues Under the Sea*.[8] The French writer mentioned that the fictional submarine was built in secret of components sent to a disguised address.[9] Subterfuge, especially when associated with an advanced weapons system, worked better in the realm of fiction than had been the case with Lairds and the two ironclads built for the South, but the fiction was derived from factual events during the construction efforts of 1862–1863.

The Ships Are Ordered

In 1862, Commander James D. Bulloch, C.S.N. arranged with shipbuilders Lairds to construct two oceangoing ironclads in Birkenhead. The two sisters were identical at 224 feet, 6 inches in length; 42 feet, 4 inches in beam; and protected with a main armor belt of 4½ inches of iron over teak planks. Each had an armament of four 9-inch muzzleloading rifles, which were housed in two turrets (two guns per turret) behind 10 inches of iron plating on the turret faces. Fitted with three masts, sails would (theoretically) assist the steam engines on long voyages. The second ship of the class would be fitted with two experimental tripod masts in an effort to reduce braces and ropes required for the sailing rig and thus allowing for greater arc of fire for the turrets. With a displacement of 2,751 tons, the two engines on each ship were estimated to drive the ironclads at what was then a respectable speed of 11 knots.[10]

Commander Bulloch went to great lengths to arrange the details of a sale to a French firm who was intending to resale the ironclads to Egypt. This was a paperwork blind, but the Union spies, sponsored by American diplomats and supported by wealthy shipowners from Boston and New York, tirelessly followed up every lead and rumor to ferret out the truth. Bulloch's subterfuge was not working. A severe winter had forced Lairds to put up temporary sheds on the site and gas lamps were installed to speed additional work during hours of darkness. Reportedly, the ironclads were intended for Egypt; however, this ruse failed to explain the urgent need for the vessels. Clearly the armored men-of-war were intended for the Southern States. Bulloch worried over the delays, as the "whole character of the work was new, and builders cannot make close calculations; great labor and unexpected time required to bend armor-plates; and the most important part of the work, the riveting, is far more tedious than anticipated."[11]

The hulls were built with a submerged, bulbous, iron ram bow to assist the smashing power of the four heavy guns. The first of the class was to have been commissioned as the C.S.S. *North Carolina*, yet she floated upon the Mersey with the false Egyptian name *El Tousson*. Her sister, the *Mississippi*, was built as hull number 295 and launched on 29 August 1863. She was christened as the Egyptian man-of-war, *El Monassir*.[12]

Confederate Navy Secretary Stephen Mallory put much hope in these ships and stated that "they could restore to us New Orleans."[13] Instead, Bulloch imagined that the armored rams would surprise the inhabitants of Portsmouth, New Hampshire, by bombarding the navy yard there.[14] Frank J. Merli writes in *The Alabama, British Neutrality, and the American Civil War* that among historians, the consensus holds that the Laird rams did not represent as great a crisis in U.S. affairs with Britain as had the Trent Affair. This view is too dismissive of the slower-building crisis over the Laird rams. Merli's statement is based, in part, on a weaker U.S. Navy in 1861, and it also fails to take into account the well-developed northern intelligence network in operation in Britain by 1863. Although the crisis over the Birkenhead rams was not as immediate as had been the Trent affair, it was a dangerous time when a diplomatic miscalculation or overreaction could have produced damaging consequences.

In Richmond, Virginia, one newspaper wrote of "bright visions ... conjured up of the blockade broken and the enemy's cities bombarded" when the rams appeared off the North American coast.[15] These hopes were dashed through the candid letters sent by the United States Minister to the Court of St. James, Charles Francis Adams, to the Foreign Secretary, Earl John Russell. The loopholes in British neutrality laws, chiefly the Foreign Enlistment Act of 1819, did not prevent the sale of men-of-war and armaments to a non-combatant nation. Regarding the seeming inability of the British government to prevent the impending departure of these two armored rams from the

Mersey, Adams issued his famous demarche to Lord Russell: "It would be superfluous in me to point out to your Lordship that this is war."[16] Adams overstepped his position by continuing to preach to Lord Russell when he wrote, "If Her Majesty's Government have not the power to prevent the harbors and towns of a friendly nation from being destroyed by vessels built by British subjects, and equipped, manned, and dispatched from her harbors ... then all international obligations, whether implied or expressed, are not worth the paper on which they are written."[17]

Russell would reply to Adams, "There are passages in your letter ... that plainly and repeatedly imply an intimidation of hostile proceeding towards Great Britain on the part of the Government of the United States unless steps are taken." Russell's response was firm when he stated that Her Majesty's government would not "overstep the limits of the law" and warned it "will not shrink from any consequences of such an action." Adams quickly apologized and allowed the issue of the Laird rams to run their course through Whitehall without additional drumbeats of war.[18] London ordered Treasury officials to seize the two rams on 9 October 1863 after it was feared that foreign agents would stage a "forcible abduction" of the *El Tousson* while she was underway from Birkenhead on her anticipated trial run.[19]

As Howard J. Fuller demonstrates in his work *Clad in Iron*, Lairds and other privately owned shipyards provided both industrial capacity and a pool of skilled labor that the Royal Dockyards could not surpass.[20] The British government needed Lairds and could not afford to alienate them. The acquisition of the two rams would strengthen the Royal Navy by denying them to the other power that had wanted to purchase them—the United States. Prime Minister Lord Palmerston had warned the First Lord of the Admiralty, stating, "If the Federals get them they will strengthen the Yankees against us if they should be disposed and able next year to execute their threatened vengeance for all the Forbearance we have shewn [*sic*] them; if we get these Ships they will give us Moral as well as maritime strength."[21] The confiscation of the armored sister ships was resolved with a purchase by the Treasury to prevent their entering service for the Confederate Navy. The seizure also prevented additional damage to the already strained relations with the United States. After months of legal arguments, the Admiralty acquired the two incomplete vessels on 8 August 1864.[22]

Fuller also contends the Laird rams were purchased for the Royal Navy not merely in response to Union diplomatic pressure, but to augment the number of British ironclads available to counter other potential threats, especially from France. The additional need to strengthen the fleet against a French buildup was well-expressed in James P. Baxter's classic *The Introduction of the Ironclad Warship*. Regarding the mid–1860s state of European armorclad design, Baxter points out that the advantage regarding "compactness, and homogeneousness would be on the side of France—individual power on the side of England—a superiority—nowhere."[23]

The Lairds-built armored rams have been given less attention by historians; indeed, they are almost always mentioned with the *Alabama* and in terms of the U.S. diplomatic efforts to halt their acquisition by the Confederacy. When the two sister ironclads are mentioned, the information is confused, and the assessments are usually brief and almost universally indifferent. In his 1984 overview, *The Fighting Ship in the Royal Navy AD 897–1984*, E.H.H. Archibald summarized their service in a few lines: "They had been acquired for the wrong reasons, and there was no really useful role for them to play."[24] Others were not so quick to condemn. Writing during the time when they were still in service, Captain S. Eardley-Wilmot, R.N., gave a more complimentary assessment, claiming that had they gone to sea under the command of an experienced Confederate officer, "skillfully handled, they should have made short work of the Northern monitors, to which in all points of construction they were greatly superior."[25]

In Service

Both Lairds-built ironclads were purchased for the Royal Navy with the H.M.S. *Scorpion* commissioned first and the second ram hoisted her pennant later that month (October 1865) as H.M.S. *Wivern*.[26] They were valuable additions to the armored squadrons of the Royal Navy but were poorly adapted to a blue water role. The *Wivern* was the first of the sisters to have any activity of note when in October 1867, she sent a boat crew to Holyhead to search for members of a Fenian plot.[27]

Several years later, the Laird rams were already outclassed and ill-suited for work in home waters. The noted naval architect Edward J. Reed remarked (in 1869) that the *Scorpion* and *Wivern* were considered "the weakest of our armorclad fleet ... have never exceeded 10 knots at their very best." Despite this claim, the *Scorpion* was able to slightly outpace her sister as she reached 10½ knots on at least one occasion. Their flat bottoms, which were more suited for operations off the American coasts or on the Mississippi River, made them "bad sailors" as they "rolled up to 27 degrees each way in a heavy sea."[28] The turret ship was less compatible with sails and rigging than the broadside ironclad and this merger slowly fell away as the two Laird rams were reshaped with almost every trip they made to the dockyard, especially in their early years.

As other ships entered service, the Laird rams were assigned duties as coastal defense vessels. The *Scorpion* was first to leave British waters, steaming (sometimes under tow of an escort) to her new home in Bermuda in 1869.[29] In early 1880, the *Wivern* was ordered to Hong Kong due to problems with Russia over Russian border tensions with China. *Wivern* left Devonport, steamed up the channel and anchored at Spithead to correct "defects in her machinery" and to be fitted to carry two 2nd-class torpedo boats. She would not receive the boats or extra equipment needed by them as the boats added too much weight to the low-hulled ironclad.[30] Edward Reed was quick to warn that "the Wivern is utterly unfit to carry extra top-weight of any kind" and the Admiralty sensibly put the torpedo boats aside on her outbound voyage. The naval architect continued to force his opinions when he publicly stated, "for general service in China waters she is, in my opinion, dangerously unfit."[31] Nevertheless, the Laird rams had been modified several times since their first commissioning in 1865. Bulloch stated that he had "designed these ships for something more than harbor or even coast defense" and based in the colonies they would get more of a chance at occasional active service to prove their worth.[32]

Historians regard the Laird rams as unsatisfactory men-of-war, but they were only partial failures and at that, primarily for only the first years of their existence. Archibald's comments that they entered service with the Royal Navy for the "wrong reasons" and they had "no really useful role" is flawed on both counts.[33] The ships were acquired "for prudent reasons," as their procurement by Britain prevented a serious breach with the United States at the height of the Civil War.[34] As Eardley-Wilmot noted, the Laird rams were "superior" (in construction) to the Union monitors, and in this sense gave the Royal Navy a qualitative seagoing edge relative to the Federal turret ships, but also in regards to the French fleet.[35]

Not originally intended to fly the White Ensign, the Laird rams were the first of over a dozen armored ships constructed in British yards to foreign orders but acquired by the Royal Navy during times of international tensions. Oscar Parkes criticized the Laird rams as "among the worst of the bad bargains."[36] Referring to a time when the rams were under construction (1863–1864), Stanley Sandler claimed the ironclads were of "very problematical worth."[37] He also claimed these sister ships were "useless away from protected waters" but affirmed that the roles the Confederacy intended for these vessels (breaking the blockade and coastal operations) were "admirable."[38] These assessments need further qualification. When originally acquired, the Laird rams did not perform well in the fleet, but when utilized in a role more suited to their original design characteristics, they proved up to the tasks. They were not ideal ironclads, but they did provide useful service far longer than larger, more expensive armored vessels from that time.

Intended for another country's navy, the Laird rams never fired a shot in anger and served in a Royal Navy which never had a clear, active-duty role for them. Despite this, they stood watch at the distant fortress bases, ready for service in a significant, but largely forgotten role as coastal defenders at distant points of the British Empire.

One

Industry and Innovation

*Building the Laird Rams
1862–1863*

The two Lairds armorclads, built from 1862 to 1865, reflected concepts of naval power in transition, from the broadside of multiple guns to the rotating armored gun platform with only a few pieces of ordnance. During these years, the ironclad was a new innovative weapons system armed with guns of increasing size and ballistic power. The design of ironclad men-of-war was understood during these years to represent what had been termed a "revolution" in naval affairs. The standards of what constituted sufficient armor and superior firepower were rapidly changing, and governments searched to create a suitable ironclad design that could "stand such shot as improved science will bring to bear against them."[1] The Lairds-built armored vessels were bold attempts to answer that design dilemma.

The Lairds ironclads were built around offensive concepts for warships at that time: the ram and the turret. The sister ironclads were a manifestation of both innovative designs and compromises, packed into what was then considered to be a moderate-sized hull.[2] They were hybrid men-of-war, designed and built for a Confederate Navy desperate for effective armored vessels. The builder, though highly experienced in the art of iron shipbuilding, improvised as construction on the two vessels progressed. Confederate and Union officials in Europe also adapted to circumstances by using legal precedent and subterfuge to accelerate or stop the building of these potentially decisive warships.[3]

Rarely mentioned by historians, and usually only in the context of the Civil War, these two sister ironclads have been dismissed, largely based upon limited accounts of their early years. Yet they were game changers, not only in terms of a potential fight against armored warships, but also for technological advancement and the precedent they offered for international relations. They were "first" in several aspects of the development of the ironclad warship, both during their building stage and later during subsequent refits.

These armored vessels, built by Lairds of Birkenhead, were intended to buy time for the beleaguered Confederacy during the Civil War and would have complicated the Federal prosecution of the conflict. Because of this, completion and planned deployment of these warships was pursued by the Confederate Navy with skill and urgency, while the Union sought all diplomatic means to prevent their acquisition by the determined foe.

The Laird rams were of vital importance for both the North and the South, and the Union efforts to block their sortie from the Mersey estuary strained relations between London and Washington to the breaking point. Union Navy Secretary Gideon Welles received reports that caused "serious apprehensions" among some of his admirals on blockade duty over fears the Lairds-built armorclads should leave the Mersey under Confederate colors.[4] The fears were justified as Confederate Navy Secretary Stephen Mallory intended to use the vessels to raise the blockade, and at the outbreak of the war, regarded the procession of "an iron-armored ship as a matter of the first necessity."[5]

Completed in 1865, the two Laird ironclad rams were seen as failures. Reed described them as being perhaps the poorest examples of British armored vessels.[6] The comparison was made largely against broadside ships, as the Laird armorclads were considered when building to have "possessed a combination of qualities."[7] The qualities and shortcomings of the two turret rams would come to light during their sea trials, subsequent voyages, and refits in the late 1860s, but they were among the first seagoing turret ships built, and represented a bold evolutionary step for warship design. The experience gained by Lairds during the construction of the rams also advanced Britain's technological edge over France during the ironclad race between the two powers in the early to mid–1860s.[8]

Indeed, the Lairds armorclads were failures, but only as they were originally (and incompletely) constructed. A more inclusive answer needs episodic qualification as the ships were adapted to new weapons and role changes throughout their service lives. This chapter will attempt to illustrate efforts to build, under some secrecy, two of the most advanced warships of the 1860s.

These two warships were known in both the American and British press as the "Laird rams," but that description is somewhat of a misnomer.[9] The first portion of the identifier is correct and without contention, for they were built by the Lairds shipyard of Birkenhead and incorporated design features from those master shipbuilders. The pair of Lairds armored vessels were blends of innovative design features merged with more accepted forms of propulsion and weapons. The Confederates selected Lairds to build the two warships primarily for two factors: location and reputation.

In the mid-nineteenth century, Britain was the determining factor in terms of finance and industrial products necessary to fight a modern war. By 1860, Britain produced 53 percent of the world's iron, 50 percent of its coal, and took in almost half of the raw cotton produced globally

Gideon Welles, U.S. Secretary of the Navy, 1861 (Library of Congress).

Stephen R. Mallory, Confederate Secretary of the Navy, 1861 (Library of Congress).

for her cloth mills.[10] Britain was acknowledged as the leading industrial and mercantile power, with economists referring to her as the center of global trade. Britain's markets and financial houses held the world's purse strings and her industries had the capacity to build and transport every deadly instrument for the arsenals and navies of both the North and the South. This was certainly true for warship construction, and the Southern States sent agents to Britain to acquire men-of-war in the shortest possible time.

Confederate flag officer Josiah Tattnall served as the commander of a hodgepodge of requisitioned tugs, packet steamers and the few underpowered ironclads outfitted and armed to defend the Confederacy's Carolina and Georgia coasts, and confided to a visiting British journalist during the war, "Long before the South has a fleet to cope with the North, my bones will be whitening in the grave."[11]

British shipyards and factories had the means, both in terms of capacity and skilled hands, to make up for what the secessionists lacked. British neutrality laws were also less strict than were those of France, as French subjects were prohibited from assisting with the armament of a warship intended for either of the American belligerents in "*any manner whatever.*"[12] The ambiguity of British legal definitions of what constituted equipment and armament left the door open for the Southerners to seek out shipbuilding contracts in the leading industrial nation on earth. The French were expanding their dockyard capabilities but, as one Confederate Naval officer noted, "A practical man who wanted a first-class ship and engines, or a large quantity of well-made arms for quick delivery, or a batch of great guns in which he could feel confidence, or any heavy iron or steel work, would almost instinctively come to England to supply his want."[13]

The major British iron shipbuilders had a clear advantage of established reputations based upon long-nurtured mechanical skills. London was a major shipbuilding center; however, the real strength lay in the builders' yards near the coal and iron ore further north. Rail rates for transporting coal and iron were high, yet labor costs were lower in other parts of Britain than in the south of England. The advantages in experience and reputation, which had long proven beneficial to the yards and workshops on the Thames, changed in the mid–1850s with the advances in iron shipbuilding. London's specialized shipbuilding trade unions were slower to adapt to changes in iron manufacture.[14] The linkage between shipping, rail, and manufacturing firms in closer proximity to the coal fields cast Merseyside to the forefront. The region offered an enticing list of capabilities for the Americans (both Confederate and Union) interested in ships and equipment for their navies and weapons for their armies.[15] Shipyards on the Thames were not an option for the Confederate Navy's ironclad program, as the shipyards were too close to the U.S. Mission in London and Union spies could too readily gain access to any ship under construction on the river.[16] Unlike the commerce raiders, armored warships could not be disguised as merchant vessels while under construction.

The shipbuilders on the Thames created quality vessels for the higher prices charged, but another factor prevented their selection by the Confederates. London had a higher proportion of shipwrights skilled in wooden shipbuilding and smaller numbers of boilermakers and ironworkers. The yards in other areas of the United Kingdom could build iron ships faster than the highly unionized shipbuilders of London.[17] Time was a crucial factor for the Confederates, and they were willing to sacrifice some issues of quality in favor of having an armored warship ready for service at the earliest possible moment.

Selecting Lairds

The Lairds shipyard was an ideal choice to build ironclad warships as they were early pioneers of iron steamship construction, and remained innovators in the trade during the era. Beginning as a boilermaker in 1824, the grandfather of the clan, William Laird, expanded into iron shipbuilding five years later.[18] One of the first iron steamers in the United States, the *John Randolph*, was purchased in 1834 from Lairds for use around Savannah.[19] The engine was built in Liverpool by Fawcett, Preston and Company and shipped to America with the hull sections of the *Randolph*.[20] The sections of the "well arranged" hull were made from rolled boiler plate, fitted together by a five-man work crew sent out by the shipbuilder to create the 100 foot long vessel.[21] This utilization of boiler plate, and similar construction techniques, revealed a natural progression of Lairds from the manufacturer of boilers into the field of iron shipbuilding. The success of the *Randolph* prompted her owner, G.B. Lamar, to acquire two more iron steamboats from Lairds in 1836.[22] Lairds established its reputation in America as a premier builder of the most modern steamships to be had. This reputation would grow beyond Savannah as more clients recognized the durability of the iron-hulled steamship.

In 1839, the British government ordered its first iron-hulled steamship, the packet *Dover*, from Lairds shipyard, which was officially known as the Birkenhead Iron Works.[23] The iron-hulled steamer/auxiliary gunboat *Nemesis* was built by the shipyard, somewhat in secret, in 1840 for the Bengal Marine of the East India Company. Begun in a likely speculative venture before she was acquired for Indian service, the then-largest iron vessel in the world was sold in what one writer described as "a piece of inspired salesmanship" and provided vital gunfire in the First Opium War.[24] Additionally, the *Nemesis* served as proof that Lairds could discreetly build warships that could influence decisive outcomes in distant waters against a numerically superior enemy.[25] After over two years of service in Chinese and Indian waters, the *Nemesis* docked in Bombay and her hull was examined. Although the iron plates of her flat bottom were dented and some were bent inward several inches as a result of striking rocks and occasionally going aground, she remained remarkably seaworthy. Despite the mishaps, her six watertight compartments had contributed to her strength and durability on distant coasts. An official report stated the *Nemesis* remained "as tight as a bottle."[26]

In the tense aftermath of the Texas Revolution, Lairds built the 778-ton iron warship *Guadalupe* for Mexico in 1842.[27] The ship sailed for Mexico with British officers and crew and in so doing, presented the British government with a legal dilemma contrary to the neutrality law enacted by Parliament in 1819. Mexico and Texas had become rivals as a result of an ill-defined border between the two republics, and the Laird ship, along with another iron-hulled steamer built in London (both vessels had British crews), gave Mexico a qualitative naval superiority. This issue was resolved due to the client failing to adhere to the financial terms of the contracts. The ships were transferred to British owners before they reached the waters of the Gulf of Mexico following repossession due to non-payment.[28]

The Royal Navy laid down its first iron-hulled frigate from Lairds, but she would not enter service in her intended role. This ship was commissioned in 1846 as a troopship after the Admiralty became uneasy over the use of an iron hull in a man-of-war.[29] Beginning with gunnery experiments against the small iron steamer *Ruby* at Portsmouth that year, cannon fire had proven (for the moment) that iron did not have sufficient durability to withstand shot at close range. Wooden hulls received damage, but timbers could be easily replaced. Early iron hull plates used in the target ship were "open and very jagged" following shots from 32-pound smoothbore muzzleloaders (SBML) and 8-inch guns, which had raked the *Ruby* from end to end. The guns "so tore the ribs and plates that it was evident that a similar vessel so situated would be in danger of being instantly sunk by one well directed shot."[30]

Lairds would build their frigate-turned-troopship to the best standards of modern iron construction then available. In spite of her iron construction, the ill-fated H.M.S. *Birkenhead* sank on 27 February 1852 after striking rocks at the aptly named Danger Point on the Cape of Good Hope, resulting in the loss of over 400 lives.[31] It was later determined that modifications to convert her for duties as a troopship had weakened her iron structure and contributed to her rapid break up on the rocky coast of South Africa. Openings were cut into the bulkheads "to make more easy the passage from compartment to compartment in the hold."[32]

This tragedy did not severely damage the reputation of the shipbuilder on the Mersey and almost 300 vessels, many of iron hulls, had been built by the Laird family from 1829 to 1861.[33] Lairds had expanded briefly across the Mersey and took on another Liverpool yard at Dingle in order to build mortar vessels for the Royal Navy during the Crimean War (1854–56). This temporary move was in response to the Birkenhead facility being remade into a more complete shipbuilding operation, purpose-built for the limited riverfront space available.[34] The designs of London architect James Abernethy recast the Birkenhead yard with four graving docks and a gridiron platform, which allowed repair of ships at low tide when space was not available in the docks.[35] New workshops, 600 feet by 60 feet, were erected during the Crimean War and lined the outer confines of the shipyard.[36] The workshops were "requisite for carrying on the business of building and repairing ships of iron and wood, and of making boilers and repairing machinery."[37] By 1861, the privately held Lairds shipyard had arguably become "the most complete of the kind in the country" and had grown into an important shipbuilder employing 3000 men, complete with workshops that manufactured boilers and marine engines of 80 to 450 horsepower.[38] The shipyard was a late entry into the field of marine engine manufacture, and did not produce its first steam engines for ships made at their adjoining slipways until 1857.[39] One noted civil engineer remarked in 1866 of his colleagues that men of John Laird's type "had to acquire our professional knowledge as best we could, often not till it was wanted for immediate use, generally in haste and precariously, and merely to fulfill the purpose of the hour."[40]

The men who built iron-hulled ships, boilers, and steam engines to propel them learned by doing. This knowledge was won through application of the shipbuilders' arts, business acumen, and the special ability to lead the thousands employed. Rising costs and constrained construction schedules brought on by iron shipbuilding moved Lairds to embrace new methods in labor-saving machines while simultaneously maintaining the benefits of a hands-on management style. One account hailed the owners/operators of this shipyard as reaching a point of achievement, which placed them second to none in the United Kingdom. When compared to other shipyards in Britain, this Merseyside industrial hive was renowned for craftsmanship and was recognized by the British government and foreign customers for the iron steamers it built.[41] By the middle of the nineteenth century, private shipbuilders in Britain achieved an advantage when securing Admiralty contracts. Although the work was divided between commercial shipbuilders and the Royal dockyards, "at all times a part only of the naval tonnage of Britain was built in the Royal dockyards; the rest of the construction was let out by contract to private firms."[42]

The spirit of constant improvements in shipbuilding and management methods made Lairds a shipbuilder sought by both American combatants. By mid–1861, it was apparent that the Civil War would not be over after a short, single campaign. That year the Laird sons, William, John the younger, and Henry, had assumed day-to-day operations at the shipyard as their father took his seat as the Liberal MP for Birkenhead. John Laird had retired from shipbuilding to support local projects and had stood for Parliament, winning his seat in December 1861.[43] This was the city Laird and his family had been the driving force in recreating from a collection of villages into a manufacturing center.[44] By mid-century, Birkenhead was "the city of the future with expectations which the reality by no means disappointed."[45] A planned municipality complete with parks, sewers and gas lines put in before the streets, houses, and shops, this booming, shipbuilding city was—second to much larger Liverpool—the other contributor to Merseyside. The expansion of shipbuilding, manufacturing, and trade on both sides of the river was termed "the grandest monument which the nineteenth century has erected to the genius of Commerce and Peace."[46]

Commerce would take precedent over peace and Lairds had honed their skills in order to build warships for both the Admiralty and others. Lairds was chosen to build the Confederacy's pair of sister ironclads not only due to their reputation for expert craftsmanship and business skills, but also for their willingness to work with the secessionists. They also had the ability, as demonstrated by the *Nemesis*, to work in secrecy.[47] The Lairds-owned Birkenhead Ironworks was the obvious choice. However, an experience gap existed which had been overlooked when construction began in 1862. Lairds had never completed an armored warship before this contract.[48]

Securing the Contract

The Laird family business was too proficient to be ignored without consequences, and the contract was an avenue for influence with industrial leaders as well as with some government elites in Britain. Through financial arrangements with British industrial concerns, the warring Americans could link key leaders in Britain to their cause or deny access to their opponent. This bitter lesson was to be learned by the Union after Confederate purchasing agents in Britain secured contracts with key manufacturers early in the war.

John Laird, 1861 (author's collection).

The Union was first out of the blocks, but stumbled badly in the race to acquire British-built men-of-war. Assistant Secretary of the U.S. Navy Gustavus Vasa Fox supported the idea of building two double-turreted ironclads in Britain with which the Federal Navy could attack the key South Carolina port of Charleston.[49] This plan was relayed through John T. Howard of New York, who had approached Lairds to seek their estimates. Fox proposed a pair of ironclads that would be equipped with two revolving turrets and protected by iron plates 4½ inches thick on each low-hulled vessel. The turrets, or "towers" as he called them, would house a single 11-inch gun in each, fitted to a hull that had a proposed length of 205 feet, a beam of 47 feet, and a draft not to exceed 14 feet, later reduced to 12 feet. The ironclad as envisioned was "not a sea boat," but was intended as an oceangoing floating battery.[50]

These armored vessels were to have a deliberately low-hull height above water in order to present a harder target for the gunners of Confederate forts and shore batteries. The Fox-Howard ironclads were designed as mastless steamers and were equipped with one rudder at the bow and another at the stern to ensure steering, even if one section was damaged by shellfire. These were not defenseless iron steamers devoid of armament. Resembling a New York ferryboat, these armorclads were designed to get into a contested harbor and return without having to come about if mauled by enemy batteries. In Charleston, Confederate defenses were positioned as close as 300 yards from the main channel, but these twin rudder ironclads would have been able to go astern and quickly maneuver away from the guns if the action was too mauling.[51]

The Assistant Secretary wanted them "finished complete, with guns and everything appertaining."[52] The letters from Fox to Howard and his subsequent discussions with Lairds clearly revealed that a British shipbuilder was asked to build two men-of-war for a belligerent, not to provide unarmed iron-hulled vessels that could be converted into warships once acquired by the United States Navy.[53] The eldest of the Laird brothers, William, traveled to New York and arrived on the Cunarder *Persia* on 21 May 1861, with the intention of securing a contract to build two ironclads for the government in Washington.[54] The attempt failed.

Had Fox engaged William Laird to build ships for the United States in those uncertain days in the summer of 1861, the Birkenhead Iron Works would have had a contractual obligation to the North. The Assistant Secretary had given in to pressure from Welles to have a fleet of armored ships built only in the United States as the Navy Department was pressured by Congress to support Union shipbuilders. Washington lost its best opportunity to kill off the Confederate Navy's efforts in Britain before they matured into custom-built cruisers and the much more dangerous ironclad rams.[55] Had the Union utilized a few contracts to keep shipyards such as Lairds busy with orders for Federal armored warships, the Confederates would have been frozen out of the British ironclad market, or at the very least greatly constricted, as Lairds was already engaged with an Admiralty contract and had building capacity for a few more ironclads during the early to mid–1860s.[56]

In that era, business relationships were considered confidential undertakings and governments only reluctantly intervened. Lairds would later claim, "It is a rule well recognized in all Trading Establishments, that an Order whilst under Execution is the property of the person giving it, and that a builder has no right to make public the orders or instructions of his employers."[57] John Laird, the senior member of the shipbuilding firm (until 1861), was to state that contract negations were "of a confidential character" and his decision to keep that confidence was also influenced by what he termed in 1863 "the present state of law in America."[58] Lairds was anxious to protect their American clients (both Confederate and Union) from American prosecution.

Despite the blockade, the relationships between the representatives of the Confederate government in Britain, key shipowners/financiers like Liverpool-based George Trenholm (a native of South Carolina), and Merseyside merchants and shipbuilders served the South well in the laissez-faire approach to business then prevalent.[59] Where the North was restricted by too much bureaucratic oversight and interference, the Confederate agents in Liverpool had a free hand to make contracts and allow the merchants and shipbuilders to speculate in the arms trade with only minimal direction from the Confederate government in Richmond, Virginia. By early 1862, Southern agents had successfully linked Lairds with the Confederacy for the duration of the war. The Union would pay a heavy price for delay and official Washington intransigence.

James D. Bulloch was the Confederate Navy's key officer assigned to Britain. His desk was located at the offices of the Southern shipping and financial magnate

George Trenholm, at 10 Rumford Place near the Liverpool waterfront.[60] This office was the epicenter of Confederate operations in both Britain and continental Europe. The selection of Bulloch as the Confederate Navy's purchasing agent was perhaps the best foreign posting made by the Southerners during the war. As a former lieutenant in the peacetime U.S. Navy, Bulloch had gained experience in American men-of-war, merchantmen, and select mail steamers on scheduled runs from New York.[61] After resigning his commission, he rose rapidly in the merchant marine to command steamers along the eastern and Gulf coasts of the United States.[62] In December 1861, Bulloch, having joined the new Confederate Navy, led the Greenock-built steamer *Fingal* through the blockade with stands of Enfield rifles, pistols, gunpowder, medicines, blankets, sabers, and four cannon: enough arms to equip a division.[63] At no time during the remainder of the war was a cargo of weapons and military supplies in such quantity ever again shipped through the blockade.[64]

While in Savannah, Bulloch saw the river steamers, in the service of the Confederate Army, conveying men and supplies to the fortifications down river. One such iron-hulled vessel was the vintage *Chatham*, another Lairds-built steamer still in operation after over twenty years of service.[65] Bulloch had to only look over the side of the *Fingal* to see efficient and dependable examples of that iron shipbuilder's art. Lairds was a preferred choice for the Confederate Navy's chief purchasing agent in Britain even before his return. Bulloch's attention to duty, his discretion, and his drive for results made him irreplaceable for the Confederate war effort. He would never again go to sea in the service of the South, neither through fault nor failure, but as the cost of his success in the *Fingal* and subsequent efforts in Britain.

The Liverpool merchants, A.E. Byrne & Co., were the go-betweens who introduced Bulloch to shipbuilders and brokers.[66] Andrew and Thomas Byrne assisted Bulloch in obtaining ships and contracts for his blockade runners, cruisers, and armorclads.[67] Andrew Byrne had purchased the *Fingal* for Bulloch, and they were paid a 1 percent commission by Lairds for the contract to build the Rebel cruiser, C.S.S.

Commander James Bulloch, CSN, 1865.

Alabama.⁶⁸ Although their role is not fully understood, A.E. Byrne & Co. may have introduced Bulloch to the Lairds when he first came to Liverpool. Byrne & Co. were also paid a commission by Lairds (likely a higher rate than that for the more conventional *Alabama*) when the Birkenhead firm secured the contract to build the two rams for the Confederacy.⁶⁹ The amount of commission paid by Lairds to Byrne & Co. for the two Bulloch armorclads is unknown, but in 1870 the Dutch Consul in Liverpool, Mr. J.W.S. May, brought legal action against Lairds for their failure to pay him a 2½ percent commission for the Dutch turret ship *Prins Hendrik Der Nederlanden* and other smaller coastal ironclads the Birkenhead shipbuilder was engaged to build for the Royal Netherlands Navy.⁷⁰

During the Civil War, the closely attuned interdependent merchants on Merseyside proved to be a valuable source of expertise for the Confederacy. Access to both key industrial leaders and material needed for the war effort proved to be a pivotal diplomatic, and especially mercantile, victory for the South. Without these business agreements, which were nearly as ironclad as the armored ships themselves, Lairds and their associates would not have become as dependent on the South for their profits as they eventually came to be. Washington lost leverage just as the Confederate gained their desperately needed entrée to British shipyards and factories. The Birkenhead Iron Works proved to be a vital link to the chain of access. In May 1861, Mallory obtained permission from the Congress of the Southern States, then meeting in Montgomery, Alabama, to construct armored vessels in Britain or France.⁷¹ Mallory intended the armored vessels to be equipped with Armstrong breechloaders, but he informed Bulloch the armament required careful investigation and if the breechloaders were not suitable, then other guns of "equal merit" could be substituted.⁷²

Following the Battle of Hampton Roads in March 1862, Bulloch entered into a contract with the Laird brothers for the construction of two armored rams at a cost of £93,750 each.⁷³ The timing of the Lairds contract was ironic as it was influenced by Bulloch more than by the battle between the American ironclads. The contract was signed soon after Bulloch's return to Britain following his voyage on the *Fingal*, which had been his priority, as previous instructions from Mallory ordered him to deliver the urgently needed supplies to Savannah.⁷⁴

The design of the ironclads had been modified from William Laird's proposed armored men-of-war first offered to the Union in 1861. Each ship was now designed with a length of 224½ feet, a beam of 42½ feet and a draft of 15½ feet forward, increasing to 17 feet aft with engines, coal, guns, equipment and supplies loaded. The hull and armor weighed 1870 tons, with armor alone comprising almost a sixth of that amount. Equipment comprised another 860 tons for a total displacement, when all combined, of 2,750 tons.⁷⁵ Armor plate 4½ inches thick protected the sides of the vessels with thinner 3-inch plates forward comprising the bow and 2-inch plates aft for the stern. The armor belt descended 3¼ feet under the waterline and provided extra protection against enemy shot or attack by a ram. Teak added to the already robust design with thick 10-inch planks on the sides and 8-inch planks providing backing at the bow and stern.⁷⁶

Each ship was heavier than the original 1861 design, and the concept for their employment had also changed. No longer intended to force their way into Charleston harbor around the forts guarding the entrance, these ironclads were modeled with a new objective. The Laird ironclads were refashioned to attack Federal warships near the American coasts and to raise the blockade of Southern ports. Attacking land defenses was now but a secondary consideration and these armorclads were built to stand up to the Union monitors then coming down the ways.

The Laird sons had a flair for ship design. William headed the drawing department at his father's yard, but the other brothers would soon take over crucial positions in the firm as the business grew. During the Crimean War, John the younger visited friends in Marseilles, also observed French builders in Toulon, and would later copy some of their business practices.[77] Henry was the principal design talent, having apprenticed in the drawing department of the French yard of Messagerie Maritimes (also known as the Messagerie Imperiales) of La Ciotat near Marseilles.[78] Although the shipyard was described as "nothing warlike ... a mere shipyard of an ordinary kind" after the Crimean War, it was visited by a Russian engineer who was on a mission to observe its operations in order to obtain ideas for the redevelopment of a shipyard in Russia.[79]

The La Ciotat facility did not remain "ordinary," and by early 1859 was developing an iron shield designed to protect the single cannon and the men for each of the eleven light gunboats it was constructing for the French government.[80] The shield of armored plates moved with the gun as it rotated on a swivel platform, and the oval iron "shed" was designed to deflect enemy shot. The mechanism that rotated the gun shield was itself armored, and its separate iron cap was designed to turn when struck and thus not fully absorb the impact of a direct hit.[81]

These French ideas for a rotating iron gun shield were undoubtedly observed by Henry Laird, who incorporated this design knowledge into his work when he returned to Britain. He took over the drawing department of the Birkenhead Iron Works from William after his return from the Continent, and it was probably he who was instrumental in designing and modifying plans of the armored ships that would later become Bulloch's rams.[82] The willingness to apprentice and collect data on French shipbuilding practices gave the Lairds a keen appreciation of the rapidly changing aspects of their art and an insight into the latest building techniques.[83]

The British press remarked on the flurry of activity at the Birkenhead Iron Works, confusing a suspected Confederate cruiser (later named the *Alabama*) with an ironclad Lairds had under construction. In 1862, the *Sheffield Independent* observed:

> It had been known for some time that a large and powerful iron vessel was being constructed at the dockyard of Messrs. Laird, Birkenhead; but monsters of the deep are so much the order of the day at this establishment that no one troubled his head much about this new production, or cared to remark the extra thickness of the plates which were being used.[84]

Although the newspaper did not give particulars of the warship under construction, the headline clearly identified her intended customer as the Confederacy.[85]

Bulloch was fortunate as he had contracted with a yard daily gaining experience in the art of armored warship construction. The practice of differing paces of work was not usual in British shipyards during the nineteenth century in order to satisfy the more profitable foreign contracts.[86] The work on an armored warship intended for the Royal Navy provided the Birkenhead Iron Works with a large work force, which could flex to speed up work on the two armored turret ships intended for Bulloch. The armored ship ordered by the Admiralty was allegedly delayed to advance the work on the two smaller ironclads. The work on Admiralty contracts in private shipyards was reported in the British press as "subordinate" to the work on foreign contracts and lesser iron projects such as bridge work.[87] Lairds were allegedly "just jogging on" at a steady pace on the frigate H.M.S. *Agincourt* while the Confederate rams were pushed forward with "spirit," but the claim was based on superficial evidence as the rams were then in the earlier stages of construction.[88] The Admiralty had also contributed to the delay on the *Agincourt* and other iron steam frigates under construction for the Royal Navy to await gunnery trials against the different varieties of armor plate then being produced in Britain.[89]

Historians refer to the ships built for the Confederates with the shipyard numbers assigned in the builder's book, but rarely mention the ships assigned between the numerical gaps linking those ships built for Bulloch.[90] The contracts between the Confederate ships were an unintended benefit for Bulloch as the Union spies mistakenly attributed some of the work to his mission, whereas they were contracts for the Admiralty and private shipbuilders.[91]

The Confederate commerce raider *Alabama* was the 290th vessel laid down by Lairds and was referred to by her number during most of her time at the yard. She put to sea as the unarmed steamer *Enrica* on 29 July 1862.[92] Hull 291 was ordered on 2 September 1861 and laid down on 30 October in Lairds' already-crowded yard.[93] This vessel was Lairds' first armored warship, the *Agincourt*, second of the *Minotaur* class, and was among the largest ironclads constructed to that time.[94] *Agincourt* had a length of slightly more than 400 feet and was to become one of the longest single-screw armored men-of-war ever constructed.[95] Hull 292 was the 140-ton steamer *Defiance*, intended for the river trade in China.[96] This small paddle steamer was soon in operation for her owner, Liverpool shipper James Breazley, whom John Laird would later lightheartedly refer to as "a most suspicious character" after local newspapers speculated that the *Defiance* would soon sail not to the Far East, but toward the Confederacy.[97] In addition to shipbuilding, the Birkenhead Iron Works had also established a good reputation for repairing damaged steamships and overhauling local tugs and ferryboats, with work praised for thoroughness.[98]

Hull 293 was the paddle tug *Columbus*, built for Henry Cruse and his partner, a Mr. Downham of the "Hercules Steam Tug Company of Liverpool" in late 1862.[99] Proclaimed as the fastest tug on the Mersey, she was fitted with two steam engines, which combined at 90 horsepower to propel her at a top speed of 14 knots and contributed to her "first-rate towing qualities."[100]

On 10 June 1862, Bulloch received instructions from Mallory directing him to negotiate contracts and begin construction of two ironclads in Britain. This dispatch was dated 30 April but had been delayed by the necessity of circumventing the Federal Blockade. Bulloch had already consulted with the "eminent" shipbuilders (Lairds) and had sought plans for two ironclads to be made by the same firm, saving £1,250 off the price of each vessel.[101] As they were built from the same set of plans, the result was a savings in both cost and time.[102] Here again, the Lairds' business acumen reduced costs for their client and prevented any slack in the construction schedules.

The 10 June dispatch from Mallory was belated official approval for the verbal agreements Bulloch had made with Lairds to build two ironclads for the Confederate Navy. These two vessels would be referred to by their builder's numbers, "294" and "295," a practice that aided the accounting shorthand for the various parts and components that went into each ship, and also assisted Bulloch's efforts to obscure the intended end user of the two armored men-of-war. In addition, Bulloch had also entered into a verbal agreement with the shipbuilder to facilitate subcontracting for the armor plate work.[103] Lairds allowed for the blending of business alliances to speed the work on the ironclads. Through the Birkenhead shipbuilder, Merseyside was closely linked to the Confederacy's naval building efforts.

Return of the Ram

The second identifier used by contemporary accounts to describe the sister armorclad warships under construction at Lairds in 1862 was the moniker of "ram." The latter part of the description is misleading for the ram was but an auxiliary weapon of the ships, whose key features were the armored gun turrets. This throwback weapon from the ancient Hellenic time of oar-powered vessels, had returned to the industrial world of the 1860s due to the advances in marine engine manufacture and improvements in the art of metal casting. The iron-hulled, steam-powered ship, fitted with a reinforced prow, could achieve a predetermined velocity and would (in theory) deliver a blow against an enemy vessel without incurring substantial injury to herself in the process. The ram did not overcome the heavy gun, but it permitted a means to deliver a critical strike against a stationary or slow-moving enemy in a sea fight. This was a close contact weapon from which there was no assured defense.

The ram reemerged as a conceptual naval weapon with the adoption of steam as more than an auxiliary form of propulsion. The return of the ram had several points of origin, with one deriving from an early nineteenth century maritime tragedy. In 1834, the officer commanding the U.S. Navy Yard at Philadelphia, Captain James Barron, proposed that the Navy Department consider his patent for the construction of a steamship fitted with a "prow" or ram.[104] Barron claimed that the idea came not from ancient history but from the loss of the Nantucket whaling ship *Essex* in 1820.[105] That event resulted in the ship sinking after being rammed by a whale, and influenced not only Barron, but also Herman Melville, and served as the inspiration for *Moby-Dick*.[106] In 1839, Nicolas-Hippolyte Labrousse, a lieutenant in the French Navy, observed the H.M.S. *Archimedes* demonstrate the then-new form of steam propulsion, the screw propeller, and realized a screw-driven ship could effectively carry a ram.[107] In February 1843, the French Navy conducted tests at Lorient with a ram attached to a chest weighing some fifty tons. The weighted ram would slide down an incline to crash against stationary targets simulating wooden and ironclad ships. The test results proved a ram would inflict damage against the side of another ship, but iron shipbuilding was not ready for the realities of a purposeful collision at the required speeds.[108]

In Britain, Vice Admiral G.R. Sartorius, R.N., proposed the building of ram-equipped, armored men-of-war to make Britain safe from a French invasion. The admiral proposed steam batteries armed with heavy guns and a ram to challenge an enemy fleet and render wooden warships particularly vulnerable. The steam battery as it existed in the mid–1850s did not have sufficient speed or maneuverability to be of service in a battle at sea. His proposal was ridiculed in the British press and his steam rams were compared to "a couple of infuriate buffaloes." The ram-equipped, armored men-of-war were dubbed "experimental baubles," concepts for Emperor Napoleon III to waste his money upon as "an absurd means of revolutionizing the whole system of modern warfare."[109] The proposal to build a screw-driven warship equipped with an armored prow would remain an idea until the seagoing ironclad came of age. For the Royal Navy, the steam ram came into its own in 1861 as a counter to the more expensive armored steam frigates.[110]

The ram-equipped steamship became a reality during the first year of the Civil War in 1861, when the Confederacy and the Union converted or built ships fitted with rams (both ironclads and unarmored vessels) to fight in close-range encounters. The ram was best suited for work in the shallow coastal waters and rivers, especially along the Mississippi.[111] Although rams were fitted to a mixture of steam vessels fighting in American coastal waters in the 1860s, the screw propeller made the iron spur a viable weapon as both could be almost completely submerged and impervious to enemy fire.

John Laird's name would forever become linked with the ram. The firm he and his sons had grown into a leading builder of iron warships was acknowledged for its proficiency in providing international clients with this weapon of secondary importance (the ram), whereas their real contribution was in the construction of the oceangoing turret ship. A feature incorporated into the two Laird rams were six main watertight bulkheads, with a special emphasis on the forward compartments, built to take the impact of ramming.[112] These athwartship bulkheads also gave the ironclads structural support and were designed to prevent the sides from crumpling when the ram "struck a heavy blow."[113] Other iron bulwarks were positioned longitudinally to provide each ship with about twelve watertight bulkheads, divided at key positions with sliding doors, which were also able to "resist the pressure of the water."[114]

With the launching of the French ironclad *La Gloire* in 1859, Britain and France embarked on their ironclad race, and the ram reappeared spontaneously from the annals of ancient history. After Britain responded to the iron threat across the Channel with the ironclad frigates H.M.S. *Warrior* and her sister, *Black Prince*, the shipyards building iron-hulled warships for the Royal Navy built ram bows almost instinctively.[115] Rapid evolution in the size of naval ordnance was not matched with improved accuracy, as guns grew to hurl larger shells against iron hull plates of increasing thickness. Battering mattered in terms of guns and the ram.[116] John Scott Russell, the builder of the S.S. *Great Eastern*, would later remark that the ram was the true decisive weapon for a warship: "Give her the stem is the order of battle...."[117]

Britain's first iron-hulled ram warship, the frigate H.M.S. *Resistance*, was launched from the yard of Westwood & Baillie of Millwall, London, on 11 April 1861.[118] Over 100 feet shorter than the *Warrior* but with a beam almost as wide, *Resistance* was, according to one London newspaper, "ungainly.... Indeed, to call her simply ugly is a flattery to which we are unwilling to stoop."[119] Other British newspapers showed less invective as they focused on her offensive capabilities and strength of construction. The 12 April 1861 edition of the London *Morning Post* remarked the ironclad ram would "be comparatively invulnerable even to the modern improvement of rifled gunnery ... her power would be tremendous even if opposed to a fleet of timber-built vessels."[120] The following day, the *Newcastle Journal* remarked of her, "a better built ship was never sent afloat."[121]

Royal Navy oceangoing ironclads of the 1860s were as varied an assortment of designs as were many armored warships of other nations during that time of transition. They were not all graceful nor ungainly, just as they were not all handy nor good sailors. One British Admiral who served in many Royal Navy ironclads of this era precisely summed up the deception of appearance over performance, noting, "good looks do not always accompany good qualities in naval architecture any more than in other things."[122] When placed in commission, the *Resistance* (referred to affectionately by her crew as "Old Rammo") and her sister, *Defence,* had one distinction other ironclads lacked. Their long, single-gun decks were painted in the black-and-white checkered pattern of the old wooden frigates. This nod to the familiar Nelsonian paint scheme was short-lived, and they were covered over in black around 1862.[123]

The hulls of the 294 and 295 were built with a submerged iron ram bow to complement the heavy guns. The shape of the ram was as an arch, curving upward from the keel, similar to that of the *Resistance*.[124] Union warships equipped as rams were of mixed hull design, with some extensions also curving upward from the keel, and other appendages or "overhang" extending from the prow downwards to rejoin the forepeak midway down the submerged bow.[125] The ram, as first used in the Civil War, was a tacked-on afterthought. The first steam-driven armored vessel to enter combat was the converted icebreaker/towboat restyled as the C.S.S. *Manassas*. Taken to a New Orleans dockyard, cut down, and fitted with a rounded deck, the one-inch-thick iron plating was intended to protect her until she could close with an enemy vessel.[126] Equipped with a single 32-pounder SBML limited to fire ahead only, the little ironclad was also fitted with a cast metal projection at her bow described as "a formidable mass of iron ... in the form of a knob."[127]

In the early hours of 12 October 1861, the *Manassas,* with a small Confederate flotilla of converted wooden gunboats, attacked Union warships at anchor in the stretch of the Mississippi River just north of the Gulf of Mexico, known as the Head of the Passes.[128] At 4:40 a.m., the *Mana*ssas came down through the fog to strike the steam frigate U.S.S. *Richmond* as the larger warship was coaling.[129] The *Richmond* had been struck a glancing blow on her port bow and suffered only a small hole five inches in circumference when the ram collided.[130] Only three planks had been stove in two feet below the waterline, and the damage was not the catastrophic hull-tearing smash that the Confederates hoped for.[131] The *Manassas* got the worst of the encounter as the force of impact caused her to "vibrate like an aspen." The impact also caused one funnel to fall on her turtle-back upper deck, one of her two engines was rendered inoperable, and the ram was broken off.[132]

When the ironclad C.S.S. *Virginia* buried her prow into the Federal sailing sloop U.S.S. *Cumberland* on 8 March 1862, the action confirmed the steam ram had become a viable weapon in close quarters naval combat. The sloop sank in broad daylight in the anchorage of Hampton Roads, the wide estuary referred to as a "natural naval amphitheatre" where several rivers empty into Chesapeake Bay.[133] The *Virginia* had delivered the dramatic blow in front of thousands of opposing Confederate and Union troops lining the shore. As Labrousse had predicted, the ram had overcome a numerically superior enemy and had been proven to be a seemingly essential weapon for the armored warship.

A lack of machine works compelled the Confederates to hammer rams out of scrap iron with whatever blacksmiths were available. Mistakenly, the Confederates devoted valuable dockyard resources and skilled manpower to the task of making the ram a designed extension of the hull instead of a disposable spur used once as a shock weapon and then forgotten to focus on what really mattered in a sea fight: gunnery. As the war progressed, the ram on Confederate ironclads was tapered into the prow with at least one Southern ironclad (*Atlanta*) carrying a sawtooth fixture on the bottom edge of the ram to cut down into a Federal warship.[134]

The ram, as fitted to oceangoing ironclads, was of different design, but the feature also degraded the performance of many warships while at sea. The overhanging fixture on most Confederate and some Union river and coastal warships would have undoubtedly kept the heads of many of them submerged into the waves had they ventured out from their harbors. By late 1862, the Federals were rethinking the design for their oceangoing armored men-of-war, with the ram fashioned to reassemble the undershot curve of European ironclads. The steam frigate *Roanoke* was reassigned from Hampton Roads to the Brooklyn Navy Yard and cut down to take iron plates and three Ericsson turrets.[135] The *Roanoke* also had a ram fitted to the forward plates, which had extended several feet forward of the stem. A solid piece of iron was fitted to the tapered iron bow frames, and the spaces in between "filled up with solid timber, all firmly bolted together."[136]

As the Laird rams were under construction at the Birkenhead Iron Works, the Union was struggling to complete a formidable ironclad frigate in New York. The ram *Dunderberg* was originally intended as a combination ironclad with casemate and twin turrets for her 15-inch guns.[137] The twin turrets design of the Laird rams may have influenced this massive Federal armored vessel as the Birkenhead-built ships and the *Dunderberg* were designed to house two guns in each turret, with 11-inch Dahlgren guns also carried below the turrets in the casemate of the New York ironclad.[138] Additional indications of competing designs influencing the builders of the *Dunderberg* and the Laird armorclads were similarities involving the ram and hull. The hull of the massive 378-foot iron ship taking shape in the yard of shipbuilder W.H. Webb was "dead flat the whole length" and similar to the Laird turret ships, but she also had armored subsurface extensions from the casemate that protected her wooden hull. These armored belts were capable of "presenting a resistance to the enemy's rams or projectiles." The forward weapon namesake of this Union "ram-frigate" was described as:

> About as formidable a looking object as one can conceive; the entire forefoot of the vessel is prolonged thirty feet from the hull proper, and, rising easily up from the keel about half the distance from the waterline, is there rounded, presenting a blunt end in shape like the profile of an axe edge.[139]

With this prow plated over with iron and the hull compartmentalized, the great warship was seemingly impervious to catastrophic damage at the bow. The wooden body of the ram was noted to project "inside of the hull almost as far as it does outboard," but this bulk was not considered as essential to the ship's structural integrity, for "even should the whole of it be knocked off in an affray the builders say that the hull will be water-tight."[140]

In Britain, the ram was intended for a unique purpose and was of different construction than the American-made counterparts. In the House of Commons, debate occurred between those who championed forts as additional protection against a possible French invasion and those who maintained that the Royal Navy was still Britain's best defense. On 10 July 1862, while debating the question of funding expanded fortifications, the question was broached over the need to raise troops for those positions. One MP, Sir Frederic Smith, sought to "strike a blow" against the forts with their new heavier guns and permanent, well-trained garrisons to man them "before it had taken too deep a root."[141] France would not be able to amass an invasion fleet of warships and wooden-hulled transports without being detected. The guns of the Royal Navy were ready to meet the French warships in the Channel and the French transports would have been vulnerable to British ramming attacks as "three or four steam rams would be able to run into and destroy a great number of them."[142] The concept called for the use of the ram as a shock weapon, with the heavy cannon on British ironclads keeping their French armored opponents busy in a gun duel. The ram was a cheap secondary weapon, a supplement to armor plate, and the gun, and when properly utilized, able to defeat funding for land defenses.

As stated, the British-built ram mounted on her first-generation ironclads was different in construction from those in America. The description of the fabrication of the ram on each of the two Lairds-built turret ships contracted by Bulloch is limited, but another ironclad built in Scotland during the Civil War offers a likely model. Confederate naval officer Commander James North had contracted with the Glasgow shipbuilding firm of James and George Thomson to build an ironclad frigate mounting 20 guns in broadside and fitted with a ram.[143] The iron prow of this "Scottish Sea Monster," as she was dubbed (she was referred to by the builders as the "No. 61," her hull number), extended from the keel and curved upward, midway from the bottom of her bow along the stem to the waterline.[144]

This ironclad was beyond the Confederates in every respect. With more than 4,700 tons displacement, her draft of 20 feet would have kept her out of every harbor in the Southern States. Requiring an impossible-to-obtain complement of approximately 520 men, she would have been a veritable "Flying Dutchman" never able to travel to her intended homeland.[145] The keel of "North's Ship" was an iron plate 14 inches in height and 4 inches thick, extending forward to receive the ram.[146] The ram on British-built armorclads was not a bulky iron wedge fixed to the bows, but a knife-like projection blended into the bows to permit better performance at sea. Forward from the collision bulkhead on "No. 61," bent iron plates referred to as "breast hooks" less than an inch thick were placed about three feet apart and then riveted to iron frames also positioned forward of the collision bulkhead. This iron webwork formed the structural fabric, which would support the ram. The ram itself was "to be made of the greatest possible strength on the most effective plan, so as to resist as much as possible the shock of collision."[147]

Commander North's ironclad was built with a network of iron frames, creating a shock absorber for the larger casting, which was the contact point of the ram. The ram on the Lairds turret ships was likely constructed with a similar support structure to fit into the swan breast curve of the prow. The curved extension was "to be forged solid of the best hammered scrap iron and formed as a projecting beak below the waterline to give the blow when the vessel is used as a ram." The ram was cast as a single forging of varying measurements calculated from the height of the deck to "the point of the beak."[148]

The Turret

In the spring of 1862, Lairds began construction of the 294, the first purpose-built turret ship in Britain. However, the designation of the first British-built armored ship with a *rotating* turret is properly assigned to the Glasgow shipbuilders Napier and Sons and their ship built for the Royal Danish Navy, the *Rolf Krake*.[149]

The armament of the Laird rams, or more accurately the housing of the guns, proved problematic, at least initially. Bulloch had originally favored building fixed turrets amidships for the few large rifled muzzleloaders (RMLs) to be carried aboard the two ironclads as the main armament. He was concerned that permission could not be obtained that would allow the utilization of Captain Cowper Phipps Coles' patented design for rotating turrets. As a result, the original plan called for the fitting of three unmovable turrets equipped with steam valves to raise and lower the gunports.[150] This idea was discarded when Captain Coles reached an agreement with Lairds in December 1862, whereby each ironclad ram built for Bulloch was authorized to be fitted with two of his turrets, although in a slightly modified form.[151] The belated approval granted to Lairds to use the Coles turret patent placed Napier in the position as the first shipbuilder in Britain to construct an armored ship with a rotating turret. On 28 August 1862, Napier signed a contract to build a warship fitted with two Coles turrets.[152] In July 1863, the *Rolf Krake* became the first turret ship to be commissioned in Europe.[153]

On 10 December 1862, the three Laird brothers and Coles agreed to the construction and fitting of two armored cupolas, or "shield and patent apparatus &c," to the 294, then building at Birkenhead.[154] Coles was paid a fee of £209 17 s. per each ship (295 was covered under a separate contract signed the same day) with the contracts denying Lairds permission to place the Coles shields in any other ship, and did not imply a warranty on any rotating gun structure. These licensing agreements did allow for the installation of each turret "with or without any subsequent modifications improvements additions or alterations" as approved by Coles.[155]

The contracts granted Lairds permission to use the Coles turret, but also gave the shipbuilders (and Coles) the legal ability to match their contractual obligations with advances in design to give the two rams the most up-to-date armored cupolas. This flexibility was recognition by all parties that advances in naval gunnery and metallurgy were an almost-daily occurrence, and the ships would be the best Lairds had built to date. The then–"established axiom ... that to stand still is retrograde" was fully understood by Lairds and Coles that the Captain's "shield" had evolved since his patents were taken out in March and September 1859.[156]

The original Coles turret was an armored cone, and closely resembled the modern single gun mount carried on today's frigates and destroyers. It was, according to Coles, "a large convex shield covered all over with thick iron and mounted upon a platform or frame which is capable of revolving after the manner of a turntable, and which also carries the gun upon any suitable carriage."[157] The turntable, or "Rollerway," distributed the weight of the heavy iron shield and enclosed armament upon the iron rollers in order to avoid the reliance "upon spindles as in American Monitors."[158] John Ericsson's *Monitor* carried the turret upon her main deck and was turned by hoisting the iron cylinder (complete with guns, slides, crew and ammunition, etc.) upon her great central iron spindle, the lower edges of the turret making a slight contact with the deck when rotated. Once positioned at the required angle from the beam, the entire cased armament platform was lowered to the deck, ready to fire.[159]

By 1862, the Coles turret was remade into a similar-sized iron cylinder capable of housing one or two guns. Unlike the Ericsson model, the Coles turret was fitted over a hole in the main deck and extended below to rest upon the rollers.[160] This turret also had a central iron spindle. The spindle was not a hoisting mechanism, but rather a device to secure the turret to the interior of the ship and provide an auxiliary means (via a capstan) to rotate the shield, if damaged in combat.[161] One American periodical scoffed at the Coles turret, calling its machinery as "delicate, compared with the duty required of it, as watchwork."[162] Intricate, perhaps, but the Coles shield performed admirably. It was easily turned, not by steam but by manual rotation through hand winches, which linked the gear teeth near the turntable to identical iron teeth under the turret base.[163]

The Coles and Ericsson turrets were also different in their above-deck construction. Both had evolved as round iron cylinders with gunports and iron gratings on the turret roof for ventilation, but the construction of each type of armored shield was different in notable ways. Coles' design had benefited from the September 1861 tests aboard the floating ironclad battery H.M.S. *Trusty* at Shoeburyness.[164] Although the ironclad had been commissioned too late to see action in the Crimean War of 1854–56, the experiments with Coles' iron gun shield cast the *Trusty* as the first ship in the world to carry an armored turret.[165]

When battered by solid shot from 68-pounders and rifled shell, the Coles shield held up well with only a single plate being destroyed—one that was not properly fitted in place.[166] The armored shield had been fired at by one hundred rounds from a 100-pounder Armstrong gun (reportedly only 33 rounds struck the turret), at the close range of 400 yards, and "shot after shot was seen to strike the shield, glance off rapidly and fall into the sea without affecting any apparent injury."[167] The 99th round made a deep indentation, and the 100th round hit the same spot, tearing away the plate.[168] The other plates were not impervious and, indeed, some damage had occurred to the other iron panels, though they were merely riddled, not completely torn away. Clearly, more armor was required inside the turret wall and on the exterior face by the gunports if sufficient protection for the gun crews inside the cupola was to be achieved. Despite the drawbacks, the Coles turret gave "so much satisfaction" that it was worthy of more serious consideration as a method of housing guns aboard some of Britain's warships.[169]

The Admiralty was suitably impressed by the latest round of tests with Coles' armored cupola aboard the *Trusty* and ordered another test with bigger guns. Days after the Shoeburyness experiments against the floating battery, another version of the Coles turret was built. The turret was expanded in diameter to carry two heavy guns instead of the single 40-pounder carried in the *Trusty* turret. A wooden mockup was built aboard the hulk *Hazard* for further tests.[170] Both the Coles- and Ericsson-designed turrets initially progressed at a similar pace, but the press of the Union war requirements freed Washington bureaucrats from the need of more trials. On 4 October 1861, Ericsson and the U.S. Navy contractually agreed to begin construction of his turret ship, the *Monitor*.[171]

Britain was not far behind. Less than a month after the Confederate and Union ironclads *Virginia* and *Monitor* fought a draw at Hampton Roads on 9 March 1862, the Admiralty ordered (on 3 April 1862) that work at the Portsmouth Dockyard on the 121-gun ship-of-the-line H.M.S. *Royal Sovereign* be halted. The steam-driven three-decker was to be remade on the stocks, and work crews were reoriented to cut her down to her lower decks in order to follow a new set of plans.[172] She was to be fitted with armor plate and four Coles iron shields with five heavy guns. The forward cupola was slightly larger as it carried two heavy guns and the others a single heavy gun each, all mounted on the centerline. Britain would convert this three-decker into the Royal Navy's first true turret warship. When commissioned in 1864, the *Royal Sovereign*, armed with five identical pieces of heavy ordnance, would predate the all-big-gun *Dreadnought* by more than forty years.[173] The next step was to construct a purpose-built iron turret ship, rather than convert pre-existing wooden hulls. The Admiralty quickly followed up the *Royal Sovereign* conversion with an order to build an iron-hulled, armored man-of-war equipped with Coles turrets. The London–based iron shipbuilders Samuda Brothers received the contract on 8 April 1862, and the *Prince Albert* was planned as the first turret warship built from the keel up for service in the Royal Navy.[174]

Upon initial glance, the Coles and Ericsson turrets were only similar in appearance: Both usually housed two heavy guns, but the turret of the *Monitor* was smaller in internal dimensions—20 feet in diameter and a height of 9 feet.[175] The Coles turrets for the Laird rams were 23 feet in diameter and stood only 5 feet above the deck when placed aboard.[176] The *Monitor's* turret had been assembled from curved plates, each a single inch thick and bolted onto each preceding plate to form a laminated, armored cylinder 8 inches thick.[177] Turrets used by the U.S. Navy would grow in diameter as heavier guns were fitted to successor monitor-type ironclads, but the construction methods remained the same during the 1860s. A turret for a Union warship would be built around a circular oak frame with each of the eleven curved iron plates fitted around the wooden pattern that resembled "the skeleton of a giant cistern."[178] Each inch-thick plate was an "iron board" 9 feet in length, 3 feet wide, and bent to the required curve on a hydraulic press. After each succeeding plate was curved on the press, it was wheeled to the turret shell where a pine stick with white paint on the end was thrust through the rivet holes on the previous plate to mark the exact spot where the next holes were to be punched through by machine. With each plate fitted in like manner, the layers of each "course" were positioned to overlap with the plates on the layer below to prevent an alignment of the plate juncture, or to "break joints" so as to prevent a joint becoming a single vulnerable place for an enemy shell to strike and weaken the structure of the entire turret.[179]

The great engineer Isambard Kingdom Brunel reportedly told Coles as early as 1855, "You only need a breechloader to make your shield perfect."[180] This was a vision of the effective use of limited space in a turret interior, but a suitable gun was a generation in the future. During the *Trusty* tests, breechloaders failed as "vent-pieces, if made of steel are broken and driven through the breech-screw; or if made of wrought iron, they are bent into an oval form ... and jammed tight into the annular surface of the closing screw."[181] The mechanisms of early breechloaders were too delicate for the demands of black powder and the service conditions of the 1860s. Metallurgical arts had not yet advanced to enable the casting of breech mechanisms which could stand the high heat required of rapid firing and safely meet the effectiveness needed in combat conditions. Thus, the muzzleloader in all its forms remained the weapon of choice throughout the 1860s.

The two guns carried in the forward cupola on the *Royal Sovereign* changed the turret into a more suitable armored platform with room for the crews to work the heavy guns and pass up shot and powder from below. Gone was the original capsule shape of Coles' early designs. The sides of the dual gun turret (and three single gun turrets) on the *Royal Sovereign* were not inclined inward, but perpendicular in order to provide more space for heavier guns than the 40-pounder tested in the armored shield aboard the *Trusty*.[182] Bulloch reported in a dispatch to Richmond that "even Captain Coles has straightened up his turrets" to make room for the new guns, but he kept the same floor plan of his earlier shield.[183] Unlike the Ericsson model on the *Monitor*, the rivets on the Coles turrets were likely recessed into the curved plates.[184] The earlier Coles sloped, capsule-like turret would return when steel breechloaders made the advanced design concept viable. Without the need for crew space to load the heavy muzzleloaders of the 1860s at the edge of the gunport, the sloped turret and the breechloader would reemerge in a complementary blend of form and function as steel became the substance of choice for both the shipbuilders and gunmakers at the end of the ironclad era.

The circular plates of the iron shields fitted on the *Royal Sovereign* would not serve as the identical pattern of turret built for the Laird ironclads, as those were changed to meet the requirements of a Confederacy deficient in the means of rapidly constructing and repairing ironclads. The willingness to modify a patented design showed Coles as an inventor ready to make changes as required. He was likely eager to get the Laird ironclads at sea and into action to prove his concepts under fire.

The Coles turrets constructed for the Laird rams were built around an iron skeleton of T-shaped beams spaced apart at 20-inch intervals fitted over an inner ½-inch thick iron skin of boiler plate.[185] Teak wood filled in the spaces between the inner skin and the support beams. Over this iron and teak blocked frame was a metal basket of ¾-inch iron strips to hold the pieces together, and outside of this was another 8 inches of teak.[186] East India teak had been selected due to its elastic qualities. Teak did not warp with changes in temperature—a necessary feature for ships operating in warmer climates.[187] In December 1863, *Scientific American* observed the Royal Navy's preference for "the universal teakwood, like unto which there is none other in John's (Bull) opinion."[188] Over the outer teak layer of the turret were fitted the iron plates, each 5½ inches thick to resist enemy shot and shell.[189] These vertical plates were arranged in a 21-sided polygon to provide for time-saving fitting, and to prevent repair delays if damaged in combat. The mechanic-deprived South did not have the industrial equipment required to reroll damaged armor plate (especially not plate of that thickness), nor the skilled manpower in sufficient numbers for overly complicated dockyard repair work.

Around the gunports of the modified turrets, another course of plates, each 4½ inches thick, were fitted to provide 10 inches of iron armor around the turret faces.[190] Bolts ran the entire distance from the turret exterior to the thin boiler plate within to bind the entire structure together. The armor on the *Trusty* had (except for the one plate torn away) suffered "only one or two screw nuts off, and a very few bolts started" inside the vessel as a result of her pounding during the Shoeburyness tests.[191] Loosened screws and bolts represented a danger of broken bits flying off upon impact during action and ricocheting around the turret interior, injuring the gun crew. The thin inner lining of iron sheeting inside the turrets on the Laird rams would have gone some way in mitigating this danger.

The turret interiors were also modified to meet the requirements of Bulloch and his (unofficial) sponsor, the Confederate government. Coles suggested (perhaps to Lairds) that the turntable of the turret be staggered in such a way as to allow for proper balancing when the guns were run out.[192] Another modification was an incline for the slides, which would allow the heavy guns to become "Self-Acting" after firing.[193] Recoil would shove the guns back into the turret, but after reloading, the guns would, with the aid of gravity, slide back to a ready position with muzzles protruding from the gunports. A few quick adjustments by the crew as directed by the gun captain to align with the next target, and the RMLs would be ready to fire again.

The above-deck hull bulwarks attached to the ship's sides were armored flaps, five feet tall and hinged at the lower edges to fall outboard, thus permitting an arc of fire for the turrets on each beam.[194] The "novel" bulwarks were topped by a wooden rail (likely teak), which was "removable at pleasure" to clear another support, which held the moveable iron sides upright until the guns were needed.[195] The flaps would fall from each side to give "the required sweep of the guns in training" for broadside fire, or slightly off beam forward and aft. The clear path of fire for the guns was limited, as the forward turret was restricted by the foremast and forecastle and the guns in the aft turret by the mizzen and poop.[196]

The guns would have been positioned abreast 4½ feet apart in each turret, with oval gunports capable of allowing the muzzle of each gun 12 degrees of elevation and 5 degrees of depression.[197] Depression was restricted to those few degrees as the ports were only five inches above the deck and only of sufficient width to allow a crewman to see an object beyond the side of the barrel.[198]

Armor Plate

The iron plate produced for the Laird rams was primarily from local sources. On 3 September 1862, Thomas Haines Dudley, the U.S. Consul at Liverpool, wrote to U.S. Secretary of State William H. Seward to report on the early progress made on the Lairds ironclads.[199] Dudley, a Quaker lawyer from New Jersey, was perhaps the most able American diplomat of the war and provided the Union with a steady flow of usually accurate intelligence on Confederate activities in Britain.[200] According to Dudley's sources, the Mersey Steel and Iron Company in Liverpool was producing 1,500 tons of armor plate, most of which was intended for the Laird rams, with the remainder to be shipped to the Southern States.[201] The size of the plates directly associated with the Laird rams were not mentioned, but others created for the Confederate Navy offer an indication of what was likely a standard size of plate to speed production. Some plates viewed by Dudley measured 18 feet in length, were a foot wide, and 2¼ inches thick. This rapid output was respectable considering sections of the Mersey Steel and Ironworks had been torn down and rebuilt to make way for a railway then building south to the Liverpool docks.[202]

The Mersey Steel and Ironworks had originated in 1812 and had grown over five decades into a cannon and armor producer of international reputation. Ericsson, the Swedish inventor/designer of the U.S.S. *Monitor*, had previously designed two 12-inch iron prototype heavy guns for installation on the U.S. steam frigate *Princeton* in the early 1840s.[203] One gun, the "Peacemaker," was cast in America, and the other, known as the "Oregon," was cast at the Mersey Steel and Ironworks. The Mersey-built gun was reportedly still in use during the Civil War, but the "Peacemaker" burst with tragic effect during a trial voyage down the Potomac River on 28 February 1844. That explosion killed the U.S. Secretary of State, the Secretary of the Navy, and four others, and wounded several more.[204] Ericsson's reputation unjustly took a battering as a result.

The Mersey works were also tasked with crafting huge iron pieces, such as the propeller shafts, for the ironclads H.M.S. *Achilles* and *Northumberland*.[205] This

Thomas Haines Dudley, 1874 (author's collection).

Rolling Mill at Mersey Ironworks, 1863 (Artokoloro/Alamy Stock Photo).

manufactory cast and crafted the 40-ton stern post for the *Agincourt,* their expertise being possible by steam-driven hammers described as being of "immense" size.[206] The steam hammer, invented by James Nasmyth in 1842, was one of the wonders of the Industrial Revolution. So great was its transforming impact, one historian wrote "For myself, I would be prouder to say that I was the inventor of that motion, than to say I had commanded a regiment at Waterloo."[207] The Nasmyth steam hammer grew apace with the rush of industrialization, and the impressive appearance of one such engine was described in a New York periodical as looking "like the gateway of a Gothic church."[208] The skill required to work those great machines was prized by the factory owners, as a well-trained hammer man could crush down on a piece of iron or steel with a force that caused the entire structure to shake, or he could feather down gently for a light tap. With skilled hands so close by, Lairds would undoubtedly have contracted with the Mersey works to also craft the stern posts and critical propeller shafts for the two rams being built in his Birkenhead yard.

The Mersey Steel and Ironworks was something of a misnomer in the early 1860s as the first metal was not the preferred metal. An advertisement from a September 1865 edition of the *Liverpool Daily Post* listed the products of the "Mersey Steel and Iron Company" with iron forgings and castings of "the highest quality and largest size" and armor plate available for the Admiralty or for export "with dispatch and care."[209] Steel was mentioned almost as an afterthought. Steel was utilized only in small batches and usually for very select purposes. Lairds built the first steel-hulled yacht in Britain in 1858 with plates cast by Mersey Steel and Iron; she was the "very neat screw-steam" yacht *Deerhound* built for the Duke of Leeds.[210] That same year, Lairds had built the paddle steamer *Ma Roberts* for Dr. David Livingstone's African explorations up the Zambesi River, with "puddled" steel plates also supplied from the Mersey works.[211] Ironically, the *Deerhound* was present when another Lairds-built ship, the raider *Alabama*, was sunk in the engagement with the Union steam sloop *Kearsarge* in the Channel on 19 June 1864.[212]

A British newspaper from September 1863 mentioned one of the Lairds-built turret ironclads as having a steel ram.[213] This report was false, as steel was a lightweight material in ship construction and was too brittle, except the small batches used as armor piecing caps on some shells.[214] In 1856, William Clay, the managing director of the Mersey works, experimented with Bessemer converters, but the metal produced was not satisfactory and was referred to as "rotten hot and rotten cold."[215] Nevertheless, experiments with other processes continued, and hard steel (usually for machine tools) was manufactured at the Mersey factory during this time. The preferred method then in vogue was not Bessemer's, but a more labor-intensive system to create puddled steel known as the "Rieppe patent."[216]

Iron used for the Laird rams also came from other suppliers as the Mersey works were unable to provide the entire requirement within the strict time frame.[217] John Brown of the Atlas Ironworks in Sheffield provided some armor plates for the *Agincourt* then building at Lairds. It is likely that arrangement was also carried out with the two ironclads built for Bulloch. The Lairds turret ships were constructed with iron from another outside source as a weight savings measure. Iron from the Yorkshire foundry known as the Low Moor Ironworks provided the thin, light but tough plates used to fabricate the watertight bulkheads.[218] The Low Moor works were well known in America for their high-quality iron used in such items as railway carriage axles, "semi-steel" locomotive tires, and the "best qualities of boiler plate."[219]

Building Begins

The keels of the 294 and 295 were laid down in April 1862 and consisted of an iron plate 2 ft., 3 in. in height, and a width of 11/16th of an inch.[220] A Dublin newspaper described the "two iron-clad shell-proof rams, of peculiar shape and construction, rising into shape adjacent to ... where the famous 290 was put together."[221] The Birkenhead shipbuilder was utilizing every spare space and hand to maximize output. With the *Alabama* gone from British waters that summer, the men of Lairds were fully engaged with the *Agincourt*, and especially Bulloch's turret rams.

Patrick Barry's work *Dockyard Economy and Naval Power* provided descriptions of many shipbuilding firms and ironworks in operation in Britain in the mid–1860s. Although this account provides rare photographs of the shipyards, iron foundries, engine shops, and rolling mills in operation at that time, a photo of Lairds is conspicuously missing from Barry's work. Originally published in 1863, the author saw the Laird rams under construction but, because any photograph could have been used as evidence against the shipbuilders, he left what appears to be a deliberate hole in this account of British iron shipbuilding and armor manufacturing firms. Nevertheless, Barry provided a rare glimpse of the rams under construction, and he described the first of the pair building in No. 3 slip and the hull of the second ram was then being assembled in No. 4 slip.[222] The shipyard, crisscrossed with traveling cranes mounted on iron rails, conveyed the iron plates and frames to the workmen laboring in the adjacent slips. The steam cranes were likely built by the engineer James Taylor in his Britannia Ironworks, near Lairds shipyard in Birkenhead. His steam cranes were of such utility that they were used not only in British ports but in harbors around the world.[223]

The 6,621-ton ironclad *Agincourt* was laid down in Graving Dock No. 3 of Lairds.[224] The interior of the shipyard was taken up by the slips, graving docks, and cranes. Along the exterior wall of the works were sheds and shops for the engineers, fitters, boilermakers, and other artisans who made the vital components and frames for each ironclad.[225] The works ran parallel along Church Street, the main entrance was bordered on the south by Mersey Street, and on the north by the railway station, which linked Birkenhead with the industrial centers of Manchester and Birmingham.[226] A tunnel connected the railway with the shipyard through a "cartway," which provided direct access for heavy equipment and individual iron sections forged in other workshops outside the confines of the shipyard. These cartway rails merged with the rails for the traveling cranes and provided a means by which heavy armor plates, engine parts, boilers, etc., could be shunted around the shipyard in an almost continual flow.[227]

The buildings that housed the machine shops and furnaces for bending plates and bending frames were three stories in height and shielded the shipyard and workers from the growing city of Birkenhead and prying eyes eager for an up-close look at the progress on the ironclads. The river was a different matter. A ferry traveled from the railway station at the north of the Lairds yard to Liverpool. Another ferry landed near Mersey Street on the south side of the Birkenhead Ironworks, permitting a limited view of the two iron men-of-war under construction.[228] At a fare of only two pence, the Mersey would have been crossed by a ferry every 30 minutes.[229] Anyone determined to survey the progress on the Laird rams would have regular and cheap access from the river.

Aside from the keels, the frames of the 294 and 295 were the starting points of construction for the two vessels. The "large and spacious apartment" section of the yard, known as the molding loft, was where frames were bent and fashioned to required specifications.[230] There, angle iron 5 inches by 3 inches was heated and hammered into shape on heavy blocks, each frame held in place by pegs previously positioned around a chalk outline indicated by either letters or numbers.[231] Once completed, each frame was perforated at predetermined intervals by a punching press for an assigned number of rivet holes, then hoisted by heavy cranes and positioned around the keel to form the skeleton of each ship.[232] In late 1862, the Continental Ironworks in New York City were building three monitors for the Federal Navy. Details of their fabrication suggest some basic similarities of iron construction techniques likely utilized at the Birkenhead Ironworks. A September 1862 article from *Harpers New Monthly Magazine* described the fitting of plates to the ribs to form the iron hulls:

> These plates and ribs are riveted together in the most elaborate manner ... bent each to its exact shape and the countless holes have been punched, every one being to a hair's-breadth in its appropriate place, before the pieces are brought to the stocks where they are built up. Upon each vessel are a hundred or two hundred workmen, seeming to cling like bees to its sides. Little portable furnaces at short intervals are heating the rivets, which boys are carrying around to the places where they are needed.[233]

The hive-like semblance was a familiar sight at Birkenhead when the frames of the Laird rams were "spaced 21 ins apart" from the center of the keel plate during the formation of the skeletons of the sister ironclads.[234]

Other Design Features

Steering in battle was a concern as the exposed wheel on any warship was likely to be shot away in a close fight. The 294 and 295 each had a double wheel on the poop, but this station would have been abandoned in action. When in battle, each ship would have been steered from a safer position below decks via a double wheel, positioned aft of the forward turret and forward of the boiler room.[235] Bulloch suggested that an armored oval "Sentry Box" plated over with 5½ inches of iron be placed on deck over the steering gear directly below.[236] From this armored box (iron over the ever-present teak), the commander of the ram could direct his ship from his slightly elevated position forward of the funnel. Additionally, armored casing around the funnel base provided some added protection as the rear of the conning tower was likely unarmored, but also of sufficient height to provide a view over the top of the forward turret.[237]

The shape of the stern was built with defense as the primary consideration. The stern was not squared off to allow room for the captain's cabin as on traditional warships, but rounded and bluff to give protection to the aft section of the ironclad. Bulloch acknowledged the "peculiar shape is not pleasing to the eye" but unlike the graceful ironclad frigate *Warrior* and other first generation oceangoing British ironclads, the rudder and the screw were almost completely submerged.[238] This somewhat mitigated the danger of exposed propellers "inviting well-aimed shots" from enemy gunners.[239] With the bluff stern extending aft in an oval curve and a ram bow extending forward of the somewhat rounded prow, they were not slender, but similar to other British-built ironclads of the middle and later 1860s: "full-breasted and full-buttocked as a canal barge."[240]

The 294 and 295 were built to "a very uncommon form," yet this design was intended to blend offensive and defensive aspects into a seagoing armored turret ship equipped with the best heavy guns available in Britain.[241] This stern design had appeared in the Royal Navy with the ironclad H.M.S. *Achilles* (launched in 1863) and contributed to an improvement in handling. The large, overhanging stern of the wooden navy (and converted ironclads) was done away with and substantial weight savings achieved as a benefit.[242]

The 294 and 295 had many unique features; however, the propulsion systems were not innovative, but typical of many British warships of the 1860s.[243] A pair of horizontal direct-acting engines were installed on each of the Lairds turret ships, and the engines were equipped with a single cylinder, 56 inches in circumference with a stroke of 33 inches.[244] The Laird rams had four rectangular boilers per vessel, typical of those carried on warships of that era.[245] The boilers, each with six furnaces, were built for a pressure of 20 pounds per square inch (another source reported that that the pressure was slightly higher at 22 psi), also considered typical for British warships of the mid–Victorian years.[246] Although greater steam pressure was used in Royal Navy warships during this era, the higher pressure was not considered worthy of risk in terms of the wear and tear on the machinery, especially in a climate warmer than Britain, as higher steam pressure would wear on the engines and "require more care on the part of the engineers."[247]

The comparison of the Laird rams with their half-sister, the armored turret ram *Prins Hendrik der Nederlanden*, offers a key reference point to determine likely similarities, as the three ironclads were built by Lairds within months of each other. Constructed from 1864 to 1865 for the Royal Netherlands Navy, the *Prins Hendrik* was a slightly larger copy of the two ironclad ships ordered by Bulloch, and when commissioned, the Dutch ship would more closely resemble the 295 with her then-unique fore and main masts.[248] The *Prins Hendrik* was equipped with four box boilers for a total grate area of slightly more than 208 square feet. The two Confederate-intended rams had a larger grate area of 250 square feet in their boilers, but the Dutch ship could produce an additional five pounds of steam pressure per square inch, and her engines were more powerful at 400 horsepower.[249] The Birkenhead Iron Works continued to modify their construction techniques and constantly sought ways to improve upon their latest designs and shipbuilding practices. Before the Birkenhead ironclads of the mid–1860s were launched, innovation and change were daily practices, and the experience of building each hull (mostly side-by-side) gave the skilled workmen, designers, foremen, and owners an invaluable knowledge pool, which permitted them to build armored warships of increasing complexity.

Lairds engines were not advanced, but were well-built and known for their reliability: "From their simplicity, these engines are kept in repair at a very modest cost, and they are also very economical in fuel, and for these reasons they appear likely to be very generally adopted."[250] Available records reveal that the two engines constructed at Lairds for the 295 were engine numbers 80 and 81.[251] This implies that engine numbers 78 and 79 were built for the 294. These engines were made from "one set of patterns" arranged on the second floor of the Engineer's Fitting and Erecting Building in an area reserved as the Pattern and Millwrights shop.[252]

The engines were likely of the familiar "Penn Trunk Engines" design, so named for the well-known marine engine manufacturer, John Penn of Greenwich.[253] Penn developed his engines to resolve the problem of linking the crank shaft to the propeller shaft by placing the connecting components directly on the end of the piston.[254] Installation of the horizontal direct-acting engines on a large British ironclad warship of the time (such as on H.M.S. *Minotaur*) frequently placed the cylinders of each engine on the port side of the shaft and the condensers on the right side, to provide balance.[255]

The trunk engine also had the advantage of components of limited height, allowing the whole of the machinery to fit below the waterline, and thus, protected from shot and shellfire. Penn-built engines were known for their high quality of iron castings and careful workmanship. In 1854, Penn had discovered that by fitting the hardwood, lignum vitae, in strips at key positions in the shaft tube at the stern, the addition would greatly reduce the wear not only on the shaft tube, but also the bearings.[256]

The London-based engine builder Maudslay, Sons and Field was considered the senior of the marine steam engine manufacturers in the United Kingdom during this era, and was seen as the "mecca" for early precision tool makers such as James Nasmyth.[257] During the Crimean War, Maudslay and Penn built one hundred and fifty sets of engines for an urgent Admiralty order for shallow draft gunboats. The use of interchangeable plans for this order was the "first example of mass production in marine engineering."[258] By the mid–1860s, Maudslay, Sons and Field and Penn each employed approximately 1,500 skilled workers and were both considered "easily the foremost in world" in the field of marine steam engine manufacture.[259] Lairds was new to engine building, having only added that capability when the new Birkenhead Iron Works was constructed in 1857.[260] Limited experience in engine building was

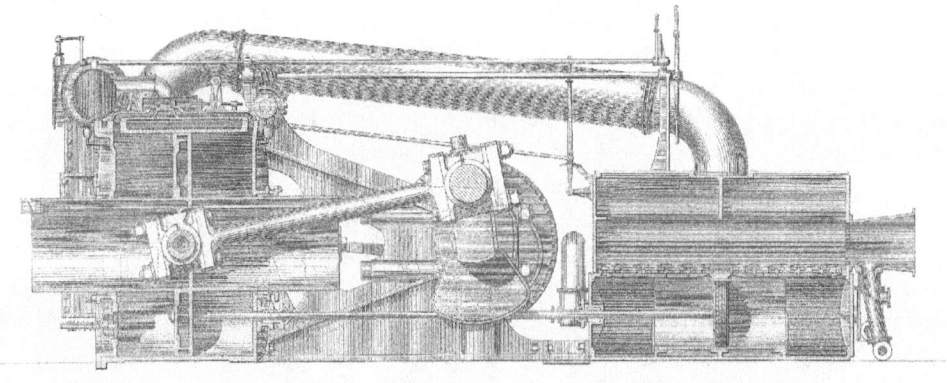

Marine trunk steam engine, 1860s (author's collection).

likely why the Laird rams had engines of 350 horsepower (total per each ship), adequate for the size of the *294* and *295* but not sufficient for the larger ironclads then building for the Royal Navy.[261]

The two Laird rams were each fitted with a single shaft to drive a single screw.[262] Some experimental ships, such as the ironclad battery H.M.S. *Meteor* (1858), were fitted with three screws but results were not favorable, as the *Meteor* experiment was an attempt to merge the machinery drive techniques of the factory shop floor with the engines of a warship.[263] The ships were not suitable for sea service, as they were criticized as being "unable to sail, steam or steer" and were considered "not altogether satisfactory."[264] For serviceability and performance, most British ironclads of the 1860s relied on the dependable large diameter, single screw propeller.[265]

The engines on the 294 and 295 rotated the shaft at a maximum of 70 rotations per minute and turned the single, three-bladed 14 foot, 6 inch screw at a maximum speed of slightly more than 10 knots.[266] The screw was fixed at a 20-degree pitch and the three blades allowed for a measure of improved performance at speed, but the pitch and the drag produced by the third blade would later prove a detriment when the Laird rams attempted to operate under lower speeds or sail alone.[267] The screw was fixed and could not be disengaged and hoisted on deck, as with other British warships of that era. Due to the propeller configuration, the Lairds ironclads were impaired under sail and slight steam, as "screw drag" scooped up water at slow speed.[268] The 294 and 295 were built as men-of-war with an eye toward labor savings while at sea. Although they operated efficiently while under adequate or full steam, they lacked the necessary qualities of endurance and were therefore not suitable as long-range commerce destroyers. They were compromises of design and restricted to only a moderate speed for the whole of their lives.

The sails were problematic for ironclads, and especially for the low-hulled turret ships. Bulloch favored a new system of self-reefing topsails as another way to keep down the required number of crewmen. In a dispatch to Mallory, Bulloch included a set of drawings for his armored ships with specifications "as minute as they can well be made."[269] The Laird rams were equipped with sails to provide maximum canvas over an area that could be handled without too great a reliance on well-trained seamen (another vital resource sorely lacking in the Confederate States). Bulloch explained with an almost resigned air his willingness to try a novel masting plan: "The object in this peculiar rig was to get a good amount of canvas in such a shape as to require the smallest possible number of seamen, properly so called."[270]

Bulloch was not the first to adopt this "peculiar" yard and sail system. The first British patent for this method dated from 1806, and the designs were periodically modified. In 1850, Royal Navy officer H.D.P. Cunningham took out a patent for rolling topsails around their yards.[271] Cunningham's "application of mechanical science" was preceded by others, but his had the added benefit of coming along at the right time.[272] The discovery of gold in both California and Australia enticed many an able seaman to desert his ship for the mining camps.[273] To make up for the loss in men, the ability to reef sails from the deck of a merchantman was adopted as a method to keep down crew numbers and prevent clippers from being abandoned in the harbors of San Francisco and Melbourne.

Double topsails served as a pattern for the Laird rams, and the iron steam frigates H.M.S. *Resistance* and her sister the *Defence* were the first in the Royal Navy to carry them.[274] The two steam frigates employed these yards and sails (as did other British warships in the early 1860s) in what was known as the "Cunningham System" where (theoretically) the upper part of the sail was rolled up as the yard was lowered, "similar in its effects to the spring blinds to a window of a railway carriage."[275] This proved to be better adapted to the less-pressing demands of commercial sailing ships than the unforgiving stresses of a man-of-war. The concept proved a failure as wet sails wadded up when the yard was lowered, quickly fouling other rigging. The Royal Navy discarded Cunningham's invention after only a year in service.[276]

Despite years of modifications, new methods for masting, and improved arrangement of yards and ropes, the blend of sail and steam was never fully successful on men-of-war fitted with turrets. Rotating gun platforms offered the advantage of a readily moveable armament, but stays and shrouds restricted the angle of fire. As armor grew thicker and guns grew heavier, masts became more of a concern regarding the center of gravity on a turret ship. Masts and yards also took time to clear away for action. Yet despite the masts, yards, rigging and canvas being a cluttering inconvenience in regard to the room needed to work the guns, they remained an accepted form of auxiliary motive power to supplement the engines and single screw. Another decade would pass before navies began to permanently discard sails and the armored warships would be altered to take on a form more suitable to their key attributes of protection and firepower.

Main Guns and Secondary Armament

The question of which type of guns would be carried on the Laird rams was not resolved immediately, as Bulloch was following the latest ordnance advances and gunnery tests. Acknowledging "the whole matter of armored [sic] ships and their armament being still in a transition state," he wanted optimal firepower combined with the need for reliability, safety, and most importantly, ease of handling.[277] Lacking sufficient hands, many gun crews manning the Confederate ironclads in America had come from the artillerymen of the army.[278] Quickly pressed into service in the crowded, unfamiliar environment of an armored warship, the artillerymen would have needed a familiar weapon to work in the closed-up spaces of a turret. Bulloch decided on a set of two 9-inch RMLs (each gun weighing 11 tons) per turret, built by the Confederacy's preferred British ordnance manufacturer, former Royal Artillery officer Captain Alexander T. Blakely.[279]

The Blakely rifles were the model for heavy guns made in the Confederacy under the direction of ordnance expert and naval officer Lieutenant John M. Brooke, C.S.N. The Blakely and Brooke guns (copied by other ordnance manufacturers) were recognized by iron banding around the breech, which provided extra strength for the larger powder charges needed to hurl the heavier shells against armored warships, and by a method of rifling within the bore known as "hook-slant."[280] Brooke guns provided the main armament of most ironclads built in the South, but the Blakely rifle was a weapon of choice for Confederate cruisers. The *Alabama* and *Florida* were among those commerce raiders that carried at least some Blakely guns on their world-ranging voyages.[281] Blakely produced heavy guns that were so technologically advanced, Confederate General Beauregard, the commander of the garrison at Charleston, wrote of two 600-pounder Blakely RMLs as being "magnificent specimens of heavy ordnance ... different in construction from anything I had ever seen."[282]

Bulloch was not an ordnance expert, but he sought to maintain a flow of heavy guns to the Confederate Navy from dependable sources. Those were the RMLs as manufactured by subcontracted firms in Britain under the direction of Captain Blakely. One business contracted to produce heavy RML Blakely guns was the Liverpool engineering firm Fawcett & Preston, which had manufactured the engines for the *Florida*.[283] This establishment, dating from 1758, was an early leader in marine engineering and cannon manufactory. Fawcett & Preston built the first iron steamship on the Mersey in 1829 and were acknowledged for their capacity to construct guns of various calibers and their ability to construct limbers of wrought iron as a substitute for the shortage of suitable wood.[284]

Bulloch compromised on another gun type for his ironclads. Two 70-pounder Whitworth RMLs were to have been carried aboard as secondary armament, with one to be placed forward and another aft to provide end-on fire.[285] The secondary armament was more complicated and expensive than the venerable 32-pounder smoothbore, and the system of rifling the barrel was debated between naval officers as to which (Blakely or Whitworth) was more effective against armored ships. Another Confederate naval officer in Britain remarked that the cost of the 70-pounder Whitworth RML was £700 per gun, £5 per shell and exclaimed the sum "almost takes away one's breath."[286]

These cannon were manufactured by Joseph Whitworth from his Sackville Street factory in Manchester.[287] Whitworth had trained at Maudslay's works in London and had opened his own machine tool factory in Manchester in 1835.[288] His machines and tools were created with precision and were of such robust design that comparatively unskilled workmen could craft quality products from his mechanisms, which were "almost self-acting."[289] By 1851, Whitworth turned his expertise to ordnance manufacture, and his skill contributed to the body of knowledge that enabled the building of rifled guns with reduced "windage" in the bore, while also building guns able to withstand the higher pressures from larger powder charges.[290] On 25 September 1862, during tests at Shoeburyness, a Whitworth gun pierced a target designed to replicate the armor of the *Warrior*. Subsequent trials proved that the flathead Whitworth shells could puncture armor plate with a neat hole, but guns such as the larger Armstrong RMLs would fire a shell, which while not armor-piercing, could smash against a larger area, thus buckling the plates upon impact.[291]

Although costly, the Whitworth guns were prized for their strength, but they were also considered complicated cannon to work. The field artillery pieces were more problematic, as they were not gunner proof and suffered damage in the stress of battle. In 1861, one Richmond newspaper relayed a report claiming with some justification that the Whitworth field pieces were "too excellently fashioned" for the average artilleryman.[292] The English traveler–war tourist Captain Edward FitzGerald Ross had observed Confederate forces in Virginia and North Carolina in the summer of 1863 and remarked on the Whitworth artillery in service. Ross observed a Confederate artillery park and commented, "There are a few Whitworth guns, which are very accurate and of great range, but require much care. The breech has been blown off or disabled through carelessness in loading. This is especially the case with breech-loading guns. I understand that the Whitworth guns which are now sent out are muzzle-loading guns."[293]

Despite the skills required to load both the breech and muzzleloaders from this manufacturer, in the hands of well-trained and patient artillerymen, the Whitworth cannon were exceptional. In North Carolina, a young artillery officer gained "much reputation for accuracy and rapidity" with his select gun and crew.[294] At the port of Wilmington, a Whitworth gun set a record "for extraordinarily accurate practice" when a shell hit the blockader U.S.S. *Connecticut* at the then-astonishing range of five miles.[295]

Bulloch stated that the type of gun he wanted (as the main armament) for his Birkenhead ironclads was the one "which will throw the largest shot with the greatest initial velocity." The secondary armament was not chosen for shell size, but for its capability within the limited spaces available fore and aft. The Whitworth rifles were to have had a limited arc from either the forward or aft positions. This arc would have been restrictive as the guns would have been placed behind their own iron-plated shields or bulwarks in the forecastle and poop, as these crew spaces were not armored.[296] The forecastle and poop structures were added after the hull was half complete and were not built directly into the main hull frames, but fitted to provide accommodation room for the men forward and the officers aft. They were of "light structure, sufficiently strong to resist any force of the sea," but built to be removed in a dockyard or shot away in battle to give the ships all-around fire (from the turret guns) if needed.[297]

Another addition, though not considered unusual on wooden and iron broadside warships, were racks to stow hammocks near the gun positions. On the Laird rams, these racks would permit the stowage of hammocks three deep around the upper edge of the turret roofs. The protection provided by the rolled hammocks were for marine riflemen to lie down on each turret roof and fire at the crew of any nearby enemy vessel, or down to clear their own decks of a hostile boarding force.[298] This was not an ideal position as the concussion from the main armament would have been disorienting to the riflemen, and the presence of the marines on the roof of the turret would have also interfered with the gunlaying if done from the roof top hatches.

The Search for the Ideal Ironclad Warship

The building of the French *La Gloire* and the immediate British response in the form of the *Warrior* set off an ironclad race between the two great rivals that redefined the measures of what constituted a first-tier naval power. The venerated three-decked ship-of-the-line, already forced to adapt to the screw propeller, had been outclassed by the large, rifled muzzleloading gun and early breechloader-equipped steam frigates disliked by naval purists for their single-deck "streets of guns."[299] Britain embarked on a massive building/conversion program to construct ironclads in order to not only keep pace with the French, but to take the lead in the number of armored ships afloat. Between 1859 and 1861, ten new ironclads were laid down in British yards, and another seven two-deckers still on the stocks were converted into single deck armorclads.[300]

In the Commons, the First Secretary to the Admiralty Lord Clarence Paget stated in July 1861, "It is no use denying that the whole world is commencing the construction of these (ironclads) ships. Every maritime nation has completely given up the thought of building wooden line-of-battle ships," and added he did not want "to excite alarm throughout the country, but rather to engender a proper confidence, that we are determined to maintain our maritime position in its integrity."[301] The newly-built ironclad frigates and the cut-down sisters (each originally intended for 91 guns) of the H.M.S. *Bulwark* class would give Britain an edge over the French, as the wooden walls were eclipsed by the unwieldy iron-plated sides of major warships on both sides of the Channel.[302]

The *Bulwarks* were still in the frame when the order to remake them into ironclads was given and when launched, their converted hulls had a less-refined appearance than the rakish *Warrior*. These cut-downs had a rounded stern, a bow with only a slight angle to the waterline, and no ram. The squat appearance of these converted ironclads led to their being referred to as "double enders" by the seamen who shipped aboard them.[303]

One British periodical of the day reflected on the sudden shift to ironclad warships in a poem titled "Iron-clad Jack" published in April 1862. This fabricated sea song blustered:

> In armour case fo'ard, amidships, abaft
> In our sides neither crevice nor crack,
> All safely we steam in our blacksmith-built craft:
> Naught to fear now has Ironclad Jack
> 'Nor of splinter or shot feel a dread;
> Pound away as he will, boys, we'll never say die!
> For we're proof 'gainst steel, iron and lead.
> We've no woodwork to riddle, alow or aloft,
> No canvas to shift or to tack;
> Not an inch in the ship that is shaky or soft,
> Shot and Shell proof is Iron-clad Jack![304]

The poem mentioned Jack safely steaming along in his ironclad, but the armored vessels of this era were cumbersome ships. An 1863 edition of *Scientific American* denounced the "lumbering old iron-clads of England and the ... unwieldy carcasses of France" as "good examples of old fogyism."[305] The editorial went on to criticize the deep draft British ironclads, with their "uncouth bows and sterns," as being unable to approach the shoreline of North America unless with great care, as their weight of armor caused them to "heave prodigiously upon the troubled sea."[306] The argument was partially refuted by another American periodical printed earlier that year. Although European ironclads were "ponderous ... with their lofty sides and many vulnerable points," Union ironclads were barely seaworthy and those few that could undertake a sea voyage without undue fear were not impervious to enemy guns.[307]

European ironclads were too deeply laden to reach all ports in North America, but several major ports in the Union could be entered, and chief among them was New York. One editorial in January 1863 noted the limitations of coastal fortifications and remarked, "When the attack is made by iron-clad steamers, the peril to a city is fearfully increased. We think we are fully justified in the opinion that the *Passaic* or the (New) *Ironsides*, the *Warrior* or the *La Gloire* could enter the harbor of New York unharmed in spite of all the fortifications which defend it."[308]

Stopping a force of enemy ironclads within gun range of a great metropolis was a troubling prospect for any nation dependent on oceanic trade. The Confederacy and the Union followed the customary path of other established or aspiring naval powers, and sought British expertise in the ways of armored naval warfare. British-built fast cargo ships transported weapons and material, which kept the Confederate forces supplied with enough arms and equipment to stave off a war-winning Union victory on the battlefields of the South for most of the conflict, but only armored men-of-war could lift the blockade of the seceding states.

The *New York Times* noted that the Laird rams had the ability to elevate their turret guns to bombard distant towns and forts, "while ships of the Warrior class would be perfectly useless for such service."[309] Bringing guns to bear was a concern not only in terms of elevation, but also for aligning the armament onto a target at the optimum time. A crewmember of the Federal monitor *Nahant* wrote that the turret did not stop when required, and on occasion, had to be reversed several feet or put through a complete rotation in order to bring the target into alignment with the guns. The Laird rams rotated their turrets manually; the mechanical defects on the steam-rotated turrets of the Federal monitors would have impaired their efficiency in a fight with other turret-armed ironclads.[310] The Laird rams presented a threat in the form of oceangoing armored vessels able to both withstand fire from most Union warships and deliver well-aimed shot and shell at range with a marginally higher rate of fire.[311]

The Bulloch contract with Lairds to build the sister armorclads represented a technological forward leap in naval warfare. The industrial capacity and manufacturing skills of Britain were utilized to produce a pair of warships to offer an effective challenge to the evolving might of the Union Navy. These sister ships were an amalgam of design features incorporated into armored hulls built at the very edge of marine engineering practices at that time. They were created not only as a response to the Federal monitors, but were also built as evolutionary models of the next phase in the development of the armored man-of-war. The ironclads under construction on the Mersey were understood by all observers to be something unique and powerful—so powerful as to contest the Union command of the sea around the beleaguered Confederacy. These two ships, with their armor plate, heavy ordnance, and moderate endurance on a light draft, were power projection weapons the South desperately hoped to have at sea under their flag. With each frame and plate fitted at Lairds shipyard, the Federals viewed progress on the ironclad rams with increasing alarm. These two new turret ships under construction in Birkenhead were viewed as direct threats to the Federal Navy and the coasts of the Union itself.

Two

Reluctant Actions

Seizure and Acquisition of the Laird Ironclads 1863–1864

The two armored warships being built at the Birkenhead Iron Works during the early 1860s had become something of a legend for the belligerents during the Civil War. For the Confederates, they were the best chance for raising the blockade of their coasts. Union officials saw them as a threat they could not assuredly counter despite their latest ordnance and larger monitor-type ironclads. The U.S. envoy in London, Charles Adams, complained to the British Foreign Secretary that the lead ship was "a steam-vessel of war, of the most formidable kind now known."[1]

Historians have approached the Laird rams during the vital stage of their construction (1863) with too much of a retrospective view. This strain in Anglo-American relations is seen as "largely resolved before it began. As a *casus belli*, the Laird rams crisis of later 1863 has been much overrated."[2] However, a more detailed review of events is needed in order to determine aspects of what was a slow-brewing diplomatic dilemma that later came to a near crisis. The predicament concerning the Laird armorclads was not as clear as is commonly supposed, and they influenced naval plans and operations for both the Confederacy and the Union.

The Civil War was not as delineated to many living in those times as it is in retrospect. War news certainly had an impact on British investors and politicians, as it did on the American opponents, and the results of the dual Confederate disasters at Gettysburg and Vicksburg in early July 1863 "did not always have symmetric effects on North and South," nor did those two events have an irreversible effect on British opinion, as many historians previously stated.[3] By the summer of 1863 the war was far from over and the Laird rams contributed to the apprehension felt in the North as the conflict continued in the aftermath of Union victories, some smaller setbacks, and the ill effects of the New York draft riots.[4]

Attitudes in Britain were "more complex than once supposed," and although many wanted the end of slavery, many also identified with the Confederacy's fight for independence.[5] Palmerston had decided in October 1862 that the British government should "continue merely to be lookers-on till the war shall have taken a more decided turn."[6] In a speech given in the Commons on 23 July 1863, he identified the key issue surrounding the Laird rams as one of ownership. After debating the nature of ships converted for use as commerce raiders, the Prime Minister turned to warships under construction for foreign customers, saying, "There is a further difficulty. I will suppose a ship built of such a character that we might safely say it was built for warlike purposes. Then you must prove whom she is intended for."[7] The situation had not changed enough for London to intervene with the Laird rams then under different stages of construction in Birkenhead during the summer of 1863. The crisis would have to run its course.

Adams did not overstate the threat these warships posed to the United States when he wrote, "All the appliances of British skill to the arts of destruction appear to have been resorted to" in their creation.[8] They represented the cutting edge of design and construction of the ironclad warship, and it was believed they could have a major, even a critical impact on the outcome of the war. The construction of these two ships would redefine the rules of diplomatic protocol and clandestine intelligence collection, and ultimately influence a reinterpretation of international law and the definitions of neutrality.

Work on the two Laird rams progressed rapidly in the early stages and Bulloch was able to report to Secretary Mallory by 11 August 1862, "The armor-clad ships are getting on finely..." and on 24 September, Bulloch again wrote to Mallory, "I have nothing to add except that the ships are progressing as rapidly as could be expected, and that I am more pleased with them every day."[9] Bulloch, like many ship owners, extended the construction timeline by requesting additions and modifications as the ships were building. In a report to Richmond he stated, "The ships being of entirely new design, I see reasons to modify the plans from time to time but only in immaterial points not involving important alterations."[10]

By the autumn, the weather affected the Birkenhead Works, and new measures were taken to regain lost time caused by rain and cold. In a November dispatch to Mallory, Bulloch reported on the slow progress on the two armorclads: "An unusual amount of bad weather has somewhat interfered with a certain portion of the work upon the ships of this description; but the builders are as anxious as I am to have them ready in the stipulated time, and have covered them with comfortable sheds, and have even introduced gas, so as to ensure additional hours for work during the short foggy days of this climate."[11]

Beginning in the spring of 1863, the issue of how or whether to stop the Laird rams from leaving British waters was discussed in Parliament on several occasions. The issue would grow in importance and intensity as the ships progressed in their stages of construction. In response to the difficult questions of how to stop an ironclad ostensibly building by a neutral party for a belligerent power, the broader issue of the Foreign Enlistment Act of 1819 was also debated. Rising to defend his name and the involvement of the Birkenhead Iron Works in the building of the *Alabama*, John Laird systematically countered the claims of his critics in the Commons that he had violated the law and outfitted a warship for the Confederate States, and was in the process on building ironclads for them. The member from Birkenhead referred to the verbal wrangling over what constituted a violation of neutrality as "childish fuss." Calling the opposition to task for providing arms to the Northern States, he questioned why Manchester arms manufacturers shipped thousands of rifled muskets, swords and percussion caps from Liverpool to ports in the United States with cargo deceptively labeled "hardware."[12] Laird then dropped a bombshell when he read aloud to the Commons the 1861 letters from Union representatives asking his sons to build ironclads for the North: "On the 14th of August, I received another letter from the same gentleman, from which the following is an extract:—I have this morning a note from the Assistant Secretary of the navy, in which he says, 'I hope your friends will tender for the two iron plated steamers.'"[13] Laird continued by claiming "to talk of freedom in a land like the Northern States of America is an absurdity." Not content to rest there, Laird went on to declare that his friend (he was likely referring to Bulloch) was followed by detectives, and that spies were employed in his sons' shipyard in Birkenhead and in other factories in the United Kingdom. In his closing remarks, Laird addressed his response against his critic (John Bright) by stating, "I would rather be handed down to posterity as the builder of a dozen Alabamas than as the man who applies himself deliberately to set class against class, and cry up the institutions of another country which, when they come to be tested, are of no value whatever, and which reduce the very name of liberty to an utter absurdity."[14]

Laird's words stirred not only in Parliament, but also resonated across the Atlantic. In the Confederacy, excerpts of the fiery speech were relayed via telegraph and courier as far away as northern Louisiana. The 4 May 1863 edition of the *Shreveport Weekly News* reported that the shipbuilder-turned-M.P. had forcefully argued that the weapons shipped to the Federals were as dangerous as the unarmed ironclads building in Birkenhead.[15]

John Laird caricature (author's collection).

The U.S. Secretary of the Navy was upset by Laird's allegation and denied that the Federal Navy had contacted the shipbuilder to request the building of ironclads for the North. Welles wrote in his diary on 2 May 1863, "It is wholly untrue, a sheer fabrication. The truth is, our own shipbuilders, in consequence of the suspension of work in private yards early in the war, were clamorous for contracts, and the competition was such that we would have had terrible indignation upon us had we gone abroad for vessels, which I never thought of doing."[16] The Navy Secretary was intensely bitter over Laird's claim, and after penning a denial to U.S. Senator Charles Sumner, Welles wrote in his diary on 19 May, "He (Laird) is in my opinion, a mercenary hypocrite without principle or honesty, as his words and work both show."[17] The denial was released to the Northern press and on 10 August, the *New York Daily Tribune* opined that Laird's allegation was false and that he had "been the dupe of some adventurer."[18]

On 13 August, Welles became despondent when he received a telegram reporting that a letter from Fox may have entangled the Navy Department with Lairds. Washington intriguers crept out of the background, and the Navy Department's Chief Clerk W.H. Faxon reported to Welles his opinion that the Assistant Secretary "has been forward, and too ready with his letters substituted for those for the Secretary or chiefs of bureaus."[19] Faxon suggested that Fox had taken it upon himself to contact Mr. Howard, the Brooklyn, New York–based interlocutor between the U.S. Navy Department and Lairds in 1861. Faxon also thought that Fox may have corresponded with one of the Lairds before Welles squashed the proposal early in the war.[20] The Navy Secretary, feeling battered by the Northern press, gave credence to Faxon's allegations by writing in his diary on 13 August 1863, "There may be something in these surmises." Welles wrote that he did not feel that the Assistant Secretary was purposely going against his instructions, but that Fox was "perhaps anxious to do something to give himself notoriety."[21]

Welles had reason to be cautious around his assistant, as Fox was connected through marriage to the influential Postmaster General Montgomery Blair, who sometimes had the ear of Lincoln.[22] Welles did not have this degree of access, and resented the standing of both Secretary of State William Seward and the Secretary of War Edwin Stanton. Regarding Stanton, Welles noted, "Not unfrequently [*sic*] he has a private conference with the President in the corner of a room, or with Seward in the library." Blair would later confide to Welles, "Strange, strange, that the President who has sterling ability should give himself over so completely to Stanton and Seward."[23] Welles was of a different temperament than Seward and Stanton. According to biographer John Nevin, he was more introverted, more of a background worker: "Welles was a wire-puller for thirty-five years, a politician's politician...."[24] In light of the Navy Secretary's isolation from Lincoln's inner circle, he both admired and distrusted those with a bold, direct air, including his Assistant Secretary. Welles came closer to the truth regarding the drive and political skill of his deputy when he wrote in his diary (also on 13 August), "Fox is shrewd."[25]

Fox was also a connected "wire-puller" in his own right, but not a directly political one. A former officer in the U.S. Navy, his pre-war career mirrored that of Bulloch as Fox rose to the rank of lieutenant while in the Navy, and commanded a mail steamer in civilian life.[26] Fox would use his naval connections to cut through red tape and bureaucratic indifference. It was this willingness to act boldly that put him occasionally at cross purposes with the careful and cautious Welles. This difference in experiences, both in sea service and politics, contributed to the Navy Department's embarrassment in light of Laird's speech in Parliament, which connected the Birkenhead Iron Works with a proposal for ironclad warships, however tenuous, from Washington in the summer of 1861.

Perhaps from caution, or perhaps from embarrassment, the Assistant Secretary made no mention of the Laird revelation in his correspondence. One of only a few references to Laird and his ships in Fox's letters was ever made. On 13 August 1862, Rear Admiral Samuel F. Du Pont, on blockade duty off South Carolina, wrote to Fox: "To ease my mind and yours about the Charleston division—the *Powhatan* should be the base there; she can run down those within, if they venture out, as well as crush the 'Laird' boat and other ironclads from England."[27]

The Union Navy was confused about the size and dimensions of the Laird ironclads. These ships were not the low-hulled armored turret ships originally envisioned in 1861. Perhaps the Union Naval authorities thought the Birkenhead-built ironclads were based on the earlier designs and more like the monitors with their shallow draft and low freeboard. This could explain the belief that a paddle frigate like the U.S.S. *Powhatan* could run down the Laird armorclads in a manner similar to what the U.S.S. *Mississippi* (another paddle frigate) had attempted against the damaged Confederate steam ram *Manassas* during the Battle of New Orleans on the night of 24 April 1862.[28] The *Powhatan*, despite her vulnerable paddle wheels, was one of the largest ships in the Union fleet. She had been recently overhauled and fitted with ten 8-inch and one 11-inch Dahlgren smoothbores.[29] A well-armed, handy ship with dependable engines, she could maintain 10 knots in most weather, but she was no match for the improved Laird turret ships.[30]

One reason for this early confidence on the part of Du Pont and Fox concerning the Laird rams likely originated from inaccurate information reported through the British press. The 10 February 1863 edition of the *London Evening Standard* claimed the Lairds "cupola corvettes" would not be armored.[31] Rather, these two ships were reported as having "a mere skin of iron" with no heavy armor or thick teak timbers for protection. The article opined that if ships such as the Laird corvettes, "costing no more than ordinary iron transports," were built instead of the more expensive *Warrior* and *Agincourt*, they could "choose their own fighting distance, and by that means in the end overcome an iron-cased adversary."[32] This same article favored a warship design that would emerge over 40 years later as the powerful, but dangerously flawed battlecruiser. The reporter likely toured Lairds yard before the armor plates were put on and thus drew the wrong conclusions about the "corvettes."

On 3 February 1863, Bulloch reported to Richmond via a cipher dispatch that the work on the ironclads at Birkenhead had been delayed due to "insurmountable difficulties."[33] The weather contributed to the delay, but the work to bend the plates was slowed by the machinery limitations of the yard. Lairds had only "two or three very light hammers for small forgings" and the fitting of the plates was undoubtedly slowed by these restrictions. Furthermore, the slow progress on the much larger *Agincourt* was described in February 1863 as "not in a very forward state."[34] The armor plates required an almost painstaking degree of exactness to fit on to the hulls of the rams. Bulloch wrote, "No armored ships for the Admiralty have ever been completed in time and the most important part of the work, the riveting, is far more tedious than anticipated."[35] Lairds was an experienced iron ship builder, but it was new to the work on armored men-of-war.

Lairds was also protective of its reputation. Bulloch was impatient with the delays encountered building the *Alabama*, but the shipbuilders would not be rushed.[36] The launching of the wooden-hulled cruiser was delayed in part by the exacting builders rejecting defective stern posts until the right one was found and properly fitted.[37] This same attention to detail and exactness of construction was another reason for delay on the iron corvettes. The armor plates were dovetailed to interlock when attached to the hulls of the turret ships, and the work was done "so accurately, that the joints are scarcely perceptible."[38] Another observer noted the plates were "beautifully planed and fitted, that it is almost impossible to tell whether the vessels are plated or not."[39]

Bulloch was a careful man, and he knew his moves were being watched. He had written to Mallory on 7 November 1862 that his plan for evading British neutrality laws had to be revised after the departure of the raiders *Alabama* and *Florida.* He wrote of the need for careful preparations, as the departure of the first armored ship had "to be conducted with such caution and secrecy that I fear to mention the plan even in this way" (via a ciphered dispatch) to Richmond.[40] Bulloch had to devise a unique plan of subterfuge for each ship, and he kept those plans to himself until the pressure by Union agents required a different tactic that went beyond the direct dealings with Lairds.[41] Rumors about the two ironclads had swirled around the docklands and out to the British press. One story held that the armorclads were destined for service with the Chinese government, but the claim was not believed due to the presence of Bulloch at Lairds, "who is daily in attendance superintending their progress."[42]

The Eastern connection was a confusion of facts related to ships building for the Imperial Chinese Navy at the time. A flotilla of approximately eight smaller men-of-war were under construction in Britain for the emperor, then battling against the Taiping Rebellion.[43] This squadron, usually referred to as the Lay-Osborn Flotilla, was named after the British Inspector-General of Customs in China, Horatio Nelson Lay, and the man selected to command the ships on their passage to the East, Captain Sherard Osborn.[44] The unarmored Chinese flotilla and the Laird rams were intertwined both in the British press and the Federal spy network, as two of the ships intended for China were built at Lairds.[45]

Rumors over the Laird rams were also fueled, in part, by newspaper reports from the Confederacy, which filtered back to Britain. Bulloch warned Mallory that "indiscreet persons who should have known better have written to private persons at [sic] the South on such matters, and I am not surprised at the result."[46] The 22 November 1862 edition of the Richmond *Daily Dispatch* relayed from a New York newspaper a report of "three immense iron steam rams, the most powerful ever constructed" with one building on the Clyde and the latter two on the Mersey built by "John Laird, M.P. who built the pirate Alabama, and is pushing them rapidly to completion."[47] Discretion was not exercised by the Richmond newspaper and on 24 November of that same year, the *Daily Dispatch* relayed the disingenuous claim that after the *Alabama* sailed from Birkenhead, "no further contracts have been undertaken."[48] This statement backfired and, instead of confusing the Federals, added to further speculation about the mysterious iron ships being built under the covered sheds (known as the "annexe") at the Lairds yard.[49] Information continued to leak that "two of the most formidable specimens of naval architecture that Liverpool ever has produced" were taking shape at Lairds.[50] Arguably, the knowledge that men were working on the two ships night and day contributed to information about the two armorclads having "oozed out that they are intended for the Confederacy."[51] The builders were pushing their men to complete the turret ships for a foreign power in urgent need of these ironclads and the Confederate States was the only client hard-pressed enough to require such an extended work schedule.

From his flagship, Rear Admiral S.P. Lee, U.S.N wrote to Fox to convey his views on the increasing danger presented by the ironclads building in Britain. In his letter dated 29 March 1863, Lee wrote: "The use the rebels have made of the extensive English workshops to provide a formidable seagoing ironclad ram navy, is the worst feature of the war."[52] This fear was justified as the Laird armorclads had developed a reputation for quality workmanship even before they were completed. Almost a year later, *Scientific American* would claim "no better specimens of war ships [*sic*] have ever been constructed than the two rams built by Messrs. Laird at Birkenhead."[53]

British Neutrality and the First Stage of the Civil War

Britain declared her neutral stance when the Civil War had been underway only a month. On 13 May 1861, Queen Victoria signed a declaration whereby the British Empire would "maintain a strict and impartial neutrality in the contest" between the "Government of the United States of America and certain States styling themselves as the Confederate States of America."[54] This declaration announced that a law enacted in 1819 forbade direct involvement in a conflict by British citizens, and the Queen prohibited her subjects from participating in the American war "as they will answer to the contrary at their peril." The proclamation continued at some length and also warned against entering into military service for a foreign power and made specific reference to sea service prohibiting the enlistment of:

> Any natural-born subject ... shall, without such leave or license ... serve in and on board any ship or vessel of war, or in and on board any ship or vessel used or fitted out, or equipped, or intended to be used for any war-like purpose, in the service of or for or under or in aid of any foreign power....[55]

The law, as echoed by the proclamation, forbade Britons from building warships for a foreign belligerent, while the United Kingdom remained neutral as they were not to:

> Equip, furnish, fit out, or arm, or attempt or endeavour to equip, furnish, fit out, or arm, or procure to be equipped, furnished, fitted out or armed, or shall knowingly aid, assist, or be concerned in the equipping, furnishing, fitting out, or arming of any ship or vessel, with intent ... to cruise or commit hostilities.[56]

Further, those who violated the law and were indicted could face fines or imprisonment or both and warned that ships fitted out with:

> The tackle, apparel, and furniture, together with all the materials, arms, ammunition, and stores, which may belong to or be on board of any such ship or vessel, shall be forfeited; and it shall be lawful for any officer of his Majesty's customs or excise, or any officer of his Majesty's navy ... to make seizures under the laws of customs and excise, or under the laws of trade and navigation.[57]

The Queen's declaration commanded her subjects to "abstain from violating or contravening" the law regarding neutrality, and gave the strongest warning that those who deliberately violated the law "will in no wise obtain any protection from us."[58] The mention of those who sought to *contravene* the law was a point of focus for Confederate agents, Union diplomats and their solicitors. If a direct violation could not be proven, the subsequent legal move was to show a violator as purposely taking steps to avoid the conditions of the law by staying outside its ill-defined legal edges. The strict adherence to the not-so-well-defined text of the law allowed shipbuilders and arms manufacturers to carry on their trade with both the Confederacy and Union to such an extent that rendered the law, known as the Foreign Enlistment Act of 1819, almost unenforceable.

The differentiations between what was legal and what was not expressly excluded by the neutrality laws and the proclamation would prove to be a source of continual friction between Britain and the United States throughout the war. The building of the Laird rams strained the relations between London and Washington to near the breaking point. Tensions had risen several times during the conflict, but the events of 8 November 1861 almost resulted in war when the Federal steam sloop U.S.S. *San Jacinto* stopped the British mail steamer *Trent* in the Bahamas and took off two Confederate commissioners.[59]

During the winter of 1861, as the Royal Navy was preparing its ships for a war with the United States, Britain's ironclads were seen as an eventual factor should a conflict ensue. One British newspaper remarked, "We have not mentioned the Warrior nor the floating batteries, as we do not suppose there would be any intention during the winter months of sending across the Atlantic any iron-plated ships." The British press had apparently forgotten that an ironclad was on station at Bermuda and in service.[60] The ironclad floating battery *Terror*, one of the first generation steam armorclads intended for service during the Crimean War, was in commission at Bermuda under the command of Captain F. Hutton, R.N, the first Captain-in-Charge of the naval base at the island fortress.[61] Armed with sixteen 68-pounders, this ship provided the heavy broadsides needed to defend the island base or attack an American fort at close range.[62]

The *Terror* was the third of the *Erebus* class of floating batteries, laid down a year after Britain's first ironclads of the *Aetna* class were begun as part of an Anglo-French plan to build armored gun platforms with which the allies could bombard Russian coastal fortifications at close range. The *Terror* and her sisters were almost identical to the *Aetnas*, but they carried two extra 68-pounders, their hulls were built of iron instead of wood, and their greater horsepower permitted a slightly increased speed. These batteries were designed to steam up to an enemy fort under their own power, but to get to the foreign shore, they had to be towed by larger vessels.[63]

The paddle sloop H.M.S. *Devastation* had charge of the *Terror* during her voyage (mainly under tow) to Bermuda in the autumn of 1857.[64] Useful for intended close combat but unwieldy in service, this ironclad was the mobile armored defender of a crucial naval base near a hostile shore. *Terror* became Britain's first ironclad to be stationed overseas, and the first armored ship to cross from the eastern to the western hemisphere. During the *Trent* crisis, the *Terror* was provided with a crew, and several ships were available at Bermuda to tow her if required.[65]

A difficulty arose regarding manning of British ships suddenly called into commission in anticipation of combat with the United States. The 7 December 1861 edition of the *Huddersfield Chronicle* warned, "our only anxiety is the want of 'trained seamen.'"[66] The men of the Royal Navy reserve were eager for the call up and in a spontaneous display of patriotic zeal, men paraded through the streets of several cities with Union flags and marching bands. In one procession, some Jack Tars carried a flag with the motto "Ready, aye ready."[67]

In Bermuda, the crew of the *Terror* was assigned from other warships in the squadron. By November 1862, the *Terror* was manned by a crew detailed from the steam frigate H.M.S. *Ariadne*.[68] The ironclad floating battery was considered to be "so heavy and clumsy to be almost immovable," but she provided vital protection to the naval base and stood ready to meet a foreign challenger, especially as the United States Navy grew in strength from 1861.[69] To man the warships in times of crisis, the admiral on station would decide to move men from various crews to man the reserve component. This was especially true for guardships like the *Terror*: ready when needed, but most of her crew had to be detailed for temporary duty on the unwieldy armorclad.

Here was a pattern that would reoccur throughout the mid-nineteenth century. The Royal Navy could husband ships and resources during times of peace and mobilize during times of international tensions, but manning was always a concern. With Britannia challenged on the seas, patriotism would send previously reluctant, trained men marching in the streets and Britain's wealth of seamen would come to the colors. Yet this was a surge capacity of manpower for the pull of commerce, and the needs of industry drew the reserve sailors and trained men back to merchant ships and factories as foreign crises abated.

The *Trent* affair was the lightning rod event in the autumn and early winter of 1861. By Boxing Day, Seward had convinced a recalcitrant cabinet and a hesitant Lincoln to acquiesce to London's demands and turned the Confederate commissioners over to "British Protection" and thus, let the crisis subside.[70] In Washington, Ambassador Lord Lyons had upheld British honor through tact and determination in his discussions with Seward, and both men helped to avert war through their diplomatic maneuvers.[71] The *Trent* crisis ended when the United States freed the Confederate commissioners and their two secretaries in early January 1862.[72]

The senior Royal Navy officer in North American waters, Vice-Admiral Sir Alexander Milne, had taken steps to prevent inadvertent acts by his commanders from aggravating the already tense peace. From his flagship H.M.S. *Nile* at Halifax, he had ordered in September 1861 that warships of his squadron were "positively enjoined" not to enter a Confederate port or salute the Confederate flag. If a Southern warship or fort fired a salute, the British captain could return it, "though you are to be most guarded not to encourage or invite in any manner such proceedings."[73] Vessels of either belligerent carrying war material were not to be interfered with in a British port, nor were they allowed to be interfered with by a warship flying the opposing flag.[74] Milne also advised his commanders that the previous practice of cruising with U.S. warships for the purpose of suppressing the slave trade was discontinued, "as it might lead to an infringement of the strict neutrality."[75] The admiral usually did not range too far afield as he had to maintain contact with the Admiralty and especially Lord Lyons in Washington. Halifax was directly linked to the Union capital city via telegraph lines, and to keep his fleet war ready, the admiral was instructed to watch for a coded message. If relations with the United States were to be severed, a telegram sent from Lyons reading, "Could you forward a letter for me to Antigua?" would be the order to commence hostilities.[76]

Liverpool and the Laird Rams

The British Foreign Secretary, Lord John Russell, undoubtedly read reports with a mixture of resignation and bewilderment regarding the symbiotic relationship between the commercial interests of Liverpool merchants and the Southern States. Russell noted that the merchant class of Liverpool was of a "port specially addicted to Southern proclivities, foreign slave trade, and domestic bribery."[77] Liverpool had strong commercial links with the South for decades. Those links only strengthened when imports of cotton dwindled, but arms and war material made up for the dislocation in trade. One Merseyside sea captain noted that blockade running had relit "a spirit the like of which has not been known since the palmy days of the slave trade."[78] Liverpool had the advantage of location as it was near the cotton mills of Lancashire and linked via railway and canal to the ironworks and armament manufactories of Britain. Connected by established business relationships to the belligerents, "the great American trade is mostly within the grasp of Liverpool."[79]

The deprivation inflicted by the cotton famine was largely recovered in other industries. Merchants in the wool trade "reaped a [sic] unexpected harvest of gold," and the munitions makers "waxed fat and greasy."[80] The war offered a tradeoff for British industry, with one observer noting: "In the kingdom as a whole the number of persons on relief did not rise materially during the war, for as heavy as was the unemployment in textile areas, other industries enjoyed a compensating boom."[81] The war encouraged merchants to avoid the neutrality laws and develop clear ways to bypass trade restrictions.

As mentioned earlier, the U.S. Consul in Liverpool was the determined lawyer Thomas H. Dudley. With his offices on the waterfront, he and his agents were well-positioned to survey the Mersey for ships arriving and departing.[82] The office of U.S. Consul at the great port city was a plum position, considered "one of the most lucrative of the foreign appointments in the Presidential gift."[83] The post required an active occupant due to the pressing commercial requirements of oceanic trade between Liverpool and America. The outbreak of the Civil War increased those duties and obligations multifold, but Dudley was to prove equal to the task. However vigilant, he was frustrated by his failure to prevent ships from sailing for the Confederacy laden with arms and munitions. In May 1862, he sent a dispatch to Seward complaining of Liverpool's loyalties: "The people of this place if not the entire kingdom seem to be becoming every day more and more enlisted" in service of the Confederate war effort.[84]

At Birkenhead, Bulloch took advantage of the cooperative relationship with Lairds and their suppliers to propose changes to his ships in order to adjust to new concepts of naval warfare. In a letter to Mallory, Bulloch reported that the ironclads would have bowsprits "fitted with a hinge so as to be turned inboard when the ship is to be used as a ram."[85] He did not mention how the bowsprit would be brought back, but the Ship's plans indicated the bowsprit was hinged to the forecastle.[86] When readied for close combat, the giant boom would be unshipped and hauled directly aft, lifting the bow sprit on end and clear of the forepeak, allowing the ram to crash into an enemy hull with minimal threat of fouling the rigging. This was not a new concept. A similar approach to a non-fixed bowsprit had been tried out in the *La Gloire*. The French warship had a bowsprit that was "a short, straight, stumpy affair, and can evidently be removed at pleasure."[87] In early 1862, the Admiralty considered fitting the steam frigate *Resistance* with a movable bowsprit "to draw in and out like a telescope," but decided to fit a more traditional fixed bowsprit instead.[88] Britain was not to lag behind for long, as the "beautiful yacht-like frigate" *Northumberland* was equipped

Two. Reluctant Actions 53

with a bowsprit capable of being folded backwards in order to clear the "knife-like bow projecting at the water-line."[89]

The funnel for each Laird ironclad was altered during the later stages of construction. The two known builder's models—one a profile of the first of the class, and the other a full model of the second—show a slightly ranked funnel resting on a base roughly three feet in height.[90] At some point during the building process, the funnel was fitted, not slightly raked as originally designed, but straight and capable of telescoping.[91] The original funnel (still slightly raked) as fitted on the first of the Laird rams was capable of being "lowered at pleasure by an exceedingly ingenious arrangement" likely involving an internal winch.[92] The one clear change made after the first ship was launched was the fitting of a circular armored casemate around the funnel and projecting well above the turrets' tops. Early photographs of the second Laird ram show a straight funnel elevated approximately eight feet above an armored sleeve, which stood some ten feet above the deck. Illustrations of the first Laird ram reveal the funnel was altered and the armored casemate was added after the ship was launched.[93]

Funnels aboard warships during the middle Victorian years were raised and lowered to accommodate sail or steam. An advantage of the armored sleeve was to protect the funnel from enemy shot and shell, but one experiment gave a false conclusion regarding the draft a damaged funnel could produce. On 3 June 1846, the steam tug H.M.S. *Echo* was the subject of experiments conducted by the Royal Navy

Builder's model of HMS *Wivern* (© National Maritime Museum, Greenwich, London).

at Spithead.[94] The funnel of the tug was cut with a series of holes to simulate damage from 24-pound shot, with one hole near the top of the funnel, one midway down, and the other at the "jacket" or base of the funnel at the deck.[95] An ingenious damage repair kit consisted of ready-made, curved iron sheets, two feet square, fitted with a small handle that turned two iron clasps.[96] These "stoppers" would be fitted over the shot hole and clamped in place to cover the damaged area like "the clasp of a door or cupboard." The results of the tests wrongly concluded that when the temporary repair plates were removed, the smoke continued up the funnel and no effect was observed in the speed of the *Echo* or in the performance of her machinery, although it was noted that a strong wind would have probably had an effect.[97] The tests were "most satisfactory" and led to the mistaken belief "that very little danger will occur from shot striking a steamer's funnel."[98]

This error derived from observations made of a series of holes carefully cut into the funnel instead of the impact of a ball or shell breaking and bending iron as it passed through the smokepipe. A decade before, "impact" and "initial velocity" were dubbed "scientific bosh" by some senior officers of the Royal Navy more familiar with Nelson's quarterdecks than the increased firepower of the guns produced during the early industrial age.[99] Admiral Sir Percy Scott would later remark of this time, "Gunnery officers were laughed at as mere pendants and coiners of long words."[100] Gunnery emerged during these decades to become more a mixture of science and sight than muscle and frequency of broadsides. Written in the aftermath of the Crimean War and the Indian Mutiny of 1857, the 4 June 1859 edition of *Scientific American* observed the change in warfare: "A sure aim will effect more than the shower of bullets hitherto thrown way."[101] Although that journal was referring to land combat, the inference was the same for war at sea. Accuracy mattered more than weight of fire alone. In 1857, the newly commissioned steam corvette H.M.S. *Pelorus* was one of the first ships in the Royal Navy to receive a gun sight.[102]

Almost immediately after the successful introduction of a steam-driven armored warship in combat, the funnel was proven to be a vulnerable point. During the first day of the Battle of Hampton Roads, the *Virginia* had her funnel damaged by the nearly point-blank fire from the 9-inch and 10-inch smoothbore guns (and single 70-pounder rifle) of the sinking *Cumberland*, causing the unwieldy ironclad to slow and her casemate to fill with smoke.[103] The *Virginia* suffered a loss of steam pressure and a subsequent loss in her already marginal maneuverability prior to the epic battle with the *Monitor* the following day. On the morning of 15 July 1862, the ironclad C.S.S. *Arkansas* was barely able to reach the Mississippi River port of Vicksburg after an enemy shell tore the funnel seal at the top of her casemate. The impact dislocated the breechings to the boilers and resulted in a drop of steam pressure.[104] This damage caused the *Arkansas* to slow and prevented her from using her ram with any hope of success.[105]

A lower silhouette precluded some damage to a warship's funnel, for enemy shot was not cast upwards, as would be found with a slope-sided casemate ironclad. During the second Schleswig War of 1864 between Denmark and Prussia, the Danish twin turret ironclad *Rolf Krake* was in action with Prussian shore batteries on three occasions and although she was struck one hundred and fifty times, sixteen rounds pierced the funnel with no appreciable loss in combat performance. Had the Prussians used heavier guns (some were 12-pounder field guns), the results of the funnel damage would have had a detrimental effect on steam pressure. The superior quality armor plate held up to the shot and shell, and a low hull made her a hard target for the Prussian gunners, but she received her only casualties when enemy rounds penetrated the thin deck plates, a weak point of many ironclads built during the 1860s. On 19 July 1864, during a debate in the Commons on the characteristics of armored warships, the *Rolf Krake* was praised: "The manner in which her guns had been used, her speed, and the way in which she had manœuvred, were admirable."[106]

Repairs and modifications were made to the ironclad after the actions; her funnel had been "shot through and through," and the turret tops were altered to prevent harassing fire from small arms entering through the ventilation gratings, as had occurred during one engagement. The turrets withstood the Prussian cannon fire with only slight indentations detectable, but the movable bulwarks were "shot to pieces" and the deck armor (¾ inch of iron covered with wood) proved to be inadequate protection from plunging fire, with one enemy shell piercing the deck and exploding near the engine room door.[107] Deck armor also deflected one Prussian shell into the side of the forward turret. Though this round did no damage to the turret, the steel shell penetrated the deck near the turret base, as this plating provided only limited protection against shot and shell fired on a flat trajectory.[108] Battle experience in America and Denmark undoubtedly contributed to the appreciation for more protection for the funnel of a warship from hostile fire. The telescoping funnels for the Laird rams were fitted not to only facilitate voyages under sail, but they were also protective measures proven from combat at close range with enemy guns.

Union Reactions to the Laird Rams

In December 1862, the federal government received a plan that involved a scheme to buy the Laird rams and similar potential men-of-war out from under the Confederates. The Boston merchant John Murray Forbes suggested in a letter to Fox that men "untrammeled by naval contractors, and such nuisances" would travel to Britain and posing as representatives of "Siam, or China, buy the best of the war steamers now under construction for the rebels."[109] After months of delay, Forbes business associate, financier and shipowner William H. Aspinwall of New York joined in the scheme now backed with U.S. government bonds. The bonds were to be sold via the federal government's banker in London, Baring Brothers, in order to raise £1,000,000 for the purchase fund.

Forbes arrived in Britain (29 March 1863) before Aspinwall and took immediate steps to aid Union efforts in the United Kingdom. After meeting with Consul Dudley in Liverpool, he made money available to aid intelligence collection efforts against the Confederates as the U.S. Consul was found to be "in sad need of moral & effective aid."[110] Despite efforts to conceal their real objective, the undertaking to purchase the ships was found out and reported in the British press. Aspinwall was too high in profile to avoid attention as he was an "ancient commercial oak" able to "give the Rothchilds a few ideas how to make money."[111] The attempt to purchase warships under construction for the Confederacy was unveiled before it could begin, as the British press reported that Aspinwall and Forbes were not representatives of Asian powers, but working for the government of the United States.[112]

Although the mission to obtain the ships failed, several ancillary gains were made by the two merchants. One was the sudden inflow of desperately needed cash into the coffers of U.S. Consul Freeman H. Morse in London, and especially Dudley in Liverpool. With these much-needed funds, the Union intelligence network in Britain retained expert detectives and expanded its supply of paid informants. Another related benefit of this tranche of funds for intelligence collection was to affect a division of labor between the two consuls. With their hands on the purse, Forbes and Aspinwall persuaded Morse and Dudley to avoid overlap.

Dudley was responsible for all intelligence collection in Britain north of the 53rd parallel, and Morse would manage collection in England and Wales south of the line. In addition to funding British newspapers that reported favorable articles about the United States not wanting a war with Britain, these two men were able to convince Washington to take key steps to remove impediments to better relations. They persuaded the federal government not to issue "Letters of Marque" with which the struggling U.S. Merchant Marines could be remade into privateers, ready in the event the Union went to war with the British Empire. Forbes made "careful use of the press" to highlight the efforts taken by the United States to avoid an increase in tensions with Britain.[113]

The most direct suggestion to change policy was an insistence that the Navy Department remove Acting Rear Admiral Charles Wilkes (who had commanded the *San Jacinto* when she stopped the *Trent* in 1861) from front line service. Forbes noted that the Federals must make active efforts "setting their teeth" to avoid aggravating British political leaders, and not just respond to events. Wilkes was a provocation, and his squadron achieved a fresh incident each time it dropped anchor in the West Indies. Forbes regarded Wilkes's abrasiveness as hitting "twice as hard in irritating John Bull as the same thing done by anybody else."[114] His reputation for belligerency and Anglophobia was a growing concern for the North, and this was reported in the Southern newspapers. In Texas, an edition of the *Dallas Herald* commented that Admiral Wilkes was "causing increased irritation in England."[115] As if Forbes' warnings over Wilkes were not enough, the financier Aspinwall wrote to Fox with his view that "every Englishman thinks that his appointment was a taunt to them intentionally made—& whatever he does, good or bad, is viewed with suspicion."[116] Welles would note in his diary regarding the inability of this admiral to follow orders: "Wilkes often recklessly disregards and breaks them."[117] On 22 May 1863, within a month of receiving the letters from Forbes and Aspinwall, Wilkes was relieved of command of the U.S. West Indian squadron. The British press reported that his removal was the result of "representations" made by Lord Lyons in Washington with the result that the "Federal Government desires to maintain at this time the most amicable relations with that of Great Britain."[118]

With Wilkes out of the way, more attention could be focused on the aspects of British neutrality and Confederate efforts to build ironclads and cruisers in British ports instead of defending or explaining the legal interpretations of a rogue flag officer of the Federal Navy. The Forbes/Aspinwall mission almost succeeded due to the frailty of Confederate credit. Bulloch had pulled in funds from George Trenholm's financial and shipping interests in Liverpool, but since the start of the war, the South lacked capital, and payments were late. Bulloch would write, "there was always much perplexity and embarrassment from lack of ready money."[119]

The Confederate government had been able to fund the war through bonds backed by cotton, but this method had only limited effects by mid–1863.[120] Bulloch had asked Mallory to forward his suggestion that bonds or "Cotton Script" could be sold in Britain, but the sale had to be through the established agents (Fraser, Trenholm & Co.), not left to a private individual. Bulloch warned that negotiations had to be along established business practices, as "the English like to do business in a formal matter-of-fact way, and are always suspicious of adventurers and undertakings that require to be puffed."[121]

By March 1863, the Union was also vying for funds from European lenders. Former U.S Treasury Secretary Robert J. Walker was in London as the unofficial representative of the Union and was urged to avoid any actions that would cause embarrassment to the federal government.[122] Walker did not heed the advice, but drove down Piccadilly in a carriage pulled by eight white horses from his fashionable residence there, and dropped pamphlets denouncing Jefferson Davis from a balloon as it floated over the English countryside. These antics did not produce any appreciable effect against Confederate fundraising efforts, but Walker's subsequent dissemination of statistical reports detailing federal monetary policy and trade volumes had a positive impact on leading banking houses in London and on the Continent.[123]

Nevertheless, pro–Southern agents did employ a "puffed" sell with mixed success in Europe. A more advanced speculative venture proposed by a retired French civil servant came along at the right moment to shore up funding for the South and also served as a mechanism to shield against federal attempts to outbid them in the European arms markets. As Forbes and Aspinwall were being armed with bonds from the Federal Treasury, the French banking house of Emile Erlanger & Co. of Paris floated a loan for the Confederate States.[124]

Foreign governments had been seen as uncertain investments after several newly independent South American countries defaulted on their loans in the 1820s. By 1862 this had changed, and "a distinct turn" in favor of loans to foreign governments was again circulated in the exchanges of Europe. On 19 March 1863, the Confederate loan was floated in Amsterdam, Paris, Hamburg, London, and Liverpool.[125] Erlanger used his business contacts to raise funds for the Confederacy instead of Richmond pushing its own bonds as the main source of income. This signaled hope to the Confederate government, as the loan and secret shipbuilding projects were interpreted as harbingers of more aid and perhaps direct intervention by Britain and France. This view was unrealistic, for both acts were isolated and not part of a general policy shift in either London or Paris in favor of the Confederacy. Erlanger had originally issued the loan at a higher share price to help Richmond make a good political impression in Europe.[126]

The Liverpool agents for the loan were the trusted shippers/financiers Fraser, Trenholm & Company, who received a commission from the sale of each bond and allowed Bulloch to borrow from them at will.[127] The Erlanger loan was made more attractive due to a linkage with the price of cotton at only a quarter of its then value in Liverpool.[128,129]

Cotton was a problematic commodity. The Confederates had imposed a virtual embargo on its export early in the war in a misguided effort to attract more European support. Although a decline in shipments succeeded in drawing down reserve stockpiles, especially in the cotton mills of Manchester, the move injured efforts to create a convertible resource for credit in Europe.[130] By late 1862, another product from the South was far more profitable. Turpentine had risen by 100 percent on its pre-war

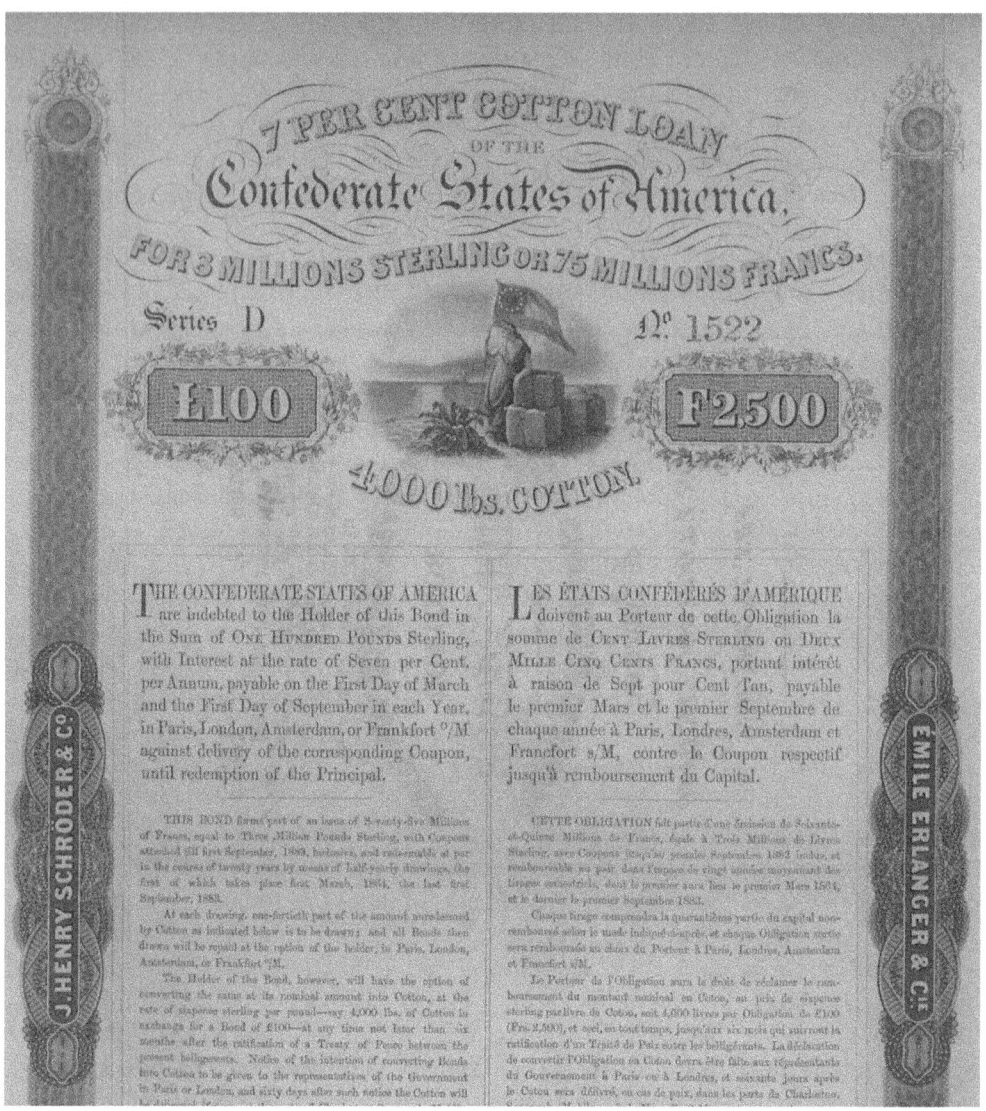

Erlanger loan certificate, 1863 (author's collection).

value, vastly outperforming cotton, which had only risen by 20 percent during the first year of the war. By 1863 the price of cotton was rising with limited supply available through the blockade, but the Confederate government failed to generate more than a trifling revenue through either taxes or export duties.[131] As a result of miscarried domestic revenue generation efforts, foreign bond sales became crucial for the maintenance of the Confederate war effort.

Most financial houses in Britain were aligned with the North, especially, according to Forbes and Aspinwall, "our steady-going friends the Barings," but Erlanger was able to persuade the London firm of J. Henry Schroder & Co. to take up the Confederate loan issue in Britain.[132] This was more than a financial godsend for the Southern States. It was also a useful propaganda tool as Schroders was a firm of "high standing and influence."[133] The Southern propagandist Edwin DeLeon, then operating from

Paris, did not like the conditions of the loan but conceded it "seemed a great success, financially and politically."[134] The success of the loan would, according to DeLeon, encounter "occasional fluctuations as the Confederate cause brightened or darkened" with each battlefield victory or defeat.[135]

The Erlanger loan did not produce steady income throughout the war, yet it provided needed revenue at a crucial time for Bulloch. On 9 March 1863, he wrote to Mallory informing him that "he [Bulloch] could not induce builders to commence more ironclads without cash."[136] The funds were delayed in disbursement, but some money did reach Fraser, Trenholm & Company and from them, payment was made to Bulloch's and other accounts on Confederate naval and military contracts.[137] Although not enough to meet the growing needs of the Southern States, the Erlanger loan provided receipts "in specie, and far larger in proportion than it [the Confederate Government] realized on any but the earliest of its domestic loans."[138]

Ownership of the Rams

Bulloch had taken essential steps to obscure the intended ownership of the ironclads and to achieve this objective, obtained legal counsel to guide him through the intricacies of British law, especially the Foreign Enlistment Act of 1819. Bulloch employed F.S. Hull, a leading Liverpool solicitor, to serve as his legal advisor throughout the duration of his mission in Britain.[139] A key restriction in the Foreign Enlistment Act, a "bewildering ... precept" according to Bulloch, was the restriction against arming, equipping or furnishing a man-of-war for use by a belligerent against a neutral power.[140] The expert advice of Hull

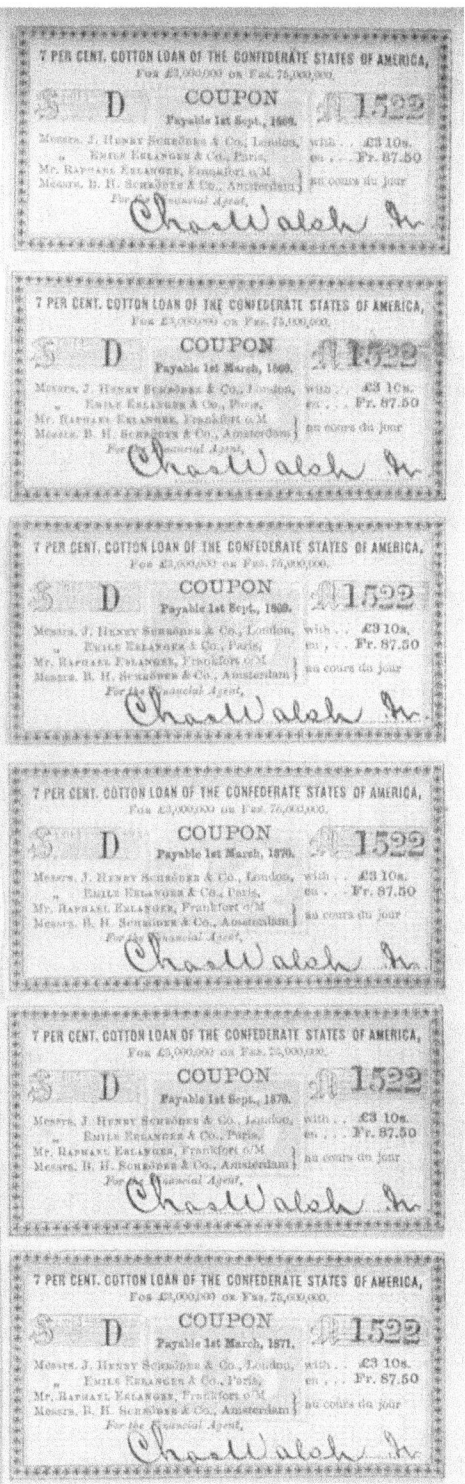

Erlanger loan coupons, 1863 (author's collection).

helped Bulloch avoid one sticking point in the "precept" regarding what was meant by "equipment." More specifically, the armor on a ship's sides was not considered "equipment," as the iron plates were not grouped as armaments and ordnance stores. Armor by itself did not pass the definition of Article 7 of the Foreign Enlistment Act as being "for war-like purposes."[141]

By April 1863, the hulls of both ironclads were completed, and the 294 had "a great number of iron armor-plates fixed."[142] At the end of June, Bulloch reported to Mallory that the engines of both ships had been ready "for several months" and the 294 would have been launched six weeks earlier, but she was held back for political considerations.[143] He also reported to his superior that spies working for the U.S. Consul in Liverpool were "daily watching their progress."[144] The Russians were also watching, and indicated they were interested in buying the two vessels. Bulloch would not wait until the ships were launched and ready for sea. He transferred ownership to thwart both the Union and Russian interlopers.[145]

Bulloch was occupied with "a good deal of management" to transfer the ownership of the rams from his name to a French firm. Bulloch had arranged to build two ironclad rams and two "clipper corvettes" with the French shipbuilder Jean-Lucien Arman of Bordeaux, and acting on orders from Richmond dated 27 March 1863, transferred the ownership of his Birkenhead ironclads to a French company in order to remove them from Britain and fit them out in France.[146] Arman was a well-connected choice to serve as facilitator. He was a politician of national standing, served in the Corps Legislatif, and had occasional access to Emperor Napoleon III.

In late March 1863, Bulloch travelled to Paris and met with the Confederate emissary John Slidell to arrange the transfer of his turret ironclads then building at Lairds.[147] Bulloch and Slidell met with Arman, who then arranged a meeting in Paris between the two Confederate officials and a suitable firm.[148] A subsequent meeting with the Messrs. Bravay proved fruitful and a "satisfactory arrangement" was made, whereby Bulloch would no longer serve as the owner of the two Laird rams.[149] The Messrs. Bravay had acquired the ironclads for a "nominal sum," but their ownership was a blind.[150] They were holders of the contract, but once the ships were finished, the former owner would reacquire the title (for another fee) and the ships would steam for America under the Confederate ensign. Bravay & Company of No. 6 Rue de Londres, Paris, was under the directorship of Adrien Bravay, with his older brother, François, providing the funds to launch the firm.[151]

François was the stuff of legend. The son of a French tradesman in "narrow circumstances," the young Bravay was apprenticed to a shoemaker, a trade that would produce his entrée to fate.[152] Taking up trade in Egypt, he was favored by chance when he repaired the shoe of Viceroy Saad Pasha. After a subsequent meeting with the viceroy, the "Lucky Shoemaker" received a contract to supply shoes for a portion of the Egyptian Army. Bravay would continue in this service of the Pasha until the death of the ruler in 1862. Following this, the wealthy François (who allegedly added to his purse through trade with Algeria) returned to France with a fortune estimated at 15,000,000 francs (£1,200,000) and stood for office.[153] After months of legal contests, he won his seat in the Chamber of Deputies.[154] The election trials and legal battles of François were likely reasons Adrien was the public face of Bravay & Company. It was through the elder brother's earlier shoe contract that the Messrs. Bravay got their proverbial foot in the door, both in Egypt and in France. Bravay was an accomplished hand at maneuvering around the intriguers in the official circles of Cairo, and even after the death of Saad Pasha, he regained his influence to such a degree with the new Viceroy, Ismail Pasha, that he was regarded as "potential as any foreigner in Egypt."[155] This linkage was the bedrock on which Bulloch's plausible storyline was built.

The Laird rams ostensibly would be sold to Egypt to build their fleet, and the transfer of the ships from Bulloch to the Bravay brothers was "a mere business transaction."[156] Lairds facilitated the transfer of ownership "in the ordinary course of business" and obtained a 2½ percent commission from Bulloch, who readily agreed to the fee, as he was "hoping that in better times we may be able to renew our business associations, which have been as satisfactory to me as our social intercourse has been agreeable."[157] The plan was believable, as the Messrs. Bravay had received an order for two ironclads intended for the Pasha. On 28 December 1862, François had written to his brother Adrien from Alexandria, reporting that he had sought to disengage from contractual obligations with the viceroy. Nevertheless, the Pasha ordered François to build "two armored frigates, after the best and most perfect designs." The ships were to come from France and the contract was not to be made public. This was due to political considerations and was likely a subterfuge to hide the purchase from the Pasha's overlord, the Sultan in Constantinople.[158]

Mallory ordered on 29 October 1862 that the Laird rams be named for the states of North Carolina and Mississippi, but he did not specify which would bear which name.[159] That was left up to Bulloch. The first of the Laird rams, 294, was to have been commissioned as the C.S.S. *North Carolina*, yet she would receive the false Egyptian name *El Tousson*. Her sister, the *Mississippi*, was built as 295 and received the cover name *El Monassir*.[160]

Despite the sale to the French firm, Bulloch was still involved with the construction of the two ironclads, only now he was less visible. The contract to build the four corvettes, and another pair of rams through Arman and his associates (two corvettes were built in Nantes by J. Voruz), was initially a good idea to diversify Confederate shipbuilding contracts, yet this would later prove to be an ill-timed distraction.[161] Bulloch had written to Mallory regarding the moves he might make to get the Laird ships clear of British waters with only a vague concept: "As I can only shape plans to suit possible changes of circumstances, it is quite impossible to go further into detail on this subject."[162] Traveling to and from Bordeaux, Paris, and back to Liverpool consumed much of Bulloch's time when delicate hands-on management of the completion and departure of the Laird ships was required. When nuance and careful steps were most needed in Liverpool, he was away in France.

Prior to transferring ownership, additional equipment was likely arranged for transport on the Laird ironclads. On 20 May 1862, when the Confederates were scouting around for British shipyards to build their oceangoing ironclads, Commander North wrote to Bulloch to report on the plan of his intended 61, the vessel later to be dubbed as the "Scottish Sea Monster."[163] North mentioned that a spare screw propeller would be carried on his ironclad as a replacement for the three-bladed iron propeller, fixed to the single shaft.[164]

The workmanship required to construct propellers was considered a high art of the iron shipbuilders' craft, and those not up to the exacting demands were regarded as "a poor tool."[165] These tasks were handled by specialized foremen, (propeller) molders, who produced the screws fabricated for ironclads built in New York and other shipbuilding centers.[166] The Confederacy lacked skilled machinists and was critically deficient in propeller molders.[167] Bulloch likely considered adding such a replacement screw to each of his rams on their voyages to the Confederacy. Transporting spare screws on deck was not unusual. When H.M.S. *Black Prince* steamed south from Glasgow to complete her fitting out in Portsmouth in 1861, she carried a propeller blade on deck as a replacement in the event the main screw was damaged.[168]

The two-bladed screw North referred to in his letter to Bulloch was probably a "Griffiths" type, capable of adjustable pitch, and was praised during a trial run in October 1862, for "scarcely any perceptible vibration."[169] The Royal Navy had adopted Robert Griffiths' pattern for all screw warships in the early 1860s, and this design offered the benefit of uniform production and greater strength. This strength was achieved by bolting the "fans" or blades of each screw propeller to the hub with flanges instead of the earlier method, which involved attaching them with a "key" and wooden wedges. This new method permitted an increased rate of screw revolution and greater speed.[170] The adoption of the Griffiths pattern required the Royal Dockyard at Woolwich to take on extra "wheelers and other artisans" to handle the increased workload of the understaffed propeller molders.[171]

The Laird rams were fitted with other modern pieces of equipment and likely included William Hornsey's patented engine room telegraph.[172] This pedestal-mounted instrument, positioned near the wheel(s), resembled a garden sundial and carried the face turned upward. The orders for changes in speed were relayed to the engine room counterpart by a lever resembling a capital letter "L" which, when pivoted over the indicated position as displayed on the face, sounded a gong in the engine room and a brass pointer would swing to the desired position on the dial.[173] An earlier version of the engine room telegraph had first been mentioned in service on the River Tay in 1821.[174] Additionally, in July 1825, the *Edinburgh Philosophical Journal* mentioned an engine room telegraph as an invention of James and Charles Carmichael of Dundee, which had been fitted on the Dundee and Fife ferry, *George IV*, and "for some time used."[175] The workings of the Carmichael-built telegraph was described by a Royal Navy officer:

> By the simple motion of a small handle, or index placed on a table, upon deck, in view and in hearing of the man at the helm and the master of the vessel, every movement which the engine is capable of giving to the paddle-wheel may be at once commanded. The vessel may be moved forward, or backwards ... or entirely stopped, at any given moment, by merely turning the handle to the places denoted by the graduations of a dial plate.[176]

The engine room telegraph was too much of a leap forward in automation for many officers in the navies and merchant fleets of that era, and the man-in-the-loop remained a familiar function of relaying commands from the deck. A series of hand signals was one method employed but when that failed, orders were relayed through voice by "bawling out the engineer below."[177] Another method used for relaying commands to the engineer was through a series of bell signals.[178] These signals, used in the U.S. Navy in the early 1860s, were detailed as "ahead slow, 1 bell; fast, 4; slow again, 1; slower, 1; stop, 2; back, 3." The U.S. Navy's method differed from the bell sequence used in the American Merchant Marine, although the Navy's system was "more complex but less ambiguous."[179] Methods of communicating from the deck to the engine room were simplified when the Hornsey telegraph was adapted for standard use in the Royal Navy in 1858.[180]

The Union Spy Network in Britain

Inspection of the work on the Laird rams was, by mid–1863, done not by Bulloch, but by others assigned by him. Lieutenant R.R. Carter of the Confederate Navy was sent through the blockade to serve in one of the ironclads (likely the *294*) but was reassigned for the duty of "inspection of work actually in progress."[181] Carter, praised for his "cheerful and intelligent assistance" by Bulloch, was appointed liaison with Lairds and those firms contracted to build Blakely pattern ordnance. Carter's duties allowed for work to continue, and Bulloch to "keep entirely out of sight in the matter" of obtaining the guns for the Laird armorclads.[182]

Bulloch had visited Lairds frequently during the earlier stages of construction, including supervising and assisting with the laying of the keels of the two rams.[183] Bulloch met with the yard foreman in charge of building his ironclads, and was seen in the company of one of the Laird brothers at the shipyard.[184] Bulloch became more cautious as Union informants had ready access to the docks along the Mersey. He was to remark on his need to maintain a low profile as "experience has taught me that it is far safer to keep our business as little extended as possible, as otherwise the chance of our transactions being ferreted out by the Federal spies, who abound even in this country, is greatly increased."[185]

Dudley's intelligence network had evolved since the outbreak of the war, and money from the Forbes/Aspinwall mission aided efforts to collect information through outside sources. The consul would be acknowledged for his intelligence gathering against Confederate plans to purchase weapons and especially to acquire warships. His tenacity paid dividends and he was later praised, for his determined efforts "in hunting for secret information appears to have been indefatigable."[186]

Dudley's attempts to obtain reports on the construction status of the rams were initially frustrated by watchmen at the Lairds yard. The consul wrote to Seward, "They are using great precautions to keep us ignorant of their doings. No stranger is admitted into their yard."[187] Dudley had to go beyond Merseyside to obtain a trusted agent to get to the men at the Birkenhead Ironworks. One leading supplier of information was London detective Matthew Maguire.[188] Maguire had obtained very detailed information about the *Alabama* while she was still building at Lairds in 1862, and his success marked him as a very effective agent for Dudley.[189] In a sworn deposition dated 21 July 1863 and related to the Confederate cruiser, Maguire was by that time living in Liverpool and kept in employment around Britain by Dudley.[190]

Men like Maguire had to be handpicked, and efforts to obtain a substratum of paid informants able to provide reliable and legally verifiable information took time. Although initially thwarted at the entrance to Lairds, the Union diplomat did obtain information regarding the armor plate being rolled for the Laird rams at the Mersey Steel & Iron Company.[191] Dudley warned Seward that the plates were much improved over what the Union fleet had to contend with from homespun Confederate ironclads. The Consul observed the plate-making process, and noted, "the metal is heated in pieces not more than a hundred pounds in weight and then rolled together ... they

12-pounder RML Blakely gun, manufactured by Fawcett & Preston of Liverpool. This gun was fired on Fort Sumter on 12 April 1861. Grant Park, Galena, Illinois (author's collection).

say the new mode is much more tenacious and its power of resistance much greater than the old."¹⁹² In 1863, one British newspaper described the art of armor plate production as an act that required "more than mere heating, and has to be cooked and watched in its cooking with as much care as if it was an omelette."¹⁹³ British rolling mills were world leaders in the production of iron cladding, and few places could match the skill and capacity of Yorkshire ironworks, as iron plate took on the sobriquet, "Sheffield carpet."¹⁹⁴

Particulars such as the one detailing the plate produced at Mersey Steel & Iron were lacking from subsequent reports sent by Dudley. The consul's workload prevented detailed analysis of all information with the result that intelligence was sometimes confused and jumbled by the sheer volume of reporting. Lines crossed with other Federal agents, and Dudley served as a facilitator and relay for intelligence obtained. He did not have the resources for always-accurate reporting. His apparatus lacked a filter.

The consul passed on information and rumor concerning the Confederate efforts in Liverpool to the commanders of Federal warships during their regular calls to British ports. On 20 July 1863, Rear Admiral S.P. Lee relayed a report to Welles regarding the disarmed steamer *Gibraltar*, formerly the Confederate cruiser *Sumter*, which had loaded at Liverpool and was waiting to clear customs on 3 July.¹⁹⁵ Her cargo reportedly included a number of heavy guns in wooden cases, including two Blakely RMLs intended for transfer to one of the Birkenhead rams when the ironclad left British waters.¹⁹⁶ The report claimed the guns weighted 22 tons each. In the holds of the *Gibraltar* were shot, shell, "other munitions of war," and the machinery likely intended to work the guns in one of the turrets of a Laird ram.¹⁹⁷ The blockade runner did carry two 13-inch RMLs, but these were destined for Charleston, not the rams. These guns (each weighing 22 tons) were too large for normal stowage and

Inscription on breech of 12-Pounder RML Blakely gun, manufactured by Fawcett & Preston of Liverpool. Grant Park, Galena, Illinois (photograph by author).

had to be positioned vertically, giving the *Gibraltar* the appearance of a ship with three funnels.[198] Although Lee's report was inaccurate in all its details, Bulloch did obtain ordnance for his ironclads from a Liverpool source. Fawcett & Preston would build several 9-inch guns (including those numbered 221, 222, and 223) as part of a five-gun order dated 8 September 1863, with four of those guns intended for the Laird rams.[199]

The presence of the Union informants in Britain was so evident by mid–1863 that "the port of Liverpool has been delivered over to a systematic espionage such as probably would be looked for in vain in despotic Russia, and could scarcely find a parallel in free America."[200] In May, the *London Evening Standard* printed a letter to the editor from a British subject recently returned to London from the continent.[201] Mistaking him for a Confederate official, the man was followed. Describing the interests in his communications, the beset Briton reported: "If the postman knocked at my door to deliver a letter an attempt was made to handle it and ascertain where it had been posted.... If I dispatched a telegram a 'private detective' was at my heels, and as soon as I left the telegraph office a bribe was offered to the young female who had received my message for the communication of its contents."[202]

Liverpool was "bristling with alarm" over the rumors of secret agents, and "every strange looking person in the streets is at once taken for a hired spy or private detective."[203] The Liverpool police, on orders from the Treasury, investigated activities related to another vessel Bulloch hoped to acquire as a cruiser, the *Alexandra*. Maguire's men and the other for-hire private detectives were functioning in an unofficial capacity and were subject to "all kinds of censure and suspicion."[204] These and other demonstrations of how the usually murky business of espionage had suddenly emerged into the public conscience were reflected in a comedy called *Finesse*; or *Spy and Counter Spy*.[205] The comedy starred a well-known favorite of the English stage, Alfred Wigan, with his wife and others in supporting roles. The farce was termed a great success with one reviewer commenting that the "applause was hearty ... the laughter incessant."[206] Bulloch was dogged by the clandestine agents of the United States and complained that their actions were increasingly invasive. The Confederate officer was to remark:

> The spies of the United States are numerous, active and unscrupulous. They invade the privacy of families, tamper with the confidential clerks of merchants, and have succeeded in converting a portion of the police of this country into secret agents of the United States, who have practiced a prying watchfulness over the movements and business of individuals intolerably vexatious, which has excited the disgust and openly expressed indignation of many prominent Englishmen, and the frequent criticism of that portion of the British press which is really neutral.[207]

The U.S. intelligence system in Britain began operations in the summer of 1861, having been established by the U.S. Consul to Belgium, Henry Shelton Sanford.[208] The consul was eager to serve the Union, and roamed between Brussels, Paris, and London in his personal quest to obtain any information regarding Confederate activities in Europe.[209] During one of his visits to Britain, Sanford was given the name of a London detective by Consul Morse when the diplomat was stopping over in the British capital. Morse informed Sanford that police detective Ignatius Pollaky was "just the man," but required £100 to start work with his team of private investigators.[210]

Pollaky worked for C.F. Field, former "Chief of the Detective Police of the Metropolis," who employed Pollaky in the role of superintendent of his foreign department.[211] Detective Pollaky had gotten married on 5 June and was undoubtedly motivated to his new line of work in the interests of generating cash for his new household.[212] Apparently Morse had read of Pollaky in the newspapers, as he was a well-known witness for Crown prosecutors.[213] By 12 July 1861, Morse had employed the investigator, and soon thereafter Pollaky and his agents were beginning their work of setting out "Posts" to be manned, and persons of interest to be followed.[214] Bulloch was a primary target on their lists, and the Confederates in Liverpool were reported on as "B. & Co."[215] Pollaky was one detective mentioned in the British press, as associated with the "Spy System considered so hateful to Englishmen." He had been previously utilized by those who sought information for pending divorce cases, forgery claims, and now, continuous surveillance work needed to track Confederate agents.[216] Morse soon found Pollaky and his men to be too heavy-handed as their techniques lacked finesse and created unwanted observation by the general public. Sanford also lacked the essential careful touch and in November 1861, proposed planting an agent on board the steamer *Gladiator* then loading with supplies for the Confederacy, and running her onto a mud bank in the Thames.[217]

The system established and paid for in part by Sanford ran afoul of Adams, who disliked Sanford's meddling where Consul Morse held the portfolio. Sanford's ad hoc network also suffered from bureaucratic redundancy as both consuls were paying for information from the same source: Pollaky. Adams disdainfully noted that the U.S. Consul to Belgium spent most of his time in Paris, and from there traveled to London for the purposes of "poaching."[218] The overlapping, dual-reporting channels could not continue, especially as the close surveillance methods of Pollaky's informants had generated unwanted press in Britain. Adams wrote to Seward, who then informed Sanford via letter that his activities had unintentionally created "some inconveniences" for the U.S. diplomats assigned to Britain, and he was to stay out of intelligence collection operations there.[219]

Dudley achieved a notable success in the spring of 1863 when he delayed a ship intended as a gift for the Confederate Navy from leaving Liverpool.[220] The *Alexandra* was a wooden-hulled screw steamer configured for rapid adaption into a commerce raider. She was launched by the shipbuilder William Miller & Sons and fitted out through Fawcett, Preston & Company, the same yard and engineering firm that had built the C.S.S. *Florida*.[221] Dudley saw this ship as the opportunity for a test case concerning the Foreign Enlistment Act and sought the assistance of A.F. Squarely, a Liverpool solicitor who had helped him during the earlier attempt to stop the *Alabama*.[222] The evidence gathered by Dudley and his solicitor was routed through Adams, who relayed it to the Foreign Secretary.[223]

The Union efforts were rewarded when officers from H.M. Customs seized the *Alexandra* on 5 April 1863. The Crown prosecutors lost their case as the ship was not armed, but the government tried again. The result was another failure, and the *Alexandra* was released in April 1864. She would eventually sail for the Confederacy later that year as a blockade runner (she had been renamed *Mary*), not as a warship.[224] Although not a decisive victory as Union diplomats had hoped, the *Alexandra* case set a precedent. Dudley had found a way to impede the efforts of the Confederate agents and their associated shipbuilders in Britain through legal (albeit temporary) intervention. The courts did not uphold the seizure, but delay became an effective tactic used by Dudley to aid the Federal war effort.

Union surveillance operations, which had continued in Britain throughout most of the Civil War, now rose to new levels of activity. The efforts centered not only on stopping arms and supplies from reaching the Confederates, but also on obtaining clear evidence for Adams to present to Russell. Dudley's background as a lawyer provided a skilled discernment regarding which testimony would carry weight at an official inquiry. Seeking more than mere information, he now moved to obtain sworn depositions from eyewitnesses. Detectives had become tainted. The Union needed a fresh approach to block the Mersey ironclads from putting to sea. They obtained men on the inside—paid informants who were skilled shipfitters in the Lairds shipyard.[225]

Especially valuable were those men who worked on or near the rams. Austin Joseph Hand was one paid informant working as a caulker in the Lairds yard. He would swear that he saw Bulloch at the Birkenhead Ironworks when the keels for the two turret ships were laid down.[226] One informant relayed a discussion he had with "Mr. Moore," one of the head workmen at Lairds, who stated with a sense of pride in the two ships, "Wait for the 294 and 295, get out and alongside the 'Alabama' and then you will soon see the Southern ports opened."[227]

Paid informants are of doubtful reliability, and soon after paying for information obtained from within the Birkenhead Ironworks, rumors swirled out that men were watching the construction of the rams and receiving coin for tale-bearing. Dudley had informed Seward that the workers he had to rely on for inside information were "not as a general thing very esteemable men, but are the only persons we can get to engage in this business, which I am sure you will agree with me is not a very pleasant one."[228] Men from shipyards suspected of building warships intended for the Confederates were reportedly offered £50, or passage to the United States and the offer of a position or "excellent situation" if they provided information to Union agents.[229]

As mentioned previously, John Laird had stated in the House of Commons as early as March 1863 that Union spies were interfering with work around the Kingdom: "Almost every detective that can be got hold of in this country is employed, and they have spies everywhere. I believe there are spies in my son's [sic] works in Birkenhead, and in all the great establishments in the country."[230] By August 1863, spies reportedly delayed progress on the rams and security was tightened at Lairds yard as a result.[231] Some informants were suspected, their positions were in jeopardy, and they were likely sacked if found out. One of Dudley's informants wrote of the social and economic costs of his involvement in the Union intelligence network, "[I would] never undertake a job like this as I have lost all my self-respect and done myself a great deal of damage. I hope you will write by return as I am getting bankrupt. Let me know to be or not to be."[232]

Austin Hand was a curious case. He had traveled with his wife to Liverpool to visit his brother-in-law, who was then employed at Lairds. His relation helped him obtain a position at the shipyard, where he returned to his trade as a ship-caulker.[233] Hand, an American citizen, supplied information to Dudley "from time to time," but when his deposition detailing Bulloch's visits to Lairds to inspect the rams was sent to Russell by Adams in London on 17 July 1863, both Hand and his brother-in-law were subsequently sacked.[234] Labeled as a spy, the unfortunate Hand had been unable to obtain work in and around Liverpool since his discharge from Lairds in August 1863, and he was eventually compelled to return to the United States.[235]

Hand arrived in New York on 28 July 1864 in a destitute state, but hoped for work at the Brooklyn Navy Yard. Unable to procure a position, Hand had reached circumstances of "great distress."[236] The story of Hand and others who assisted the American consul in Liverpool undoubtedly sent a chill through Merseyside. No one who had jeopardized the reputation and wellbeing of the area shipyards and the means to procure work for over 3,000 men working at Lairds could continue undamaged. Swearing out depositions to give to Dudley would end any semblance of a steady working life in Birkenhead and Liverpool. Once labeled as an informer for the Union, these men had to go away, some as far as America, in order to rebuild their lives. Taking the £50 from the Federal spymaster had proven to be more costly than anticipated for certain informers.

Launching the Rams

Although the public had been largely barred from the major shipyards in Britain, some newspaper reporters were permitted access, and one wrote of his visit to Lairds in September 1863.[237] That unnamed correspondent, having traveled to Liverpool and then on to Birkenhead to ostensibly visit an agricultural show, wrote: "To not have paid a visit to Messrs Laird's great industrial establishment, would have been something equivalent to being in Rome and yet visiting neither the Pope nor St. Peter's." After walking among the building ways, the correspondent found the two copula ships, which he described as "unmistakable ships of war ... evidently sea-going, very strong, yet fine in the lines, with workmen clustered upon them everywhere like bees." The atmosphere at Lairds had undoubtedly changed with a new emphasis on security, as the writer observed that "in the whole establishment there was not a single loiter ... each man seemed occupied, and even more intent than his neighbor, in close attention to his special duty."[238]

The pace of work on the two rams had suddenly picked up in the early summer of 1863. The *Alexandra* case had cast doubt over Confederate shipbuilding efforts, but the work was renewed with purpose after Lairds and Bulloch felt reasonably confident that the sale to Bravay & Company would prevent the U.S. diplomats from gaining ground with the Foreign Office. On 16 June, payment terms between Lairds and the new French owners were agreed whereby one fourth of the costs of the ships would be paid to the builders when the first ironclad was launched, and another quarter was to be paid when the first ship was completed.[239] The remaining funds would be paid under identical conditions for the second ship.[240]

The drafts of money were facilitated by a French banker, a Monsieur Langier, who had also helped facilitate the Erlanger loan.[241] Langier had reportedly signed as a guarantor for the rams, and served as the financial link between the Lairds and Bravay. On 28 June 1863, Bulloch had officially relinquished legal claim to the Birkenhead rams (which had officially begun under contract on 1 July 1862), and did "for ever [sic] quit claim" his interest in the ships.[242] Work could go ahead with renewed emphasis despite the prying of Federal informants, as the Confederate agent was out of the picture, at least as far as Lairds were concerned. Bulloch had temporarily relocated to

France to supervise the building of his armorclads at Arman's yard in Bordeaux, and only came to Liverpool for a day or two in the late summer to review letters and post his dispatches to Richmond via the Bermuda mail.[243]

The two ironclads building at Bordeaux were lesser men-of-war compared to their Laird predecessors. Shorter and of less displacement than the Birkenhead vessels, these French variants carried a 9-inch Armstrong RML in the forecastle and two 70-pounder RMLs in a fixed turret aft.[244] Like the Laird ships, both Arman ironclads were designed to operate in shallow waters (although their draft was almost as much as that of the 294 and 295) and built with rams, but the iron beaks projected much further forward than on the Birkenhead ships.[245] One French armorclad was given the cover name *Cheops* and her sister the *Sphinx* in an attempt to give the ships another Egyptian air.[246] Unlike Lairds turret rams, the Arman ironclads were wooden-hulled and coppered in preparation for use in the warmer waters of the American South.[247]

The ram on these French-built ironclads was unusual. Shaped like an elongated duck bill, it was described as "a huge round backed point, sharpened and curved as it descends under the waterline," and extended approximately 20 feet from the prow.[248] Four times as long as the five-foot tapered ram on the Laird ironclads, this feature negated the maneuver advantage of the twin screws and twin rudders on the *Cheops* and *Sphinx*.[249] The ram on the two Laird turret ships (when compared to other British-designed steam rams of the era) was likely submerged three feet below the surface, but on the Arman vessels, more of the ram was above the water at the prow unless the ships were loaded forward.[250]

Unlike the Laird ships where the ram was a secondary weapon, the Bordeaux armorclads were built with an emphasis on the ram as a first strike option. The larger surface area of the ram on the Arman ships undoubtedly cast up spray and confronted the dual rudders with more submerged mass to overcome when helm was needed. Steering was also hampered by the pronounced forward sweep of the "tumblinghome deficiency of the ram bow," as observed by Patrick Barry during his visit to the Arman yard while the French rams were under construction.[251] When the *Sphinx* belatedly entered Confederate service in 1865 as the C.S.S. *Stonewall*, her commanding officer, Captain Thomas J. Page, C.S.N, described her ram as an "elephantine proboscis" and faulted the structure as contributing to her poor seakeeping abilities.[252] Page noted the ironclad plowed into the waves "diving and coming up, after the fashion of the porpoise."[253] The ram was simply too large for a ship of 194 feet in length overall.[254]

In Richmond, Mallory was increasingly anxious to get the Laird rams away from Birkenhead. On 21 April 1863, he had written to Bulloch with his views on the two turret ships, announcing, "These vessels would be of incalculable value to us at this Time." Undoubtedly anxious for the Confederate Navy to have the wherewithal to score a blow against the Union forces, Mallory ventured a bold but highly impractical concept of operations when he wrote in the same letter about the possibility of restoring New Orleans to Confederate control. The secretary was desperate for information to allay his fears that the Confederate ironclads might not get out in time, and he concluded the introduction of his letter with an inquiry: "What prospect have we of getting them out, and when? These are all questions that intrude themselves constantly upon me."[255]

Earlier, Bulloch had written to Mallory, requesting the command of one of the

Laird armorclads. The Confederate Navy Secretary replied peevishly on 3 March 1863, "If you adhere to this desire, give the earliest notice practicable, that I may send an officer to take—not supply your place."[256] Faced with the ungracious opposition from his superior, Bulloch withdrew his request for command. When his success getting the *Florida* and *Alabama* into commissioned service for the South should have been rewarded, his plan changed to one of waiting for official gratitude to come later. On 30 August 1863, Mallory wrote to the Confederate officer selected to command the Laird rams, Captain Samuel S. Barron, C.S.N, instructing him to travel to Britain and assume the command of the first Birkenhead ram after Bulloch brought her out to France. Barron was under orders not to interfere with Bulloch's "special duties ... the department desiring to leave his judgment and action the larger scope."[257]

Mallory had tried to assuage Bulloch's disappointment at not receiving a command when he wrote in April 1863, "I know of no gentleman in our service whom I would, from my point of view, with more pleasure see in such command than yourself, while at the same time there is not one to whom I could look to supply your place for us in England." This was a shortsighted move by Mallory, a move which dampened the ardor of a man deserving of a chance to command a warship on a combat mission. Mallory suspected he overstepped and wrote to Bulloch to explain, "I may have too far lost sight of your professional esprit."[258]

Mallory was too far removed from the action to appreciate what his man in Liverpool had accomplished. A short assignment at sea would have given the chance of glory to an accomplished officer instead of overburdening him with more desk work. Mallory unwittingly removed the inspirational spark that hope provided to his most effective officer. With command a fading prospect, Bulloch pursued his tasks with a determination driven by duty, rather than one also motivated by anticipation and the hope of adventure. Bulloch switched operations to France to avoid the increased attention from Federal agents in Britain, but the Laird rams were progressing again, and he was needed most in Liverpool at this time.

Bulloch was probably hoping that one of those French-built ships would finally be awarded to him as his command. Mallory's oversight had thwarted his best officer, and in so doing probably injured the Confederacy's best chance of getting one of the Laird rams away from European waters at a crucial time in the war. Bulloch was undoubtedly disappointed at not receiving command of one of the Laird ironclads. He knew his position in Europe was crucial for the Confederate war effort, but he could not completely contain his bitterness and later wrote:

> Active service at the front wins the "Bauble reputation." The men who work in the rear are not despised or even undervalued, but they must have the nerve to stifle their ambition. They may expect fair and just commendation, but then they must not aspire to stand side by side with those who wear the "Myrtle Crown."[259]

On 4 July 1863, the *El Tousson*, the first of the Laird rams, was launched on the Mersey.[260] She was launched without her masts or turrets, and her wide beam gave her an appearance of looking "more circular than conical" when afloat.[261] As she slid down the ways, she carried the British flag astern and a French Tricolor fluttered from a temporary mast amidships in an acknowledgment of her new owners.[262] Towed to her fitting out dock at Lairds, men were detailed to work in 24-hour shifts in a renewed effort to get her ready for sea.[263] One Liverpool newspaper remarked of

294 at her launching, "She will give a good account of herself, and sustain the high reputation of her now celebrated builders."[264]

The launching was a tribute to Bulloch's perseverance; however, that same day, the Confederates had suffered two catastrophic blows that would place them on the defensive for the remainder of the war. The Confederate fortress of Vicksburg, Mississippi, the last link to the trans–Mississippi river region of the South, surrendered to Union General U.S. Grant on 4 July.[265] A day earlier, General Robert E. Lee's regiments, the crème of the Confederate Army, were defeated in the epochal encounter at Gettysburg, Pennsylvania, and began a struggle to get back to the relative safety of Virginia.[266] In one 24-hour span, the Southern States lost the initiative and became frantic for the means to divert Union forces from their now-compressed front lines.

Although the Laird ironclads were incomplete at this stage, they affected naval plans and operations for both the Confederacy and the Union. The rams offered the Confederates the means to inflict telling damage on the Union far from the battle lines. Though he could not command his armored ships, Bulloch still held influence regarding their utilization. Five days after the first Laird ram was launched, he wrote to Mallory from Paris to express his reasons why attacking New Orleans and pressing further up the Mississippi River were not valid options. The ironclads would need escorts to pass over the bar from the Gulf of Mexico. The shifting sands and mudflats at the entrance to the great river would require towboats to help pull the ironclads over the bar into the river channel. If they did not go aground, the ironclads would likely be restricted by the confines of the river "very much in the condition of a boxer with one arm tied behind his back."[267]

Bulloch proposed something much bolder, but also less hazardous than a mission along the Mississippi. He favored an attack against the New England coast, a bombardment of the naval facilities at Portsmouth, New Hampshire. The former U.S. naval officer was familiar with that port: "Opposite the town is an important national dock and building yard. The whole lies invitingly open to attack and destruction."[268] As a reprisal for the burning of Southern towns, and as a scheme to help pay for the warships, Bulloch opined that a flag of truce could be sent to the mayor of Portsmouth to demand $5 million in gold—otherwise $50 million in "Greenback" paper notes—or the Confederate ironclads would bombard the town. Enamored with the visions of his plan, he wrote with an adventurer's flair, "suppose our two ironclads should steam unannounced into that harbor on some fine October morning."

Bulloch knew they needed the best men to crew these ships, as they were not cruisers able to attract men in search of prize money, but ships with a "grim aspect and formidable equipment [that] clearly show they are solely intended for the real danger and shock of battle." Bulloch was confident that he could obtain engineers and stokers from Britain and perhaps enough men to man one gun on each ship, but he needed Southern men skilled in the arts of heavy artillery. If such men were preassigned to forts around Wilmington, North Carolina, the rams could steam through the Union blockading squadron and take the gunners on board to fill out their crews. From Wilmington, the resupplied and fully manned ironclads could take on the Federal Navy and lift the blockade on their way north.[269]

Confederate authorities knew a seaborne attack was difficult to resist. Early in the war, the Union naval attack on Port Royal, South Carolina, impressed General Lee, who wrote to Richmond, "wherever his fleet can be brought no opposition to his

Franklin Shiphouse at Navy Yard, Portsmouth, New Hampshire, c. 1870 (author's collection).

landing can be made except within range of our fixed batteries." Lee was careful to place defensive works around Savannah and Charleston in areas that could provide interlocking fire while also positioned where Union warships could not offer direct support to attacking Federal troops.[270]

A key target for the Laird rams would have been the Union Naval base at Beaufort, North Carolina. This port, captured by a Union amphibious operation in April 1862, provided coal, ammunition, provisions and repair faculties for the Union warships blockading Wilmington, North Carolina, 100 miles to the southwest.[271] Beaufort was a busy port and the coal stocks varied in size as warships came in to refuel, generally during the full moon, as blockade runners only attempted to run into Wilmington during dark nights.[272] The base was also an anchorage for ordnance supply vessels and storeships. By June 1864, Beaufort had more provisions on hand than the combined stocks of the Baltimore and Washington Navy Yards combined.

The harbor was difficult to enter due to the shifting channels and prevailing winds, but the port brimmed with flammable materials including coal, barrels of tar, and highly combustible turpentine, enough to present a fire hazard to the civilian colliers, Federal men-of-war, and supply ships that usually crowded the bay. Confederate soldiers had burned bridges in the area and their scouts were familiar with the pace of activities at the port.[273] The Laird rams (or one of them) would likely have conducted a sortie to bombard Beaufort, as the benefits of shelling that port far outweighed the risks. An attack on the key base would have disrupted Union resupply operations and would have greatly hampered the Federal blockade. With a Laird ironclad operating from Wilmington, the Union Navy would have been compelled to reassign monitors from operations near Charleston to protect their base at Beaufort should Wilmington continue under blockade. As a method of disrupting Federal operations, the base was too inviting a target to bypass if the Birkenhead ironclads were in commission under the Confederate flag and steaming near the Carolina coasts.

Union authorities had mixed views of the Laird rams, but most were growing concerned at their prospects of getting to sea. Adams was increasingly gloomy regarding the outlook of stopping the departure of the vessels later referred to as "these floating engines of destruction." One early Union casualty of the two ironclads would have been the exchange rate, as gold was sure to have risen against the Greenback upon news of their sailing from British shores.[274] The official exchange rate in 1863 was $4.85 (U.S. dollars) to £1. Greenbacks depreciated from that level and averaged 70.5 percent of their face value against gold during the mid-war years. A rise in the gold value would have damaged Union revenue from bond sales in Europe, as these were purchased in Greenbacks.[275]

Welles wrote in his diary on 17 August 1863 that he sent a response to Rear Admiral John A. Dahlgren, "who has serious apprehensions about Laird's ironclad steamers, which trouble Du Pont," and relayed a report from the State Department confirming Washington was making entreaties to Britain to prevent the Laird ironclads from sailing.[276] In his dispatch to Dahlgren, the Navy Secretary detailed a report from Seward, which relayed that Adams "had informed the British Government that if the Rebel ironclads are permitted to come out it will be *casus belli*."[277]

Fox sent a copy of plans for one of the Laird rams to John Ericsson, who scoffed at their armament (and construction) when compared with the larger guns of the new Union monitors: "Such a gingerbread affair must not come near our XV inch bulldogs in their impregnable kennels."[278] Bulloch took a different view, writing, "if one of the rams had gone into smooth water, and had suffered a 'Monitor' to make deliberate practice at her with 15-inch shot at short range ... no doubt in time her plates would have been loosened and the backing splintered; but their power and speed was such that in open water, with room to maneuver, I think they would have had no difficulty in running down any 'Monitor' then afloat...."[279]

Endeavoring to avoid alternative history, a brief discussion of ordnance available to the Union Navy, and that designed for the Laird rams, will hopefully shed some light on the results of a possible encounter. The wooden warships of the Federal blockading squadrons lacked sufficient firepower to resist one Laird ram "long enough for a second broadside"; therefore, the armament of the larger monitors in service during the Civil War provides the comparison point.[280]

The Union Navy had proven the capabilities of the 15-inch Dahlgren smoothbores, the largest naval guns in operational service in the war. Two Confederate ironclads, the *Atlanta* and *Tennessee*, had their armored casemates penetrated by shot from these guns, but lighter ordnance was ineffective against the unwieldy, Confederate-built armored vessels.[281] The 15-inch Dahlgren had an effective range of 2,120 yards at 7 degrees of elevation.[282] The four Blakely 9-inch RMLs on each Laird ram would have been able to outrange the 15-inch Dahlgren guns, but the two 70-pounder Whitworth guns intended for each ram had the distinct lead in range by better than 2 to 1 over a Federal monitor.[283] Although the 70-pounder (5-inch bore) Whitworth was considered by some in the British press to be too light when used against the heavier armor plate then entering service (in 1864), it was considered a superior piece of ordnance in terms of range and accuracy.[284]

As the 294 and 295 were armored with rolled plates of single thickness, and the

5-inch Whitworth rifle, captured from blockade runner *Princess Royal*, 1863, Washington Navy Yard, Washington, D.C. (photograph by author).

Union monitors were shielded with laminated iron, a battle could be decided by those warships armed with heavy guns capable of piercing the latest armor.[285] A confidential Admiralty paper on ordnance indicated several qualities required of heavy guns in the late 1860s, including accuracy, range, penetrating power, simplicity of use, and strength to withstand heavy powder charges. The Admiralty was clear as to which quality was most desired: "The *penetrating power* (italics in original) at ranges under 1,200 yards is certainly the most important under the existing circumstances of naval warfare. It is the most difficult to obtain, and without it all other qualities are useless."[286] The initial velocity of a shell as it left the muzzle of a naval gun was an indicator of penetrating power. The Admiralty compared several leading guns of the 1860s, and the 9-inch RML, fired with a heavy charge of 43 pounds of powder, developed a muzzle velocity of 1,340 feet per second. This compared favorably to the largest American 15-inch guns, which developed an initial velocity of 1,220 feet per second when fired with a 60-pound powder charge.[287]

For the Union monitors, a maximum powder charge firing a shell from a 15-inch gun could have decisive effects at close range. One 15-inch shell had penetrated the layered armor of the Confederate ironclad *Tennessee* at the Battle of Mobile Bay in 1864, a blow that contributed to the surrender of the vessel. Nevertheless, a charge of 60 pounds of powder in a 15-inch gun was considered "daring" and threatened to burst the barrel if not handled with great care in loading.[288]

Both Confederate and most Union ironclads were built in America with wooden hulls, mostly from green timbers, and suffered structural stresses due to the rapid deterioration of the unseasoned wooden supports and planking. The monitors also lacked enough watertight integrity to ensure they could withstand being holed below the waterline; however, the Laird rams were adequately compartmented below decks and were designed with a double bottom to withstand contact with a torpedo.[289]

Another mitigating factor was the quality of shell. Ammunition manufactured in the South suffered from mediocre quality, and the Confederate Navy's chief ordnance officer, Commander John Brooke, warned those inferior shells put their warships at a marked disadvantage against the better equipped Union men-of-war.[290] This was partially the result of a lack of adequate materials, but the main reason was the lack of skilled laborers, a dilemma referred to in a report to the Confederate Congress by Mallory as a "serious evil."[291] The Laird rams would have overcome this problem due to the superior quality of rifled guns and armor piercing shell available for the Blakely and Whitworth ordnance.

Had the Laird rams gone to sea with their intended RMLs, they would have had the edge in terms of range and accuracy in a gun duel with the most modern Union ironclads. These monitors had the advantage in terms of weight of shell during a close-range encounter, but the Laird rams also had suitable speed to maneuver out of reach if damaged. A likely outcome would have been an inconclusive battle with the Laird ram(s) giving and receiving damage, but Union naval operations along the coasts of North America would have been endangered by the arrival of the Birkenhead ironclads. David G. Surdam wrote, "Although Northern naval superiority alone probably was not sufficient to have defeated the Confederacy, it appears to have been a necessary condition for the Northern victory."[292] The Laird rams threatened to disrupt the Federal Navy's support to the overall Union war effort.

On 8 September 1863, Fox wrote to Lincoln, warning that the Laird rams represented a clear threat to the Federal Navy and the coasts of the Union: "In a naval point of view the departure of these vessels, or even one of them, requires, on the part of this Government, the gravest deliberation."[293] The Union Navy had taken steps to offer some protection to Boston and the New England fishing fleet in the event a Laird ironclad steamed near Cape Cod. One newspaper in Ohio reported the steam frigate *Niagara* had been refitted with a heavy battery of guns, but the prospect of her action against one of the Laird rams was a source of "apprehension" for the Union.[294]

The Federal Navy was urged to take other actions to make ready for the new Confederate oceangoing ironclads. Rear Admiral Dahlgren had proposed precautions in anticipation of the first Laird ironclad arriving off Charleston. The Admiral asked that a new monitor, either the *Dictator* or the *Puritan*, be ordered to Union-occupied Port Royal, South Carolina, to protect that essential supply base.[295] Dahlgren also proposed that coal and provisions be moved nearer to the Union lines outside Charleston. This would allow adequate supplies for shallow draft steamers supporting the Federal regiments outside that Rebel-held port, as the arrival of a Laird ram would drive off the larger warships maintaining the blockade.[296]

Bulloch would state years later, "the Government of the United States did not exaggerate the importance of preventing the departure of the rams from Liverpool."[297] The governor of Massachusetts also did not underestimate the rams and had dispatched Colonel Harrison Ritchie as his agent to purchase the latest RMLs from Armstrong for the protection of Boston Harbor. Ritchie wrote back to inform the governor that the purchase must be "managed with great secrecy and caution" to avoid public scrutiny.[298]

The guns from the Elswick Ordnance Works were a curious choice for the fortifications of a key base of the Union.[299] The 10 May 1862 edition of *Scientific American* denounced the transition of Armstrong guns from breechloading ordnance to larger muzzleloaders as a reflection of "the age of humbug."[300] Despite this seeming regression, the development of the Armstrong guns progressed through the early 1860s to become "very much more of a success than is generally supposed."[301] One American journal compared the Armstrong heavy pieces with similar-sized U.S. ordnance (15-inch Rodman guns and Parrott 300-pounders), disdainfully noting examples of failed American guns as "cast-iron abortions."[302]

The Armstrong patterns offered readily obtainable heavy guns for the protection of Boston, bypassing Washington bureaucracy and industrial backlogs in the Northern states. In London, Colonel Ritchie obtained the Elswick contract through a third party: the noted shipbuilder John Scott Russell.[303] The guns were delayed by slow payments and deception. Russell had made the first installment with money received from Ritchie, but diverted funds to pay off his debts and to finance his shipyard in Cardiff.[304] By the time the guns were finished, the war in America was over and Russell's embezzlement had been found out.[305]

The quality of work in armor, ordnance, and overall construction put the Birkenhead ironclads at the forefront of naval shipbuilding in the mid–1860s. Both Confederate and Union officials *believed* the Laird rams would have had a noteworthy impact on the naval war. In 1903, a New York newspaper reported a former Confederate naval officer spoke of the Laird rams, and commented, had the ironclads departed Britain and arrived off the Confederate coasts, "the effect upon the war might have been very great."[306]

Redefining Neutrality

The Foreign Enlistment Act of 1819 was, by the 1860s, at variance with the demands of trade, industrial-scale production of armaments, and the speed of transatlantic travel. One British periodical would accurately note, "in truth, the whole system of maritime warfare has been revolutionized by the introduction of steam...."[307] The neutrality law had become obsolete and so too the methods of enforcing that act.[308] Neutrality, as it was understood in the mid–1860s, was ill-defined, as it was implemented and changed at a deliberate pace more suited to the sail and the horse. New concepts of what comprised neutrality had to travel at the speed of the telegraph if officials responsible for enforcing government actions were to outrace the locomotive and the marine steam engine.

The key problem regarding enforcing neutrality was where to begin. The belligerents had imported arms and equipment, and men from Britain had been enlisted in the services of the warring powers, in both military and industrial capacities. The 1819 law warned that British subjects were not to "knowingly aid, assist, or be concerned in the equipping, furnishing, fitting out, or arming of any ship or vessel."[309] Factories in both the North and the South were in dire need of skilled hands, and the promise of high wages encouraged some to make the Atlantic crossing. John

Snowden returned to his English birthplace to recruit ironworkers for his factory in Pittsburgh, Pennsylvania.[310] Snowden was the senior partner of the firm Snowden & Mason, which built shallow draft Union monitors for service on the Western Rivers.[311] The Confederates contracted for British foundrymen to travel to the Southern States and begin work casting heavy guns. Bulloch took this mission in hand, arranging with Thomas Ludlam, the foreman of the Low Moor Iron Works in Yorkshire, to travel with a team of skilled men through the blockade in order to set up an armaments shop for the Confederate Navy.[312] Ludlam and his men were skilled tool makers, experts at the steam hammer, and one of their team was considered "a practical man of every trade, one who can ... make a horseshoe or repair an engine."[313]

Attempts by Adams to stop the Laird rams from going to sea were hampered by actions undertaken in the United Kingdom by men working on behalf of the U.S. government. Federal agents had complicated matters for the North by recruiting men in Ireland for the Union Army, and some for their Navy. One editorial called attention to the recruiting efforts in Ireland to man the Federal Army, but also questioned the legal dilemma regarding the use of weapons sent to the belligerents: "The Confederates may be shot down with English-made cannon, but the Federals must not have their cotton and tea seized by English-built ships flying the Confederate flag."[314]

Recruitment was sometimes considered deceitful work undertaken by unscrupulous men. The U.S. Navy was cautious calling at some ports due to the actions of the recruiting agents, or "Sharks," as they were sometimes called.[315] Captain John Rodgers, U.S.N., had written to Fox to report that he had lost men who had overstayed their leave, and recruiters in New York were keen to acquire seamen, especially English speakers.[316] Merchant ship captains, hoping to avoid Confederate cruisers, were reportedly paying $50 for men to sign on for a voyage to Liverpool, and the Federal Army was offering a $150 enlistment bonus.[317] When the steam frigate H.M.S. *Ariadne* visited New York in the winter of 1861–2, twenty-two men deserted the ship to take up arms for the Union. The desertions had occurred even though leave was not granted, and the *Ariadne* had anchored not near the city, but in the harbor off Staten Island. One officer on the frigate noted "nationally was of no consequence so long as the men were ready to fight."[318]

Rather than recruiting men in Ireland, the Confederates pressed able-bodied men into service wherever they found them in the Southern States.[319] The British Consuls were able to obtain release from the Confederate Army for some men, but Governor Thomas Moore of Louisiana warned that if British subjects volunteered, the local government would not intercede with the military authorities to obtain their release. The use of the bounty seemed to be a key component of military service. Whether sought out, taken under pressure, or after physical abuse, the money in hand meant to the local authorities the man was enlisted in voluntary service.[320] Despite pressure and coercion, some enlisted due to local ties and personal obligations. One Scottish machinist living in Baton Rouge, Louisiana, enlisted in a state regiment out of a sense of loyalty to his neighbors, and for "the honour of old Scotland."[321]

Crown prosecutors would later try men for operating a recruitment service in Liverpool tasked with providing crewmen for the Confederate commerce raider *Georgia* in violation of the Foreign Enlistment Act. One man, Frank Glassbrook, signed aboard under the assumed name Frank Rimmers, a name he used in the Royal Naval Reserve.[322] Three men in U.S. naval uniform appeared before a judge in Cork, Ireland, for having enlisted aboard the Federal man-of-war U.S.S. *Kearsarge*. These three men, natives of Ireland, pled guilty, but one of them stated they did not think there was any harm in their actions.[323] Both the Union and the Confederacy had enlisted British subjects in their service in breach of British law, and these were actions that were considered in Britain to be "the grossest violation of all amicable relationships which ought to exist between friendly powers."[324]

In August 1863, the Confederate warship *Florida* returned to European waters and contributed to the rising apprehension over the fate of the Laird rams. The *Florida* steamed into the French port of Brest in need of repairs to her engines and copper hull plates. Her arrival compounded the concerns of Bulloch and consumed much of the diplomatic good will he had retained through his discretion. Some 35 men from the *Florida* were discharged and made their way to Cardiff in a ragged and worn state, and unintentionally aroused suspicions over the Mersey ironclads. From Wales, they traveled to Liverpool and attracted the attention of both Union intelligence operatives and legal agents of the Crown.

A confidential letter from the Foreign Office to British legal authorities asked "whether these seamen, in so far as they may be subjects of Her Majesty, are not liable to be proceeded against" for enlisting in the service of the Confederate Navy. The law officers were less anxious to seize such a large body of men, as they appeared to no longer be in service of the Southerners, and opined the arrest and trial of these men was not worth the effort. However, the arrest of those *Florida* men "anxious to be re-engaged in the service of the Confederate States" would serve as a suitable example to discourage further recruitment.[325]

By the late summer of 1863, the pace of work at Lairds had moved the construction of the ships forward to such a point that their service at sea was becoming a near certainty. One observer of the Lairds yard described this construction as being done with a speed which was "apparently by magic" and the ever-present industrial sounds as "knocking and hammering ... such cyclopedian noise."[326] The turrets were aboard neither the *294* nor *295*, but they were being painstakingly fabricated in the yard, with the chief workmen making frequent references to the plans close by. The turret foundations were largely in place in the lower hulls, their forms resembling "neither more nor less than ordinary railway turn-tables."[327]

At 10:45 a.m. on 29 August 1863, the second ram, number 295, was launched in the presence of hundreds of spectators.[328] The *El Monassir*, translated as "Victory," was not a merchantman that could be converted into a cruiser; she was a "war-ship of extraordinary power ... of some other purpose than mere privateering."[329] She flew the French Tricolor as a matter of form, but no one was deceived.[330] The *El Monassir* and her sister were intended for the Confederates. The race to prove complicity and the ruse of both actual and intended ownership were soon to come to the fore.

The first Laird ram, the *El Tousson*, was rapidly coming together. Her masts had been shifted, boilers and engines were in place, and the ram was put on.[331] Equally worrying to the Federals, four Confederate Navy engineering officers had arrived in Liverpool on the Cunarder *Asia* from Halifax. By the time her sister was launched, the forward turret was installed, and painting was soon to begin on the first ram.[332] Several coats of thin, red lead paint had been applied to the 294 to protect the ironwork from oxidizing prior to the final painting of the hull and upper works in black, white and buff. The three coats of red lead paint applied to the exterior gave the ironclad a

ONE OF THE STEAM-RAMS IN COURSE OF CONSTRUCTION IN MESSRS. LAIRD'S SHIPBUILDING-YARD, BIRKENHEAD.—SEE NEXT PAGE.

294 fitting out at Lairds, 1863 (author's collection).

dull hue, but the color was an unmistakable signal to all who saw her.[333] The first Laird ram was nearing completion and only the installation of her aft turret, final fittings, and finishing paint work was needed to prepare her for sea.[334]

Anticipation, fears, plans of action, and intelligence reports circulated between Britain and Washington, yet the ships were not ready for combat. The guns were not aboard the Laird ironclads, but the ships had one piece of "equipment" that could not be explained away.[335] The ram projecting forward from the bow of each ship was described as "a most effective weapon of war," thus proving that Lairds were building warships for a foreign power. One British newspaper touched on the key point of the Confederate shipbuilding efforts when it proclaimed that "there must be some fault somewhere, when we see *the spirit of the law evaded*" (italics in original).[336]

The United States had pressed Britain to close the legal loopholes, which permitted a ship to leave a British port and later be transformed into a man-of-war flying the Star & Bars. One British newspaper quoted in a New York magazine stated, "there is no amendment of the law required. The Government has ample powers, and if it really wanted to put a stop to the fitting out of vessels in our ports for the Confederates, Mr. Davis would be unable to get a fishing smack out of the Mersey."[337] This position was supported in another British newspaper when it compared the Laird rams to the attempted procurement of Hale's Rockets for Hungarian revolutionaries in 1853. As with the rockets, ships could be seized in Britain, for "laws, we know, can be stretched or tightened at the will of those who are appointed to execute them."[338]

The main problem with enforcing the Foreign Enlistment Act as it applied to the Laird armorclads was the point of ownership. They belonged to a French firm, and what happened to them after the owners received them was not a point that *directly* involved the British government. Interpretations of when an activity permitted by a neutral power ceased to be neutral, and actions by a belligerent involved other nations in a conflict where they had beforehand remained apart, now (late summer to autumn 1863) became the dominant issues of transatlantic relations. In late October 1863, one British newspaper highlighted the legal dilemmas of neutral trade with belligerents when it stated, "of all the different classes of the law, the Law of Nations is the most intricate, and consequently to this hour the most unsettled."[339]

The Laird brothers brought the dilemma to a head in early September 1863 when they informed S. Edward Price, the Collector of Customs at Liverpool, of their intention to take the *El Tousson* out for a short cruise on the Mersey. They intended the voyage to be a short trial run to begin on 14 September in order to test her machinery, after which the ironclad would return to the shipyard for her final stages of fitting out.[340] This proposed run was thwarted when the Treasury ordered the Liverpool Customs office to prevent the ironclad from leaving the Mersey until government inquiries into the destination of the ship were concluded.[341] The first Laird ram was expected to be completed in early October and the second ship by early November if the work schedule was maintained.[342] The delivery of the two ironclads was an issue that could not be ignored, and the British government would soon have to choose sides in America's Civil War regarding these warships.

On 11 September, the Foreign Secretary wrote to Adams in response to his entreaties against the Laird rams, stating:

> With regard to the general duties of a neutral, according to international law, the true doctrine has been laid down repeatedly by Presidents and Judges of eminence of the United States, and that doctrine is, that a neutral may sell to either or both of two belligerent parties any implements or munitions of war ... and it is difficult to find a reason why a ship that is to be used for warlike purposes is more an instrument or implement of war than cannon, muskets, swords, bayonets, gunpowder, and projectiles to be fired from cannon and muskets.... In fact, the ship can never be expected to decide a war or a campaign....[343]

Russell was using America's recent history against Adams to prove that neutrality was open to a wide disparity of interpretation. During the Crimean War, American businesses had supplied arms, and had built ships for the Russians.[344] One U.S.-built steamer, the *America*, was built for Russia and sailed to Petropavlovsk during the Crimean War, under the command of American officers.[345] William H. Hudson, the captain of the *America*, had allegedly carried arms for the Tsar's Pacific garrison buried in the bunkers under the ship's coal.[346] Hudson would claim he only carried a few small arms, a barrel of powder and "Robin shot."[347] Colt revolvers and other arms were reportedly sent on U.S.-flagged and other neutral vessels to the then-Prussian port of Memel on the Baltic for overland shipment to eastern Russia.[348] American mechanics from Baltimore had reportedly travelled to Russia in 1855 to take the place of British railway workers who had left due to the outbreak of war the previous year.[349] Trade with the allies was more important for the United States, both in terms of ready income and relations with the big powers. American clipper ships were chartered to carry troops, munitions, supplies and horses for the British and French forces besieging Sevastopol.[350] Neutrality was still a confused concept in the mid-nineteenth century, but the application of national interest was one key factor, and another was profits. During the Civil War, one British journal was to remark:

> Ingenious lawyers and crotchety politicians may contend that there is no distinction between exporting guns and exporting men-of-war. But the results prove the contrary. The Americans have practically lost half their mercantile marine. The Confederate Government are the parties who have directly or indirectly caused these ships to be built in this country, and in so doing they entered upon a deliberate course of violating and evading the laws of England.[351]

In Washington, Lincoln was considering a declaration of war, and on the back of his calling card, wrote his instructions to Seward for him to pass to Adams. The note read: "Tell Adams to say to Palmerston that another 'Alabama' means war!"[352] Meanwhile, the British government was taking steps to determine the fate of the Laird rams.

On 22 September 1863, the British Naval Attaché to France, Captain E. Hore, R.N., met with Adrian Bravay to find out the true owners of the pair of ironclads.[353] Bravay produced the papers from Laird, proving that he was the legitimate owner, and reported that the former owner, Bulloch, was involved with the ironclads then under construction at Bordeaux.[354] The meeting also provided Captain Hore with more than supposition regarding the intended end user of the rams, as Bravay punctuated his comments with a series of winks and nods to indicate Bulloch was to be the recipient of the finished ironclads.[355]

The prime minister had also been involved in the search for a way out of the dilemma. He had written to the First Lord of the Admiralty with what was apparently a sales pitch to buy the Laird armored ships: "We are short of Iron Clads, [sic] and it takes Time to build them, we want a good many more to put us on our proper level with France; here are Two nearly finished, no doubt well built, fast sailors, and fitted as Rams...."[356] One Liverpool newspaper chided the seemingly indecisive Foreign Office, announcing that if the impasse over the Laird ships was to continue, the power would rest not in Westminster, but with "any shipowner in England to plunge the nation into war."[357] That newspaper concluded with the call, "just now we want a Cromwell, not a Russell."[358]

On 28 September, the newly appointed Chief Constructor of the Royal Navy, Edward James Reed, reported to the Admiralty the results of the interviews he had with the Lairds.[359] Reed had met with William Laird and his father, John Laird, M.P., on the 21st, 25th and 26th of that month to inquire if the two turret rams would be available for purchase by the British government.[360] The constructor found the suspicious Lairds "very reserved" at first, but they soon let down their guard and indicated that the issue of French ownership of the two rams was "apparently mere policy."[361] Work had again slowed on the ironclads due to the increased official interest in the ships, and Reed's inquiries revealed that the Lairds (and the Messrs. Bravay) would be interested in selling the armorclads to the Admiralty. This changed again by the time of his last meeting with John Laird and his son William on the 26th, as the shipbuilders apparently grew wary of Reed's insistent questionings.[362] These meetings were likely the beginning of a rivalry and distrust between Reed and the Lairds that would come to the fore several years later, and would follow the two rams throughout most of their service lives.

Reed had been censured before the Commons on 27 February 1863 for his perceived insults written in a letter to a member of Parliament.[363] A controversy had occurred around his appointment as Chief Constructor, due in part to his reported inexperience in constructing warships.[364] Laird had asked the Commons on 26 February, the day before the constructor was brought before the bar in the House, to question why accounts in the Royal Dockyards had not been properly kept, and had asked that Deptford be sold due to a lack of shipbuilding activity there.[365] Several days earlier, Laird asked that work on Reed's broadside ironclad H.M.S. *Enterprise*, and on the *Royal Sovereign*, then fitting out with Coles' revolving turrets, be pushed to early completion in order to test the benefits of each design.[366] Laird was not involved in his censure, but Reed was understandably wary of running afoul of an M.P. so deeply engaged in warship design, as well as the affairs of the naval dockyards. Suspicion was the natural outgrowth of Reed's controversial start.

Following his September visits to Merseyside, the Chief Constructor reported to the Admiralty his views that the Birkenhead Ironworks had not made sufficient progress on the ironclad frigate *Agincourt* then building for the Royal Navy, due to the apparent work priority given to the two turret ships.[367] Reed would also criticize the Sheffield iron maker John Brown & Company for delaying work on Royal Navy warships in order to export armor plate to the United States. To the Lairds, Reed likely seemed something more dangerous than a spy or a uniformed emissary from the Admiralty. He had the power to influence future contracts with the government, or he could perhaps steer away new orders from would-be foreign clients. With so much of their money undoubtedly tied in with the turret rams (the constructor had told the Admiralty the 294 and 295 might have been undertaken as "mere speculation" by the shipbuilders), the Lairds could not afford to confer too openly with the inquisitorial Reed.[368]

The constructor highlighted the pros and cons of acquiring these ships for the Royal Navy in a confidential report to the Duke of Somerset, the First Lord of the Admiralty. In his report, Reed stated the iron cladding on the rams was less at the bow and stern than the armor fitted on British warships then building or in service, and the iron ribs were "inferior in size and strength" compared to British armorclads.[369] Although low in the water, the raised forecastle and poop would undoubtedly improve the seaworthiness of each vessel.[370] Reed wrote the ships were "formed sufficiently strong to render them sound, safe, and durable," and recommended the First Sea Lord consider the "immediate" purchase of the two rams in order to add more ironclads to the British fleet.[371]

Seizing the Ships

In early September, the Prime Minister wrote to Russell expressing his satisfaction with the move to detain the Laird rams and the ironclad building on the Clyde.[372] Palmerston would later write (on 21 September) to his Foreign Minister, "politically I appreciate it would be best that the South should have them," but he understood this would not occur.[373] Palmerston knew the "ships cased in iron were intended for warlike purposes," and he was waiting for the final excuse to seize them while avoiding a change to the Foreign Enlistment Act that would run afoul of Parliament.[374] The Prime Minister suggested to Russell that the ironclads could best serve "our own interests" in a harbor defense role in British ports.[375]

The excuse came in the form of a story likely spun by Union informants regarding the discharged crewmen from the *Florida* preparing a plan to hijack the *El Tousson* on her trial run.[376] The renewed desire by the builders to send their nearly completed *294* on a short run just beyond the entrance to the Mersey presented a hazard that could not be ignored. On 8 October 1863, the Admiralty sent a coded telegram to Captain Edward A. Inglefield, commanding the ship-of-the-line H.M.S. *Majestic*, anchored in the river, with instructions to support the Customs officers after they had received orders to seize the two ironclads.[377] The following day, George A. Hamilton of H.M. Treasury informed Lairds that threats of "forceable abduction" of one or both of the rams could not be overlooked; therefore, the ships were seized by Customs officials.[378]

Inglefield ordered a gunboat moved up to the "Great Float" (the entrance gate from the fitting out basin to the Mersey), a well-armed guard boat patrolled the area at night, and a detail of twelve marines under the command of an officer was placed on board the *El Tousson*.[379] The workmen were sent ashore with their tools and no one was permitted aboard other than the Marine guard.[380] The *El Monssair* was not the focus of attention as she did not have masts, sails, funnel or rudder fitted.[381] One American magazine quoted a poem from *Punch* entitled "The Ram of Liverpool," the conclusion of which proclaimed:

> They said he was going to Egypt,
> At least so his owners states,
> But suppose he mistook the turning,
> And made for Davis's straits.
> I think that an honest drover
> Might prove where he'd made a sale,
> And not come smoothing us over
> With a cock and bullish tale.
> And I think that Policeman Russell,
> Who to keep the peace is bound,
> Has used a wise discretion
> In clapping the Ram in the Pound.[382]

The Laird rams, and ironclads in general, had acquired a reputation for near invincibility, with the *Scientific American* wryly commenting, "The majesty of the law must be the real safeguard: setting a wooden ship to 'guard' a ram is like putting a sheep to protect a bulldog."[383] The Admiralty felt the precautions were not enough and ordered the recently commissioned ironclad H.M.S. *Prince Consort* to the Mersey to watch over the Laird rams.[384] The lumbering broadside ironclad, converted from a 91-gun ship-of-the-line while still on the builder's ways, was the only British ironclad available for immediate duty and was dispatched from Plymouth with a newly assigned crew on 28 October.[385] The men were temporarily detailed to the ironclad from other ships in the dockyard; only the Chief Engineer and the Warrant Officers had been on the ship longer than three days, and no one aboard had experience on the *Prince Consort* in a variety of weather conditions.[386]

En route to the Mersey, the armored frigate encountered a severe gale in the

294 and 295 in the Mersey, 1863 (author's collection).

Channel and Irish Sea. The new ironclad struggled against the waves as she began to take water down both her hatchways and the bases of the funnel casings when seas washed over her upper deck. As the huge waves broke over the bows of the ironclad, her main (steam) pump failed, and the ship was in danger of foundering. Her captain knew he could not reach the safety of Liverpool in the face of the storm, and turned instead for Ireland as the ship's company worked the manual pumps. The crew kept to their stations and the stokers were barely able to keep the pressure up in the boilers as the water rose to their knees. It was a close-run escape, and when the people of Britain learned their overdue ironclad had not sunk as was feared, Queen Victoria sent a congratulatory telegram to the officers and men of the *Prince Consort*.[387] Afloat, but still the worse for wear, the ironclad was not to proceed to the Mersey, but on 5 November, departed Ireland for immediate repairs at the Devonport dockyard.[388]

Legal maneuvers continued between the government and the shipbuilders, with Lairds anxious to finish the ships, and the officials determined to prolong a resolution. Lairds wrote to the Treasury on several occasions to protest the "arbitrary" seizure of their vessels and pressed for permission to take the *El Tousson* on a trial run.[389] On 27 October, the Treasury responded to the builders, stating they could not take their ironclad out that week "or within any other suitable time."[390] Two days later, Lairds answered with an attempted explanation of their secrecy concerning the rams:

> It is a rule well recognized in all Trading Establishments, that an Order whilst under Execution is the property of the person giving it, and that a builder has no right to make public the orders or instructions of his employers. This is a rule of business which must be well known to H.M. Government. We are satisfied that Her Majesty's Government have lent too credulous an ear to the inventions of designing persons.[391]

Not content to let the matter lie with their opinion of rumors about their turret ships, Lairds warned: "We need hardly say that we hold the government responsible to us for the large pecuniary loss we shall sustain by these arbitrary proceedings."[392]

Squabbling over the fate and condition of the rams continued for months. Worsening weather damaged the two unfinished ironclads, now anchored in the Mersey.[393] On 7 December, Lairds wrote to inform the Treasury that an insurance policy covering fire aboard the *El Tousson* had expired and the shipbuilders asked for advice regarding the payment of insurance protection for the vessels while in government custody.[394] On the 18th, the Treasury replied, saying that the insurance on the two vessels would be paid by the government with the provision that after the fate of the ships was adjudicated, the costs of the insurance would be reimbursed to the public purse.[395]

The case of the Laird rams was finally resolved on 20 May 1864, when Bravay & Company accepted the offer of H.M. Government to purchase the two ships for service in the Royal Navy.[396] The price for the incomplete ironclads, having spent months floating on the Mersey, was £195,000, with another £25,000 to be paid to Lairds to complete the ships to planned specifications existing prior to the seizure.[397]

The purchase provided a twofold benefit by diffusing a growing American crisis, and prevented France from obtaining a numerical advantage in armored warships. The Laird ironclads were not purchased for the "wrong reasons," but were acquired to resolve two pressing strategic issues simultaneously.[398] Thus, the ships were acquired "for prudent reasons," and Britain would fit out two modern men-of-war during a time of rapid industrial change while also preventing disruption to a key shipbuilding facility.[399] Although Reed had suggested the "immediate" purchase of the two rams, their belated acquisition by the British treasury added two powerful but untested armorclads to the Royal Navy.[400] Britain had avoided a breach with the United States over the feared Confederate procurement of these ships, and the Royal Navy acquired two hybrid turret ironclad rams. Although initially the British fleet had "no really useful role" for the two Laird armorclads, the Admiralty would spend decades trying to find a suitable purpose for them.[401] That quest would help advance the role of the turret ship in the Royal Navy, while through trial and error, they would eventually fit into a crucial defensive niche.

Three

Technological Advances and Failings
The Laird Rams in Service 1865–1880

The completion and commissioning of the Laird ironclads in the autumn of 1865 provided the Royal Navy with two distinctive, but untested armored warships, built during a time of rapid and almost contradictory change. It was a time when technological inventions were perfected and adapted "rather suddenly" to introduce "new dimensions to the conduct of naval warfare."[1] Steam propulsion, iron construction, and ever-increasing ordnance power marked this time of "revolutionary" changes in naval might. Armored shipbuilding was evolving so rapidly that the warship became, as William Ashworth states, "virtually a new commodity."[2]

The purchase and completion of the Laird turret ships allowed Britain a further numerical advantage over her European rivals during the transition from wooden ships-of-the-line to armored warships. The need to strengthen the fleet against a French ironclad building program was pressing, as the armored frigates of the Royal Navy were not entering active service in enough numbers to give Britain the decisive superiority it needed. Some in London feared that a contest of ironclads in the Channel would be "an unequal one for the English Fleet."[3] The Laird turret ships gave Britain a slight edge over their French rivals and against a revitalizing naval threat from Russia. Palmerston considered the rams could prove useful in any fight against the Tsar, as they could "run down and sink the Russian ships in the Black Sea if need were."[4]

Reed remarked in the late 1860s that the Laird rams were considered perhaps the poorest examples of British armored vessels. This view was framed by the Constructor's earlier comments in a letter to the First Lord of the Admiralty in which he stated that he would not "propose the building of exactly such ships as these."[5] Constructed for a power deprived of the wherewithal of building seagoing ironclads, the Laird rams did not fit into a tailor-made niche for the Royal Navy. As stated, they were valuable additions to the armored squadrons of the Royal Navy, but were poorly adapted to a blue water role.[6] Britain established a precedent in acquiring these armored warships designed and intended for a foreign buyer. London would seize other armored men-of-war in times of crisis from British shipbuilders before they steamed off under a foreign flag, largely from the example set by the acquisition of the two Confederate-intended rams built on the Mersey. The seizure, purchase, and completion of the Laird rams also provided Britain with the first purpose-built turret ships to be commissioned in the Royal Navy.[7]

Historians credit the H.M.S. *Prince Albert* as the first true, keel-up British turret ship, but this is misleading. The *Prince Albert* was the first purpose-built turret ship *ordered* by the Royal Navy; however, she was not commissioned until 1866. Therefore, the distinction must go to the first of the Laird rams, H.M.S. *Scorpion*.[8] Overshadowed by the *Warrior, Alabama* and the tragic *Captain,* the Laird rams were innovative designs on a compact hull. Built to the specifications of a foreign customer and intended for a contest against a numerically superior enemy, they never saw combat, but they deserve more attention than they have received after 1865.

Ships' Trials

Both Laird-built ironclads were placed in service with the Royal Navy in the autumn of 1865, with the H.M.S. *Scorpion* commissioned first, and the second ram placed in commission as H.M.S. *Wivern* in October of that year.[9] The *Scorpion* had her initial run on 30 August 1864, with the British press reporting that "her machinery worked with great smoothness" and she lacked the vibration usually associated with screw-driven ships.[10] The results were measured from her initial test runs from Birkenhead, and the reports were optimistic as they recorded her performance at her highest speed before she had been fitted with her guns, equipment, provisions, or a full load of coal. It was also stated that the ironclad would draw about another foot of water when fully loaded (13 feet forward, 14 feet 9 inches aft during trials) and although the screw would be more deeply immersed, it was felt this would not affect the speed noticeably. This proved to be untrue as her best speed dropped from 12.34 knots to 10.5 when commissioned.[11]

HMS *Scorpion* at sea, 1865 (author's collection).

The *Wivern* had her trial run from Birkenhead on 8 June 1865 and reached a speed of slightly more than 10½ knots. It was estimated that she would reach a top speed of 11½ when the engines were put in order at the builders' yard.[12] It was not to be, as she too lost speed when fitted out, and she only reached slightly more than 10 knots when commissioned.[13] Fitted with three masts, sails would assist (in theory) the steam engines on long voyages as the ships carried an area of sail that was considered ample, or in the case of the second of the class, "unusually large" for ships of this small size.[14] The *Scorpion* was praised for her "handiness" but when the engines were stopped and sail utilized as the only motive power, the ships were hard to control as they steered "anywhere."[15]

Helm control was a factor when at 3:40 a.m. on 23 March 1865, the *Scorpion* collided with the merchant ship *Theresa Titiens* while the ironclad was steaming south of Holyhead, en route for her first stop at Plymouth.[16] The wooden merchant vessel reported damage to her port side when a steamer brushed into her, staving in a portion of her hull. The *Scorpion* stopped engines, furled sails, hung out lights and waited for any sounds from a sinking ship, but none were reported in the dark night. Although aboard the *Titiens* planking was torn and some of the rigging carried away, the armored vessel did not escape unscathed in the encounter. The merchantman luckily did not contact the dangerous ram extending from the bow of the *Scorpion*, yet the turret ship was "bruised" with six feet of her forecastle stove in. Unable to locate the other damaged ship, both vessels continued their voyages and arrived in their respective ports dented, scratched, and torn, but without the loss of any crewmen.[17]

The ram sailed south in an incomplete condition due to a separate mishap involving a government supply vessel, and the *Scorpion* was to be completed when she arrived at Portsmouth. Although the slides for her guns were carried in her two turrets, no armament was shipped. In late February 1865, the ordnance steamer *Balaclava* (mistakenly identified in the British press as the *Lord Panmure*) transporting the four 12-ton guns intended for the ironclad went ashore on the eastern coast of Ireland.[18] As the *Scorpion* steamed south (manned by a temporary crew from the screw ship-of-the-line, H.M.S. *Donegal*) without her guns, a recovery gang from *Prince Consort*, the one-time intended guard ship of the rams, was dispatched from Plymouth to haul up the ordnance.[19] The guns were recovered, but had to be forwarded to Woolwich Arsenal to be examined and refurbished.[20]

The gun carriages were a point of contention between those who favored turret ships and those who supported the broadsides of the central battery ironclads. The *Royal Sovereign* received wooden carriages for her guns, while Reed's small ironclad H.M.S. *Research* received more durable iron models.[21] Other ships preparing to enter service (including Reed's corvette H.M.S. *Pallas*) were given priority for iron carriages.[22] The *Scorpion* received obsolete wooden carriages of "very defective" manufacture, and the *Wivern's* turrets were unbalanced and their revolutions impaired when iron was loaded in her turrets to simulate the guns and carriages she would eventually receive.[23]

The second Laird ram was delayed joining the fleet due to a lack of suitable gun carriages. Woolwich Arsenal experienced delays due to the recent adoption of the "novel invention" of iron carriages, and struggled to manufacture the new gun mounts "as rapidly as the strength of that establishment admits."[24] The delay frustrated the attempts by the Admiralty to outfit the Laird turret ships, with

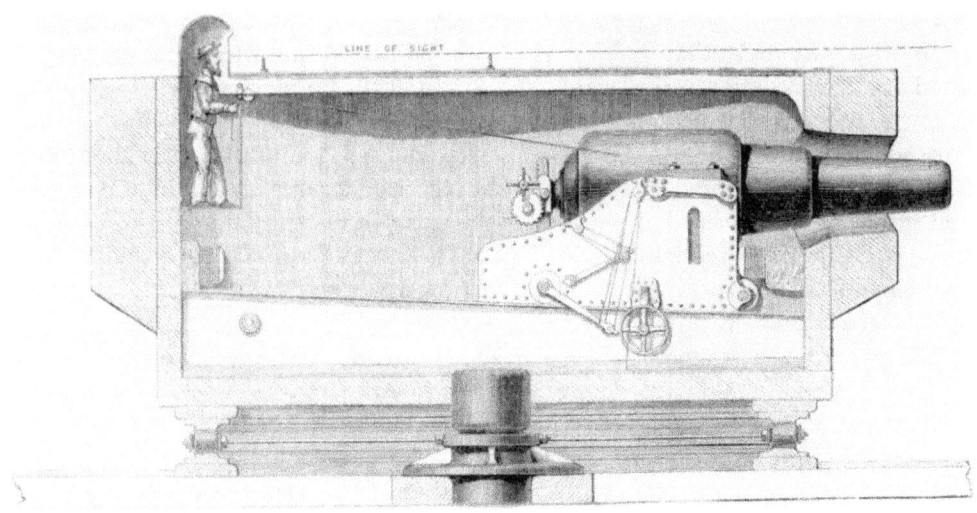

Coles turret, with 9-Inch Armstrong RML, and Scott slides (author's collection).

chains and blocks required for the *Scorpion*'s guns, and the armament and fixtures for the *Wivern*.[25] Admiralty and War Office officials (Woolwich was an Army establishment, but made guns for the Royal Navy during these years) exchanged letters during the summer and autumn of 1865 regarding the armament for the second Laird ram, with the tone changing from "as soon as convenient" to one that "demanded" the gun carriages be supplied.[26] The completion of the armament for *Wivern* was overdue as she did not have her guns, carriages, shot, and shell from Woolwich aboard until early 1866.[27] Finally, on 29 December 1865, the ordnance steamer *Lord Panmure* departed her wharf at the arsenal loaded with four wrought iron gun carriages and a supply of shot and shell for the four steel-lined RMLs to be installed on the *Wivern*.[28]

In the mid–1860s, the Royal Navy struggled with the War Office to supply the armament to all ships entering commissioned service. Guns were available, but the necessary accoutrements were sometimes lacking. The supply of adequate gun carriages continued to hamper Navy readiness, as the *Liverpool Daily Post* commented: "We are not deficient in the pieces themselves as far as the fleet is concerned, but we want a sufficiency of iron carriages or, indeed, of any carriages, to support the shock of firing from very heavy ordnance."[29] Rifled heavy guns, stout carriages, plus supply of shot and shell were part of the myriad issues affecting the ever-changing shape and makeup of ships of the Royal Navy during the transitional years away from sail to the armored steam warship.

The *Wivern* had the distinction of being the first ship in the navy to receive tripod masts, which were to improve the arc of fire for the guns by substituting the hollow iron legs in place of the numerous stays and shrouds, which would have further restricted the training of the guns.[30] The masts offered a means to work the topsails and halyards without having to send men aloft as lines passed down through the masts to positions below decks.[31] The iron masts also offered a reported advantage. They were hollow iron tubes and served as a type of ventilator for the lower decks. Later ships used lower iron masts as ventilators, but those masts were seen as a fire hazard as they created an updraft, which would have unintentionally fueled a major fire if one broke out below decks.[32]

On the rams, the iron masts would also sink when shot away and not float with rigging trailing behind to risk fouling the single screw during a fight.[33] Although the *Scorpion* was not fitted with tripod fore and main masts, both ships suffered the limiting factor of turrets on a fully rigged ship. The *Scorpion* would have to shoot away much of her lower rigging when the guns were brought into action during combat in order to train the weapons against a moving target. The *Wivern* did not have the same burden of rigging, but the iron legs of the masts still inhibited the guns so much that her captain opined they would have to be shot away to provide an adequate arc of fire during action.[34] The British press even acknowledged this inevitability: "Should it ever be found necessary in time of war to clear the decks and give both ships their true monitor form, a few powder discharges from the turret guns would speedily effect the desired metamorphosis."[35]

Sighting the two guns in each turret could be achieved through three small open hatches for the gunner to "pop his head through" on the turret roof.[36] The sides and rear of these sighting ports were protected from small arms fire by "iron bonnets" fitted over the openings. The turret arrangement was proven during the trials and "the facility with which it was worked was admirable, even with an untrained crew." The rams offered an advantage as their low silhouettes, only 4 feet, 6 inches above the waterline (amidships) when the bulwarks were lowered, presented targets that would be difficult to hit.[37] Furthermore, one writer ventured to speculate they would become very difficult to see if painted slate gray like the earlier blockade runners that steamed into the Confederate ports during the Civil War.[38] Some French harbor defense vessels were also painted this color in order to complicate enemy gunnery at longer ranges.[39]

The ironclads of the Royal Navy were painted black with white upper works, and black or buff funnels, and the masts and yards were usually painted either a bone or a red brick color. Illustrations and photographs of the Laird rams in the middle to late 1860s show them in this prescribed blend of pigment, complete with a thin white stripe or "Boot-top" running fore to aft midway along the hull.[40] The ironclads of the Royal Navy were not camouflaged or obscured; they were painted to be seen. One historian noted the uniformity of the livery schemes gave their black hulls "a fearsome and sinister" look.[41]

Appearance was not the only consideration, for in iron ships, rapid deterioration would result from exposure to saltwater and air. Paints had to be durable and elastic enough to withstand the elements and the movement of the hulls, upper works, masts, etc., especially while underway. Paints adopted from those mixed for houses or wooden ships were not suitable throughout an iron ship, as lead-based paints were electrically conductive around the positions where copper and iron were near each other, particularly near the lower hull plates, for these properties contributed to a rapid decay of the iron at those points.[42] Ship painting remained an inexact science for decades as different potions were mixed to provide properties suitable for iron and, later, steel vessels. Men assigned to coat a ship were exposed to inhalation risks from the noxious mixtures and many succumbed to "painter's colic."[43] Fast-drying paints were needed to get a ship out of dockyard as quickly as possible, and when used in poorly ventilated interior spaces like coal bunkers, the workmen were known to suffer "bleeding from the nose and ears and temporary dementia."[44]

When preparing to fire the guns, the movable bulwarks on the Laird rams would pivot from a hinge positioned on the lower edge of the iron shield and attached to the deck.[45] Other turret ships were similarly fitted with the iron bulwark supports resembling a capital letter "L."[46] The bulwark plates were each supported by two (or perhaps three for the longer bulwarks amidships) of these stanchions on a base plate, and were inclined inboard at a slight angle of approximately 10 degrees.[47] With the back of the L-shaped stanchions fixed to the 2-inch thick bulwark, the other shorter edge was secured to a base plate which was in turn either secured by "pins" or when removed, freed from the deck. When clearing away, a few men could rotate the movable iron walls over the ship's side, where these bulwarks would hang slightly above the waterline.[48]

Other design features provided advantages, but also highlighted unintended and sometimes related shortcomings. The three bladed, 14-foot propeller enabled the *Scorpion* to answer her helm with a quickness that was regarded as "remarkable."[49] The official reports on the Laird rams revealed different performance results than those listed in the press. Under sail, the *Scorpion* performed "as well as can be expected for her small sail power." The three bladed screw was a clear detriment when not steaming, as the small rudder also contributed to the ship steering "wildly" when under sail alone or at low speed. She had to have 3 to 4 knots from the screw to enable the ship to answer the helm.[50] The direction the ship was to turn was likely also an issue, as the rotation speed of the screw determined the amount of water washed against the rudder. Some ships of this era turned better when the rudder was at port, as a right-handed screw with an ample pitch would churn more water over the ported rudder than to starboard.[51] This factor undoubtedly influenced the performance of the Laird rams at low speed with a screw designed to rotate to the right.[52]

The *Scorpion* (and likely her sister) had a rudder of slightly under 17 feet 5 inches, and experience was to prove that armored warships needed larger rudders to offset the rotations of the screw(s) and hull weight.[53] This was not a new phenomenon, as some of the post–Crimean War wooden-hulled steam battleships were built with longer hulls for larger machinery spaces. These vessels gave the Royal Navy ships-of-the-line higher speeds, but at the expense of rudder control caused in part by the drag from the screw propeller.[54] The steam line-of-battle ships were fitted with a "banjo" frame, whereby the screw could be uncoupled from the shaft and hoisted inboard during sailing. Despite this ability to disconnect and pull in the screw, those steam battleships with finer hull lines did not perform as well under canvas as their earlier companions in the fleet. Some of the ships-of-the-line converted to steam also suffered in performance, as they had a tendency to roll after being retrofitted with engines.[55]

In light of these facts, the performance of the Laird rams should be examined with the performance not only of other ironclads, but with other steam warships. For most advantages gained regarding iron construction, heavier guns, steaming qualities, etc., other qualities were sacrificed. This typically meant that steering (especially under sail alone) suffered, and other unforeseen drawbacks were manifested in seakeeping and fuel consumption. Reed had remarked in 1863 that her rig was "very satisfactory," but this preliminary assessment of the masts and sails of the *Scorpion* did not hold up to performance at sea.[56] A ship that might be a good cruiser usually had to sacrifice some aspects of performance to achieve a different set of compromises required of a seagoing warship needed at different stations of the globe. This world-ranging capability generally came at the cost of a deep draft, a lack of armor, and a larger crew.

When steaming, the *Scorpion* performed well "for her horsepower."[57] The main drawback of the first Laird ram was identified while underway, as she "rolls very deeply when there is any sea on the beam, which causes her to ship large quantities of water."[58] Flat-bottomed and without a deep keel, the Laird rams had the ability to approach closer to a hostile shore while presenting a low hull profile, but this came at the cost of seaworthiness while underway off the coasts of Britain. Steaming showed the best qualities of the *Scorpion* under ideal conditions. She spent the last three months of 1865 on Home Station, where her captain observed, "she behaves very well at sea and her engines are very effective and good, driving the ship in a head sea remarkably well. A heavy head sea and strong head wind do not seem to affect her much."[59] A design feature that restricted the field of fire fore and aft, the forecastle and a poop, improved the ram's performance while underway. Her first captain noted that the forecastle kept the ship relatively dry and "the ship rises easily and buoyantly at sea." She could shrug off a head sea, but waves amidship deluged the vessel between the turrets. The *Scorpion*'s commanding officer noted that it was "dangerous" for the men to work the ship under these conditions as the water washed across the deck.[60]

The *Wivern* had the most problems of the two sister armorclads, as her trials revealed a tendency for the main shaft bearing to heat "considerably" when she was at full speed, but she performed satisfactorily when slowed to 50 revolutions per minute. This defect was not corrected until a new main shaft was put in during her first visit to Portsmouth dockyard.[61] Her turrets also did not operate as planned. The rollers did not distribute the weight of 180 tons of iron ballast substituted for the yet-to-be mounted armament (1865) and as a result, the turrets could only be worked "with difficulty and great labour."[62] Also, the turret sills were only 5 inches above the deck, and this lack of height exposed the ships to the risk of flooding the turret room and magazines unless corrected.[63] Here the advantage offered by a low gun platform, with the base of the turret below deck, was also a drawback. Unlike the American monitors with their turret bases above deck, the Laird rams also had to contend with the disadvantages of a low turret on a low hull.

Like her sister, the *Wivern*'s deck was only 4 feet 7 inches above the water at the gangway when her armored bulwarks were down. The low hull exposed the ship to flooding not only at the turret sills, but also the hatchways, whose lack of height above the deck was termed "a very serious defect" on a later cruise.[64] A heavy sea on the beam caused a great deal of water to be shipped aboard the rolling rams and undoubtedly held aboard longer than the scuppers could clear away while the bulwarks or "flaps" were up.[65] In essence, the movable bulwarks kept some water out and held some water in, depending on the sea and the position of the ship. The *Scorpion* and *Wivern* proved to be uncomfortable and flawed ships, but they were the seagoing turret ships by which other armored vessels of their type would be measured. The 8 November 1865 edition of the *Exeter Flying Post* asked, was it "possible to build an armed vessel upon the model of these rams fit for regular sea service?"[66] The answer would be found through trial and error, frequent refits, and design modifications. As originally built, the Laird rams were not suitable models for the cruising armored man-of-war, but they showed how to remake the turret ship into a suitable naval weapons platform, which would eventually overshadow and then supersede the broadside.

Port Visits and Foreign Dignitaries

On 29 August 1865, the French Channel Fleet from Cherbourg visited Portsmouth. Among the French dignitaries were Minister of Marine M. de Chasseloup-Laubat, Chief Constructor of the Navy and architect of the *La Glorie* Dupuy de Lome, and a collection of admirals.[67] The Duke of Somerset led the visitors on a tour of several new ironclads at Portsmouth.[68] Aside from the large iron frigate *Minotaur*, the Lords of the Admiralty escorted the French delegation to view the new turret ships still fitting out, the *Scorpion* and *Wivern*.[69] The French visitors also toured the foundries and armor plate workshops at the dockyard, but the ironclad men-of-war were the chief points of interest.[70]

The *Wivern* still carried the iron weights in place of her guns when she underwent sea trials from Portsmouth that autumn.[71] The ironclad would have to wait to have her deck modified with the more traditional teak planks after the Lairds innovations to deck armor were removed. Lairds had built both ships with a lightly armored iron deck to provide limited protection from plunging fire, and placed cement over sections of the deck for added defense and waterproofing.[72] The cement also had another role in that it protected the rivet heads on the deck and in the bilges. The continual wash of water in the bilges of iron ships had been found to scour the iron so that the heads of the rivets were worn away, but the application of cement delayed this.[73] The *Scorpion* had served as a test of the utility of applying cement to the iron decking for an armored warship, but the results proved to be an almost instant failure. Small channels were cut in diamond patterns, crisscrossed over the iron deck plates, and filled in with cement to provide a better footing for her crew, but the cement cracked and quickly worked out of the seams. This early experiment of what would later become an anti-slip feature more recognizable to warships of the twenty-first century was removed and not repeated as the traditional teak decking was applied over the iron.[74]

The British press lamented they were not the best vessels in the Royal Navy; however, a more recognized symbol, one of the larger armored frigates, also had problems at this time. The "masterpiece of ironclads," the *Warrior*, was in the hands of the dockyard "gutted" in the process of an extensive refit, and concerns were raised over the costs of the overhaul.[75] The *Times* remarked that the *Wivern* would not have added much to the British squadrons sent from the Channel Fleet on the earlier 1865 visit to Cherbourg, as she was very low in the water for an oceangoing cruiser and her tripod masts gave her "a most experimental appearance, anything but reassuring to a sailor."[76] The editorial was perhaps true for those more accustomed to the more traditional displays of naval might in an era of transition, but the Laird rams were a demonstration of British innovation and a readiness to adapt to meet a variety of threats from would-be hostile powers. The Admiralty was moving at a measured pace to incorporate new adaptations in iron warship construction in order to make units of variable capabilities, for the possibility of meeting rivals with varying combat potential.

The tripod mast configuration was suspect almost from the day they were fitted. During her trials, the *Wivern* was thought to roll more than the *Scorpion* due in part to the lack of armament aboard the second armorclad. As stated earlier, weights were placed in the turrets to replicate her yet-to-be completed guns during her voyage south from Birkenhead, and these contributed to her rolling.[77] The tripod fore and main masts of the *Wivern* proved to be of great strength on her first voyage, as "there was not the sign of a crack or the starting of the paint" on these stout structures.[78] Captain Hugh Burgoyne did not like tripod masts from his first experiences in the *Wivern*. He preferred masts strong enough to stand up in action, but fitted with shrouds during other times.[79] Although they reduced the amount of standing rigging required, the tripod masts would prove to be unsuitable for any ship carrying sail. One British admiral was later to remark that the stout construction of the experimental masts was a detriment, as the rigid legs reacted "to a push as well as a pull."[80] The tripod legs held the masts firmly in place, but virtually eliminated the flex of a more traditionally rigged ship of war. Without the slight movement and sway accepted in masts aboard other ships, the tripods pushed that motion into the ship's hull and also contributed to the roll.[81]

Although adequately armored and provided with sufficient internal compartments for watertight integrity, the Laird rams were poorly ventilated ships when originally constructed.[82] On her trials in May and August 1865, the temperature throughout the *Scorpion* varied noticeably. The engine room was apparently well

HMS *Wivern* at sea, 1865 (author's collection).

HMS *Wivern* at Plymouth, 1865 (U.S. Naval History and Heritage Command).

ventilated, but the stokeholds were not, and the temperatures in certain sections were sweltering. Heat ranges from deck to engine room varied markedly, but temperatures in the middle stokehold were significantly hotter than the engine room. At one point the mercury registered 122 degrees Fahrenheit, which influenced the Chief Engineer to remark to the inspectors that ventilation was "much required."[83] The layout was also found to be defective aboard her sister.

During the trials of the *Wivern* in October 1865, the ventilation of the stokehold was found to be "very faulty." This was not by accident, but was a reflection of her design influenced by the requirements of her original intended customer in preparation for a fight against a numerically superior enemy, likely at close quarters.[84] The smaller area of hatchways and "other openings on her upper deck" were designed to restrict access to the spaces below if boarders were able to attack the ship and gain access to the main deck. This was a practical measure as navies still practiced with cutlass in hand. The Royal Navy would conduct drills at boarding stations with edged weapons and small arms until 1905.[85]

Liverpool followed the news of the French visit to Portsmouth, and was proud of the efforts of the Merseyside shipbuilders and their role in providing the Royal Navy some of their latest armorclads. The *Cheshire Observer* wanted the French delegation to visit the Mersey to see a source of Britain's strength: "They will find here no yards of the splendid proportions of Cherbourg, but they will find private enterprise teeming everywhere, and performing wonders which even Imperial (French Government) resources cannot equal."[86] With several thousand workers laboring in their compact yard, Lairds was preparing the ironclad steam frigate *Agincourt* for commissioning to meet any seagoing threat Napoleon III dared send forth.[87] A distinction between the hurried activities of British yards, as compared with the slower pace of French building slips, was not lost on British observers proud of the changes reflected in the growing armored strength of the Royal Navy.

The fleet exchange visit was a clear message to Paris that Britain was ready to meet any French naval expansion with new iron ships fitted for action with broadsides or a few heavy guns behind armor-plated, revolving turrets. France would have to meet this dual challenge of the large, new iron frigates and the low-hulled copula ships or fall behind her rival. The British press would later criticize the *Scorpion* and *Wivern* as being neither very powerful nor steady as they were hurriedly built. That was the point made by Laird when he built (actually by then his sons owned the facility) the ships. They were built rapidly, their flat bottoms and lighter draft were well-suited for a role in coastal waters, and they were armed with four of the largest guns Britain manufactured at the time behind adequate armor. The rams gave the Admiralty options for defense and attack, and the foreign powers noticed. France and Russia added turret ships and rams to improve their coastal defense forces by purchasing surplus American monitors and building shallow draft ironclads.[88]

The *Scorpion* and the *Wivern* steamed together from Portsmouth to test their capabilities in the autumn of 1865.[89] Despite their failings, the rams were important acquisitions for a Royal Navy in an era of continual experiment both at home and from her would-be challengers for maritime supremacy. The British press declared, "it is satisfactory to know that the English navy alone possessed such a class of vessel as this—fit of either harbour work or ocean cruising, and having such a rate of speed at a comparatively small expenditure of power. The famous American monitors are not so fast by several knots, and they are only coast vessels."[90] The Laird rams were capable of both harbor and coastal defense roles, whereas the *Prince Albert* was designed for harbor defense, as "no provision has been made in her calculations and arrangements for carrying masts and sails, or stores for sea-going purposes."[91]

Despite their disappointing speeds, the *Scorpion* and *Wivern* could, under moderate weather conditions, reach closer to enemy home waters without having to stand offshore like the larger iron frigates. While cruising in late October, the rams struggled back into Spithead in heavy seas, disproving a rumor that the *Wivern* had foundered.[92] An observer from the shore noticed one of the vessels was seen to roll in a manner that was "very perceptible," a motion that highlighted the problems with the low freeboard and flat bottom as well as the weight of the heavy masts and lower spars, all combining to impair the capabilities of these ironclads.[93]

Seakeeping qualities were their main limitations, and ocean cruising was not a task these ships were to undertake except for limited durations. They were failures as seaboats, but the definition of a failure was highly subjective, as many early armored vessels were prone to quick and deep rolling while at sea. Storms provided a valuable reference point for the performance of ships in commission at the time, as the turret ship *Monarch* delayed her December 1869 transatlantic crossing due to heavy weather, even though she was considered to be the crack ship of the Royal Navy.[94]

Ship handling changed with the advent of the armored warship. This was especially true for short-hulled ironclads, and the low-hulled turret ships served as a new test bed for how best to run an iron-coated man-of-war. Experience with these ships demonstrated to the commanders, officers, and men of these ironclads that they had to change routines to successfully run their ships while at sea. During the short career of the Confederate ironclad C.S.S. *Stonewall*, the new warship demonstrated her propensity to plow into the green seas and so alarmed the engineers and the crew of the armored vessel that they appealed to their captain to return to port. A Confederate naval officer aboard persuaded the Danish captain, contracted to return the ship to her French builders, to press ahead, as "the only danger lay in stopping engines; that in a word, the safety of the vessel, and all on board depended entirely on the continuous movement of the engine, and the watchful care of it by the engineers."[95]

In December 1867, Captain M.H. Jansen, the commander of the Dutch turret ship *Prins Hendrik der Netherlanden*, steamed off Brest to test her seakeeping abilities.[96] Jansen later reported that although his ironclad rolled noticeably in the trough of the winter waves, she did come up slowly but steadily. When put into the wind, the performance improved somewhat. Although the funnel was caked with salt from the waves and spray, the *Prins Hendrik* was able to weather the gales.[97] Experience in the mid–1860s revealed that these ships could not be steered and worked in a manner similar to their predecessors. The turret ironclads had to be *driven* and handled like the new and touchy beasts they were.

The Laird rams were slow to obtain proper refits in the Portsmouth dockyard, as ships required for service on foreign stations received priority over those assigned closer to home. This was especially true for the rams; their schedule of alterations to modify them into more efficient seaboats was suspended or delayed as cruisers and heavier draft ironclads came in for refits. The *Scorpion* and *Wivern* suffered from the effects of bureaucratic delay as they did not meet the exact requirements for any fleet. Too unstable to use on long cruises, too untested to warrant a suitable refit when purchased, they were unready during their early years under the White Ensign.[98]

Captain Coles utilized the Laird-built rams in his press battle for the turret ship by responding to a report in the *Times*, which claimed turrets employed on Royal Navy ironclads were not viewed as "very favourable."[99] In reply to this claim, Coles struck a vital point when he defiantly called, "I challenge any one to produce a broadside square-box ship that will carry the same broadside of 300-pounders as the Scorpion and Wivern, designed by Messrs. Laird Brothers, with as much speed, the same tonnage, the same protection and equal buoyancy at sea." Coles went on to say that his rival, Reed, had no vessel in commission at that time (1866) with guns as heavy as the two rams, and touched on another key point when he stated that heavy guns would be carried on Reed's ships, then under construction, but those ships were of "enormous tonnage."[100]

As stated earlier, the heavy broadside warships could cruise the oceans, but they could not get inshore. The Laird rams were compromises of design, and reflected both those advantages and limitations in their construction and employment. They also did not need large crews. The number of crewmen reportedly varied from a high of 170, yet most reports refer to a complement of some 150 per ship to man the turrets, work the guns, steam, and fitfully sail. Britain's ironclads of the 1860s were usually crewed by hundreds of men. The *Achilles* and *Minotaur* each had 705 men aboard. Indeed, only the Reed ironclads *Research* and *Enterprise* required fewer men than the Laird rams, but only 15 fewer hands were aboard those experimental warships.[101]

Manning requirements proved to be a benefit for the Laird rams as the number of active duty marines and seamen in the Royal Navy available for shipboard duty had declined since the early 1860s, and ships on foreign station were reduced to "the minimum amount necessary for the maintenance of the honour of the country...."[102] Further cuts in manpower were pushed by Disraeli's government in an effort to keep to a fixed budget. The Prime Minister reported to the Queen on 15 February

1868, "without any material increase of expenditure, your Majesty will now have a real & we hope, rapidly increasing naval reserve."[103] Other manpower changes were enacted during the late 1860s by reducing the number of boys in the training establishments, reducing the number of stokers in the reserves (and paying seamen extra to perform that duty), and placing more officers on the retired lists. Limited budgets also meant that some candidates failed to obtain commissions, although they passed their entrance examinations, with the result that some appointments were not filled.[104] During these years, a few more ironclads were constructed to keep up with foreign rivals, but they came at the cost of fewer men and fewer ships ready for sea in the event of an emergency.[105]

Performance at Sea

The oceangoing performance of the rams was mixed. The *Wivern* steamed with the Channel Fleet to the west coast of Ireland for exercises in September 1866 to test her capabilities with an armored squadron. The fleet was battered by a western gale, with the *Research* and *Pallas* having the worst of the tempest, although the *Wivern* responded "remarkably well."[106] While underway for Ireland, the admiral in command signaled to ask if the ships could work their guns in the heavy seas. Most could not, as the ships rolled about 25 degrees in the swell. *Wivern* responded that she was able to work her guns, as did the Reed-built ironclad frigate *Bellerophon*, but they did not fire while in transit to Ireland.[107]

In the Victorian era, the dimension of the degree of a roll was calculated from the entire motion, instead of a one-way measurement from an even keel, as is done in the modern day, but the deep roll was still uncomfortable for the crews of many ironclads.[108] A printed illustration from her 1866 voyage revealed the *Wivern* rolling to port, and shipping waters up to the base of her tripod masts as waves surged over the low sides. Nevertheless, with bulwarks down, the turret ship could still "satisfactorily work" her guns, as they were further from the sea than on a broadside warship.[109] The print showed the *Wivern* struggling in a heavy sea with all sails furled, men on her forecastle, and flying bridge inclined backwards against the pitch of the ship, which seemed to prove the naysayers' claim that "she cannot do much in the way of sailing, and she is as a steamer very expensive."[110] The storm showed the limitations of several ships during that voyage as the ironclads were contending with increased weights of armor, guns, and engines, which had conversely come with a loss of seakeeping agility and crew comfort at sea. The illustration of the *Wivern* struggling in the waves also showed the funnel raised to its full height as the ironclad turret ship fought to make headway.[111]

Many ships of the Royal Navy of the 1860s had telescopic funnels, which were usually lowered in port and raised when getting underway.[112] In the early 1870s, one commanding officer adopted a unique solution to raising the funnel. Captain John Hopkins, while in command of the armored frigate *Agincourt*, had determined to improve drill aboard ship, and ordered a series of bugle calls for specific shipboard evolutions.[113] When the accepted military bugle calls were assigned to more traditional practices, an adoption of a popular tune was utilized. The captain selected the new call, briefed his bugler, and the stokers were mustered to inform them of the change in routine. When the bugler sounded the nursery rhyme "Polly Put the Kettle

HMS *Wivern* in the channel, 1866 (author's collection).

On," the stokers raced to their winches and the funnel went up in quick order.[114] The Royal Navy was adapting to mechanical changes brought about by the evolving ironclad warship, and through innovation and drill modification, the routines of shipboard life were changing with them.

During the September 1866 exercises, the fleet was ordered to practice an evolution under sail alone and the new *Bellerophon* failed to perform to satisfaction.[115] While underway, another concern arose due to unexpectedly high fuel consumption rates. The *Wivern* was the first to drop out of the exercise, as she was running short of fuel and was ordered to take on more coal at Cork.[116] The *Wivern* was singled out for additional criticism as Admiral Hastings R. Yelverton later relayed a report from her then-commander, Captain Burgoyne, that she was almost always battened down when at sea as the water threatened to pour in through her gunports.[117] It was also claimed that fires in two of her four boilers were doused by a rush of water from the deck while she was steaming down the Channel.[118]

On 26 September, the ships engaged in gunnery practice south of Bantry Bay, off the west coast of Ireland, despite a heavy swell, which caused some of the ironclads to roll up to 30 degrees.[119] Each ship was to fire fifteen rounds, but some ships could not reach that rate due to the continuing swell. Despite the seas washing over her deck, the *Wivern* was among those able to fire at the floating targets when the other broadside ships could not open their gunports.[120] The gunnery was uneven as only the *Achilles* performed well, for when firing her broadsides, she was reportedly "steady as a church" despite the loss of her main and mizzen topgallant masts in the storm.[121] The fleet gunnery practice was hazardous, as the heavy guns threatened to get away from their crews struggling on the pitching decks. The men had to contend with some guns that had their muzzles dunked and their powder ruined in the heavy seas while wrestling to keep the guns from sliding back when their ships rolled and lurched in the waves. Some ships reported their gunports were completely submerged at times.[122] The ironclad warship, in all its forms, was rarely a comfortable and efficient man-of-war during this age of rapid change.

These training cruises allowed commanders to determine the characteristics of not only each ironclad, but the performance of an armored squadron as a unit. These exercises produced new considerations regarding the various applications of ship handling needed for both attack and defense, or "all the possible evolutions which ships, divisions or squadrons may be called upon to perform while acting together." During this era, the concept of seapower transformed into two distinct expressions. Tactics were evolving into concepts of localized operations separate from the broader context of naval warfare, a different outlook defined as global or strategic in its scope.[123] This reevaluation of naval thought occurred with the advent of steam propulsion and the armored warship, and grew apace as the ironclad evolved in its different forms.

The Admiralty and the Laird Turret Rams

The Laird rams were never popular with the Admiralty. When debating naval budgets in the Commons, the then-Secretary to the Admiralty, Lord Clarence Paget, called the *Scorpion* and *Wivern* unfit vessels, remarking that the crew spaces were faulty and the men could not be kept clean.[124] The inference that the ships were dirty was disingenuous. Sub-Lieutenant Swinton Holland kept a log of his time aboard *Wivern* when he was assigned to the ship from September through the end of December 1865.[125] He made 22 references to cleaning the ship, from the holds to the turrets. Holland also mentioned the crew was issued soap and tobacco as rations.[126] The log of the *Scorpion* made references to "cleaning ship" during this time, which indicates this was a normal part of the ship's routine and not excessive duty aboard the rams.[127] The telescoping funnel aboard each ironclad was a probable contributor to coal dust aboard the rams, especially if the funnel was lowered, but coaling procedures were notorious for all steam-powered ships.

The coal used was likely the real reason the ships had to be cleaned continually. The Royal Navy used a mixture of North Country coal and Welsh anthracite during the middle Victorian years as a cost-saving measure.[128] The result was a thick cloud of smoke produced by the cheaper North Country variety.[129] Another reason for this supply concern was due to the well-established collier trade from Newcastle to London, especially by the time of the Crimean War of 1854–56. The supply of Welsh coal was relieved somewhat by the end of that war, but the need for economy meant that the dual coal supply remained in effect.[130] The Royal Navy would continue to use the dirtier bituminous coal until 1887, when the cleaner-burning Welsh coal was utilized exclusively, except when supplies were not available.[131]

In 1866, the Laird rams came in for abuse on the floor of the Commons due to their poor performance in the fleet. On 15 March, Paget had mentioned that discipline suffered as a result of the unsatisfactory conditions aboard the Laird rams, saying neither vessel was "fit to put British sailors into."[132] His comments were at variance

Officers aboard HMS *Wivern*, c. 1865 (© National Maritime Museum, Greenwich, London).

HMS *Achilles* (in background) and *Wivern*, at Plymouth, with funnel raised (U.S. Naval History and Heritage Command).

with other remarks he made in the Commons that day. Paget stated, when referring to the *Agincourt*, that he would prefer the command of smaller ships, as the larger ironclads were not as handy in turning. His remarks are also curious, as he stated that he would prefer the command of smaller ships "even at some sacrifice" to the performance and firepower of a larger ocean-cruising ironclad.[133] The remarks were a part of a verbal joust with John Laird, who had proclaimed that the rams were not failures, as they were not intended for duty as oceangoing cruisers, but they had proved to be "thoroughly seaworthy" during trials and exercises.[134] Laird also pointed out that if the rams were troublesome in a seaway, it was because they were not fully modified to meet requirements *before* joining the Channel Fleet.[135]

Laird made a clear distinction as to the real benefit of the two ironclads when he observed they had advanced the evolution of the turret ship as test beds for Coles' armored cupolas.[136] In the mid–1860s, the Admiralty had mixed views of the proper utility of a turret ship, as Paget mentioned the ironclad U.S.S. *Monadnock*, a powerful double turret monitor then en route around Cape Horn, for harbor defense duty at San Francisco.[137] Paget compared the American monitor to a rock at half tide, deck awash in a breeze, and a hard vessel on her crew, but he also called her "one of the most formidable engines of war in existence."[138] Paget had said earlier that month (March 1866) that the Laird rams, though not effective as cruisers, would be "very effective" under certain circumstances.[139] Laird claimed that the Royal Navy did not know what to do with either the *Scorpion* or the *Wivern* or how to use them properly, and as such, they remained in home waters until they found a suitable role. It would be years before the forlorn ironclads would be adequately modified for the role more suitable to their design.[140]

The *Scorpion* was the first to go out of commission when she was docked for alterations to make her "one of the most efficient of our armored vessels" as Laird had hoped, except money was not appropriated in a timely fashion and only five or six men were working on her in July 1866.[141] The previous month, the double-turreted monitor U.S.S. *Miantonomoh* anchored in Cork, having crossed the Atlantic in the company of two U.S paddle-driven warships. One British newspaper described the armored visitor as "destitute of spars and rigging," noting her low hull was barely visible above the water.[142] Her sparse arrangement of upper works attracted a curious description, as her "broad flat base and her confused superstructure ... she might very well pass for a novel description of dredging machine," claimed one British newspaper.[143] The low silhouette of the American monitor was a feature not immediately recognized for seaworthiness, yet her arrival in the United Kingdom caused a sensation due to the subsequent impressions of the vessel and the demonstrations of her 15-inch Dahlgren guns.[144] Before the voyage, the addition of a 3½ foot tall, wooden breakwater forward aided the *Miantonomoh*'s headway, although waves surged inboard, rolling "halfway up the forward turret" during the crossing.[145]

A fixture that facilitated her transatlantic crossing as much as her breakwater, waterproofed hatches, and steam-driven fans and pumps, was the "Hurricane Deck."[146] This structure, positioned between the two turrets, was described as "a latticed platform ... supported upon pillars, on which when the ship is at sea all the nautical duties are performed."[147] The fitting of hurricane decks improved conditions aboard iron warships of the time, and after the Reed armorclad *Research* received hers, she was "rendered at least safe and comfortable—and she kept her place fairly with the fleet."[148] By August 1867, the *Scorpion* was fitted with her walkway, which extended over her turrets and permitted safer passage from the forecastle aft to the poop in heavy weather.[149] The Admiralty had taken a step to render the Laird rams and other ironclads more serviceable in British waters, although the bold steps needed to reduce weight aloft and thus lessen some of the rolling would have to wait for a later overhaul. The *Scorpion* had her masts removed during the "extensive" refit, but they were placed back aboard ship near the end of her time in dockyard, and an opportunity was lost to convert her into an all-steam ironclad.[150]

Weight savings had been achieved in the mid-nineteenth century with the adaption of rope made from steel wire. Although wire rope was first made in Britain in 1832 for collieries, mine owners were slow to switch from the trusted hemp and only added wire rope when the manufacturing process evolved.[151] By 1859, the Admiralty had fitted three steam frigates with steel rope manufactured by such firms as Webster & Horsfall of Birmingham.[152] The new steel rope was also almost a third of the diameter of hemp and held up well to experimental stress tests, and by the late 1860s, both iron and steel rope were less expensive than hemp.[153] When introduced to the United States, the steel substitute was termed "an invention of great importance."[154] Traditional hemp rope continued in service as wire rope of steel and especially iron lacked sufficient elasticity until steel manufacturing processes were advanced in the 1860s. Wire rope was made from individual strands, each comprised of six wires of equal diameter. The manufacturer varied the number of strands depending on the size of rope required. Iron rope was preferred for standing rigging, as it was cheaper than steel rope, and like hemp, was sometimes tarred for waterproofing. Steel rope proved more suitable than iron for work in the various blocks carried on ships, and the use of galvanized wire ropes for both iron and steel resolved the problems of corrosion and allowed for increased flexibility over the more rigid, tarred stays.[155]

Despite these advances, the weight savings did not compensate for the increased weight of the engines and boilers on warships. In November 1867, the wooden-hulled twin-screw gunboat H.M.S. *Plover* was found to be too heavy aloft as she rolled as much as 20 degrees even in fine weather due to her heavy masts and rigging. She was subsequently reduced in both to render her more stable.[156]

Special Duty, Gun Failure and Drill Changes

In July 1867, *Wivern* was present at the Spithead Naval review held in honor of the Sultan of Turkey, Abdul Aziz.[157] Nevertheless, the refurbished *Warrior*, the *Black Prince*, and *Minotaur* were the more traditional representations of British naval might. Several turret ships were at anchor during the review, although the *Wivern* was the smallest.[158] The ship was still at Portsmouth in August when the officers placed an advertisement in a local newspaper announcing that the wardroom would not be responsible for the debts incurred by their steward. Curiously, the newspapers still referred to her by the earlier misspelling of her name, "*Wyvern*."[159]

Duty at Portsmouth had been dull for the crew of the *Wivern*, as earlier notices appeared in local papers concerning occasional breaches of discipline aboard ship. In January 1866, two boys, Charles Peacock and Joseph Windsor, were tried before the local justice of the peace and charged with desertion. After admitting their crime, the boys were returned to the ironclad.[160] Another boy, Harry Cole, had deserted the ship on 5 October 1865, and was apprehended and court-martialed years later (January

1870). He was imprisoned at Winchester and sentenced to 18 months hard labor before being discharged from the navy.[161]

In late September 1867, information concerning a possible Fenian attack in Ireland led to several warships being sent from the Channel Fleet with only a few hours' notice.[162] The *Wivern* had been held in a state of partial readiness, as she was listed as "unappropriated" in one British newspaper prior to sailing with elements of the fleet.[163] The *Wivern* was ordered to Holyhead to serve as the guardship at that harbor in response to rumors of an impending raid.[164] The ironclad left without her full complement, as her captain was recalled from leave to join his ship after she arrived at the Welsh port.[165] Emergency orders and a new station changed the routine of shipboard drill aboard the ram, and the added impetuses of possible action undoubtedly lifted morale, as no issues regarding discipline were reported on board the turret ship during her mission.

The *Wivern* had her first taste of "action" in September 1867 while at Holyhead, when she sent a boat crew to search for members of a Fenian plot who had sailed from Liverpool aboard a ship bound for Cardiff.[166] The boat searched a nearby merchant ship for the two Fenian escapees from Manchester jail, former Union Army Colonel Thomas Kelly and Captain Timothy Deasey. Kelly and Deasey had been arrested on charges of plotting an uprising in Manchester.[167] On 18 September 1867, while being transferred to prison, a Fenian gang attacked the prison van and killed police Sergeant Charles Brett, permitting Kelly and Deasey to flee and reportedly seek passage to America. The attackers were soon captured and William Allen, Philip Larken, and Michael O'Brien were sentenced to hang for their roles in the murder of police Sergeant Brett, with the execution carried out on 21 November.[168] The men would go into Irish folklore as the "Manchester Martyrs."[169]

The boarding party from the *Wivern* did not find any fugitives, but the ironclad was ready to assist with men and firepower if the threatened Fenian plot erupted into a series of full-scale riots around the country.[170] On 14 November 1867, the ship was involved in another anti–Fenian mission.[171] Shortly after midnight, a telegram from Manchester warned that a unit of armed men planned to land at Holyhead and rescue an Irish prisoner scheduled to arrive there. The Coastguard notified the commander of the *Wivern,* Captain George A.C. Booker, R.N, who responded by leading a force of marines ashore to search for the armed band. Later that morning, the turret ship fired a shot across the bow of the London & Northwestern Railway steamer and sent a boat over to search the vessel. Although no suspicious persons were found aboard, Coastguard Chief Officer Rowe and Captain Booker were later praised for the "greatest activity and vigilance" in the sweep for the reported armed men.[172]

The *Wivern* had remained on duty despite a near tragedy that occurred aboard ship during a routine training event. In early November 1867, a gun in the forward turret (incorrectly identified as the after cupola in another report) blew up during target practice after firing a shell with a 30-pound powder charge.[173] The "left hand gun" burst while the gunners were firing at a target some 1,500 yards distant, and the explosion caused the breech of the gun to be "blown clean away." Aside from the gun captain, whose legs were grazed when the breech, weighing about a ton, flew backward to strike the turret wall and then fell to the deck behind the remains of the gun, no one was injured. This despite a crew of about fifteen being in and below the turret at the time of the explosion, as the blast from the failed gun cast up above the heads of the men and the breech blew back and away from all but the gun captain.[174]

The *Wivern* was armed with four 300-pounder RMLs, two guns per turret, as was her sister ship, indicating that three men were assigned to each gun in the turret and an additional three below for each gun to pass up powder and shell and two other men to bring more ammunition from the forward magazine when needed. With the gun captain in the cupola, this would account for a fifteen-man crew assigned to each armored turret above and below decks.[175] As a result of the mishap, the *Wivern* was mentioned in the Irish press as having "A Novel Armament" and with some black humor, was referred to as having "three guns and a half."[176] The failed gun, produced at the Woolwich Arsenal, reportedly had some casting flaws in the iron, which contributed to the mishap.[177] The flawed gun was reported to be a 10½-inch, 12½ ton Armstrong RML made before an improved reinforced breech was adopted in 1863.[178]

The *Scorpion* was initially reported to carry smoothbore cannon, but these and the original armament of the *Wivern* were earlier RMLs.[179] An officer in the 18th Hussars, William Palliser, had patented the method to refurbish smoothbores into rifled guns by inserting a rifled iron and later steel inner core into the old guns. When the breech of the muzzleloader was covered with iron bands to provide additional strength for the increased powder charges, the Woolwich Arsenal (which used the Palliser patent) was able to provide inexpensive rifled guns reconditioned from old smoothbore cannon.[180] Coincidentally, the change from smoothbores to heavy rifled muzzleloading guns had occurred as the ordnance terminology was changing. By March 1864, the War Department designated the heavy Armstrong guns (and subsequent ordnance) by the size of the bore, not by the weight of the shot or shell, as had been the previous practice.[181] Palliser would later identify the screw threading of the breech plug as the weak point in these early 300-pounder RMLs. The cascable was screwed into place to seal the breech after the rifled tube had been inserted into the rear of the gun during manufacture. The screw threads had been cut from the breech wall instead of the later method of inserting a raised threaded surface for strength. With each firing of the older guns, the force of the blast worked from the inside of the breech down the screw lining to the outer threading of the cascable. Fortunately, few of these guns were made before the stronger breech closing method was adopted.[182]

As a result of the incident aboard the *Wivern*, the Admiralty ordered the older pattern guns replaced with the improved 9-inch RML.[183] The failed guns were the early Mark I versions with steel rifled tubes built up at the breech with overlapping sleeves of iron "hooked together" for supposed strength, but the breech (and the cascable screw threads) was not strong enough to contain the heavy charges.[184] For casting the improved 9-inch guns, the gunmakers had discarded the earlier method of overlying reinforced iron at the breech for fitting a thicker, single-layered iron covering from the breech to the trunnions for greater longitudinal support.[185] With each modification the gun changed, with the inner steel tube becoming more tapered and less rounded at the innermost part near the vent, and with more separation from the cast breech plug.[186] After changes to the gun, the carriages had to again be modified, as the 9-inch RMLs were termed "inconveniently heavy" for use aboard most warships of the time.[187] Naval armament had become more of a weapons system and bore less resemblance to the wooden gun trucks and iron smoothbores of the sailing navy. Industrialization was reaching the very heart of the warship and transforming the perceptions of firepower. Both man and machine had to work in precise unison to load, direct, and fire the heavy ordnance used to arm the ironclads of the middle-nineteenth century.

Large naval ordnance in a turret represented a challenge to gun drill in the 1860s. The heavy guns of British ironclads during this time were described as "short dumpy things like soda-water bottles."[188] The muzzles of these guns barely stuck out from the gunports of the turrets, and the short barrel length hampered firing due to safety concerns. In 1865, several lieutenants and some of the crew of the *Scorpion* were detailed to the *Royal Sovereign* to learn the intricacies of working turret guns.[189]

The *Royal Sovereign* was the touchstone of the turret warship for the Royal Navy, and the practical experience gained by the gunners who trained aboard her was invaluable. Originally armed with 10½-inch smoothbore muzzleloaders, the standardized armament for all turrets aboard allowed for a uniformity of storage and handling of ammunition, as well as practice at gun loading and training.[190] During gun drills in the forward double turret, marines refused to stand at the muzzle of one gun, ready to load as the other was being fired. The reason was fear of the fire from the muzzle blast of the other gun coming into the gunport while they were handling the powder charge of their yet-to-be-loaded smoothbore.[191] Two members of the Royal Marine Artillery prefaced their appeal to a lieutenant in the turret by warning, "we are experienced gunners, we have had as much experience as you have." The solution was to fire the guns almost simultaneously to prevent the blast from one gun inadvertently touching off the powder of the other.[192] An emphatic warning given by practiced experts overcame faulty procedures to produce a gun drill adapted for the larger ordnance entering service on the ironclads, especially for those guns housed within the close confines of the armored turrets.

During her first commission, *Scorpion* carried 25 marines as part of her then (October 1865) overall crew complement.[193] Divided between the crew for a turret provided from the Royal Marine Artillery (R.M.A.), the remaining ten marines would have served as riflemen positioned around the ironclad to shoot down men on an enemy quarterdeck, gunners near an open port, or at their opposites in a fighting top. The Royal Marines were flanked by the Admiralty and War Office establishments, and were separated from their naval brethren and each other by different uniforms and traditions. The R.M.A, that "splendid body of men," was considered well trained and superior to their army counterparts, although they wore blue uniforms patterned after the tunics of the Royal Artillery.[194] The scarlet-coated riflemen of the Royal Marine Light Infantry (R.M.L.I.) ranked after the 49th Regiment and before the 50th Regiment of the British Army when serving ashore, and earned the distinction of being referred to as the venerable "Forty-Ninth and a Half."[195] Marine artillerymen and the R.M.L.I. were trained to double as foot soldiers when needed for an expedition ashore, and their services afloat added an *esprit de corps* wrought from having a dual mission, which made them "particularly useful" for the myriad of duties required by the Empire.[196]

Experience aboard the *Royal Sovereign* in May 1865 proved that marine riflemen could not stand or kneel on the turret roofs as originally envisioned when Bulloch ordered the two Laird rams for the Confederates, as the double-gun turret produced a "very serious concussion" to anyone positioned immediately above the guns when fired.[197] The turret was changing drill aboard the ironclads of the Royal Navy;

although the marine riflemen were not assigned to a place atop a turret, they were undoubtedly deployed to their traditional positions aloft in the tops of the foremast or mainmast of the Laird ironclads, as these were the surviving fighting positions from the sailing navy still carried in these turret ships.[198]

The 9-inch Armstrong was the largest rifled gun afloat on Royal Navy warships of the mid–1860s. Bigger smoothbore guns were afloat under the White Ensign, but the Armstrong was the main RML in service until larger bore, heavier rifled guns could be perfected.[199] Although this 12-ton gun was the premier piece of naval ordnance aboard British men-of-war at that time, the Admiralty experienced problems with those 9-inch RMLs produced by Woolwich Arsenal, the guns considered to be "the pride of the War Department."[200] Tests at Shoeburyness had proven the advance of armor had been momentary halted, but as mentioned previously, the gun explosion aboard the *Wivern* revealed a design flaw in the earlier breech plug. Complaints in British newspapers also called attention to the bore of the Armstrong guns as they wore out rapidly when firing the heavy shells and larger powder charges. The guns usually lasted only one hundred rounds before needing repair or at least detailed inspection, as the steel rifled central tube and iron coils wrapped around the breech were unable to endure the blasts from repeated firings. Another problem was that the grooves cut into the bore reportedly contributed to the fire not being carried away from the muzzle immediately after discharge.[201] Improvements to the muzzle loading naval rifles continued, although the projectiles proved to be disappointments. One senior naval officer observed that studded shells broke up in the barrels or tumbled in flight and "went in any direction except the right one, but the guns made plenty of smoke."[202]

In Search of a Role

The British press exhibited a casual dislike of the Laird rams during their early years in service, with one newspaper exclaiming they were hurriedly built and unsteady at sea.[203] By early August 1868, *Wivern* went into the Portsmouth dockyard for a refit and to receive new guns.[204] She was to be modified along the lines of her sister ship, as the *Scorpion* had been "improved greatly" with new fittings and alterations.[205]

Despite the alterations, these two turret ships were not significant improvements over their previous configurations. Less than five years after being commissioned, the Laird turret rams were already outclassed and ill-suited for work in home waters. Reed remarked (1869) that the *Scorpion* and *Wivern* were "the weakest of our armour-clads."[206] In a rebuttal to the claim, one writer questioned Reed's mention of the armament of the two Laird rams as being light, and retorted saying, "we might admire the grandeur of thought which could contemplate a 300-pounder with such a degree of depreciation" as the guns carried in these turret ships were among the principal afloat in the Royal Navy, and only three British men-of-war carried larger guns at that time.[207]

Performance issues impacted the reputation of Laird rams during their first years in commission. The *Scorpion* was able to slightly outpace her sister as she reached 10½ knots on at least one occasion.[208] Although they achieved what was then considered a moderate speed, the Laird rams were susceptible to roll as they took seas amidships. During her 1866 cruise with the Channel Fleet, the *Wivern* rolled up to 27 degrees in a heavy sea, but this must also be read in context of the Coles-Reed battles in the press.[209] Coles had remarked earlier that two Reed-built ironclads, the *Enterprise* and *Research*, were both "dreadfully slow" and did not perform well at sea, going on to proclaim that the *Research* was an unsafe ship, and that "the Admiralty have never trusted her 100 miles from our coast since launched."[210]

The battle between Coles and Reed had been going on beyond design issues regarding the broadside versus the turret ironclad, and also delved into the fittings on the ships. As previously mentioned, the *Scorpion* was originally equipped with wooden carriages instead of newer iron carriages for the Armstrong RMLs.[211] The British press opined, "While the captains of Mr. Reed's ship get everything which they require done without a day's delay, the captains of the turret ships find all their requests treated with utter neglect, and are forced to do as they best can with what their own crews can manage to do."[212] The *Scorpion* needed adjustments to her gun carriages to render her armament more serviceable, and these modifications were undertaken by her crew.[213] The port side gun carriage in the aft turret was altered, as several bolts were too long and had to be cut down to prevent injury to the gunners in the confined space between the muzzleloaders.[214]

Turret ships of the Royal Navy lacked the room associated with an unobstructed gun deck of those broadside armed ironclads of the 1860s. The larger armored vessels carried rope netting or "mantlets" suspended from the deck above the guns in broadside in order to prevent shell fragments, broken bolts, or nuts from flying unimpeded around the gun deck during action.[215] When in place, these rope barriers (some weighing as much as 820 lbs. each) would separate each gun crew in a cage-like isolation.[216] During gunnery tests ashore, the rope mantlets did stop larger fragments and served to deaden the sounds when the guns fired, but they also presented a fire hazard.[217] When treated with a fire retardant (chloride of calcium), the rope mantlets could be made safer, as they were also considered a barricade to prevent burning powder from entering an adjacent gunport when heavy ordnance was fired from a warship during high winds.[218] The rope mantlets were a valuable method of improving safety aboard the broadside warships, but they were not suitable for the turret ships, as overhead beams were needed to secure the rope screens and would have impeded the loading and sighting of the guns.[219]

The refitted *Scorpion* participated in a mock combined arms demonstration off Dover Castle on 30 March 1869, with the *Royal Sovereign* serving as flagship of the squadron.[220] The "sham fight" involved the two ironclads reducing the shore batteries manned by the army volunteer regiments as part of their annual review, while gunboats were to provide close-in fire for the invading force. A gale delayed the exercise until the rains abated; a drummer aboard the *Royal Sovereign* beat to quarters as a signal was hoisted ordering the *Scorpion* to clear for action.[221] High waves prevented the smaller gunboats from putting to sea from Dover as the brig H.M.S. *Ferret* broke loose from her moorings in harbor and was bashed to pieces against a quay.[222]

The gale tossed the mail steamers about "as if made of cork," and the two ironclads held their positions only through the application of full steam power.[223] The storm tested the abilities of the men and turret ships, as both vessels wallowed in the heavy sea and the *Scorpion*, with her flat bottom rolled in excess of 30 degrees.[224]

Eventually the storm abated and the two turret ships prepared for action after lowering their iron bulwarks, an act the well-trained men of the *Royal Sovereign* completed "in a few seconds."[225] Some of these men were a picked crew from the gunnery training ship H.M.S. *Excellent*, and the commander of the squadron also commanded both the gunnery establishment and the Royal Naval College.[226] The flagship opened fire at 4:30 p.m. as the crew served their 9-inch guns (she had been rearmed in 1867 when her original 10½-inch smoothbore guns were removed) with a drill that was described as "smart and exceedingly well regulated" and the rotation of the turrets "worked smoothly and without a hitch."[227] The *Scorpion* joined in, and both ships did "good service" in providing the invading force with covering fire to reduce the batteries ashore.[228]

An 1869 print from the *Illustrated London News* shows both ships firing, the *Scorpion* employing the guns in her forward turret, the *Royal Sovereign* firing all but the gun from her central-most turret.[229] The ironclads have hurricane decks, permitting officers and men on the ships better forward and aft access as waves are washing over the lowered bulwarks on each ship. The *Scorpion* revealed another aspect of her refit as her armored casemate surrounding her funnel was no longer visible, indicating that the somewhat slender telescoping funnel and armored sleeve had been removed to make way for the hurricane deck and larger fixed funnel.[230] Although her topside weight had been reduced with the change to her funnel, the iron masts and yards contributed to her rolling and lesser performance at sea.

Nevertheless, the ships put on a good show. The artillery ashore fired back with 68-pounders, but their response was considered insignificant when compared with the boom of the naval guns as their reports reverberated off the cliffs. Both ships were to fire a round from each gun every three minutes, but the *Scorpion* was much slower than the flagship in her rate of fire. At the completion of the simulated bombardment, the bulwarks were raised, the guns run in, and the ships anchored.[231]

HMS *Royal Sovereign* (left) and HMS *Scorpion* at Dover, 1869 (author's collection).

The sham fight did illustrate a valuable tactical lesson. An invading force, when supported by heavy guns of armorclads within range of a vital stretch of coastline, would greatly complicate the defense. The defending force would have to have the ability to imperil the attacking warships, withstand the bombardment, and hold off the invading ground force, or be overwhelmed. The assault force was assessed to have gained the outer works of the defenders after the fire from their guns had become "ominously slacker, for the heavy artillery of the fleet had succeeded in overpowering and silencing many of the guns of the south-east bastions."[232] Although the bombardment was only a demonstration, the *Scorpion* would have been effective in a coastal assault role, as her slighter draft would have permitted a closer approach to an enemy shore in wartime. With a crew trained to handle the heavy guns in a seaway, she (and her sister) would have likely given a good account against a hostile coastal position.[233]

In April 1869, the *Scorpion* was at Portsmouth to receive new "pointers" for her guns. Artisans formerly employed by the gunwharf establishment at Portsmouth had been let go in a cost saving plan and as a result, skilled workmen had to travel from Woolwich Arsenal to carry out the fittings at almost double the cost.[234] The government responded to the claim by stating that the work was intricate and would have cost the same for the materials and the skilled labor regardless of whether the men came from Woolwich or Portsmouth. During a debate in the Commons over this expenditure, the real issue came to the fore. Skilled workmen (113 of them) had been discharged from the gunwharf as the navy was forced into cost cutting measures.[235] Some men took the offer for free emigration to Canada as a resettlement severance from government employment, and Sir James Elpinstone remarked it was "a thousand pities" for Britain to lose their hard-earned skills.[236]

Fiscal restraint was the demand from Westminster, as the Royal Navy's funding had contracted by over 40 percent from the end of the Crimean War to the early 1880s.[237] Despite the occasional funding spikes brought on by the Civil War, Franco-Prussian War, and the 1878 crisis with Russia, British domestic political gravity kept budgets under constraint.[238] Parliamentary pressure for low defense expenditure was answered at the cost of efficiency. The requirements for those ships not in the dockyard to keep to sea exacerbated the problem of defending a global empire with a navy restricted in size by budget and wear. Those ironclads not considered a success by the contradicting requirements of a service with worldwide commitments nevertheless meant they had to be retained in degrees of readiness.[239] Britain had to keep ships like the *Scorpion* and *Wivern* in the fleet to maintain enough armorclads available for service while others were in overhaul. Although smaller and slower than the large armored frigates, and in need of alteration, they were still required. To maintain Britain's maritime security, every ironclad was needed regardless of seakeeping qualities. It was a numbers game.

The *Scorpion* participated in another "sham fight" off Southsea Castle near Portsmouth on 26 April 1869 when she led a force of six "enemy" gunboats in a mock attack against the castle, supported by an attacking land force comprised of volunteers and regulars. During the simulated invasion, the castle fell after a landward attack supported by the *Scorpion* and her flotilla, with the ironclad shielding the smaller vessels until they closed the range.[240] The turret ship did not fire her guns (although they were run out and the bulwarks lowered), as it was feared that the blast from her 9-inch battery would shatter the glass of the houses near the shore.[241] A nearby lighthouse had the lenses removed as a precaution against damage from the guns of the flotilla, as "economy—even in glass" was the order of the day.[242]

After that stage of the exercise, the invading force moved up with skirmishers and field artillery toward the main objective, the fortress of Portsmouth.[243] A naval landing party led by an officer from the warships marched with the field artillery as the gunboats protected their flank. The flotilla steamed into Portsmouth (in a simulated bombardment) and was reportedly overwhelmed by the fire of the forts, whereupon the invasion collapsed under the weight of counterattacks.[244]

The event was conducted under a festival-like atmosphere as the gunboats slowly moved into position, and the volunteers, led by regulars, followed a set schedule with no adjustments for the probable response of a real enemy. The spectators enjoyed a good show and a team of inventors from London brought a pedal-driven sightseeing craft, or "velocipede yacht," to the beach to the delight of the crowds. Although termed "perhaps the prettiest spectacle yet presented in connection with the volunteer movement," the exercise was dubbed a naval "absurdity" and the field maneuvers ashore "highly indifferent as a military lesson."[245]

Two days later, after being refueled and provisioned, the *Scorpion* was at sea again, headed for her new assignment in Ireland, arriving at Queenstown anchorage on 1 May.[246] With her sister on duty as a guardship, by mid–May 1869, the *Wivern* was back in Portsmouth in the hands of the dockyard for alterations to adapt her for her more suitable role as a coastal defense ironclad.[247] Experience gained aboard one turret ship was relayed into refits and modifications with the other turret ironclads as new technology, methods of drill, and changes to ship handling remade these vessels. The turret ship was evolving.

The Guardships

In early May 1869, *Scorpion* took up her duties as guardship at Cork. from where she would occasionally put to sea, to exercise the crews at the guns.[248] On 26 July, she steamed out on what was to have been a week-long cruise along the Irish coast.[249] The vessel encountered a tremendous storm, which caused the ship to "behave very badly" in the mountainous seas to the terror of her crew.[250] The waves washed down on the turrets, the powder stores were damaged when water poured in from the turrets down into the magazines, and the men were drenched, as their berths were "in anything but a comfortable condition."[251] The ship was quick to roll and was taking water on one side of her deck as she was emptying it from the other side.

One day during the cruise, all sail was applied but the results were not satisfactory. Despite this shortcoming, her captain would later claim that when steam was used, "I thought the *Scorpion* as safe as any ship could be."[252] She answered the helm when under steam but when under sail only, her steering was described as "wild."[253] Another factor that impaired her performance in the storm was that her hurricane deck was too narrow for her crew to safely work her with efficiency.[254] With her complement exhausted from the ordeal, the storm-battered *Scorpion* returned to anchor at Cork a day earlier than anticipated on 31 July.[255] This voyage, and the experiences with the *Royal Sovereign*, likely contributed to design changes needed for other turret ships, as Reed's H.M.S. *Glatton* was fitted with a hurricane deck 11 feet wide to permit suitable room for her crew to move about while that harbor defense ironclad was underway.[256] The structure (also referred to as the spar deck) on the turret ship H.M.S. *Captain* was widened to 24 feet to provide room to work all the ropes for the sails, conduct navigation, and provide storage for the ship's boats.[257]

In August 1869, rumors circulated that the *Scorpion* had her masts removed in Cork after her crew protested that she was unseaworthy due to the experiences they endured during the July storm. This was not entirely true, but the men were wary of again going out in her.[258] Despite the claim made in the *Cork Herald* (and repeated in the British press) that the performance of the ship "occasioned such panic to her crew," the report was exaggerated. However, her captain acknowledged that the *Scorpion* was very uncomfortable in a heavy sea, and the amount of water on the deck during those conditions made it unsafe for the crew to move about except on the hurricane deck, and impossible to work the guns.[259] The low freeboard was a concern for the crew, and although "not heavily sparred for her size," the heavy iron masts and yards contributed to her top-heavy condition.[260] The double topsails in several Royal Navy ironclads of the 1860s provided little in the way of extra speed, but the weight aloft was excessive. On the larger iron frigates, as much as six tons were added, but the sails and rigging also added to the wind resistance in steam armorclads.[261]

The Laird rams were rarely known as being good sea boats, and a month after her arrival in Cork, the *Scorpion* was referred to in one Irish newspaper as a "tipsy Sinbad the Sailor."[262] Ironically, the whimsical story published in the 18 June 1869 edition of the *Cork Examiner* described the *Scorpion* as a seaman on liberty, weighted with back pay or "having much metal about his hull." The tale continued with the tar (*Scorpion*) becoming wrecked after having been "sorely buffeted by that Old Man of the Sea."[263] This intended light-hearted musing undoubtedly played on the superstitions of some members of the crew and contributed to their fear during the great storm several weeks later. The Laird rams were regarded as "equally disreputable" seagoing vessels and some members of the crew stated they would not go to sea in the *Scorpion* again after her July voyage.[264]

The issue of the ship's seaworthiness was revived when on 16 September, orders were read to the crew instructing them to steam to Bermuda to assume the duty as guardship there.[265] The men came aft and "respectfully remonstrated" against having to put to sea on a long voyage at that time of year "in a ship like the Scorpion."[266] The effect of the crew going aft was a change in the order, and the voyage into the central Atlantic was postponed in the interest of safety. After the weather cleared, the ship was reportedly ordered to proceed to Portsmouth for a refit prior to her circuitous voyage to Bermuda.[267] The armorclad did not steam to Portsmouth, but the Admiralty took the unusual step of coming to her in Queenstown. When the *Agincourt*, flagship of the Channel Squadron, anchored in the roadstead later that month, the inspecting party proceeded to the turret ship to ascertain for themselves the conditions aboard and to determine her fate. The party consisted of the First Sea Lord, Vice-Admiral Sir Sidney Dacres, Commodore G.O. Willes, and the former commanding officer of the *Wivern*, Captain Burgoyne. The report found nothing that prohibited the ram from its mission, and the *Scorpion* was ordered to proceed to Bermuda when her escort ship arrived from Devonport.[268]

The *Scorpion* was needed at the Atlantic island naval base to reinforce the station, and the somewhat modern turret warship was considered essential to defend the key installations, especially the new floating dry dock. The dry dock was indispensable for a modern fleet. It facilitated command of the local seas, for well-maintained British warships, especially armored ones, had an advantage against an enemy force far from their own home waters. The dry dock was "the pivot around which British Imperial strategy was transformed between 1860 and 1890."[269] Bermuda was the ideal location; within easy steaming distance to Canada, the West Indies, and the American eastern coasts, it was a protected base that provided Britain with a likely launch platform for raids against American harbors and shipping if war occurred. Admiral Milne referred to the island base as the "key" to the United States, and American observers agreed.[270] One Washington, D.C., newspaper commented as late as 1896 that Bermuda was "menacing our coast" and hailed the strategic location near the center of the Gulf Stream as the "Watch Station of Great Britain."[271] Significantly, the newspaper featured an etching not of a fleet at sea or great gun, but of the cradled *Bellerophon*, her bow sprit extending forward over the men posed along the upper and lower gangways of the floating dock, as an illustration of British Imperial might.[272] The colonial dry docks gave the Royal Navy an edge over most rivals, as they kept the ships of the Royal Navy not only in repair but also battle ready, for their "everyday role was to maintain speed and endurance."[273]

In the summer of 1869, the Royal Navy undertook one of the most intricate feats of seamanship since the laying of the transatlantic cable three years before. The floating dry dock *Bermuda* was towed from Britain to Maderia, then on to her namesake home in two relays. Described as "intrinsically ugly," the 381-foot-long dock was also acknowledged as a specimen of skilled workmanship that would provide the Atlantic colony with the modern means to overcome the shortcomings of poor soil and coral, which prohibited the building of a more traditional dry dock.[274] Escorted by ironclads the entire way, this tow was an example of British maritime power executing a seemingly routine transfer to a colonial station with breathtaking skill. It was also a display of naval supremacy as four of Britain's ironclad frigates, including the *Warrior* and her sister, the *Black Prince*, escorted the dock from Madeira to Bermuda after the *Agincourt* and *Northumberland* towed the *Bermuda* to the Portuguese archipelago from Britain.[275]

Weighing 8,350 tons, it was dubbed "the monster floating machine," the largest floating dry dock in the world.[276] Although able to ride on the waves "like a well corked bottle," she needed a ship to pull her back when she yawed while under tow. That function was served by the venerable paddle frigate *Terrible* after the gunboat H.M.S. *Lapwing* went ahead to inform the naval authorities of the convoy's progress. The dock arrived at Bermuda on 29 July 1869 and came to anchor at her new home at the naval base on the western edge of the archipelago. The Royal Navy now had the means to repair ships on the North Atlantic Station. The tow of the *Bermuda* to her namesake home over 4,000 miles of open ocean was an achievement justly commended by the Admiralty to the men of the ships involved in the undertaking as "an operation without precedence in the British or any other navy."[277]

In the late 1860s, Britain had naval yards around the Atlantic at Halifax, Jamaica, Antigua, Gibraltar, and the Cape of Good Hope, yet these lacked dry docks.[278] Aside from the floating dock at Bermuda, one other graving dock existed at Quebec for the use of the North American Squadron. However, due to icing up, this facility would not be available during winter.[279] Only the *Bermuda* gave the

Royal Navy the year-round strategic option of keeping an iron-hulled warship on the coasts of North America and available for service in the South Atlantic without returning to Britain.

On Tuesday, 12 October 1869, the *Scorpion* left harbor with her consort, the paddle frigate *Terrible* recently returned from Bermuda in close proximity.[280] The British press mistakenly reported that the paddle frigate had been ordered back to Bermuda in order to tow out a dredging machine for use clearing channels around the reef-bound base.[281] Details of *Scorpion*'s brief refit were only hinted at in the British press, but these likely included the removal of her double top gallants for lighter, single-yard variants to render her a safer vessel.[282]

Captain Booker (former commander of the *Wivern*) had identified several deficiencies in the ship during the July voyage and pointed to the flanges around the turrets and the hatches as the main avenues of flooding. By adding screw "buttons" to tightly hold the flanges to the iron plate that circled the base of each turret, the water would be prevented from entering the ship through the spacing between the deck and the turret wall.[283] Raising the height of several hatchways was also required to ensure the ship remained dry. These minor alterations were likely carried out before the Admiralty delegation arrived as further fittings were recommended by the inspectors. These included the installation of deadlights to the hatchways to provide more light from above, and the fashioning of angle iron to fill in the space between the funnel and pilot house in order to "carry off the sea."[284] Captain Booker had made other suggested changes, which included widening the hurricane deck and replacing the three bladed screw for a more suitable two bladed Griffiths version, but these were not implemented while in Ireland.[285] The ship had to carry out her mission and steam for Bermuda. Prior to her departure, the main armament was transferred to the *Terrible* to further reduce the weight of the turret ship.[286]

The Laird rams were not the only armored warships to have been unpopular with officers and men of the Royal Navy during the first decades of the ironclad age. Reed ships also received reproofs from the Admiralty. The Reed-designed *Vixen* and *Waterwitch* were experimental ships termed "failures" by the Navy. These small casemate ironclads had a feature referred to as "plough bow," which restricted the speed of each vessel and held the bow down in the waves.[287] Men aboard both ships were said to have come aft to protest going to sea in them.[288] One admiral referred to them as "coffins" and the naval experts refuted the subsequent claim by their designer that they were intended for river use.[289]

The Reed-designed *Viper* performed better than her unpopular sister, the *Vixen*, yet these three vessels were armored corvettes and carried a few heavy guns on a lighter draft. They suffered from the design disadvantage of a compromise on a small experimental hull form. Observers would comment some twenty years later that the ironclad warship was a compilation of concepts put forth by the gunner, the seaman, the engineer, the naval architect, and other nautical experts. The *Times* correctly referred to the rapidly evolving armorclads of the middle nineteenth century as "a marvel of theory, compromise, and complication."[290]

The *Scorpion* steamed to Bermuda via Madeira in the late autumn of 1869.[291] Towed by the *Terrible* during some stages of the voyage, the crew of the turret ironclad apparently did not suffer any mentionable ill effects from weather as the ship rolled far less than in the Irish Sea, and was only under sail for several days between

Madeira and Bermuda. While in tow of the paddle frigate, coal was conserved, as usually only two boilers were lit on the turret ship when not steaming.[292]

On 18 November, the *Scorpion* and the *Terrible* anchored at Bermuda "all well."[293] Britain had successfully dispatched a turret ship to an overseas base and soon, others followed. A turret ship stationed at a distant naval station had a distinct advantage over a broadside-equipped ironclad, as a ship fitted with twin turrets could "direct all her guns on the same object on more bearings than by any other known plan," and when the broadside armorclad was navigating an intricate harbor channel, the turret ship would have guns brought to bear while the broadside warship was end on at times and vulnerable.[294]

Maintenance and Reserve Duty

As the *Scorpion* was settling into her new role in Bermuda, modifications to the armament of the *Wivern* were made during her refit in the autumn of 1869. Her guns had been removed, and subsequently, experimental changes made to her reconditioned armament and equipment.[295] Another modification made to the *Wivern* during that refit was the installation of a hurricane deck to connect her poop and forecastle "similar to those carried out on board the Scorpion."[296] Both Laird rams had received much-needed modifications, but these changes were made incrementally. The masts were retained and the armorclads were not allowed a suitable refit to test their true abilities for their role as coastal defense warships. The Royal Navy was reluctant to cast off the large masts and heavy yardarms for armored ships propelled only by steam.

The Laird rams were needed as other ships were decommissioned, and *Wivern* was ordered to Hull after completing her refit in Portsmouth to relieve the wooden steam frigate H.M.S. *Dauntless* as guardship at that port. The men from the frigate were to be transferred to the *Wivern* when she was paid off on 31 December 1869 to give the turret ship a complement of 130 officers and men. The gunboat *Rainbow* (a Crimean War vessel built by Lairds) was to serve as a tender for the *Wivern* at her new home.[297] The arrival of the *Wivern* in Hull marked the end of the assignment aboard the turret ship for some of her crew, as this was a temporary arrangement. The remaining complement of the ironclad was comprised largely of coastguardsmen, as most of the active service seamen were transferred back to Portsmouth for duty on other ships.[298]

On the evening of 3 May 1870, the routine of the ironclad guardship was disrupted when a fire broke out at a sawmill in Hull. The fire quickly spread toward the Victoria Dock, spraying showers of sparks onto the air and silhouetting the ships stranded at the quay.[299] *Wivern* was fortunate, as she had been moored at the Albert Dock for six months since her arrival in port, and had cast off and steamed out into the roadstead only that morning.[300] One or two merchantmen had caught fire, but the flames aboard were extinguished as those ships were pulled away from the quays to anchor out with the ironclad and other ships in the safe anchorage way from the spreading blaze.[301] Assisting the firefighting efforts were fifty men from the *Wivern* who chopped away some wooden sheds near the docks and carted away timbers to slow the spread of the "fearfully grand" conflagration.[302] Rowed out from the ironclad in boats, the men were cheered when they marched up from the dock under the direction of the commanding officer of the guardship, Captain Charles W. Hope, R.N.[303]

The *Wivern* men immediately began work when the bugle was sounded, and continued for four hours without letup until the bugle called them to withdraw after the danger to the docks had passed. A report circulated that the ironclad's firefighting detail was withdrawn after a dispute occurred with the local police, but the claim was quickly proven to have been erroneous, and Hope's men were subsequently praised for their good service. Although the flames continued to spread to a nearby timberyard, the intervention of the *Wivern* men did prevent several ships and stacks of lumber from being consumed in the inferno, and thus helped slow and contain the path of destruction.[304] The discipline of the men of the *Wivern* under the direction of Captain Hope revealed the positive impact of training and teamwork for a well-drilled crew proud of their role as the home defense ship.

The outbreak of the Franco-Prussian war again disrupted the peacetime routine of the guardship, as the *Wivern* received orders to rejoin the Channel Fleet.[305] The ironclad was valued at Hull as an armored defender of the Humber River, and the town council protested her removal in a memorial to the government, noting that in the event of Britain's involvement in a wider war, only two small forts defended the coast in that vicinity and those garrisons had only obsolete artillery.[306] Despite the protests from Hull, the *Wivern* was soon on her way to the Channel, where she would form part of "a small but very formidable ironclad squadron" assembled at the Nore.[307]

Steam and armor had not only changed concepts of warship design, but had also redefined the concept of positioning for a naval battle. The tactical employment of an ironclad squadron had changed from the time-tested line-of-battle to groups of bow-on formations. By the 1870s, armored ships were expected to clash with an enemy in a manner similar to a cavalry charge, and although the line-of-battle was used, another formation, a grouping of three ships or "pelotons," was briefly in vogue. This arrangement was intended for mutual support, but even this smaller bunching was difficult to maintain with ironclad warships of different seakeeping abilities.[308]

While firing at the rocks of Bantry Bay during gunnery practice later that summer, a dangerous defect was discovered. A log entry from the *Wivern* dated 13 August 1870 indicated that the compressor screws did not hold the guns in place after they were loaded and run out.[309] With the ship rolling 15 degrees, the guns were moving back and forth on their slides and presented a danger from an accidental discharge or the crushing weight of an out-of-control heavy piece of ordnance. The new guns installed after the 1867 explosion in the forward turret had not resolved the problems of operating heavy ordnance at sea. The guns proved to be too heavy for their carriages, and the compressors attached to the slides were unable to hold the combined weight of guns and iron carriages in place. The *Wivern* had to be turned head-on to the swell to steady the ship and regain control of the 9-inch RMLs in the turrets. *Wivern*'s commander remarked that her guns could not be "fought except under extreme risk."[310]

The 1870 fleet exercise highlighted more faults in the Laird rams as the *Wivern* would need modifications to make her suitable for operations in British waters. Admiral C.W. Elliot, the inspecting officer, returned a scathing appraisal: "I cannot look upon the Wivern as being 'efficescent [sic] as a cruizer [sic]."[311] With an extensive refit, she could be reshaped into an efficient coastal or harbor defense ship for duty near home. Her guns were the immediate priority as she was in need of modern slides to render her capable of using her armament at sea. Despite her obvious drawbacks, the ironclad also was "quick and handy in turning" and had the advantage of a light draft. With a list of alterations completed in dockyard, this armored man-of-war would be made into a warship more in line with her potential.[312] Her low hull was a concern, as the sea constantly washed over the deck between the turrets, rendering it "difficult and hazardous" for the crew to pass fore and aft while underway except via the hurricane deck.

The *Wivern* was recommended for further alteration by removing her heavy iron tripod masts and fitting with light poles to carry fore and aft sails only.[313] Accepting that the sails would never move the ship, the light rig would help stabilize the ironclad in a rough sea. Seamen in the merchant navy prized the steadying effect a fore and aft sail could have on an iron ship by referring to the stabilizing stretch of canvas as a "flopper stopper."[314] With her tripod masts removed, *Wivern* would cut down a considerable amount of topside weight, the loss of which would contribute to an increase in stability. To correct the defect in communications between vital compartments on ship, voice tubes were to be added between the forward pilot position and the engine room, and a speaking tube from the pilot position (forward of the flying bridge) and the aft turret was also proposed.[315]

The *Wivern* was placed in the 4th Division reserve that autumn to await her turn in the dockyard.[316] She arrived at Devonport on 27 September 1870 and her captain, with the officers and some crew, were transferred to one of Reed's new central battery ironclads H.M.S. *Invincible*, as the *Wivern* was decommissioned.[317] The ironclad ram was also recommended to receive two 64-pounder muzzleloading rifles to give the ship greater arcs of fire and supplement the restricted turret guns, but the new guns were never installed.[318] Her refit was again incremental as she was docked in Devonport in October 1873 to have her hull scrapped and painted with two coats of "Hay's Protective Varnish."[319]

Ironclads were frequently in the hands of the dockyards for hull maintenance and refit as the reoccurring problem of marine growth was one shared by all iron-hulled vessels. Although iron provided strength to longer hulls and solved the escalating costs associated with timber shortages, the iron hull was fouled by marine growth at a much faster rate than copper-sheathed, wooden-hulled ships. If not cleaned and painted regularly, the iron bottom of any warship would resemble a "lawyer's wig" of shell and sea grass in short order.[320] In 1871, the *Scorpion* was in the hands of the dockyard in Bermuda to examine the condition of her hull.[321] One section amidships on the starboard side was found to have been "honeycombed," with the corrosion reaching a depth of 1/16 of an inch into the plates, and some of the rivet heads partially eaten away.[322] The remainder of the hull was found to have been in good condition, which was a likely indication of the different qualities of iron used in her construction, and a justification for using Hay's Protective Varnish to impede fouling and corrosion.[323]

Hay's compound was in general use for the iron warships of the Royal Navy, and was advertised has having "met with the approval of the Lords of the Admiralty."[324] Hay, who worked as the chief chemist at the Royal Dockyard at Portsmouth, also produced a "prepared putty" and other protective substances that bore his name.[325] Early anti-fouling substances contained mixtures of copper, mercury, and arsenic, and "probably killed many painters as well as barnacles."[326] These toxic blends were necessary, as after six months in home waters without docking, an iron ship would accumulate enough marine growth to decrease performance while underway by 25 percent. Most anti-fouling substances would last about a year before a ship would need to be sent back to dry dock, but more frequent attention was needed if in warmer waters. Despite the need for more regular hull maintenance, the anti-fouling paints saved the admiralty the additional weight per hull by avoiding more expensive and drag-inducing solutions.[327] *Warrior* received coats of the stuff after a visit to dry dock in 1863, and Hay's concoction was termed "invaluable" in the preservation of the submerged sections of her hull.[328]

Another problem that vexed the merchantmen and men-of-war during the mid–Victorian years was the short lifespan of the boilers aboard all steam vessels. This was particularly true for warships, due in part to the improved performance of engines and the subsequent decline in the sailing abilities of ships of war, most notably in the ironclads. The box boiler favored in this era had grown to the limits of its capacity. A Parliamentary committee established to investigate solutions received a dire report from the Admiralty that announced, "boilers in the Navy did not last more than five or six years."[329]

Another resource tried by the Admiralty was tubes made from brass. These tubes were installed in the boilers of the seagoing ironclads like the *Warrior* and later *Alexandra*, as brass corroded less than iron.[330] The *Scorpion* also had brass boiler tubes, likely a detail foreseen by Lairds in the original construction.[331] During a Bermuda dockyard overhaul in 1873, iron tubes were fitted to replace the brass tubes on the turret ship, which had become foul from the effects of burning bad coal.[332] Despite advantages, brass boiler tubes were expensive and, as such, were phased out aboard most Royal Navy warships around 1882.[333] Iron was the cheaper product, but only with the advent of steel in the construction of the components of the water tube boiler could the necessary high steam pressures be obtained with safety and efficiency.[334] Iron was at its limit.

Refit and a Foreign Station

In March 1878, the British press reported that the *Wivern* was to enter dockyard at her birthplace to undergo a six-month refit.[335] The turret ship was long overdue for more than a short-term patching over as she was towed by the paddle frigate H.M.S. *Valorous* and assisted by the paddle tug H.M.S. *Scotia* to Birkenhead.[336] *Valorous*, the last wooden-hulled paddle frigate commissioned in the Royal Navy (1852), was well-suited to the task, as her paddle wheels dampened most rolls of the waves while at sea.[337] Her hull length and freeboard also contributed to her being recognized as an "easy" ship due to her superb handling under sail and steam. The ability to use the paddles independently allowed her to remain in position or to maneuver with only slight turns of the helm.[338] Although one Irish newspaper referred to the frigate *Terrible* in 1867 as being as "ancient as a trireme," these obsolete paddle warships were useful, even preferable, to other vessels for the more routine tasks of ocean surveys, coastal patrols, and the underappreciated but vital assignments of towing ungainly armored men-of-war.[339]

After the ironclad frigate H.M.S. *Iron Duke* had completed her refit at Lairds' shipyard, the *Wivern* was turned over to her builders, not for a refit and the installation of new components, but for a long-needed remaking.[340] The *Scorpion* was also slated for an extensive alteration, and on 24 June 1878, the Admiralty approved Lairds' offer (for £1340) to construct a new funnel, uptakes, and boiler mountings for refitting that ironclad at the Bermuda dockyard.[341] By Christmas, the *Wivern* and the ram H.M.S. *Hotspur* were still at Lairds in overhaul. Merseyside was experiencing

Hoisting a Whitehead torpedo aboard a British ironclad, c. 1875 (author's collection).

a slowdown in ship orders at the time, and work on the navy rams was most welcome during a period of "considerable decline" compared with the previous year. The *Wivern* received new boilers, her engines were reconstructed, and she received attention to her hull as part of the extensive alterations undertaken to make her more suitable for steaming to an overseas outpost.[342]

In February 1880, the Admiralty announced that the *Wivern* would be dispatched to Hong Kong to provide a naval defense for the colony.[343] The decision to send the *Wivern* to Asian waters was ridiculed in the British press as the turret ironclad and her sister were called "the weakest of our armor-clad fleet."[344] She was slow and rolled in heavy weather, but she was available for service in the Far East. Despite her shortcomings, the *Wivern* was the right fit for a defensive role on the China coast. Modifications were made to her again after her stay at the Merseyside shipyard. New fixtures were to have been added at Portsmouth, but she had to steam to Devonport without the new machinery aboard. This back-and-forth steaming was due in part to issues of heavy loading of support equipment on an already deeply laden hull.[345] Reed criticized the decision to send her to the Orient and, referring to her new role, proclaimed, "for general service in China waters she is, in my opinion, dangerously unfit."[346]

The Admiralty did not share Reed's view, as the old turret ship had undergone "considerable improvements" which had made her "a safe and efficient vessel for the services for which she is intended."[347] To prevent overloading the hull, the ironclad would pick up some components at Malta, dispatched prior to her departure from the Channel.[348] Other new weapons would be sent out on separate ships, especially two 2nd class torpedo boats (TBs) originally intended to be carried on davits amidships on the *Wivern*.[349]

The boats first intended for the *Wivern* were damaged in a mishap on the night of 5 February, during a mock attack on their carrier ship H.M.S. *Hecla* at Spithead. One

2nd class torpedo boat, c. 1890 (author's collection).

TB was painted black to render her nearly invisible to the lookouts on the mother ship. Although she was observed while closing on the *Hecla*, the other attacking torpedo boat did not see her. The second boat, painted gray to obscure the outline of her features, collided with the hard-to-see black boat, and both were damaged in the mishap.[350] Although the thin, steel-hulled boats were both pierced and torn, the watertight compartments held, and none of the personnel aboard were injured. With repairs ordered for the camouflaged torpedo boats, two more 2nd class TBs were substituted for eventual assignment to the *Wivern*.[351]

Almost two decades after they were accepted by a reluctant Royal Navy, the *Scorpion* and the *Wivern* were still mentioned in Parliament as unsuccessful ships. The *Scorpion* and her lightly armored harbor defense cohorts at the Atlantic island fortress came in for abuse when Lord Henry Lennox proclaimed that he hoped that Bermuda would never find itself confronted by a serious opponent. Lennox asserted that if the *Scorpion*, *Viper*, and *Vixen* were all the colony had for naval defense, then their best course of action was not to engage, but withdraw.[352] The *Scorpion* and the other gunboats on that station would, from "within the ring of Bermuda reefs," cooperate with the shore batteries and protect the minelaying crews to defend the channels and harbors (especially the naval station and dockyard) at the island base.[353] The *Wivern* was also criticized in the Commons, as she was among a handful of small ironclads singled out as being no more efficient as seagoing ships than Noah's Ark.[354] This curious reference was an unintended compliment, for like the ungainly ship from the Bible, the *Wivern* was serving her true purpose and was soon to depart for a new station.

Both the Laird rams were to find their optimum roles as coastal defense ships and the Admiralty spokesman, Sir Thomas Brassey, corrected the opposition for speaking

HMS *Scorpion* on duty anchored outside the breakwater off the floating dry dock *Bermuda* with another warship inside for cleaning and repair, c. 1874 (author's collection).

"very lightly" of these (and other small ironclads), emphasizing that they were quite useful in a defensive role, and they enjoyed the added benefit of being in very good repair.[355] Although slow and not worthy of the van of a battle line, these ironclads had a task to defend far-off stations while other warships patrolled the oceans to show the flag and intimidate Britain's enemies.

The low-hulled Laird rams would never again make the voyage home. Nevertheless, these old armored guardships had more years of service life in them, keeping the White Ensign flying at distant and vital bases while modern corvettes and ironclad frigates were busy on other "needful duties."[356] The Royal Navy needed more modern ships to meet the growing combined threats from the French and Russian navies. The old turret ships and the other forlorn ironclads remained in harness until newer ships could be built, their crews properly trained, modifications made and tested, and then the more modern warships would be sent out to defend the seaways. The *Scorpion* and *Wivern* helped give the Admiralty the breathing space it needed to build up the fleet as European rivals launched their own versions of improved armored vessels. The Laird turret ships bought Britain time.

FOUR

Naval Weapons and Power Projection

The Laird Rams on Foreign Station 1874–1923

British ironclads no longer suitable for front line service in home waters or the Mediterranean were remade into armored guardians to deter would-be aggressors further afield at the outposts of the Empire. Small turret ships, such as the *Scorpion* and *Wivern*, not only relieved other "sea-going" warships for more urgent tasks, they also remained on hand for defensive operations and some were held in readiness for a possible attack against an enemy coast in the event of war.[1]

Scorpion and the Bermuda Dockyard

In the early 1870s, the three ironclads of the "Inshore Defence Squadron," the *Scorpion* and the smaller *Viper* and *Vixen*, were periodically exercised at sea. These maneuvers occurred rarely as the ships suffered problems with manning and mechanical malfunctions.[2] During a drill in April 1873, the *Scorpion* experienced defective boiler safety valves and was stopped almost immediately after weighing anchor.[3] The ironclad also suffered the effects of corrosion on internal and topside iron surfaces, and a repair was deemed necessary. To both improve her performance and avoid a total refit, her heavy masts and spars were removed, and boilers were overhauled. The storerooms and cabins aft had to be cleared away to repair and paint the rusting iron hull frames below the water line. As a cost-saving measure, the storerooms and the cabins were not reinstalled as the ship was assigned to harbor and coastal defense duties and would likely not cruise far afield.[4] Refit of the *Scorpion* created a more streamlined defender capable of employing her turret guns with greater effect after the clutter associated with a sailing warship had been removed. Local naval authorities took necessary steps to maintain a degree of readiness without exhausting limited budgets. This was a sensible move as the iron ships at Bermuda appeared to have suffered advanced corrosion in the warm, wet climate.

The problem of suitable coal stocks continued to influence naval operations at Bermuda. The British press had stated that the supply of coal from Nova Scotia "gives us an overwhelming advantage over any European combatant who might endeavour to cripple our Atlantic trade," but that advantage was only a short-term benefit. Poor quality coal had damaged the *Scorpion*'s boilers and sentenced her to frequent care of the dockyard.[5] As mentioned in the previous chapter, the use of inferior coals continued until 1887, when cleaner-burning Welsh coal was ordered for Her Majesty's warships, except when supplies were not available.[6] The need for economy and the requirement to maintain fuel stocks meant that supplies of cleaner-burning Welsh anthracite could not always be maintained.

Weather was an additional factor, and the Bermuda dockyard was particularly susceptible to tidal surges. On 28 August 1878, an Atlantic gale damaged the crucial floating dock when the *Bermuda* was lifted by the storm surge and rammed into the breakwater. The dock had been careened for repairs but with the pending arrival of the storm, it was temporarily "flooded down" by filling her with water in an effort to limit damage. For generations of Bermudians, the sight of the dock sinking without a ship awaiting repair was the sign a hurricane was imminent. The *Bermuda* was pumped out and salvaged by crews detailed from the warships on station and the dockyard workers reassigned to repair the floating dry dock.[7] In late August 1880, the island base was struck by another severe hurricane, but the floating dock "remained immovable" as the *Scorpion* was inside, keeping the great structure in place at her berth.[8]

Bermuda was the key link in the chain of British dockyards and military bases in the New World. Halifax, Bermuda, and the Bahamas were referred to as the "guardians" of the Gulf Stream, "freighted ... with the exports of half a continent."[9] Bermuda was at the center of that ring of bases, and the dry dock was the crucial component. An adjacent addition near the floating dry dock was the massive sheerlegs built by James Taylor & Company of Birkenhead. Shipped and installed at the naval base in 1875, this 195-ton structure augmented the heavy repair capabilities of that Atlantic station.[10] A photograph, circa 1878, provided a rare glimpse of a Bermuda ironclad, likely the *Scorpion*, moored under the sheers for an extensive alteration. The vessel looked less cluttered with masts removed, new funnel fitted, and canvas awning rigged where the aft turret once stood. The armorclad had probably received her new boilers, and this stern view revealed her riding high without her earlier fittings, turrets, and guns.[11]

Despite the dockyard improvements, Admiral J.E. Commerell, a former commander of the *Scorpion*, did not like Bermuda and termed it "one of the most tempestuous spots in the world." Commerell warned that an ironclad that suffered a flooded compartment in the winter months would have a "lively time of it" waiting offshore for the right conditions of wind and tide to get over the bar and into the dry dock. He also pointed out the necessity of bringing laborers from Britain to repair the dock and to conduct the necessary upkeep of chipping and painting the "enormously expensive" structure. The Admiral feared the health of the workmen shipped from Britain would "surely break down," adding to the costs of maintaining the dry dock. Despite these misgivings, Bermuda would remain the key facility for the Royal Navy in the Western Hemisphere until a large dry dock was built at Halifax in the late 1880s.[12]

Condemned in the British press in 1876 for being "failures as seagoing vessels," the small ironclads "stowed away" at Bermuda were overhauled in anticipation of service in local waters.[13] To refer to these ships as "failures" discounts another factor that influenced their construction. When launched in the mid–1860s, these ships had armor as thick as that of the *Warrior*, although they were armed with only a few heavy guns. Despite being poor sea boats, they had another advantage. The *Scorpion* and the smaller experimental ironclad rams, *Viper* and *Vixen*, were capable of steaming

Warship, likely HMS *Scorpion*, under the sheers at Bermuda, c. 1878 (National Archives, Kew, London).

up the St. Lawrence as far as Montreal to provide heavy naval firepower should the United States threaten open hostilities. The *Viper* and *Vixen* had the additional advantage of shorter length, beam, and draft to permit the transverse of the locks at Montreal if required, into Lake Ontario should tensions with Washington reoccur.[14]

The shoals, difficult currents, and slender channels of Bermuda made the Atlantic fortress the ideal base for the rams.[15] An American geographer observed that the main shipping channel (St. George's) was so narrow "that one could easily toss a biscuit to either shore."[16] At Bermuda, the speed of the more modern man-of-war was not a necessity. Here, a warship's position and accuracy of fire were the determining factors in a conflict with any enemy willing to hazard an attack. A ram would have an ample opportunity to fire on, and crash into, an enemy vessel threading its way between the shoals. Bermuda was, according to Richard Gould, "one of the few places in Britain's overseas empire where geography, in the form of surrounding reefs, and narrow channels, favored the use of steam-powered rams."[17]

The North American and West Indian Squadron and the Russian War Scare of 1877–1878

Rivalry between Britain and Russia over Russian advances against Turkish forces in the Balkans threatened to break out into open conflict in 1877–1878. The purchase of several fast U.S. merchant steamers for the Imperial Russian Navy in 1878 marked a return to the debates over neutrality and the threat of commerce raiding on the Atlantic by would-be auxiliary cruisers. A Philadelphia banker named Wharton Barker was the official owner of the steamers *State of California, Columbus,* and *Saratoga*, but he served as a blind for the real owners, the Russian government.[18] Barker was well-positioned to facilitate the purchase of the American ships for Russia, as he was a personal friend of Captain Leonid Pavlovich Semetschkin, the Tsar's naval emissary chosen to arrange the purchases. The issues of contractual obligations and the enforcement of laws related to neutrality came to the fore as it had during the building of the Laird rams, and the *New York Herald* warned that Barker's purchase of the steamers had brought the "Washington government face to face with the great question of international duty toward the two great nations," Britain and Russia.[19]

British activity had not gone unobserved. The *New York Times* noted most of the Royal Navy's North American and West Indian Squadron had assembled at Bermuda by the first week in April 1878, where they "were constantly at ball practice."[20] Increased readiness at the island base was in response to Russian attempts to purchase the commerce raiders in America. British authorities were confident in their preparations and acknowledged that although a Russian steamer converted into a commerce raider might have initial success on the Atlantic, that success would be short lived: "We might have some trouble at first," yet the Russians were "more likely to fall victims to our cruisers than to inflict damage on our merchantmen."[21]

At Bermuda, the pace of activity increased as the ships in reserve were slated for immediate overhaul. The *Scorpion* was to receive two new boilers from Britain, and the small ironclad rams *Viper* and *Vixen* were also in the hands of the dockyard, in preparation for active service.[22] Armored warships with heavy guns, when combined with the ram and/or torpedoes, provided a suitable defense against any then-likely naval enemy capable of making an effort against the island fortress. Bermuda received a supply of torpedo stores in the summer of 1876, and these weapons were held in readiness for defensive or offensive operations. Additionally, Halifax had received a shipment of torpedo-related supplies that year.[23] These weapons, when augmented by the refitted warships, allowed Britain a renewed capability against the handful of cruisers Russia could deploy into the Atlantic.

While warships conducted gunnery practice and troopships shuttled replacements and reinforcements to Bermuda and other points of the Empire, the great Atlantic island storehouse was supplied by the visiting schooner or hired steamer. As Whitehall prepared for a possible war with Russia, British merchantmen were contracted to supply naval bases and garrisons at overseas stations. The steamer *Lady Tredegar* was chartered by the Admiralty to carry the two new boilers destined for the *Scorpion*, along with 80 tons of provisions, 50 tons of shot and shell, and another 200 tons of ammunition for the army garrison and the naval forces at Bermuda.[24]

The *Wivern* to the Far East

The opening of the Suez Canal in 1869 led to a decline in Russian overland trade with China. The primary route to Beijing from central Russia wound down Siberian rivers and across Lake Baikal to the edge of the Tsar's empire. From 1879–1880,

Russian expansionism in Asia contributed to a border dispute with China over control of Kuldja (also known as Kuldzha), a frontier town some 100 miles southwest of Lake Balkhash.[25]

Russia's response to border tensions with China was marked with a steady buildup of military and naval forces dispatched to Asia. Vladivostok was vulnerable to Chinese troops across the Amur River, and the Russian government responded to this threat by chartering ships to convey 1,500 men to this strategic port. Russia also made arrangements with Japan to supply her ships with coal and provisions. Six torpedo boats were dispatched to Vladivostok to defend that port, freeing the Tsar's Pacific cruisers for offensive operations. Russia prepared to blockade Chinese ports to counter their preponderance of ground forces during these tensions, and warships were rushed to the Far East to give Russia, as a British newspaper noted, "a naval influence in the Pacific superior to any she has ever enjoyed in that quarter of the globe."[26] The Russian build up was followed closely in the British press: "Russia, free from the entanglements of Constantinople and Merv, will be ready to carry fire and sword to the pagodas of Pekin [sic]."[27] China also stepped up military preparations on the Pacific frontier, and a Chinese spy was reportedly captured near Vladivostok with a map of the city.[28]

Russia ordered modern vessels, including the ironclad frigate, *General Admiral*, to Vladivostok in order to augment forces already in those waters, which included the armored frigate *Minin*. The *Minin* was the first Russian ironclad to arrive in Asia, and her armament was considered superior to that of the British flagship in those waters, the *Iron Duke*.[29] Russian ironclads and cruisers were fitted to carry torpedo launches "constructed after the most approved models," and the *Minin* was assigned three.[30] More men-of-war arrived in Vladivostok, and Russian capabilities on land were enhanced with the assignment of marines from these warships. The British government was not content to remain idle, and the *Wivern* was ordered to Hong Kong in response to the Tsar's naval buildup. Despite this increase in Russian activity, the Admiralty was questioned in the British press over its decision to send the *Wivern* to Hong Kong, as that port had "little to fear for years to come" and reportedly, no enemy armored vessels were stationed in the Far East.[31]

The *Wivern* had undergone engine tests and minor modifications after she arrived at Plymouth on 14 February 1880.[32] The men removed ammunition into lighters, and the dockyard workers effected repairs as the ship neared her departure time. The crew went about their duties "as requite" including cutlass drills, cleaning ship, and preparing boats for the voyage to the Far East.[33] A photo from this time reveals a ship transformed by extensive refits. Gone were the heavy iron tripod masts and yardarms. In their place were three light masts carrying only fore and aft sails to steady the ship while at sea; the pretense of an actual sailing ability had been abandoned. The image, taken from the ship's starboard side, revealed that the earlier telescoping funnel had been replaced by a larger, more standard oval-shaped stationary version. The bulwarks were in the up position and the ship was painted white in preparation for her voyage to Asia. A boat was alongside and hooked to a boom forward of the gangway, with two other cutters secured to davits on either side of the poop. Four empty crutches were visible amidships, awaiting one of two torpedo boats she would obtain at her new homeport. Positioned around a newly added superstructure amidships, forward of the funnel, were bell-mouthed iron ventilators.[34] These, combined with the two smaller versions forward on the forecastle, were a far cry from the canvass sacks suspended from mast or yardarm utilized in 1865 in an attempt to provide increased air flow to the engineering spaces below.[35] The raised forecastle and poop were cut back and angled inward towards the deck, permitting a greater radius for the turret guns. Devoid of a jib boom, and fitted with only the most rudimentary rigging, the rebuilt *Wivern* had a less cluttered, more rakish look.[36]

When the *Wivern* steamed to Hong Kong in 1880, she was to have sailed with two 2nd class torpedo boats aboard. Her plans indicated that torpedo boats were to have been hoisted aboard, one each side of the funnel, at the height of the hurricane deck, with "torpedo spars" stowed amidships for the use of the two intended torpedo boats. These auxiliaries, TBs No. 51 and No. 53, were not embarked, as they would have added extra weight during her long voyage out.[37] The ironclad was also to have sailed with a "water heating arrangement," which would allow the two torpedo boats to quickly get up steam and set off on a separate or supporting mission. This apparatus was not ready when she departed Britain, and it was sent forward for loading at Malta.[38] *Wivern* was fitted with a "railway" on the forecastle, and related handling gear for her Whitehead torpedoes, but these weapons were not loaded in the ship on her outbound voyage.[39]

The ironclad was to have been accompanied by the frigate H.M.S. *Raleigh*, but that vessel was required to transport replacement crews to Australia. As a result, the corvette *Curacoa* was assigned the duty of escorting the turret ship to China.[40] However, that corvette was delayed by dockyard repairs at Devonport, and the *Wivern* sailed alone on 13 March, bound for Gibraltar.[41] Her complement consisted of 13 officers, 34 petty officers, 85 seamen, 16 marines, and 4 boys for a total crew of 152 personnel.[42]

HMS *Wivern* at Plymouth, 1880 (Naval History and Heritage Command).

Crew drill with light RML on field carriage, c. 1890 (author's collection).

The *Wivern*'s plans were retained at Devonport, and revealed a ship incorporating some of the latest weapons in anticipation of her service on the China Station. The turret tops revealed only a central circular grating over each pair of heavy guns and no bonnets or hatches for sighting. Twelve Nordenfelt machine guns were carried aboard (only four were part of her permanent armament at this stage), with two forward (one on each side on the forecastle), two positioned aft of the funnel on the superstructure, two stowed (not ready for immediate use and further aft on the superstructure), two stowed on the poop, and four positioned (two on either side of the poop) to provide complete coverage of the vessel. She transported some of the stowed guns for other vessels on the China Station and with only 150 Nordenfelts available for service in the Royal Navy by October 1880, the guns were in short supply. On the poop, a Gatling gun and a rifled 7-pounder gun, both on field carriages, were lashed in place, intended for close-in fire support and later service ashore, when the *Wivern* arrived at Hong Kong.[43]

The Gatling was one of about 50 in service with the Royal Navy at that time. It likely was the six-barreled variant in .450 caliber (which had been adopted in August 1874), with the rounds (400) carried in the top-mounted Broadwell drum magazine. The British Gatlings were made under contract by Sir William Armstrong & Co. of

Newcastle, and this weapon (likely due to the field carriage) carried on the *Wivern*, may have been one of the twelve issued from Woolwich Arsenal to the Royal Navy by March 1878.[44]

The 7-pounder was a versatile light artillery piece, suitable for service ashore when mounted on its field carriage or placed on a small naval carriage and slide for boat operations. Like the slightly larger 9-pounder, these dual-use RML boat guns were shipped aboard British men-of-war to provide a landing party with the ability to fire a shell over three kilometers when elevated to the maximum. The guns were known to have been stamped with the numbers "1° 30" when manufactured by the Royal Gun factory at Woolwich. This reminded the gunner that the barrel deflected to the right, as all British guns were rifled to be "right handed." Designed for simple loading and sighting, these guns were recognized as "weapons of some versatility." With their rugged and portable design, the small-bore muzzleloaders were in service throughout the Empire as mobile light guns with the Royal Horse Artillery and the Royal Navy for over thirty years until the end of the century.[45]

The Nordenfelt gun was available in multiple variations, but these particular versions were four-barreled weapons, capable of shooting a four-round volley as rapidly as a crewman could move the charge handle forward to fire and to the rear to reload.[46] This close-in weapon, with its 1-inch shell, was designed to counter torpedo boats and deemed of sufficient size to penetrate the light steel skin of an attacking craft. Additionally, the gun was nimble enough to retrain to a rapidly shifting target. The four barrels of each gun were necessary for an adequate amount of fire to ensure a hit against a fast-moving attacker.[47] The machine gun, either the Nordenfelt or rival Hotchkiss, was seen as the naval weapon of choice for an ironclad to sink a TB during the 1880s. One Royal Navy officer stated, "Suffice it to say, that either of these machine guns, if properly handled, will render a torpedo-boat attack a service of extreme difficulty and danger."[48]

Another feature on the modernized *Wivern* was a single wheel, positioned immediately forward of the iron conning tower. Within a pace to the port side was the engine room telegraph and speaking tube. Although the *Wivern* retrained her wheel aft, it was now of only secondary, even tertiary, importance. Steering had reached an impasse with the development of the large iron steamship and in 1867, John McFarlane Gray invented a steam-powered mechanism for the unwieldy *Great Eastern* to overcome the limitations of manual steering. Gray's machine was the first to employ a "feed-back" system, and permitted the large double and triple wheels familiar to sailing ships to be replaced by smaller, single variants positioned forward.[49] With steering located at a vantage point forward of the funnel on the *Wivern*, the need to communicate to the helmsmen aft, through shouted commands or by hand signals, was eliminated.[50] The steam steering gear was likely manufactured by Forrester & Company (of the Vauxhall Foundry in Liverpool) to Gray's patent, as more modern ships in the Royal Navy and mercantile service used this device, which was hailed as "one of the most important of modern inventions connected with navigation."[51] Although still open to the elements, the "bridge" of the *Wivern* was marked by an elevated wooden grating where a quartermaster and a detail of men could pilot the ship. With binnacles on either side of this forward edge of the superstructure, the ironclad had made another evolutionary step away from sail.[52]

Crew drill with the Nordenfelt, c. 1895 (author's collection).

After the *Wivern* arrived at Gibraltar on 18 March, the crew readied the ship for the next leg of her voyage.[53] The following day, as some members of the crew were engaged coaling ship and loading stores, the gunner armed one of the cutters and trained select men in firing details. This detail fired dozens of shells and some canister from the light 7-pounder. Another weapon, a launcher tube designed to fire 24-pound Hale rockets, discharged only two rounds.[54]

Britain officially adopted the Hale rocket in 1867, replacing the earlier guidestick-stabilized Congreve rockets popularized in the American national anthem.[55] The Hale 24-pounder was slightly over two feet in length and painted red to protect the iron casing from rust. The most distinctive feature was a raised triskelion at the rear of the casing with three vent holes to induce spin when the rocket was fired from its tube.⁵⁶ The tube went through several iterations and one version employed for shipboard and boat operations was designed by Lieutenant, later First Sea Lord, John Fisher.⁵⁷ The rocket, referred to as "the soul of artillery without the body," was an erratic weapon that offered the advantage of blast and incendiary capability, but was susceptible to damage as the casing was prone to expand or contract when used in climatic zones of extreme temperature variations.⁵⁸ When utilized on colonial campaigns, Hale rockets offered the benefit of range (approximately 1,200 yards), were lightweight, were effective at dispersing enemy formations (especially cavalry), and were frequently employed to burn down grass hut villages. Their main drawback was their erratic, slow flight path, which occasionally resulted in the rocket ricocheting against trees and turning back toward its launching point.⁵⁹ The Hale Rocket, propelled by gunpowder, suffered from a short shelf life and the Admiralty required them

Shipboard Hale rocket launcher, c. 1880 (author's collection).

to be returned to arsenal for examination every five years. The rocket was useful for brush wars, as it "spread danger over a wide area," but was also considered "almost as dangerous to the firers as to the enemy."[60]

The *Wivern* departed Gibraltar on 23 March 1880, bound for her next refueling stop at Malta.[61] While at sea in the central Mediterranean, the crew exercised firing the main 9-inch guns, the Nordenfelts, and discharged a few volleys from their Martini-Henry small arms rifles. During the gunnery exercise, the left 9-inch RML of the aft turret was disabled after the slide split from the effects of the recoil of the gun and carriage. The ironclad also developed a leak and when she arrived at Malta on the 28th, she was placed in dockyard to make good her defects, which included examination of her screw by a diver.[62]

The armorclad departed Malta for Port Said, on the north coast of Egypt, on 4 April, and the crew was employed in the usual shipboard routines of muster, drill, and painting. On 6 April, rough weather precluded some training as seas washed over the deck, but boat crews were later instructed in rockets and lights.[63] As the *Wivern* steamed westward, the British press noted that Edward Reed described her, and other older ironclads, as being outdated, with "armour which is no longer worthy to be called armour." Nevertheless, Reed acknowledged the "ironclads of the old type ... have been rightly and widely repaired and refitted."[64]

The *Wivern* began her voyage through the Suez Canal shortly after dawn on the 11th. While under the control of the pilot, the ironclad exhibited her propensity to yaw at slow speeds, and although engines were reversed, the Ironclad's port side touched the bank of the waterway and the ship grounded. After a short ten minutes aground, the *Wivern* was off and underway. By the 14th, the man-of-war was steaming south through the Red Sea, bound for Aden. The ship's log revealed that her captain, Commander T.G. Jones, kept the men busy painting ship, conducting routine repairs, and hoisting sail to compensate for the ship traveling at half speed. The *Wivern* was slowed to conserve fuel, yet waves washed over her main deck, indicating that higher speeds were preferable to maintain suitable headway in storm-prone waters. Jones kept to routine as much as possible in the rough seas, ordering firefighting practice, boats swung out, and a cutter's men provided with life jackets or "cork dresses" for lifesaving drills.[65]

By 21 April, the *Wivern* was at Aden, where she was refueled and provisioned, and her crew conducted target practice with the Nordenfelts, the Gatling, and the 7-pounder. When underway on the 24th, a log entry indicated that coal stored on the upper deck was used for fuel.[66] This reference revealed that refits had increased the stability of the ironclad and permitted her to ship extra coal on her deck. Coaling stations had become a new part of naval strategy as sail was a diminishing consideration for mobility.[67] It was not uncommon for warships to carry a temporary coal supply on their decks to extend range. During the 1869 voyage to tow the massive floating dock to Bermuda, the ironclads *Warrior* and *Black Prince* each carried extra coal on their main decks to ensure adequate and available fuel. This was recognized as an unsafe practice, as warships that carried loads of coal on deck were "unfit to meet an enemy and doubtfully fit to meet extremes of wind and sea."[68] This fear was justified when the new sloop, H.M.S. *Condor*, disappeared in a storm off Vancouver in December 1901. The load of 48 tons of extra coal carried on her deck was assessed to have been a contributing factor in her loss.[69]

After her arrival at Singapore on 21 May 1880, *Wivern* conducted her usual routine of recoaling, provisioning, and repainting. She also took on another seaman, but this man was excluded from duty as he was a supernumerary and bound for the military hospital at Hong Kong, another facility that differentiated that naval base from a commercial port or coaling stop.[70]

On 2 June, *Wivern* steamed into Hong Kong harbor and made ready for her new mission as reserve guardship. Awnings were spread for protection from the sun, and the ship was guided to her anchorage at No. 4 buoy. Four men were discharged to hospital, and the crew began the tasks of offloading stores for shipment ashore and cleaning ship. Three days later, the log of the *Wivern* noted the arrival of one of the American-built Volunteer cruisers, the *Aziya*, as she steamed into Hong Kong harbor flying the flag of a Russian rear admiral. With the *Wivern*'s crew parceled out in predetermined assignments to other British warships in the Far East, on 14 June, the turret ship was paid off and her pennant lowered for the end of her first commission on the China Station.[71]

The *Wivern* was ideal for this role. She was selected to protect the harbor of Hong Kong and the smaller adjacent islands viewed as potential positions where a hostile warship could bombard the shore while safely shielded from fire by land batteries. Forts were, in this scenario, "useless" against an enemy sheltered within the islets, and the turret ship was available to chase off all but the largest armored man-of-war. Additionally, her two torpedo boats posed a fast-moving threat and would further complicate the actions of a hostile force.[72]

With British coastal defenses in Asia and Australia improved after the arrival of armored turret ships at key bases, the Royal Navy had the "strategic flexibility" to attack enemy harbors and hunt down hostile cruisers.[73] One key British foreign policy goal in the second half of the nineteenth century was to maintain China's stability. The *Wivern* was available for defensive duty in the event renewed Russian tensions with China escalated into war and the Royal Navy became involved.[74] The *Wivern* gave the Royal Navy freedom of action in Asian waters, as more British warships were available for operations without leaving Hong Kong exposed.

A permanently based armored warship in Hong Kong was a welcome sight for colonial officials at that vital possession. One newspaper in the colony summed up the new addition as "the best fighting ship of her size" on station.[75] The Colonial Governor, Sir John Pope-Hennessy, said in his speech on 10 October 1880, "We have in the harbour at this moment a most efficient turret-ship, the *Wivern*. That ship is here for local purposes. The Admiralty will not carry her away from us...."[76]

Duty on the China Station

The *Wivern* gave Britain an edge over the other Pacific powers. She remained in local waters while the larger ships of the squadron went out to show the flag or, in the event of conflict, hunt the enemy. Following the *Wivern*'s arrival at the Asian colony, officers not remaining on board were divided between the old wooden receiving ship, *Victor Emmanuel*, the flagship *Iron Duke*, and gunboat *Kestrel* to round out wardroom billets. Crewmen were also reassigned as needed. As a caretaker ironclad, the *Wivern* was available for service, but she was not fully manned.[77] Nevertheless, she was ready for immediate service, and the Hong Kong press noted that her presence "can hardly mean that she will lie in this harbour all her commission."[78] Indeed, she did not remain idle, as she was regularly utilized for training voyages.

The turret ship was a subject of particular interest for Governor Hennessy. The governor was invited to travel aboard the ironclad for a trial trip on 6 January 1881, and was impressed with the performance of the ship and her gunnery practice during the journey. In a report to his superior Colonial Secretary, the Earl of Kimberley, Hennessy judged the ram to be "a most efficient ship" for the purpose of harbor defense. The governor also included "colonial defence" in his description of the *Wivern*'s role in Hong Kong. The ironclad was, in Hennessy's estimation, "of more value than a regiment of soldiers," and he asked for Kimberley's support, requesting that the Admiralty man the *Wivern* with a full complement and place her on active service. During the trial trip, the crew had been borrowed from then-flagship *Iron Duke*. With the turret ship fully manned, wrote Hennessy, a battalion (he referred to it as a "wing") of the British regiment then stationed in Hong Kong, could be available for deployment elsewhere or returned to Britain, thereby reducing costs on the Imperial establishment.

The Admiralty declined the request, as the expense of taking the ironclad out of reserve and providing her with a full complement of officers and crew would have been "considerable." Cost savings was the focus of all branches of the imperial machine, and the priorities of one service inhibited a unity of effort in the colony. The Admiralty was not prepared to take on the additional costs of keeping another ironclad in service without an increase in funds. The *Wivern* was placed in reserve to augment the China Squadron in the event of hostilities, yet her role was not envisioned as that of a static guardship. The ironclad gave the Admiralty options, and they specifically mentioned her light draft and heavy armament as useful not only in defense of Hong Kong, but on rivers where her big guns were likely to be more powerful than those an enemy was expected to bring to bear.[79]

The Admiralty forwarded Governor Hennessy's proposal to Vice Admiral G.O. Willes, but it was clear that if the ram went back into service, the crew would come from ships already on station. Willes had suggested that the Admiralty post to Hong Kong twenty-five Royal Marine Artillerymen (all assigned to the books of the *Victor Emmanuel*) in order to man the guns of the *Wivern*. The marines would serve as a nucleus around which more men could be assigned to build a temporary crew in order to provide the turret ironclad with a full complement during times of crisis. Willes' suggestion was overruled by the Admiralty, as they did not consider it necessary for "so large a number" of marine gunners to be utilized for a standby mission on the *Wivern*. Nevertheless, they promised to send out ten marine gunners when "an opportunity offers" for the use of Willes as he saw fit. Around these men, a partial crew could assemble to man the *Wivern*'s guns and when augmented with several additional hands from the squadron, could prepare the ship for commissioned service.[80]

As stated, the turret ram was not relegated to remain at Hong Kong on a continuous basis. In December 1881, she steamed to Canton to show the flag and train her delegated crew, assigned from the sloop H.M.S. *Pegasus*, in the ways of their temporary charge.[81]

In January 1882, the *Wivern* visited the nearby Portuguese colony of Macao and steamed once more towards Canton.[82] In early February 1883, *Wivern* was again at sea with a crew borrowed from the sloop H.M.S. *Albatross*, after that vessel was dry-docked for repairs.

On 5 February, while steaming down river to Hong Kong from Canton, the ironclad ran aground on a bank in the river while in charge of the pilot. Attempts to tow her off were unsuccessful, and the torpedo boats and ammunition were offloaded to lighten ship. On 9 February, with assistance from a civilian paddle steamer and the gunboat H.M.S. *Swift*, the ironclad was pulled free.[83] After reloading the turret ship, the *Wivern* steamed down river in company with the *Swift*, and both vessels returned to Hong Kong on 11 February. The following day, target practice was conducted with the main battery as the ironclad steamed off Hong Kong. After firing four rounds from each 9-inch RML, the torpedo boats were lowered for practice runs with their Whiteheads. The log entry notes the *Wivern* increased to full speed "as requisite for firing torpedoes," indicating at least two of these weapons were launched not from the TBs, but from the ironclad. On the 17th, the crew was ashore assisting with undocking procedures for the *Albatross* and after days spent returning equipment to that vessel, their mission was completed. The *Wivern* hauled down her pennant at sunset on 23 February 1883.[84]

A problem with a new gun occurred aboard the new flagship in December of that year. On 21 December, the *Audacious* was at target practice off Hong Kong when a gun captain, Leading Seaman William Haynes, was injured as Number 33 gun, a 4-inch rifled breechloader (RBL) was discharged. During the shoot, a vent sealing tube flew backwards and into the chest of Seaman Haynes as the gun fired. The new

Docks at Canton, (Guangzhou) China c. 1890 (author's collection).

breechloader had been fitted aboard only on the 12th of that month, and this firing was likely one of the first aboard ship. Firing from the new breechloaders was halted until the problems with the tube and the failure of the breech "shutter" to hold the tube in place were corrected.[85] The British press noted the problems with the China Station, especially concerning the age of some of the warships and their "rubbishing guns." Of the few vessels noted as being "worth a rap" in those waters, the *Wivern* was listed among them.[86]

Colonial Defense and the Torpedo Boat

The Civil War had proven that the torpedo had changed naval warfare, at least in coastal waters. British newspapers feared the new weapon as a force equalizer, and one commented, "A little powder, an old and worthless boat frame, a simple apparatus for ignition, directed by one or two cool and resolute men, may in a minute send to the bottom all the labour, science, money and valour embarked on vessels such as the *Warrior* or *Royal Sovereign*."[87] The torpedoes, and the boats and crews that carried them, were becoming weapons to contend with and prepare for.

After she arrived at Hong Kong, the *Wivern* acquired a secondary but important role. As a torpedo boat tender, she was to serve as a floating school for those men chosen to man the torpedo boats and work the new guns. The flagship *Audacious* sent men to her for training, and one torpedo party rowed over to the turret ship on 16 February 1883.[88] Aboard the *Wivern*, the gunners and torpedomen of the station maintained and improved their skills on the rapidly evolving new generation of weapons, especially the rapid-fire light guns and the self-propelled Whitehead torpedoes.[89]

By the early 1880s, the self-propelled torpedo evolved into a sophisticated projectile, and the expertise required to work on those machines had to be guarded in part by non-disclosure agreements signed by those bluejackets selected to maintain these temperamental weapons. On 17 January 1882, the Admiralty dispatched a letter to the China Station commander, Vice Admiral Willes, requiring all torpedo personnel in his ships to sign form S-321 to protect "the secret of the Whitehead Torpedo."[90] Restrictions regarding the Whitehead were imposed with "painful exactness" as the training manual was to be left aboard the torpedo training ship, and junior officers were not allowed to remove it for their private study after duty.[91]

In 1883, the Admiralty approved the plan to have more torpedo boats stationed in the colony (but only with partial crews) and sent two 1st class torpedo boats to Hong Kong. With only one full crew available for the new boats, the craft would be swapped into and out of service at regular intervals following their arrival from Britain. A single 2nd class torpedo boat would also be placed in service by combining most of the men from the two TBs assigned to the *Wivern*. This rotating plan of manning was a positive step forward in readiness for the embryonic torpedo boat section in the colony, but the Royal Navy continued to be undermanned in those waters. The makeshift situation on the China Station is illustrated by a letter written by Lieutenant Douglas Gamble, the torpedo officer assigned to the *Victor Emmanuel*. Gamble requested a gig and crew be permanently assigned to him in order to perform his duties as the officer in charge of the torpedo boats. Gamble was required to move

Four. Naval Weapons and Power Projection 139

from the warships at anchor, the dockyard and his four direct charges by borrowing a boat and crew from the Chief Engineer of the *Wivern* in order to make his rounds. Gamble had the duty of ensuring that all machinery on his boats were "kept in a state of efficiency," for the little flotilla had to perform at least six runs per quarter with Whitehead torpedoes to maintain proficiency with those weapons. This duty was complicated by the *Wivern's* Chief Engineer, as the boat was frequently needed by

Rigging anti-torpedo nets, c. 1880 (author's collection).

this more senior officer, who was also tasked with keeping the turret ship in a state of readiness, visiting the dockyard, and conducting his additional duties aboard the gunboats *Elk* and *Tweed*.[92]

In 1882, the Admiralty sent out 50 torpedo nets from Britain for the protection of naval assets in Hong Kong. The flagship already had a complete set; therefore, the new nets were assigned to the *Wivern*. The Admiralty also specified that the five corvettes on station were not to be supplied with nets, for in the 1880s, nets were generally provided to armored ships.[93] These were likely the nets of steel wire rope, which were "incredibly flexible," yet "wonderful for strength and evenness of texture." Made by William M. Bullivant of London (based on his wire rope patent of June 1878), these nets were used by the Royal Navy and foreign powers alike.[94] Each section of net (held out from a ship's side by spars) was 25 feet in length, 20 feet wide, and suspended to a depth of nine feet.[95] These nets gave ships an added degree of security against torpedo attack, especially while at anchor, and were acknowledged later as "an unglamorous but essential phase of naval warfare."[96]

The burdens of cost continued to influence colonial defense planning in the 1870s and early 1880s. In a letter to Governor Hennessy in April 1880, former Colonial Secretary Sir Michael E. Hicks-Beach wrote to inform the governor that Hong Kong could be safeguarded with smaller vessels, as they would be "most useful & certainly the least expensive form of defence of this kind."[97] Nevertheless, the turret ships and other, smaller ironclads were considered in these years as "the most effective means of defending the larger ports" rather than coastal fortifications, as the armored ships were able to offer protection for area sea lines of communications and for harbor facilities, especially the crucial coaling stations and dockyards.[98] During debates in the House of Commons on 1 August 1882, Sir John Hay, a former First Lord of the Admiralty, asked the pointed question about coastal defense ironclads: "How are we going to replace them?"[99] These vessels were not replaced. They were repaired, refitted, and remade to meet the changing requirements of an imperial establishment increasingly aware of its vulnerabilities. Like the dockyards, coal depots, and cable stations, they were an essential part of the infrastructure of empire.

The Royal Navy and Deterrence in the Far East

In January 1885, a Washington, D.C., newspaper observed, "the ironclad fleet of Great Britain cannot be intelligibly classified. It embraces not less than twelve distinct types."[100] That article went on to claim the British ironclads, built over the preceding twenty years, "represent the transition period of naval architecture ... and present a variety of type, class, and design that not only bewilders the non-professional mind but often confuses the expert."[101] Despite their differing types, the ironclads of the Royal Navy were acknowledged in one Salt Lake City newspaper from that year as comprising the force that represented Britain's "floating peace-makers."[102]

British and Russian rivalry over Turkey, China, and, later, Afghanistan usually simmered below the diplomatic surface during the late 1870s and 1880s. This did not preclude planning for offensive operations. In 1878, Russian naval planners envisioned a sudden attack against Hong Kong, Singapore, and Australia. British intelligence agents intercepted the plans, and these likely influenced efforts to reinforce Hong Kong.[103] The *Wivern* was regarded as being able to "do good service" defending the colony (especially when supported by one or two gunboats) against a foreign naval threat that was termed "very far from imaginary."[104] In Hong Kong, one local newspaper noted the Tsar's military pressure on Afghanistan and observed, "Russia can hardly repudiate a treaty, before the ink is dry."[105]

The French naval build-up of the mid–1880s in Asian waters caused a stir in British newspapers, but with warships including the *Wivern* held in reserve at Hong Kong, Britain had "far from an 'insignificant fleet' out here, in spite of the croaking of alarmists at home."[106] Nevertheless, all was not completely secure. In a December 1884 London newspaper article, Admiral Sir J.C. Dalrymple feared that Britain was unprepared to meet a French surprise attack launched on a global scale. In his fanciful "Kreigsspiel," he stated "that modern wars begin without declaration" and then described how French Admiral Anatole Courbet's squadron at anchor in Hong Kong would suddenly spring to a pre–Christmas attack upon receipt of secret, sealed orders from Paris.[107] With his four ironclads, Courbet would ram the *Audacious* and the "nondescript" *Wivern,* sinking both, and thus put Hong Kong at his mercy. The colony would have been forced to surrender or the port, dry dock, and shipping would have been put to the torch. Recoaling from captured stockpiles, Singapore would have been next to fall under the guns of the attacking ironclads. The fast-moving and unhindered French would then have charged into the Indian Ocean by early January 1885, seizing coal and destroying dockyards as they went. If the coastal defense ironclads *Abyssinia* and *Magdala* put up a fight at Bombay, they too would have been sunk in a similar attack run to that faced by the hapless Hong Kong ironclads. This was Dalrymple's alarmist "coup" where the ram featured prominently in this fictitious surprise thrust against the British Empire.[108]

The China Station and the Russian War Scare of 1885

In March 1885, Russian forces attacked an Afghan army position at Penjdeh on Afghanistan's northern frontier with the Russian Empire and in response, William Gladstone's government in London prepared for war.[109] Russian expansionism into Afghanistan (and the advance toward British India) had come not from individual officers acting rashly, but as part of a combined War and Foreign Ministries cooperation, which "made Russian polices unusually flexible and vigorous."[110] The British resolute answer to the incursion forced the issue in St. Petersburg, and belatedly, the Admiralty and the Minister of War were compelled to admit to the Tsar that Russia was not ready for a conflict with the British Empire.[111] Despite this revelation, events moved with their own momentum, and both Britain and Russia prepared for open conflict. Although Russia was only a "second rate" naval power, the Tsar's admirals had "made a very good disposition of her forces abroad" in preparation for a war with Britain.[112]

In Hong Kong, the *Wivern* had been reconditioned in anticipation of a return to active service. On 11 February 1885, she went out to fire her guns while the fleet commander was aboard. She had been fitted with two iron fighting tops, both of which were equipped with a Nordenfelt, as part of the overhaul to render her "into first class fighting efficiency."¹¹³ The masts no longer carried sails, but were two "posts that supported the circular framework" of the fighting top. With the machine guns behind iron shields, the Nordenfelts could fire "a bullet as big as a pigeon's egg" against any hostile target within range.¹¹⁴ The military mast of the late Victorian era was considered by one New York journal to be "a position perhaps the most dangerous in all naval warfare." Describing the difficulties of manning that position during a battle, the newspaper commented, "It is no easy task to fire from a platform placed at the bob end of a pendulum, swinging irregularly, and the results attained testify to the value of the drill and to the physique of the individual."¹¹⁵

The British press reported the *Wivern* was to be commissioned in preparation for steaming to join the British warships off Vladivostok, yet the China Squadron needed reinforcements, and was "fully occupied" with the needs of local defense.¹¹⁶ The land defenses of Hong Kong were considered inadequate, and the *Wivern*, with her torpedo boats, was in demand. Nevertheless, her status as a reserve warship escaped the attention of one observer, Charles-Dominique-Maurice Rollet de l'Isle, aboard the French warship *Primauguet*. The French officer wrote, "The British do not have a large naval force in the region ... they have quite a few gunboats in China, but most of them are obsolete, wooden craft. They won't put up much of a fight against the new Russian cruisers and ironclads."¹¹⁷ The local press noted the Royal Navy had only two ironclads on station, the *Audacious* and *Wivern*, but the Russians had the armored frigates *Vladimir Monomakh* and the *Minin* in nearby Asian waters, and another armorclad frigate, the *General Admiral*, was en route. The new turret ship H.M.S. *Agamemnon* was steaming for the Far East via the Suez Canal, but the advantage in size of the ironclads lay with the Russians, as a Hong Kong newspaper felt the "contrast is not pleasant."¹¹⁸

In 1885, the numerical advantage in armored ships in the Far East remained with the Russians as the *Wivern* was to be held back (at least initially) in order to be available for "judicious use" to supplement the Hong Kong fortifications in the event of a Russian attack.¹¹⁹ As discussed, Rollet de l'Isle made no mention of the *Wivern* or her torpedo boats during his visits to Hong Kong. The French officer likely did not observe the turret ship during his brief visits to the colony; he only saw a limited part of the city, as his ship was assigned to an anchorage reserved for warships, whereas the *Wivern* would likely have been anchored closer to shore near Kowloon, where her guns could protect the coal depot.¹²⁰

Lieutenant Gamble would have agreed with the French officer's subsequent observation regarding the difficulty of loading torpedo launches aboard a warship at sea.¹²¹ Gamble reported his concerns that the two TBs carried on the *Wivern* would have been damaged by the blast from the main turret guns, and noted the boats could not be hoisted out unless in a calm sea "as the derrick only just-takes the boat clear of the Ship's side." Gamble proposed that a permanent facility be built ashore at Kowloon to house the torpedo establishment. Until that facility was completed, the turret ship would continue in her dual role as coastal defense ironclad and depot ship for the torpedo boats.¹²²

Despite her limitations, the *Wivern* was valued in Hong Kong. An assertion made in the *Pall Mall Gazette* (in late 1884), that British gunboats on the China Station were "slow tubs mainly manned by Chinese," generated some ire in Hong Kong. This article, combined with Sir Edward Reed's claim that the *Wivern* was "a weak old gunboat," was met with some surprise in the China Squadron. The retort against the false claims of the London newspaper criticizing the preparedness of the China Station was continued in the *Hong Kong Telegraph*, which proclaimed the "Wivern is undoubtedly the most formidable fighting ship of any nation ever seen in Hong Kong Harbour."[123]

The *Wivern* was recommissioned for active service on 19 April 1885, with a crew gathered from other warships recalled to Hong Kong. During a short gunnery exercise in April 1885, the turret ship conducted target practice, although the weather conditions were described as "unfavourable." The effects of her reconstructions and frequent maintenance were telling, as the practice was termed "very satisfactory" despite the bad weather.[124] Commissioning the *Wivern* was a temporary measure to provide security for the port with more foreign ironclads on station, but she was placed back into reserve when armed British merchant steamers were ready to receive their crews at Hong Kong. In this instance, speed was a priority over armor and heavy guns. The Royal Navy did not have enough men to fully crew all ships in reserve and also provide the complements for the auxiliary cruisers temporarily acquired to patrol the shipping lanes.[125] The *Wivern* was returned to reserve status and her improvised crew sent back to their ships on 22 July 1885, but the local authorities were "very undecided as to be the proper course to adopt." The uncertainty was due in part to war tensions with Russia, yet health was another consideration, as cholera outbreaks were reported along the southern coast of China, and getting men back to sea was likely a precaution.[126]

The Royal Navy needed a convenient harbor from which to blockade or attack Vladivostok and constrict Russian naval activity in the Pacific. London did not wait until Russia presented another *fait accompli* as it had in Afghanistan, and the Admiralty was ordered to occupy a strategic position on the southern coast of Korea—the islets of Komundo, collectively referred to as Port Hamilton.[127] From this location, the Royal Navy had a forward base from which to attack Vladivostok 850 miles to the north.[128] To help secure the anchorage, the auxiliary merchant cruiser *Pembroke Castle* sailed north from Hong Kong with marines and stores aboard, ready to disembark as a nascent garrison.[129] A detail of eight men (including a Lieutenant) were transferred from the *Wivern* to provide part of the 150-man crew of the auxiliary cruiser.[130] Britain had taken the bold step of occupying Port Hamilton and in this sortie had forestalled another Russian land grab. In Germany, the news was viewed as a bold display of military agility, with one newspaper calling the British move "a political and military masterstroke."[131]

"The Last Relic": The Final Years of the *Scorpion*

Mention of the *Scorpion* was rare especially after the mid–1880s, and those are usually brief. One reference in the local *Royal Gazette* reported that in July 1887, the Royal Bermuda Yacht Club used her as a stationary marker on their race through island channels.[132] Duty was infrequent for the iron warship, but a modern feature of the *Scorpion* was utilized for service at the dockyard in 1895 during the Navy ball, when her dynamo was employed to help produce electricity for the 200 lights slung in the sail loft, which had been converted into a temporary ballroom.[133] Two years later, the old ironclad played center stage in the colony's festivities held as part of an Empire-wide celebration marking the Diamond Jubilee, the sixtieth year of Queen Victoria's reign. The *Scorpion* was immaculate with her white hull, sparse rigging, and her three pole masts bedecked with flags as she anchored in Hamilton harbor.[134] Among the flags she probably hoisted aloft were also the ones for her assigned signal letters, "GTPV."[135] Shortly after 10:00 a.m. on 22 June 1897, the governor and his staff were brought to the ironclad, which then fired a 60-gun royal salute. Following hours of the march past of the various garrison troops and bands, a thanksgiving service, and reception, nightfall brought a display of colored lights throughout the city.[136] At 9:00 p.m., the *Scorpion* fired a gun to signal the commencement of a torchlight tattoo and fireworks display. The ironclad added her searchlight to a light show until the festivities concluded at 11:00 that night.[137]

In 1898, the *Scorpion* was readied for operations, as Royal Marine Light Infantrymen were detailed to her in response to "some war scare."[138] A detachment of 110 officers, NCOs, and men were to provide the majority of her crew if the ironclad was ordered into commission. The marines exercised at gun drill, and one of their officers also received machine gun training onboard the ship. That officer, Lieutenant H.T.R. Lloyd, RMLI, did not like duty aboard the old ironclad and recorded in his diary on 26 February 1898 that he had taken his men down to the *Scorpion* "hopefully for the last time."[139] On 22 March, the flagship signaled, asking how many marines could be ready to man the old ironclad and prepare her for sea. Lloyd and his brother officers were surprised by the signal and answered none were available. On the 24th, the *Scorpion* put to sea without the marines in a simulated attack on the dockyard.[140] The failure to provide a detail of men when the signal came from the flagship was likely not forgotten, as the Vice-Admiral then commanding was Sir John Fisher, and "Jacky" was never satisfied with anything but "Full Speed."[141]

HMS *Scorpion* at Bermuda, 1895 (author's collection).

Four. Naval Weapons and Power Projection   145

HMS *Scorpion* fires salute during the Diamond Jubilee celebration, Hamilton, Bermuda, 1897 (author's collection).

As the nineteenth century came to a close, time was catching up with the refitted and somewhat modernized *Scorpion*. Despite her refits, she was mostly forgotten in the British press, with one magazine stating that Bermuda was "destitute of ironclad vessels."[142] On 3 May 1900, the *Scorpion* completed her last exercise as a member of what was then termed the "Reserve Squadron" at the island colony. With a temporary crew from the premier ship on station, the First Class cruiser H.M.S. *Crescent*, the old armorclad steamed out into the Atlantic, accompanied by the gunboats *Medway* and *Medina* to test the ad hoc crews of these reserve warships. The voyage on 3 May only lasted a few hours, and having completed their steam and gunnery trials, the Reserve Squadron returned to the dockyard and made fast by late afternoon. The temporary crew detailed to the *Scorpion* returned to their regular duties on the *Crescent*, the flagship of the North America and West Indian Station commander Vice-Admiral Sir Frederick Bedford.[143]

At 1:33 p.m. on 14 May 1901, the *Crescent* and the *Scorpion* steamed out from the dockyard and proceeded up the coast, coming to anchor between two shoals at a bay on the western shore of St. George's Island known as "Murray's Anchorage."

HMS *Scorpion*, Bermuda, c. 1898 (author's collection).

HMS *Scorpion* Bermuda, c. 1900 (author's collection).

HMS *Crescent*, c. 1897 (author's collection).

An officer assigned to the flagship recorded the event in a series of three photos kept in his personal scrapbook. The *Scorpion* was anchored with her port side seaward, broadside to the cruiser. Five flags flew from her three pole masts, her turrets turned to port and her guns run out. A slight wake appeared at her stern and her engines were under light steam. She had been painted gray with two large white dots on her hull roughly the area of several gun ports, one dabbed fore and the other aft. These spots served as range markers positioned at equal distance on the hull from stem and stern, midway between the deck and the waterline.[144] Near the flagship, the torpedo boat H.M.S. *Quail* carried the governor and his staff to witness the gunnery tests against the old ironclad riding at anchor.[145]

With the temporary crew removed from the *Scorpion*, the *Crescent* opened fire, with her light 3-pounder and 6-pounder quick firing (QF) guns at a range of 1,000 yards. Extending the range to 3,000 yards, her battery of 6-inch QF guns fired on the target ship.[146] A photo reveals the *Scorpion*'s forward turret pockmarked by no less than 13 hits from the 6-pounders. One turret-mounted 9-inch gun on the ironclad may have received a glancing blow against the lower rim of the muzzle from another 6-pound shell. More damage was evident on the underside of the hurricane deck above the turret, and revealed the occasional hole from a shell fragment cast up after striking the turret. Gun port lids had been removed, and the 3-pounders likely concentrated on the upper works as the 6-pounders focused on suppressing simulated fire from the 9-inch main guns of the *Scorpion*. Under a steady hail of fire from the light guns of the *Crescent*, the crew of the old ironclad would have been killed, wounded or driven below before her own light guns got within range to answer.[147]

Wooden dummies representing the crew had been positioned on the *Scorpion* to depict men at their stations. The hail of smaller shells from the *Crescent*'s light

Target ship *Scorpion*, Bermuda, 1901 (© National Maritime Museum, Greenwich, London).

guns swept the decks of the anchored turret ship, inflicting "great havoc" among the mock crew and everything topside not protected by her iron-plated armor. The firing was, reportedly, mixed after the range was extended to 6,000 yards. The 6-inch guns fired on the *Scorpion* as the flagship had worked up to full speed in a simulated one-mile combat run, with disappointing results. Following the extension of range, the accuracy of the rounds from the 6-inch guns dropped considerably.[148] The *Crescent* fired some twenty rounds at that range with most of these larger caliber rounds falling within a short radius of the ironclad, and the firing was termed "bad." Although the cordite charges produced "a faint bluish haze," the demise of gunpowder as a propellant eliminated the clouds of that "old familiar puff of dense

Forward turret, HMS *Scorpion* Bermuda, 1901 (© National Maritime Museum, Greenwich, London).

white smoke" so characteristic of the gunnery exercises held only a few years earlier.[149] The *Scorpion* was hit by only two or three 6-inch shells, yet those proved sufficient to cripple her. One shell penetrated the armor and exploded with a force that "practically wrecked everything on board."[150] Changes in propellant design and fabrication had shown the damage a well-aimed, high velocity shell could inflict on an older ironclad warship.

The reasons for the less than satisfactory performance of the 6-inch guns hitting the target were a combination of factors. Vibrations from the reciprocating engines on a warship of that era rendered gun laying problematic, especially at full speed.[151] In addition, the gray paint scheme undoubtedly helped to obscure some finer features of the *Scorpion* that would have stood out had she remained in her peacetime livery of black, white and buff. Nevertheless, the primary reason for the ironclad being harder to hit at range was an aspect of her original design features. Her low profile and scant upper works contributed to most shells missing the mark from that distance.

A work detail from the *Crescent* was sent over to the *Scorpion* in order to pump her out and prepare her for further trials. During the late morning of 16 May, a 180-pound mass of guncotton was exploded against the side of the ram to simulate the effects of a hit from an 18-inch Whitehead torpedo. After the denotation of the guncotton charge, divers and a "diving engine" were sent to the target ship to survey damage and affect repairs. By the morning of 17 May, the hulk was maneuvered into shallow water and placed on a reef to prevent her from sinking. Firing from the *Crescent* briefly resumed before noon and the tests were concluded shortly thereafter. The following day, a work detail boarded the ironclad to survey the damage. The old armorclad had been severely mauled; however, the strength of her construction and her internal compartmentalization led one observer to note that she had stood up better than had been expected.[152]

She was raised and patched by February 1903 in order to be taken away and broken up for scrap.[153] Word slowly filtered out that she was to be sold off, and interest

6-inch bow chaser gun crew, HMS *Crescent*, 1901 (author's collection).

was piqued by those who valued the old hulk for more than her broken bits of iron. The warship had been purchased at the price of £736 for scrap; however, some Confederate veterans were interested in acquiring the vessel with the idea of towing her to a port in the Southern United States in order to preserve the old ironclad as "a souvenir of the lost cause." Referred to as perhaps "the last relic of the navy of the Confederate government," some Southern veterans hoped to raise the issue of purchasing the *Scorpion* at their annual convention, which was held in New Orleans that year, but news of her disposal by the Admiralty arrived after the convention adjourned. Despite this, neither the old veterans nor the shipbreakers would have her.[154]

The British tug *Powerful* towed the *Scorpion*, along with her maintenance crew of fifteen men, from St. George's, Bermuda on 10 June 1903, bound for Saint John, New Brunswick. She had been purchased by Thomas Butler & Company of Boston and was to be delivered to the Canadian port, where she would be turned over to the shipbreakers at the Portland Rolling Mills and torn apart for an estimated $40,000 in scrap.[155] During her slow voyage north, *Scorpion* struggled in the face of a severe northeasterly storm two days out from Bermuda, yet she was able to remain buoyant despite developing a leak. The storm continued unabated and Captain Harding, commander of the ironclad, directed his men at their stations until the pumps gave out on the 14th. Nothing remained but to abandon ship, and Harding signaled for the *Powerful* to send a boat to take his men off as "terrific seas" crashed over the *Scorpion*. The waters near this location, some 500 miles northwest of Bermuda, were treacherous, as "the currents in vicinity of George's Shoal are very irregular and at times

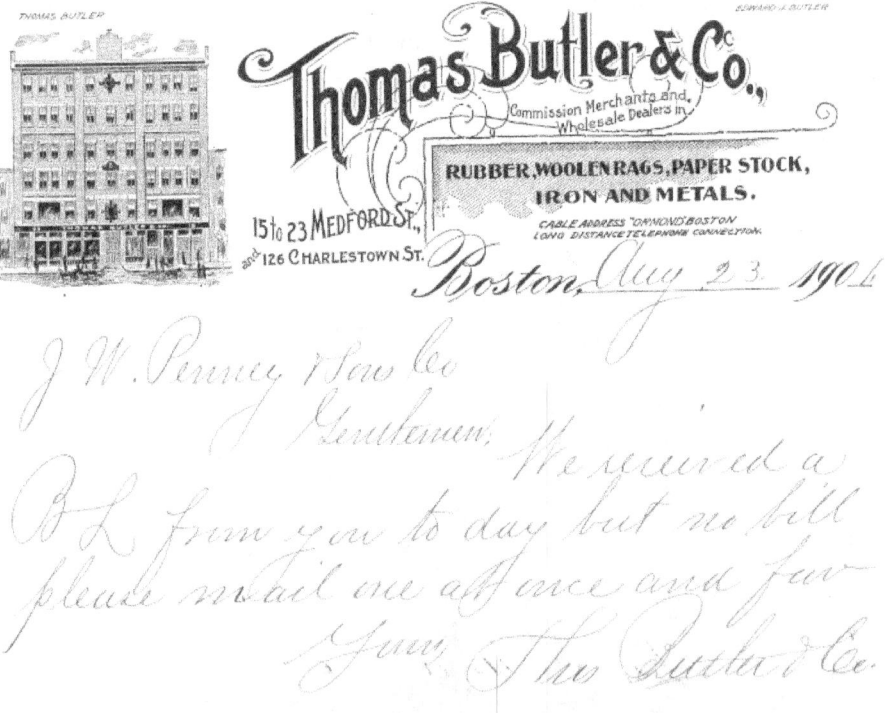

Thomas Butler billhead. This firm purchased the *Scorpion* in early 1903 (author's collection).

Four. Naval Weapons and Power Projection 151

St. John Harbor, New Brunswick. The shipbreaker here was the intended last stop for the *Scorpion* **(author's collection).**

very strong."[156] After three laborious trips in the small boat, the men were rescued from the ironclad, which, although abandoned, managed to remain above the waves for several hours before finally succumbing. The *Scorpion* sank 80 miles off Georges Shoal (located some 150 miles east of Cape Cod) on 16 June 1903. Her tow now gone, the *Powerful* steamed to Boston where Captain Russell, her commander, deposited the men from the old hulk and reported the news of her loss.[157]

The Old "Warhorse": The Last of the *Wivern*

Although her sister in Bermuda remained largely within sight of the dockyard during most of these years, the *Wivern* was, by contrast, quite active. After a short local cruise in early May 1888, the *Wivern* returned to her Hong Kong anchorage and her temporary crew was dismissed to their regular duties around the squadron. The cruise was a regular occurrence for keeping the men of the China Station and the reserve ships in a state of readiness. In addition to local voyages to keep the ship and men ready, the *Wivern* would, usually on an annual basis, steam up the Pearl River as far as Canton to show the flag.[158] Undoubtedly, she flew her recognition signal "GVMN" during this and her other cruises on the Chinese coast.[159]

At other times, the turret ship would conduct evolutions in local waters to try out new tactics. From 11–12 September 1889, the ironclad was underway and flying the Commodore's flag. That night, with her searchlight sweeping, the old turret ship repelled a mock attack by two torpedo boats in a nearby bay. After having expended ammunition, including some rounds from her main battery of four 9-inch rifled muzzleloaders in the two turrets, the reserve ironclad steamed back to Hong Kong and was secured to her buoy on the afternoon of the 12th. Machine guns were removed from her fighting tops and awnings spread to shield the crew from the sun as the ram returned to her harbor-bound lull.[160] The break in activity proved to be damaging to the morale of the few men actually assigned to the *Wivern*. Boredom took its toll on at least one bluejacket when, in April 1890, the British press reported that Daniel Murphy, a gunner on the *Wivern*, had been tried at court-martial for leave-breaking, resulting in a loss of one year seniority in service.[161]

In April 1893 the *Wivern* was re-commissioned and put to sea, and the gunboat *Tweed* followed astern as an escort. During this training voyage, the men on the ironclad were exercised at fire stations, put out collision mats, closed watertight doors, and went to general quarters to practice repelling boarders. The *Wivern*'s boats were armed and manned, and defensive preparations continued as the crewmen practiced "burning" the electric searchlight. The following day, 13 April, the crew of the *Wivern* conducted target practice and expended a quarter of her ammunition, including 1-inch rounds from her secondary battery of Nordenfeldt guns and .45 caliber rounds from her Gatlings. That evening, two torpedo boats came alongside to receive water.[162] Those torpedo boats—No. 8 and No. 20—had been serviced and received water from the ironclad in preparation for an exercise night attack. After inspection by the commander of the China Station, Admiral Sir E.R. Freemantle, on the 14th, the ironclad was moored stern to stern with the *Tweed*. Shortly after midnight on the 15th, the watch observed an "enemy" gunboat with two TBs and two armed pinnaces entering the anchorage. The *Wivern* opened fire (likely with a few blank rounds) on the torpedo boats, which had managed to fire two unarmed Whiteheads, one of which "struck" near the bridge on the port side of the ironclad "presumably" sinking the ship, but the *Tweed* was credited with putting the remainder of the battered attackers out of action. The exercise concluded after sunup and the *Wivern* took her cutter and the *Tweed* in tow.[163] The *Wivern*'s log entries from this voyage reveal the exercise was not the action of an elderly, quayside harbor defense ship, but a new concept of defense based on the practiced evolutions of a dependable unit of the reserve flotilla.

In late April 1894, the *Wivern* was out again with several gunboats for target practice and drills "as requisite." The next day, 26 April, was to be the highpoint of that year's exercise. After the ironclad fired her "full quarter" allowance of ammunition at a target, Torpedo Boat No. 8 was hoisted aboard for maintenance. Lowering TB 8 and sending her off with dispatches, a mock battle was the next log entry, with the old ironclad firing blank rounds at the gunboats, *Alacrity* and *Rattler*, as they entered the bay. TB 20 was later hoisted aboard after the mock cannonade ceased, also likely for routine maintenance, and a short time later lowered over the side again in preparation for night practice. The *Tweed* was moored stern on to the *Wivern*'s bow and the *Alacrity* was linked likewise (stern on) by hawsers to the ram's stern, the defensive arch providing protection against a torpedo boat attack. The close formation apparently proved successful as the *Wivern*'s searchlight swept the approaches and the linked ships repelled the attack by the torpedo boats in a hail of simulated fire. The following morning (27 April) the ironclad weighed anchor and transferred two men "wounded by accident" to TB 8, which then transported them to hospital in Hong Kong. At noon on the 28th, she was back at her usual mooring in Hong Kong with the crew stacking provisions and ammunition on deck in preparation for a

Firing the Gatling from a fighting top, c. 1875 (author's collection).

return to storage. By sundown, the stores and ammunition were gone, the fires were out in all four boilers, the men returned to their usual ships, and the pennant was hauled down until the next exercise.[164]

In the autumn of 1894, the *Wivern* was again on active duty as a replacement for the cruiser H.M.S. *Undaunted*, which was in the hands of the dockyard for repairs. This assignment stood as an example of the important, but poorly appreciated contribution made by the coastal defense ironclads on distant stations of the British Empire. Ships in dockyard provided an opportunity to try new tactics and exercise designated crews for special duty. The *Wivern* served an important role not only for local gunnery training, but also as a fill-in for warships out of service. The old ironclad was also held in readiness to steam to Shanghai if required while the cruiser was in the dockyard.[165]

The Laird rams were old and, as far as London was concerned, largely dismissed as inadequate. Indeed, Thomas Brassey stated in 1895 that they "can hardly be considered effective ships."[166] They were also described by Sir Edward Reed, writing in one American magazine, to be nothing more than "unimportant, small vessels." The old coastal defense turret ships were frequently looked upon as antiques; however, Admiral G.A. Ballard saw their true worth. He compared them to be like "full-armoured knights riding on donkeys, easy to avoid but bad to close with."[167]

In 1895, the *Wivern* was an active ship, although she remained in port most of that year. Her marines practiced infantry drill, gun crews from other ships of the China Station maintained their proficiency through exercises held in her aft turret, and a boiler was lit to raise steam pressure to test the compressed air for one of her Whitehead torpedoes. Most other activities revolved around the usual ship routine of holystoning decks, painting, repairs, and inspections.[168]

The *Wivern* returned to gunnery practice in early April 1896. Gunnery consisted of firing 9-inch shells with propellant charges (black powder) of 33 and 50 pounds per gun, one hundred 1-pounder Nordenfelt rounds, and two hundred from the Gatlings. After a full-speed run (of slightly less than 10 knots) lasting just over an hour, the *Wivern* was secured to a buoy and the ship and her crew, recently collected from ships of the squadron, were inspected by the admiral commanding. March 1897 brought more target practice to fire off a portion of her quarterly allotment of ammunition and a few days of steaming and "General Quarters" drill (putting out collision mats, closing watertight doors, etc.) for the old ironclad to keep her assigned crew proficient.[169] Although derided in the British press as being of "little value ... except for harbour defence," the *Wivern* remained a trusted and familiar feature of seasonal training in Hong Kong.[170]

In 1897, the old ironclad was mentioned in the dramatic booklet warning of Hong Kong's fall entitled *The Back Door*. In this fictional account, Hong Kong was attacked in a surprise assault by a combined Franco-Russian amphibious force while the modern British warships were away on other duties. The hodgepodge of warships left to defend the colony were several "old fashioned" men-of-war, including the *Wivern* and the gunboat *Tweed*—two warships that had been derided in the fabricated description as "gross flattery to call harbour defence vessels." *The Back Door* continued with a thinly disguised reference to the real pace of the station: "The Wivern had only the week before had her half-yearly commission and cruise, so she was coaled, but her provisions and ammunition had been returned into store." The account described a battle in which the *Wivern*, *Tweed* (both hastily resupplied with ammunition) and six torpedo boats fought the invading Russian flotilla to a near standstill.

The tale described the sinking of several Russian TBs as the *Wivern* made good use of her QF guns and 9-inch main battery before she was struck by two Russian torpedoes, one on the port beam and other on the port quarter, which sent the old ram down stern first shortly thereafter. Although *The Back Door* was criticized for errors, one reviewer observed that a surprise attack could not be ruled out, as "it should be remembered that a declaration of war has not invariably preceded hostilities even amongst the most civilized powers."[171]

The pace changed for the *Wivern* two years later with a voyage upriver. From 11 to 30 September 1899, the turret ship was cruising between Canton and Hong Kong with a temporary crew transferred from the port receiving ship H.M.S. *Tamar*.[172] Unlike previous voyages, this one was not an exercise, as the old ironclad was on a mission that brought her into circumstances where she was ready to fire her guns in anger.

Piracy and lawlessness had increased in areas around Canton, causing merchants there to warn buyers that they could not meet their contract deadlines as hoped. The flow of silk and money to and from the old port on the Pearl River was in jeopardy. British gunboats were dispatched there to restore order and keep cargoes moving, yet these were only of limited effectiveness.[173] Attacks against foreign shipping on the rivers had occurred at the end of 1898 and some attacks against British ships took place in daylight. A few of these attacks occurred near Chinese coast guard stations, as local authorities were not inclined to offer assistance against the marauders.[174] The gunboat, *Tweed,* and a torpedo boat were ordered to Canton to suppress area pirates, but they did not have the desired impact on the local brigands and their protectors.[175]

The *Wivern* was dispatched to Canton in an effort to have "a moral effect on the Viceroy, who has shown himself as adept at giving trouble." The viceroy, Li-Hung Chang, was caught in the midst of a ground swell of Chinese patriotism, imperial intrigue, and the desire of other Western powers to expand their holdings further into China. The situation had deteriorated to the point where the imperial court in Beijing asked the southern viceroys for both money and troops as skirmishing broke out with Western forces. The South, however, refused to join in this Boxer wave of nationalism.[176]

Near the end of her service life, the *Wivern* once again proved her worth as she rode at anchor, heavy guns run out for action, and secondary armament bristling in readiness. Her appearance was enough to quiet tensions for a time. Old but still relevant, the turret ship illustrated the willingness of the Royal Navy to enforce the rights of navigation on Chinese rivers and adjacent waters. This cruise, along with her deployment to Hong Kong almost twenty years before, underscored her main purpose. The *Wivern* and her sister served most effectively in the deterrence role. The Canton appearance of the heavily armed ironclad persuaded the viceroy, local warlords, and area brigands to keep out of direct involvement in the anti-Western conflict.

Denied the opportunity to fire at a hostile warship or force ashore, she fired her guns to keep her crew in practice. Returning from Canton and while near Hong Kong, the *Wivern* fired at a target with her main battery and her light close-in self-defense weapons, the Nordenfelts and Gatlings. The results of the firing were not reported, but one shipboard "casualty" was a barometer shattered by the blast of one of the 9-inch muzzleloaders.[177]

By the dawn of the new century, the *Wivern* was termed "ineffective" in the Hong Kong press. This report came as a response to the Admiralty, which had counted the "little monitor" and her sister as coastal defense warships still on the effective list. In Britain, the press reported several warships of the China Station as "hopelessly obsolete" and singled out the *Wivern* with the uncomplimentary description of "death-trap."[178]

Despite her age and continual lack of favor from the press, both in Britain and at home, the "little monitor" had one more exercise in her. *Wivern* was commissioned for the last time on 4 March 1901, with the practiced routine of getting underway with a borrowed crew, dropping off the target, and blasting away with the Nordenfelts and her RMLs. The crew also accumulated more experience looking for "hostile" torpedo boats while the searchlight was "burnt." *Wivern* was back at her buoy in Hong Kong harbor by the afternoon of the 6th. The following day, ammunition and supplies were returned to the arsenal and storehouses. *Wivern* became surplus.[179] Her days as a coastal defense ship (and a training ship) at an end, she was "relieved" of her boilers and guns in preparation for her envisioned fate. *Wivern* was to be towed to the British treaty port of Wei-Hai-Wei and used as a target. This, however, turned out not be her final role, for she was retained as a hulk and remained in Hong Kong.[180] By the dawn of the twentieth century, time and technology had left the first generation of turret ships behind. Refits could not coax much more out of the ancient iron hulls, and the *Wivern* was simply too old to perform her reserve duties. Although still carried on the Admiralty lists into the first years of the new century, she was clearly beyond mere obsolescence.

The *Wivern* was dubbed "an interesting relic of bye-gone times" by a Hong Kong newspaper in 1902, and was recast in a new role that year as a distilling ship in response to a severe local drought. A sum of $38,000 was appropriated to refit the old turret ship with new machinery in order to provide warships of the China Station and the naval base with enough distilled water to "cover such difficulties in future." The receiving ship *Tamar* detailed Engineer Commander J.E.D. Graham to the old ironclad in order to ensure the machinery was in good order.[181]

Wivern was finally sold to Chinese shipbreakers around September 1921. She was stripped of all useful equipment before she was to cast off for the last time. As she was towed away on the morning of 13 March 1923, one Hong Kong newspaper mentioned a few interesting facts about the "obsolete ironclad," which the newspaper also referred to as the "old, crippled warhorse." One aged resident of the colony was the primary source of the article, which mentioned the ironclad was out of date when she arrived in Hong Kong and also observed that "seaworthiness was hardly the term that could be applied to her." The article incorrectly stated that she "remained practically stationary in these waters" after her arrival, but also declared she had a heavy battery "of sufficient value to make a showing in these waters."[182]

Dismantled of her turrets, funnel, main guns, and secondary battery of light weapons, only two masts (with fighting tops still fitted) remained above her rust-streaked hull. It was a suitable tribute for the "old warhorse" that she had a full complement of men lining her sides and peering through the stern gun ports to send her off not as a discarded hulk, but as an honored veteran of a bygone era.

Conclusion

*Exit the Ironclad:
The Laird Rams in Perspective*

By the late 1880s, few of the Royal Navy's ironclads were similar, as each had been built around competing developments of armor and ordnance, and were reflections of the technological moments when they were completed. Rapid changes in armored warship design of the middle Victorian years manifested as a peculiar collection of differing types and hybrids, so much so that Admiral Sir John Commerell remarked in 1887 that some British warships looked like something "between a clock case and a bathing machine."[1] Many older armorclads, like the *Scorpion* and *Wivern*, were refitted and provided with a few modern apparatus to keep pace with technological developments. If the costs of repairs and refits were not excessive, a man-of-war received dockyard attention, as it was "extremely difficult to draw the line at the precise stage at which a ship becomes obsolete as a vessel of war."[2] This was especially true for ironclads, as armor, even if penetrated at close range, offered protection at longer distances and gave the armored ship under fire "a utility out of all proportion to its ability to withstand shot on the proving ground."[3]

The coastal defense role was the one best suited for the Laird rams, but that role had two distinct components: one was "coastal assault," and the other was for defense of a local area from a seaborne threat.[4] The low-hulled ironclads could be used for either mission, but some British low-hulled ironclads were intended more for the assault.[5] Which coastal defense vessels would be assigned an attack mission and which were to remain closer to home port depended largely on *where* these ships were stationed when a conflict threatened. In an 1884 war plan against France, British Naval Intelligence detailed which types of ships could be used in a series of rapid global strikes and which would remain behind. The *Scorpion*, *Wivern*, and the other coastal defense ironclads in colonial waters, like the *Cerberus* at Australia near Melbourne and the two in Indian waters at Bombay, the *Abyssinia* and *Magdala*, would not steam away in order to attack a distant shore. These small ironclads were not to be earmarked for an attacking force, as "they will be required and used for the protection of the several ports they are intended for and are allotted to, and will not therefore be available to take part in an *offensive* (italics in original) policy."[6]

The types of offensive missions each station was to conduct also restricted the role of the coastal defense ironclads, especially for those assigned to colonial ports. While the major British warships assigned to foreign stations were to hunt for enemy men-of-war and attack or blockade hostile ports, the coastal defense armorclads were to provide security for the main British bases.[7] It was the difference between utilizing ironclads for attacking enemy-held harbors and defending key ones, or what has been referred to as the "contradiction between coastal assault and coastal defence."[8] As an element of the various concepts of naval attack plans and needs for protection both at home and in key colonies, the coastal defense ironclad remained an essential element of British naval strategy for offensive and defensive purposes, until the end of the century.

Size had become an issue for the modern warship of the later Victorian era as, according to one writer of that time, "you cannot put a quart of power into a pint of displacement."[9] The Laird rams, fitted with armor plate and the heaviest guns in use aboard the warships of the Royal Navy in the mid–1860s, had proven it could be done, but technological advances outstripped the pint-sized *Scorpion* and *Wivern*. Technology transformed the man-of-war into a new being. It became a vessel with steam-powered engines and a host of electrical motors for the ever-growing capital warship, a vessel of "monster" proportions, a "Frankenstein" of the sea.[10] The armored warship in all its forms had, by the end of the nineteenth century, become "a floating factory." It was, according to one Hong Kong newspaper, "a machine crammed with other machines," requiring more space to house the new devices.[11]

The sturdy Laird-built ironclads ordered by Bulloch decades before defied description and full appreciation throughout their existence. The 1880 plans used to reconstruct the second of the sisters revealed an exquisite detail of drawings and ornate script, yet an accurate categorization was not achieved. The plans, probably reused from the builders after the ships were acquired by the Royal Navy in 1865, were inscribed in the elaborate copperplate so popular in that era that the terms "Iron Cased Cupola Screw Steam Rams" was an attempt to affix a defining label to the ships that identified them by their Egyptian names, *El Tousson* and *El Monassir*. The names "Scorpion" and "Wivern" were merely scribbled under the previous names as an afterthought.[12] Despite this identity problem, the *Scorpion* and *Wivern* were hosts to almost astonishing transformations within their armored hulls. From the hesitancy to surrender sail to the domination of steam in the first part of their service lives, these ships would later receive more than a token share of new devices. From the fittings of their light guns with hydraulic recoil, new boilers, automatic weapons, the torpedo, rockets, and even the electric dynamo, these ironclads were test beds for the more deadly hardware of the twentieth century until iron armor gave way to steel plate.

The primary question regarding these ships: *Were the Laird rams failures?* The answer must be no, as they were successful warships when utilized for colonial defense. The British coastal defense ironclads of the Victorian navy, incorrectly termed as "almost valueless," were in fact "required" as area denial weapons on foreign stations.[13] They never fired a shot in anger, but like the famous *Warrior*, "it does not matter the battles actually fought but those prevented."[14] The Laird rams were not failures, as they best served the Royal Navy as coastal defense ships and performed well in that role until the modern steel navy arrived. They proved that iron, steam, and turret, when divorced from the weight and tether of sail, could defend the important bases at the edges of the British Empire. They deserve a better reputation than that imposed on them in most histories of the ironclad warship.

Glossary of Terms/Abbreviations

C.S.S.—Confederate States Ship

C.S.N.—Confederate States Navy

H.M.S.—Her Majesty's Ship

ILN—*Illustrated London News*

IJNH—International Journal of Naval History

LOC—Library of Congress

M.P.—Member of Parliament

NMM—National Maritime Museum

NYT—*New York Times*

PSI—Pounds per Square Inch

ORA—*The War of the Rebellion: A Compilation of the Official Records of the Union and Confederate Armies*

ORN—*The Official Records of the Union and Confederate Navies in the War of the Rebellion*

RBL—Rifled Breechloader

RML—Rifled Muzzleloader

R.M.A.—Royal Marine Artillery

R.M.L.I.—Royal Marine Light Infantry

R.N.—Royal Navy

RUSI—Royal United Services Institute

SA—*Scientific American*

SBML—Smoothbore Muzzleloader

S.M.S.—Seiner Majestät Schiff (His Majesty's Ship)

S.S.—Steamship

TB—Torpedo Boat

TNA—The National Archives

U.S.S.—United States Ship

U.S.N.—United States Navy

WA—Wirral Archives

Chapter Notes

Introduction

1. James Phinney Baxter III, *The Introduction of the Ironclad Warship* (Originally published Cambridge, MA, 1933, Annapolis, 2001), 204.
2. "Note on Naval Estimates," *Wrexham Advertiser*, 23 March 1861, 3.
3. Howard J. Fuller, *Clad in Iron, The American Civil War and the Challenge of British Naval Power* (Annapolis, 2008), 143, 240.
4. Jules Verne, *Paris in the Twentieth Century* (New York, 1996), 133.
5. "A Trifling Chronological Error," *Punch,* 26 April 1862, 163.
6. James Dunwoody Bulloch, *The Secret Service of the Confederate States in Europe; or, How the Confederate Cruisers were Equipped*. II (London, 1883, reprinted 2009), 202, 203. The Confederate casemate ironclads suffered from weight and armament overload and all were too large for their underpowered engines. Referring to the ironclad C.S.S. *Tennessee*, which defended the Alabama port of Mobile, Bulloch noted "she had neither the speed nor the ability to reverse quickly which are so essential in an armored vessel with a fixed battery and designed to be used also as a ram."
7. "Vulcan Arming Neptune," *Punch,* 19 April 1862, 157.
8. Jules Verne, *20,000 Leagues Under the Sea* (New York, 1966), 94.
9. *Ibid.*, 94.
10. "The Rebel Pirates. Ironclads on the Mersey. Description of the Vessels," *New York Times (NYT)*, 16 September 1863, 1, 2, TNA, ADM 1/5842, *Admiralty Correspondence*, "Specification of Cowper Phipps Coles Masts," 10 April 1862, Patent No. 1027, was for Coles' tripod masts design, referred to as "Improvements in Masts for Ships."
11. James Dunwoody Bulloch, *The Secret Service of the Confederate States in Europe; Or, How the Confederate Cruisers were Equipped*. I (London, 1883, reprinted, 2012). 391, 395.
12. *The Official Records of the Union and Confederate Navies in the War of the Rebellion (ORN).* II, 2 (Washington, 1921), 584–586.
13. *Ibid.*, 407.
14. *Ibid.*, 455, 456.
15. "An Important Confession," *Daily National Republican*, 3 November 1863, 1.
16. David Hepburn Milton, *Lincoln's Spymaster: Thomas Haines Dudley and the Liverpool Network* (Mechanicsburg, 2003), 91.
17. Amanda Foreman, *A World on Fire. Britain's Crucial Role in the American Civil War* (New York, 2010), 522.
18. *Ibid.*, 522.
19. LOC, "Correspondence Between Her Majesty's Government and Messr. Laird Brothers Relative to the Iron-Clad Rams." *United States Serial Set*, Number 1397, Senate Executive Department No. 11, Volume 4, 41st Congress Appendix No. XIII (Washington, 1869), 264, 267, 276.
20. Fuller, *Clad in Iron,* 15–17, 22.
21. *Ibid.*, 232.
22. Arnold A. Putnam, "The Building of Numbers 294 & 295: The Laird Rams." *Warship 1999–2000*. Edited by Antony Preston (London, 1999), 14.
23. Baxter, *The Introduction of the Ironclad Warship* (2001), 319.
24. E. H. H. Archibald, *The Fighting Ships in the Royal Navy AD 897–1984* (Poole, 1984), 111.
25. Captain S. Eardley-Wilmot, R.N. *Our Fleet To-Day and its Development during the Last Half-Century* (London, 1900), 125. Howard J. Fuller, "John Ericsson, the Monitors and Union Naval Strategy," *IJNH*, 2 (December 2004), 18. The Monitors were, according to Fuller, part of the "conflicting aspects of Union naval strategy which a single ship design could not possibly hope to resolve." Fuller makes a distinction in naval missions for these ironclads, between coastal defense against enemy warships, and coastal assault against enemy fortifications.
26. Baxter, *The Introduction of the Ironclad Warship (*2001), 320–321.
27. "Kelly and Deasey—Searching a Greek Vessel," *Dublin Evening Mail*, 2 October 1867, 4.
28. Edward James Reed, *Our Iron-clad Ships. Their Qualities, Performances, and Costs* (London, 1869, reprinted Cambridge, 2011), 96, "Naval and Military Intelligence," *Times,* 14 February 1880, 8.
29. "Naval and Military News," *Hampshire Telegraph*, 15 December 1869, 2.
30. "Naval and Military Intelligence," *Times,* 14 February 1880, 8.

31. "H.M.S. Wivern," *Times*, 20 February 1880, 12.

32. Bulloch, *The Secret Service of the Confederate States in Europe*. I, 394.

33. Archibald, *The Fighting Ships in the Royal Navy AD 897–1984* (1984), 111.

34. "The use of armour in the Royal Navy," *Hampshire Telegraph*, 30 January 1886, 2.

35. Eardley-Wilmot, *Our Fleet To-Day and its Development during the Last Half-Century* (1900), 125. Regrettably, Eardley-Wilmot does not give specifics to support this claim.

36. Oscar Parkes, *British Battleships: "Warrior" 1860 to "Vanguard" 1960. A History of Design Construction and Armament* (London, 1966), 78

37. Stanley Sandler, *The Emergence of the Modern Capital Ship* (Newark,1979), n42, 294. The First Lord of the Admiralty, the Duke of Somerset, opined that the rams "are not good for much," but this view was written in a letter dated 18 February 1864, before the ships were completed.

38. *Ibid.*, 85, 187.

Chapter One

1. Colin F. Baxter, "Lord Palmerston: Panic Monger or Naval Pacemaker?" *Social Science*, 47 (autumn, 1972), 205. Baxter quotes from the October 1860 *London Quarterly Review*, 296–297, regarding the "Revolution" of ironclad shipbuilding. Also see "Iron-Plated Frigates," *Dublin Evening Packet and Correspondent*, 2 October 1860, 2, and the "Revolution" in ironclad construction: "The gorgeous Line-of-battle ship [*sic*] which inspired our youth…is doomed."

2. Warren F. Spencer, *The Confederate Navy in Europe* (Tuscaloosa, 1983), 83.

3. David Hepburn Milton, *Lincoln's Spymaster: Thomas Haines Dudley and the Liverpool Network* (Mechanicsburg, 2003), xix, xxii.

4. *The Diary of Gideon Welles*, I. 1861–30 March 1864 (Boston, New York, 1911). 407. Welles reported to his admirals that the Union was threatening war with Britain if the rams departed for the Southern States.

5. *ORN* II, 2 (1921), 64, 69. In describing the armored vessel he had in mind, Mallory referenced European broadside ironclads as the best example to confront the Federal Navy and lift the blockade.

6. Reed, *Our Iron-clad Ships* (2011), 96.

7. William P. Roberts, "James Dunwoody Bulloch and the Confederate Navy." *The North Carolina Historical Review*, 24, 3 (July 1947), 332.

8. Baxter, "Lord Palmerston: Panic Monger or Naval Pacemaker?" *Social Science*, 47, 4 (autumn, 1972), 203, 210.

9. Raimondo Luraghi, *A History of the Confederate Navy* (Annapolis, 1996), 205.

10. Paul Kennedy, *The Rise and Fall of the Great Powers* (New York, 1989), 151

11. *The Confederate Navy; The Ships, Men and Organization, 1861–65*. Edited by Dr. William N. Still, Jr (London, 1997), 91.

12. Roberts, "James Dunwoody Bulloch and the Confederate Navy." *The North Carolina Historical Review*, 24, 3 (July 1947), 319.

13. Bulloch, *The Secret Service of the Confederate States in Europe*. II (2009), 2. That same officer (Commander James D. Bulloch) remarked that "in the great mechanic arts, in building ships and manufacturing the heavy engines to propel them especially, Great Britain has outstripped all competitors"

14. "Description of the Birkenhead Iron Works," *The Practical Magazine* (London, 1874), 5–6, S. Pollard, "The Decline of Shipbuilding on the Thames." *The Economic History Review*. 3 (1950), 76.

15. Brian Tunstall, *The Realities of Naval History* (London, 1936), 200.

16. Harriet Chappell Owsley, "Henry Shelton Sanford and Federal Surveillance Abroad, 1861–1865." *Mississippi Valley Historical Review*, 48 (Sep. 1961), 212, Thomas R. Neblett, "Major Edward C. Anderson and the C.S.S. Fingal," *The Georgia Historical Quarterly*, 52, 2 (June, 1968), 136. Neblett relates an account (autumn, 1861) from Major Edward Anderson, a Confederate artillery officer assigned to Britain in order to obtain war material. Anderson was soon followed by detectives hired by the United States government, and on one occasion, a clean-shaven "shadow" in a dark suit and dark hat was across the street when Anderson left his London lodgings and went by cab to a railway station to buy a ticket for Liverpool. After Anderson purchased his ticket, he noticed the same man standing nearby in a white hat, different collar, different shoes, and a mustache. Anderson spoke to the detective (a man reportedly named Brett) and stated that he had seen him in front of his residence a few minutes before wearing different clothing. This detective was thereafter removed from his surveillance mission and another assigned to watch Anderson.

17. Pollard, "The Decline of Shipbuilding on the Thames." *The Economic History Review*. 3 (1950), 77, 81.

18. "Mr. John Laird. The Birkenhead Ironworks and Docks," *Liverpool Daily Post*, 29 July 1861, 3.

19. Alexander Crosby Brown, "The John Randolph: America's First Commercially Successful Iron Steamboat." *The Georgia Historical Quarterly*. 36, 1 (March 1952), 32. The steamboat *Codorus*, built by John Elgar of York, Pennsylvania, launched on 14 November 1825, was arguably the first iron-hulled steam vessel in America.

20. *Ibid.*, 37.

21. *Ibid.*, 36.

22. *The Advent of Steam*, Editor Robert Gardiner, Consultant Editor Dr. Basil Greenhill (London, 1992), 62. The Lairds-built vessels of Lamar's company were among a fleet of towboats which

were "kept very busy" on the Savannah River in the decades before the Civil War.

23. *Ibid.*, 26, Basil Greenhill and Ann Gifford, *Steam Politics and Patronage: The Transformation of the Royal Navy, 1815–1854* (London, 1994). 129. David Lyon, Rif Winfield, *The Sail & Steam Navy List: All the Ships of the Royal Navy 1815–1889* (London, 2004), 177.

24. Greenhill and Gifford, *Steam Politics and Patronage* (1994), 130.

25. Edgar C. Smith, *A Short History of Naval and Marine Engineering* (Cambridge, 1938 reprinted 2013), 112.

26. *Ibid.*, 113–115.

27. Baxter, *The Introduction of the Ironclad Warship* (2001), 34.

28. *Ibid.*, 34–35.

29. David Lyon and Rif Winfield, *The Sail & Steam Navy List* (2004), 174.

30. Baxter, *The Introduction of the Ironclad Warship* (2001), 37, 39, The iron shipbuilders criticized these results and claimed that the *Ruby* was a poor example of a properly built and maintained iron ship as her deck had been partially removed, her rivets were rusted and her iron plates were "no thicker than half-a-crown."

31. Lyon and Winfield, *The Sail & Steam Navy List* (London, 2004), 174.

32. Smith, *A Short History of Naval and Marine Engineering* (2013), 130.

33. "Mr. John Laird. The Birkenhead Ironworks and Docks." *Liverpool Daily Post*, 29 July 1861, 3

34. Lyon and Winfield, *The Sail & Steam Navy List* (2004), 146.

35. "Iron Shipbuilding at Liverpool." *Illustrated London News (ILN)*, 25 October 1856, 417.

36. *Ibid.*, 417, Birkenhead Map, Ordnance Survey Office, Southampton (1875).

37. "Iron Shipbuilding at Liverpool." *ILN*, 25 October 1856, 417.

38. *Ibid.*, 417, "Mr. John Laird. The Birkenhead Ironworks and Docks," *Liverpool Daily Post*, 29 July 1861, 3.

39. J. R. Parkinson, *The Economics of Shipbuilding in the United Kingdom* (Cambridge, 2011), 40.

40. Smith, *A Short History of Naval and Marine Engineering* (2013), 171.

41. "Description of the Birkenhead Iron Works," *The Practical Magazine* (London, 1874), 6–7.

42. Pollard, "Laissez-Faire and Shipbuilding," *The Economic History Review*. 5, 1 (1952), 105. Pollard reported that the commercial shipbuilders also had the advantage in Admiralty contracts of not being directly under government supervision, as "private yard had fewer changes to vessels building after the dockyard-built models" were created.

43. "The New M.P.s." *Morning Chronicle*, 25 December 1861, 6.

44. *Ibid.*, 6, *ORN*, II, 2 (1921), 380.

45. "Visit to Birkenhead." *Living Age*. 6, 60 (5 July 1845), 25.

46. *Ibid.*, 25–26.

47. Greenhill and Gifford, *Steam Politics and Patronage* (1994), 130.

48. "John Laird's Contract for the New Iron-Clad Frigate," *Cheshire Observer*, 14 September 1861, 5.

49. Baxter, *The Introduction of the Ironclad Warship* (2001), 271–272.

50. *Ibid.*, 274.

51. *Ibid.*, 270–272.

52. *Hansard*, 27 March 1863, 170, cc 70.

53. Baxter, *The Introduction of the Ironclad Warship* (2001), 271–272.

54. *Ibid.*, 272, "Passengers Arrived," *New York Times (NYT)*, 22 May 1861, 8.

55. *The Diary of Gideon Welles*, I, 1861–30 March 1864 (Boston, New York, 1911), 291.

56. *Ibid.*, 291, 394, 395, Ari Hoogenboom, *Gustavus Vasa Fox of the Union Navy* (Baltimore, 2008), 354, n9, Douglas H. Maynard, "The Forbes-Aspinwall Mission." *The Mississippi Valley Historical Review*, 45 (June 1958), 68, "Iron-Cased Shipbuilding," *London Evening Standard*, 10 February 1863, 3.

57. The National Archives (TNA), TS 25/1285, "IRON CLAD SHIPS: Vessels under seizure: To Determine their Destination and Ownership," letter dated 29 October 1863

58. *Hansard*, 27 March 1863, 170, cc 71.

59. Wesley Loy, "10 Rumford Place: Doing Confederate Business in Liverpool." *The South Carolina Historical Magazine*, 98 (October 1997), 358.

60. *Ibid.*, 358.

61. Bulloch, *The Secret Service of the Confederate States in Europe*. I (London, 1883, reprinted, 2012). 31–32.

62. *Ibid.*, 2.

63. Stephen R. Wise, *Lifeline of the Confederacy: Blockade Running During the Civil War* (Columbia, 1988), 53–56, The weapons and supplies were immediately dispatched to Tennessee and Richmond to outfit new recruits.

64. *Ibid.*, 56, J. Thomas Scharf, *The Confederate Navy* (New York, 1996), 639, Bulloch, *The Secret Service of the Confederate States in Europe*. I (2012). 112.

65. Wise, *Lifeline of the Confederacy* (1988), 293.

66. Andrew Bowcock, *CSS Alabama: Anatomy of a Confederate Raider* (London, 2002), 7.

67. *Ibid.*, 7, *ORN*. II, 2 (1921), 379.

68. *ORN*. I, 12 (Washington, 1901), 228, Bowcock, *CSS Alabama* (2002), 7.

69. Bowcock, *CSS Alabama* (2002), 7.

70. "Assize Intelligence," *Morning Post*, 23 August 1870, 7.

71. *ORN*. II, 2 (1921), 64, 68, 70–72.

72. *Ibid.*, 64. (Also see William N. Still, Jr. *Iron Afloat: The Story of the Confederate Armorclads* (Columbia, 1971), 9–11.)

73. Parkes, *British Battleships* (1966), 78.

74. *ORN*, II, 2 (1921), 65.

75. Parkes, *British Battleships* (1966), 78, 80.
76. *Ibid.*, 78.
77. Kenneth Warren, *Steel, Ships and Men: Cammell Laird, 1824–1993* (Liverpool 1998), 34, "John Laird," *Engineer.* Volume 85, 28 January 1898, 88.
78. Warren, *Steel, Ships and Men* (1998), 34, "The Premier Gas," *Morning Chronicle*, 18 September 1858, 7, "French and Sardinian Preparations" *Western Daily Press*, 25 February 1859, 3, "Henry H. Laird," *Engineer.* 75, 2 June 1893, 467.
79. "The Premier Gas," *Morning Chronicle*, 18 September 1858, 7.
80. "French and Sardinian Preparations," *Western Daily Press*, 25 February 1859, 3. These gunboats were prefabricated in sections to facilitate overland transportation and were designed to be reassembled in "an incredibly short space of time."
81. *Ibid.*, 3, "A New French Gunboat," *Falkirk Herald*, 7 March 1861, 2.
82. Kenneth Warren, *Steel, Ships and Men: Cammell Laird, 1824–1993* (Liverpool 1998), 34.
83. "Henry H. Laird," *Engineer.* 75, 2 June 1893, 467, "John Laird," *Engineer.* 85, 28 January 1898, 88.
84. "A New Confederate Iron-clad," *Sheffield Independent*, 18 August 1862, 4.
85. *Ibid.*, 4.
86. Pollard, "Laissez-Faire and Shipbuilding," *The Economic History Review.* 5 (1952), 107.
87. "Iron-Cased Shipbuilding," *London Evening Standard*, 10 February 1863, 3.
88. *Ibid.*, 3, Lyon, Winfield, *The Sail & Steam Navy List* (2004), 235–236
89. Pollard, "Laissez-Faire and Shipbuilding," *The Economic History Review.* 5 (1952), 105, "The Navy," *Dublin Evening Mail*, 15 July 1862, 1, Hansard, 12 March 1863, 169, cc 1361.
90. Merli, *The Alabama* (2004), 200.
91. Owsley, "Henry Shelton Sanford and Federal Surveillance Abroad, 1861–1865." *Mississippi Valley Historical Review*, 48 (Sep.1961), 214.
92. Bulloch, *The Secret Service of the Confederate States in Europe*. I (2012), 274.
93. Stephen Chapin Kinnaman, *The Most Perfect Cruiser* (Indianapolis, 2009), 43
94. Lyon, Winfield, *The Sail & Steam Navy List* (2004), 235–236, 322.
95. *Ibid.*, 235–236, Kinnaman, *The Most Perfect Cruiser* (2009), 43.
96. "The "292," *Dublin Evening Mail*, 20 November 1862, 3, "Mr. John Laird, and the Birkenhead Ironworks and Docks," *ILN*, 27 July 1861, 74.
97. "Launch of a Government Troopship at Birkenhead," *Liverpool Mercury*, 24 November 1862, 3.
98. "For Sale, The Fine Paddle Tug Steamer Lion," *Liverpool Daily Post*, 29 July 1863, 8.
99. Wirral Archives (WA) ZCL/5/195/4), "The Fastest Tug-Vessel on the Mersey," *Liverpool Daily Post*, 14 January 1863, 5.
100. "The Fastest Tug-Vessel on the Mersey," *Liverpool Daily Post*, 14 January 1863, 5.
101. Bulloch, *The Secret Service of the Confederate States in Europe*. I (2012), 382, 385.
102. "H.M. Turret-Ships Wivern and Scorpion," *ILN*, 4 November 1865, 282.
103. Bulloch, *The Secret Service of the Confederate States in Europe*. I (2012), 385.
104. Lieutenant Commander Claude G. Berube (USNR), "American Thunder Childs," *Naval History*, 24 (June 2010), 61.
105. *Ibid.*, 62.
106. Nathaniel Philbrick, *In the Heart of the Sea: The Tragedy of the Whaleship Essex* (New York 2000), xiii.
107. Larrie D. Ferreiro, "The Social History of the Bulbous Bow." *Technology and Culture*, 52 (April, 2011), 340. Labrousse would predict, "as in Rome, the ram will re-establish equilibrium in favor of courage, and diminish superiority founded on greater numbers."
108. Baxter, *The Introduction of the Ironclad Warship* (2001), 57, 63.
109. "The Steam Ram of Sartorius," *Hampshire Telegraph*, 18 September 1858, 4.
110. Ferreiro, "The Social History of the Bulbous Bow." *Technology and Culture*, 52, 2 (April, 2011), 341.
111. Berube, "American Thunder Childs," *Naval History*, 24 (June 2010), 64.
112. Arnold A. Putnam, "The Building of Numbers 294 & 295: The Laird Rams." *Warship 1999–2000*. Edited by Antony Preston (London, 1999), 10. Smaller bulkheads protected the bow and stern, with the forward collision bulkhead providing additional protection should ramming occur.
113. *ORN*, II, 2 (1921), 453.
114. WA ZCL/005/0195/039/040, Description of Laird Rams, likely for Bravay of Paris, dated July 1863.
115. Baxter, *The Introduction of the Ironclad Warship* (2001), 109. 159. Also see Daniel A. Baugh, *The Journal of Interdisciplinary History,* 27 (Summer 1996), 123–124, review of C. I. Hamilton, *Anglo-French Naval Rivalry 1840–1870* (New York, 1993): "It was probably the first clearly defined modern technological arms race and was initiated by the challenging power, France." Nevertheless, "Britain had a much greater industrial capacity in respect to iron working and steam-propulsion manufacturing."
116. Stanley L. Sandler, "The Day of the Ram," *Military Affairs*, 40, 4 (Dec. 1976), 177.
117. *Ibid.*, 176.
118. Baxter, *The Introduction of the Ironclad Warship* (2001), 159, "Launch of the Resistance," *London Evening Standard*, 12 April 1861, 3.
119. *Ibid.*, 3. The ironclad careered down her ways stern first into the Thames and narrowly missed a steamer and tug, to the relief of the 10,000 in attendance, as the armored warship would have "annihilated anything less impervious than a granite mountain."

Notes—Chapter One

120. "Launch of Her Majesty's Iron-Cased Screw Frigate Resistance," *Morning Post*, 12 April 1861, 5.
121. "Launch of the Ironcased [*sic*] Frigate 'Resistance,'" *Newcastle Journal*, 13 April 1861, 3. This account also stated her ram was admired for its shape, as the contour resembled "the curved line of a swan's neck and breast."
122. Admiral G. A. Ballard, *The Black Battlefleet* (Greenwich, 1980), 230.
123. *Ibid.*, 166, 168.
124. Parkes, *British Battleships* (1966), 78.
125. Alexander L. Holley, "Iron-Clad Ships and Heavy Ordnance," *Atlantic Monthly*, 11 (January 1863), 93.
126. Charles L. Dufour, *The Night the War Was Lost* (Lincoln, 1994), 71.
127. *Ibid.*, 72.
128. *Ibid.*, 77.
129. Still, *Iron Afloat* (1971), 50.
130. *Ibid.*, 50, Baxter, *The Introduction of the Ironclad Warship* (2001), 233.
131. Baxter, *The Introduction of the Ironclad Warship* (2001), 233.
132. Dufour, *The Night the War Was Lost* (1994), 79; Still, *Iron Afloat* (1971), 50.
133. Still, *Iron Afloat* (1971) 25–27, 29.
134. *Ibid.*, 06, 107.
135. Guernsey, "Iron-Clad Vessels," *Harpers New Monthly Magazine*, 148 (September 1862), 440.
136. *Ibid.*, 444, 445. The *Roanoke* was also given a curved iron extension or "hood" aft to protect both her screw and rudder.
137. Tony Gibbons, *Warships and Naval Battles of the Civil War* (New York, 1989), 71.
138. *Ibid.*, 71.
139. "The 'Dunderberg,'" *Scientific American (SA)*, 8, 14 March 1863, 162.
140. *Ibid.*, 162.
141. *Hansard*, 10 July 1862, 168, cc 163.
142. *Ibid.*, cc 163.
143. Luraghi, *A History of the Confederate Navy* (1996), 202.
144. *Ibid.*, 202–203. The Confederates planned to name her the *Glasgow* or *Santa Maria*, likely as an initial moniker in an attempt to deceive Union spies, until she was safely at sea. Once equipped with her guns, ammunition and stores she would have probably been named for a southern state after she hoisted the Confederate naval ensign.
145. Gibbons, *Warships and Naval Battles of the Civil War* (1989), 67, Luraghi, *A History of the Confederate Navy* (1996), 203.
146. *ORN*, II, 2 (1921), 193. The stem was "of hammered scrap iron with part of keel forged on same" and served as the connection point between the separate ram forging and the keel plate.
147. *Ibid.*, 194.
148. WA ZCL/005/0195/039/040, Description of Laird Rams, dated July 1863.
149. Hans Christian Bjerg, "When the Monitors Came to Europe: The Danish Monitor Rolf Krake, 1863," *International Journal of Naval History (IJNH)*, 1 (October 2002), 3.
150. *ORN*, II, 2 (1921), 453, Putnam, "The Building of Numbers 294 & 295." *Warship 1999–2000* (1999), 10, Roberts, "James Dunwoody Bulloch and the Confederate Navy." *The North Carolina Historical Review*, 24, 3 (July 1947), 332.
151. WA 5/195/39 & 40, Captain Coles License for ships 294 and 295, 10 December 1862.
152. Bjerg, "The Danish Monitor Rolf Krake, 1863" *IJNH*, 1 (October 2002), 4.
153. *Ibid.*, 1, 5.
154. WA 5/195/39 & 40, Captain Coles License for ships 294 and 295, 10 December 1862.
155. *Ibid.*
156. Bowcock, *CSS Alabama* (2002), 184, WA, 5/195/39 & 40, Captain Coles License for ships 294 and 295, 10 December 1862.
157. Baxter, *The Introduction of the Ironclad Warship* (2001), 186–187.
158. H. W. Wilson, *Ironclads in Action; A Sketch of Naval Warfare from 1855–1895, With Some Account of the Development of the Battleship in England*. II (London, 1896), 224.
159. "The Ericsson Battery," *SA*, 6, 5, 1 February 1862, 73.
160. *Ibid.*, 73, Admiral G. A. Ballard, "The First Mastless Capital Ship H.M.S. Devastation." *The Mariner's Mirror*, XXII (1946), 6, 9.
161. Baxter, *The Introduction of the Ironclad Warship* (2001), 188–189, *ORN*, II, 2 (1921), 453.
162. "The Foreign Ironclads" *SA*, 9, 24, 12 December 1863, 377.
163. Putnam, "The Building of Numbers 294 & 295." *Warship 1999–2000* (1999), 11. Reportedly, a crew of 18 men could turn the armored copula one complete revolution in only a minute. An additional account claimed a crew of eight men could carry out a rotation in 90 seconds.
164. "Naval and Military Intelligence," *Essex Standard*, 27 September 1861, 4.
165. Lyon and Winfield, *The Sail & Steam Navy List* (2004), 241.
166. "Naval and Military," *London Daily News*, 2 October 1861, 3. The copula cast off most of the rounds, and based on the superficial damage, "a very large number of the shots glided off without injuring the plates."
167. "Naval and Military Intelligence," *Essex Standard*, 27 September 1861, 4; Baxter, *The Introduction of the Ironclad Warship* (2001), 191.
168. "Naval and Military Intelligence," *Essex Standard*, 27 September 1861, 4.
169. "Multum In Parvo," *Liverpool Mercury*, 7 October 1861, 7.
170. Baxter, *The Introduction of the Ironclad Warship* (2001), 192–193.
171. *Ibid.*, 260–261.
172. Lyon and Winfield, *The Sail & Steam Navy List* (2004), 239.
173. *Ibid.*, 239.
174. *Conway's All the World's Fighting Ships 1860–1945*. Editor Roger Chesneau (London,

1979), 19–20; Lyon and Winfield, *The Sail & Steam Navy List* (2004), 240.

175. "The Steam Battery 'Monitor,'" *SA*, 6, 22 March 1862, 177; *SA*, "The Laird Rams," 11, 1 October 1864, 224.

176. Putnam, "The Building of Numbers 294 & 295." *Warship 1999–2000* (1999), 11.

177. "The Steam Battery 'Monitor,'" *SA*, 6, 22 March 1862, 177

178. Guernsey, "Iron-Clad Vessels," *Harpers New Monthly Magazine*, 48, September 1862, 440.

179. *Ibid.*, 440.

180. Wilson, *Ironclads in Action*. II (1896), 220.

181. "The Armstrong Gun," *Dublin Evening Mail*, 10 October 1861, 1. The ordnance maker Sir William Armstrong disdainfully referred to the breechloaders of that era as "gimcrackery" with justification.

182. Baxter, *The Introduction of the Ironclad Warship* (2001), 192.

183. *ORN*, II, 2 (1921), 310.

184. Photo NH 61923, *"U.S.S. Monitor (1862),"* U.S. Naval Historical Center, Washington.

185. Putnam, "The Building of Numbers 294 & 295." *Warship 1999–2000* (1999), 11.

186. *Ibid.*, 11.

187. "Description of the Birkenhead Iron Works," *The Practical Magazine*, (London, 1874), 28.

188. "The Foreign Iron-Clads," *SA*, 9, 12 December 1863, 377.

189. Putnam, "The Building of Numbers 294 & 295." *Warship 1999–2000* (1999), 11.

190. Parkes, *British Battleships* (1966), 78.

191. Baxter, *The Introduction of the Ironclad Warship* (2001), 154.

192. *ORN*, II, 2 (1921), 310.

193. Wilson, *Ironclads in Action*. II (London, 1896), 220.

194. Parkes, *British Battleships* (1966), 79. James Reed claimed the "turn-down" iron bulwarks were four feet high and made in lengths of about eight feet. See TNA, ADM 1/5842, *Admiralty Correspondence*, "Steam Rams on the Mersey," Letter written by James Reed, 17 September 1863, 8–9.

195. "The Laird Rams," *SA*, 11, 1 October 1864, 224.

196. *Ibid.*, 224, *ORN*, II, 2 (1921), 225.

197. *ORN*, II, 2 (1921), 265.

198. TNA, ADM 135/417, Office of the Controller of the Navy Ship's Book Series 1, H.M.S. Scorpion," *ORN*, II, 2 (1921), 265.

199. *ORN*, I, 13 (Washington, 1901), 331.

200. Milton, *Lincoln's Spymaster* (2003), xix, xxii.

201. *ORN*, I, 13 (1901), 331. The plates were "made in a new manner" of "the best iron" in the rolling mill of the Mersey works.

202. "Progress of the New Railway into Liverpool," *Liverpool Daily Post*, 20 September 1862, 5.

203. Baxter, *The Introduction of the Ironclad Warship* (2001), 14.

204. *Ibid.*, 14, "Launch of the Valiant," *Lloyd's Weekly Newspaper*, 18 October 1863, 1.

205. "Prince Alfred in Liverpool," *Blackburn Standard*, 25 September 1861, 4, "International Exhibition," *Kentish Chronicle*, 31 May 1862, 2.

206. "Launch of the Agincourt," *London Evening Standard*, 28 March 1865, 6, "The Japanese Ambassadors in Liverpool," *Liverpool Daily Post*, 29 May 1862, 5.

207. David Evans, *Building the Steam Navy. Dockyards, Technology and the Creation of the Victorian Battlefleet 1830–1906* (London, 2004), 58.

208. Guernsey, "Iron-Clad Vessels," *Harpers New Monthly Magazine*, 148 (September 1862), 436.

209. "The Mersey Steel and Iron Company, Limited" *Liverpool Daily Post*, 26 September 1865, 7.

210. "Launch of a Yacht at Birkenhead," *Liverpool Mercury*, 17 July 1858, 9.

211. Kenneth Warren, *Steel, Ships and Men: Cammell Laird, 1824–1993* (Liverpool, 1998), 95.

212. "The Week's News," *Cheshire Observer*, 25 June 1864, 4.

213. "Another 'Ram' for a 'French' House," *Liverpool Daily Post*, 31 August 1863, 5.

214. "Trial of Mr. MacKay's New Gun," *Cheshire Chronicle*, 16 April 1864, 3.

215. "Experiments with Bessemer's Process," *SA*, 12, 1 November 1856, 64.

216. "To Make Steel from Pig Iron," *SA*, 3, 10 November 1860, 308.

217. "Liverpool News," *Glasgow Herald*, 2 July 1864, 7.

218. "Launch of Her Majesty's Ironclad Frigate Lord Warden," *Sheffield Daily Telegraph*, 30 May 1865, 3, *ORN*, II, 2 (1921), 224.

219. "Patent Railway Axles—Interesting Chance in Extending a Patent," *SA*, 4, 14 April 1849, 235; "Semi-Steel Locomotive Tires [sic]" *SA*, 4, 5 January 1861, 3; "The Exhibition of Iron and Steel," *SA*, 16, 15 June 1867, 374.

220. Putnam, "The Building of Numbers 294 & 295: The Laird Rams." *Warship 1999–2000*. Edited by Antony Preston (1999), 10, Parkes, *British Battleships* (1966), 78.

221. "Lord Clarendon at Liverpool," *Dublin Evening Mail*, 16 October 1862, 4.

222. Patrick Barry, *Dockyard Economy and Naval Power* (London, 1863, reprinted, 2005), 301. Likely in the interest of speeding the work along, and to best use available space at the shipyard, one of the rams was built stern on to the Mersey, the other bow on.

223. "Obituary," *Manchester Courier and Lancashire General Advertiser*, 15 September 1894, 13.

224. "Iron-Case Shipbuilding," *London Evening Standard*, 10 February 1863, 3.

225. (WA), Birkenhead Map, Ordnance Survey Office, Southampton (1875).

226. "Description of the Birkenhead Iron Works" *The Practical Magazine* (1874), 3.

227. Ibid., 3.
228. Ibid., 26.
229. "Visit to Birkenhead," *Living Age*, 6, 5 July 1845, 25–26.
230. "Description of the Birkenhead Ironworks," *The Practical Magazine*, (1874), 26.
231. Putnam, "The Building of Numbers 294 & 295." *Warship 1999–2000* (1999), 10.
232. Ibid., 10, "Description of the Birkenhead Ironworks," *The Practical Magazine*, (1874), 26.
233. Guernsey, "Iron-Clad Vessels," *Harpers New Monthly Magazine*, 148 (September 1862), 442.
234. Putnam, "The Building of Numbers 294 & 295." *Warship 1999–2000* (1999), 10.
235. Ibid., 12.
236. *ORN*, II, 2 (1921), 364, R.F. Scheltema de Heere, "The Prins Hendrik der Nederlanden," *The Mariner's Mirror*. 17 (Cambridge, 1931), 44.
237. Putnam, "The Building of Numbers 294 & 295." *Warship 1999–2000* (1999), 12; Scheltema de Heere, "The Prins Hendrik der Nederlanden," *The Mariner's Mirror*. 17 (1931), 44; Parkes, *British Battleships* (1966), 78.
238. *ORN*, II, 2 (1921), 453.
239. "Defects of the British Ironclads," SA, 1010, 13 February 1864, 101.
240. Ballard, *The Black Battlefleet* (1980), 63.
241. "Shipbuilding on the Mersey," *Chester Chronicle*, 29 November 1862, 7.
242. Ballard, *The Black Battlefleet* (1980), 42, 63–64.
243. Putnam, "The Building of Numbers 294 & 295." *Warship 1999–2000* (1999), 10.
244. "The Double-Turreted Ship Wyvern," *ILN*, 16 December 1865, 594.
245. Parkes, *British Battleships* (1966), 78; *Steam, Steel & Shellfire. The Steam Warship 1815–1905*. Editor Robert Gardiner, Consultant Editor Dr. Andrew Lambert (London, 1992), 175.
246. "Miscellaneous, Return of a Blockade-Runner, Departure of the Scorpion," *NYT*, 8 April 1865, 2, Lyon and Winfield, *The Sail & Steam Navy List* (2004), 252; Parkes, *British Battleships* (1966), 78.
247. Antony Preston, "Creating an Inshore Navy: Royal Navy Littoral Warfare Forces in the Russian War 1854–56." *Warship 1999–2000*. Edited by Antony Preston (London, 1999), 23; Robert V. Kubicek, "The Design of Shallow-Draft [sic] Steamers for the British Empire, 1868–1906." *Technology and Culture*, 31 (Jul. 1990), 433.
248. Parkes, *British Battleships* (1966), 80; Scheltema de Heere, "The Prins Hendrik der Nederlanden," *The Mariner's Mirror*. 17 (1931), 51.
249. "The Double-Turreted Ship Wyvern," *ILN*, 16 December 1865, 594; Scheltema de Heere, "The Prins Hendrik der Nederlanden," *The Mariner's Mirror*. 17 (1931), 45.
250. "The Fastest Tug-Vessel on the Mersey," *Liverpool Daily Post*, 14 January 1863, 5.
251. WA Z/CL2/9/0000/005, "Records of Cammell Laird and Co. H.M.S. Wivern, Engines No. 81, copy of plans.
252. "H.M. Turret-Ships Wivern and Scorpion," *ILN*, 4 November 1865, 282; "Description of the Birkenhead Ironworks," *The Practical Magazine* (1874), 2, 26.
253. Ballard, *The Black Battlefleet* (1980), 28. This type of engine was described as having "occupied the minimum of floor space (within the hull of the vessel) without loss of stroke, and for a horizontal lie offered the further advantage of large surfaces for the sliding parts, which reduced wear."
254. Richard Sennett, Henry J. Oram, *The Marine Steam Engine: A Treatise for Engineering Students, Young Engineers, and Officers of the Royal Navy and Merchant Marine*. (Reprint of London, 1898 version Bremen, 2012), 7.
255. WA ZCL/005/0195/039/040, Description of Laird Rams, dated July 1863. Ballard, *The Black Battlefleet* (1980), 194.
256. *The Advent of Steam*, Editor Robert Gardiner, Consultant Editor Dr. Basil Greenhill (London, 1992), 100.
257. *The Dynamics of Victorian Business: The Problems and Perspectives to the 1870s*. Edited by Roy Church (New York, 2006), 90, 91.
258. S. B. Saul, "The Market and Development of the Mechanical Engineering Industries in Britain 1860–1914," *The Economic History Review*, 20 (April 1967), 117.
259. Ibid., 88, 89 102.
260. Warren, *Steel, Ships and Men* (1998), 34.
261. Putnam, "The Building of Numbers 294 & 295." *Warship 1999–2000* (1999), 10.
262. Parkes, *British Battleships* (1966), 78.
263. Lyon and Winfield, *The Sail & Steam Navy List* (2004), 240–241. This floating battery (and perhaps others of the five-ship *Aetna* class) built in Britain during the Crimean War was adapted from a single screw armorclad to carry two wing propellers in addition to her original central screw, with those side screws likely driven by belts connected to the single engine.
264. Wilson, *Ironclads in Action*. I (London, 1896), xxxiii.
265. Ballard, *The Black Battlefleet* (1980), 194.
266. Parkes, *British Battleships* (1966), 78; *Liverpool Daily Post*, 10 October 1865, 10.
267. TNA, ADM 53/9512, *Ship's Log* H.M.S. *Scorpion*, 2 December 1868 to 31 December 1869.
268. Ballard, *The Black Battlefleet* (1980), 194. *Liverpool Daily Post*, 10 October 1865, 10.
269. *ORN*, II, 2 (1921), 452, 453. He matter-of-factly explained the drawings of the sail plan with only a passing reference to a labor savings appliance aloft: "I will merely say that the upper topsails roll up as the yards are lowered."
270. Ibid., 453.
271. "Reefing Topsails," *London Daily News*, 16 September 1861, 2. "Cunningham's Self-Reefing Topsails," *Hampshire Telegraph*, 23 May 1857, 5.
272. "Reefing Topsails," *London Daily News*, 16 September 1861, 2.
273. Ibid., 2.

274. "Naval and Military Intelligence," *Morning Post*, 21 March 1862, 2.
275. "Ship Launch," *Sussex Advertiser*, 18 January 1859, 6.
276. Ballard, *The Black Battlefleet* (1980), 166.
277. *ORN*, II, 2 (1921), 310.
278. Luraghi, *A History of the Confederate Navy* (Annapolis, 1996), 175, 192.
279. *ORN*, II, 2 (1921), 178, 310, George M. Brooke, Jr. *John M. Brooke, Naval Scientist and Educator* (Charlottesville, 1980), 263.
280. Brooke, *John M. Brooke* (1980), 264.
281. Wilson, *Ironclads in Action*. I (1896), 147, 152.
282. C. R. Horres, Jr. "Charleston's Civil War 'Monster Guns,' the Blakely Rifles," *The South Carolina Historical Magazine*, 97 (April 1996), 123, 130.
283. "Ordnance in the London Exhibition," *SA*, 6, 21 June 1862, 391, Gibbons, *Warships and Naval Battles of the Civil War* (1989), 24.
284. Bowcock, CSS *Alabama* (2002), 7, "The International Exhibition," *Hampshire Chronicle*, 17 May 1862, 3; "Liverpool News." *Glasgow Herald*, 30 September 1861, 5.
285. *ORN*, II, 2 (1921), 290, 310.
286. *Ibid.*, 301, 310.
287. *Ibid.*, 360, 668.
288. Marshall J. Bastable, "From Breechloaders to Monster Guns: Sir William Armstrong and the Invention of Modern Artillery, 1854–1880." *Technology and Culture*, 33 (April 1992), 234.
289. W. T. O'Dea, "A Century of British Engineering," *Journal of the Royal Society of Arts*, 99 (4 May 1951), 466.
290. Saul, "The Market and Development of the Mechanical Engineering Industries in Britain 1860–1914." *The Economic History Review*, 20 (April 1967), 121; Karl Lautenschlager, "Technology and the Evolution of Naval Warfare," *International Security*, 8 (fall 1983), 10.
291. Bastable, "From Breechloaders to Monster Guns: Sir William Armstrong and the Invention of Modern Artillery, 1854–1880." *Technology and Culture*, 33 (April 1992), 234, 238.
292. "The Whitworth Gun," *Daily Dispatch*, 22 June 1861, 4.
293. Ross FitzGerald, *Cities and Camps of the Confederate States* (Urbana, 1997), 132.
294. "The Siege of Washington N.C.," *Daily Dispatch*, 16 April 1863, 1.
295. Ross, *Cities and Camps of the Confederate States* (1997), 151
296. *ORN*, II, 2 (1921), 290.
297. *Ibid.* 453.
298. *Ibid.*, 454.
299. J. H. Ward, Commander, U.S. N. *Steam for the Million: A Popular Treatise on Steam and its Application to the Useful Arts Especially to Navigation* (New York, 1864), 96. See Howard J. Fuller, "The *Warrior*'s Influence Abroad: The American Civil War," *IJNH*, 10 (October 2013), 6. The *Warrior* also influenced the building of the *Monitor* and "Union naval policy towards counter-deterrence-or coastal defense first, and coastal assault-against the Confederacy-second."
300. Lyon and Winfield, *The Sail & Steam Navy List* (2004), 233, 236.
301. *Hansard*, 26 July 1861, 164, cc 1633.
302. Lyon and Winfield, *The Sail & Steam Navy List* (2004), 193.
303. Ballard, *The Black Battlefleet* (1980), 116.
304. "Iron-clad Jack: A Sea-Song of the Future," *Punch*, 12 April 1862, 146.
305. "The Foreign Iron-Clads," *SA*, 9, 12 December 1863, 377.
306. *Ibid.*, 377.
307. Guernsey, "The Revolving Iron Tower and Its Inventor," *Harper's New Monthly Magazine*, 26 (January 1863), 247.
308. *Ibid.*, 245. It is noteworthy that the first ironclad mentioned in the editorial was the only monitor, and the other three ironclads were the traditional broadside equipped ocean-going armored vessels. Despite the advances achieved by the Union Navy during the Civil War, their ironclads were not ideal examples of seaworthiness. Getting to the scene of combat was half the battle, and the monitors built in America were regarded as coastal warships.
309. "Miscellaneous, Return of a Blockade-Runner, Departure of the Scorpion." *NYT*, 8 April 1865, 2.
310. Alvah Folsom Hunter, *A Year on a Monitor and the Destruction of Fort Sumter*. Edited by Craig L. Symonds (Columbia, 1987), 89.
311. *Ibid.*, 35, 66. Here, Hunter describes how the guns on the monitor U.S.S. *Nahant* had to be swabbed out and reloaded with long-handled sponges and rammers through the open gunports after the turret was turned away from the enemy. Later when "sectional" rammers and sponges were used, gunports were left closed and the turret did not need to be rotated, but the rate of fire did not improve as the "sectionals" were complicated to use. See Gibbons, *Warships and Naval Battles of the Civil War* (1989), 30.

Chapter Two

1. TNA, FO 412/11 "Correspondence Respecting the Two-Ironclad Vessels Building at Messrs. Laird's Yard, Birkenhead," dated 11 July 1863.
2. Merli, *The Alabama* (2004), 23.
3. William O. Brown Jr., and Richard C.K. Burdekin, "Turning Points in the U.S. Civil War: A British Perspective," *Journal of Economic History*, 60 (Mar. 2000), 217, 218, 230.
4. "America," *Morning Post*, 27 July 1863, 5.
5. Joseph M. Hernon, Jr. "British Sympathies in the American Civil War: A Reconsideration," *Journal of Southern History*, 33 (Aug. 1967), 357–360.
6. *Ibid.*, 359.
7. *Hansard*, 23 July 1863, 172, cc 1271.
8. TNA, FO 412/11 "Correspondence

Respecting the Two-Ironclad Vessels Building at Messrs. Laird's Yard, Birkenhead," dated 11 July 1863

9. Bulloch, *The Secret Service of the Confederate States in Europe*, I (2012), 389, 391.
10. *Ibid.*, 391.
11. *ORN*, Series II, 2 (1921), 292.
12. *Hansard*, 27 March 1863, 170, cc 33, 38, 70–72.
13. *Ibid.*, cc. 70.
14. *Ibid.*, cc. 70–72.
15. "Telegraphic," *Shreveport Weekly News*, 4 May 1863, 1.
16. *The Diary of Gideon Welles*, I, 1861–30 March 1864 (1911), 291.
17. *Ibid.*, 307.
18. "Secretary Welles and Mr. Laird," *New York Daily Tribune*, 10 August 1863, 4.
19. *The Diary of Gideon Welles*, I (1911), 401; "The Federal Government and Mr. Laird," *Dundee, Perth and Cupar Advertiser*, 25 August 1863, 8.
20. *The Diary of Gideon Welles*, I (1911), 401
21. *Ibid.*, 401. Welles was distrustful, perhaps even envious of Fox as he continued in his diary entry of 13 August, writing, "There are little weaknesses which others as well as Faxon detected. Admirals Smith, Lenthall and Dahlgren were vexed by Fox's 'officious manner and order.'"
22. Doris Kearns Goodwin, *Team of Rivals, The Political Genius of Abraham Lincoln* (New York, 2005), xvi, 335, 629.
23. *Ibid.*, 525. 526.
24. John Niven, *Gideon Welles: Lincoln's Secretary of the Navy* (Baton Rouge, 1994), viii.
25. *The Diary of Gideon Welles*, I (1911), 401.
26. Hoogenboom, *Gustavus Vasa Fox of the Union Navy* (2008), 46–49.
27. *Confidential Correspondence of Gustavus Vasa Fox*, I (New York, 1918), 145–146.
28. Dufour, *The Night the War Was Lost* (1994), 265, 274, 275, 279, 280.
29. Gibbons, *Warships and Naval Battles of the Civil War* (1989), 36, 138–140,166.
30. *Ibid.*, 139.
31. "Iron-Cased Shipbuilding," *London Evening Standard*, 10 February 1863, 3.
32. *Ibid.*, 3.
33. Bulloch, *The Secret Service of the Confederate States in Europe*, I (2012), 395.
34. "Iron-Cased Shipbuilding," *London Evening Standard*, 10 February 1863, 3.
35. Bulloch, *The Secret Service of the Confederate States in Europe*, I (2012), 395.
36. Kinnaman, *The Most Perfect Cruiser* (2009), 102.
37. *Ibid.*, 102.
38. "The Steam Rams at Birkenhead," *Chester Chronicle*, 26 September 1863, 2.
39. "Launch of Iron Steam Rams at Birkenhead," *Birmingham Daily Post*, 31 August 1863, 4.
40. Bulloch, *The Secret Service of the Confederate States in Europe*, I (2012), 391.
41. *Ibid.*, 392.
42. "Vessels Building for the Confederates," *Liverpool Mercury*, 13 February 1863, 6. This edition inquired as to Bulloch's role: "Does this gentleman hold his commission from his Celestial Majesty or from Jefferson Davis"?
43. Merli, *The Alabama* (2004), 160, 162.
44. *Ibid.*, 162, 165.
45. *Ibid.*, 167.
46. Bulloch, *The Secret Service of the Confederate States in Europe*, I (2012), 394.
47. "The Confederates iron-clad navy-Yankee information on the subject—What England is doing about it." *Daily Dispatch*, 22 November 1862, 1.
48. "Later from the North," *Daily Dispatch*, 24 November 1862, 1.
49. "Lectures on the American Crisis," *Liverpool Mercury*, 7 February 1863, 6.
50. "Gunboat Building on the Mersey," *Westmorland Gazette*, 22 November 1862, 8.
51. *Ibid.*, 8.
52. *Confidential Correspondence of Gustavus Vasa Fox*, II (New York, 1918), 252.
53. "Defects of the British Ironclads," *SA*, 1010, 7, 13 February 1864, 101.
54. "The Neutrality Proclamation," *The Spectator*, 18 May 1861, 521.
55. *Ibid.*, 521.
56. *Ibid.*, 521.
57. "Royal Proclamation," *Reynold's Newspaper*, 19 May 1861, 10.
58. *Ibid.*, 10.
59. *ORN*, Series I, 1 (Washington, 1894), 138–143.
60. "The British Forces on the North American & West India Station," *Yorkshire Gazette*, 7 December 1861, 11.
61. "Stations of the Royal Navy in Commission," *Morning Post*, 5, December 1861, 6, Lt. Cdr. (Ret.) Ian Stranack, *The Andrew and the Onions. The Story of the Royal Navy in Bermuda 1795–1975* (Bermuda, 1990), 143.
62. Lyon and Winfield, *The Sail & Steam Navy List* (2004), 241.
63. *Ibid.*, 241.
64. *Ibid.*, 160, "The Navy," "H.M. Gun-battery 'Terror,'" *Royal Gazette*, 20 October 1857, 2.
65. "The North America and West India Station," *Exeter and Plymouth Gazette*, 6 December 1861, 10.
66. "Our Naval Position in the Event of War," *Huddersfield Chronicle*, 7 December 1861, 6.
67. "The Royal Naval Reserve," *Carlisle Journal*, 6 December 1861, 8.
68. TNA, ADM 53/8205, *Ship's Log* H.M.S. *Terror*, 16 Dec. 1861–31 Dec. 1862, entry 29 November 1862.
69. "The Yankee Blockade of Bermuda," *Newcastle Journal*, 30 October 1862, 3.
70. Goodwin, *Team of Rivals* (2005), 398.
71. "Return of Lord Lyons from Washington," *Caledonian Mercury*, 17 June 1862, 3.
72. "Arrival of Mason and Slidell," *Berkshire*

Chronicle, 1 February 1862, 6. After being released from their confinement at Fort Warren in Boston harbor, the steam frigate H.M.S. *Rinaldo* carried the party to Bermuda, where they arrived on 9 January.

73. NMM, MLN/114/9, 1st Bt., Sir Alexander Milne, Admiral of the Fleet. "Additional Instructions for the guidance of Cruizers employed in the Protection of British Commerce on the East Coast of America." 9 September 1861, 10.

74. *Ibid.*, 12.

75. NMM, MLN/114/9, 1st Bt., Sir Alexander Milne, Admiral of the Fleet. "Additional Instructions for the guidance of Cruizers employed in the Protection of British Commerce on the East Coast of America." 12 November 1861, 6.

76. Amanda Foreman, *A World on Fire: Britain's Crucial Role in the American Civil War* (New York, 2010), 103, 413.

77. Spencer, *The Confederate Navy in Europe* (1983), 101.

78. Wesley Loy, "10 Rumford Place: Doing Confederate Business in Liverpool." *The South Carolina Historical Magazine* 98 (October 1997), 353. So tightly intertwined were the Merseyside merchants with the Southern States that Liverpool reportedly flew more Confederate flags than were seen even in Richmond.

79. "The Wonders of the Port of London," *SA* 9 (5 December 1863), 357. Trade in "metals, hardware, earthenware, &c" were mostly disguised to obscure the real contents, which were weapons intended for the war in America.

80. Lance E. Davis & Stanley L. Engerman, *Naval Blockades in Peace and War* (Cambridge, 2006), 129.

81. *Ibid.*, 130.

82. Bowcock, *CSS Alabama* (2002), 7.

83. Horatio Bridge, "Personal Recollections of Nathanial Hawthorne," *Harper's New Monthly Magazine* 502 (March 1892), 510. In 1853, the office was held by the poet Nathaniel Hawthorne, who wrote to a friend to lament that his "official duties and obligations are irksome to me beyond expression."

84. Herman Hattaway and Richard Beringer, *Jefferson Davis Confederate President* (Lawrence, 2002), 138.

85. Spencer, *The Confederate Navy in Europe* (1983), 82.

86. Putnam, "The Building of Numbers 294 & 295: The Laird Rams." *Warship 1999–2000*. Edited by Antony Preston (1999), 12–13.

87. "The Mechanics of Modern Naval Warfare," *The North American Review* 103 (July 1866), 201.

88. "Naval and Military," *London Daily News*, 27 January 1862, 2.

89. "The Great Exhibition," *Dundee Advertiser*, 10 May 1862, 3.

90. WA 2/527, NMM, "HMS Wivern (1863) Service Vessel; Coast Defence Ship," Repro ID: F8955–001, "One of the Steam-Rams in Course of Construction in Messrs. Laird's [*sic*] Ship-Building Yard, Birkenhead," *ILN*, 26 September 1863, 321.

91. "Her Majesty's Ship Majestic Keeping Watch Over the Steam-Rams in the Mersey," *ILN*, 28 November 1863, 552; U.S. Naval Historical Center (USNHC) Photo #NH 48145, "Engraving of Confederate ironclad built by John Laird during the Civil War"; USNHC Photo #NH 52526, "HMS Wivern in the Hamoaze River, Plymouth, England, in 1865"; USNHC Photo #NH 71211, "HMS Wivern off Plymouth, England."

92. "Ship Launches on Saturday," *Liverpool Daily Post*, 6 July 1863, 5; Ballard, *The Black Battlefleet* (1980), 161.

93. USNHC Photo #NH 71211, "HMS Wivern off Plymouth, England," "The Anglo-Rebel Pirates—One of Laird's Steam-Rams," *Harpers Weekly*, 17 October 1863, 661.

94. "Portsmouth, June 6, 1846," *Hampshire Advertiser*, 6 June 1846, 5.

95. "Portsmouth, May 30, 1846." *Hampshire Advertiser*, 30 May 1846, 5; "The Experimental Squadron," *Morning Chronicle*, 5 June 1846, 3.

96. "Portsmouth, May 30, 1846," *Hampshire Advertiser*, 30 May 1846, 5.

97. *Ibid.*, 5.

98. *Ibid.*, 5, "The Experimental Squadron," *Morning Chronicle*, 5 June 1846, 3.

99. Commander Geoffrey Penn, R.N. "*Up Funnel, Down Screw!" The Story of the Naval Engineer* (London, 1955), 48.

100. Admiral Sir Percy Scott, *Fifty Years in the Royal Navy* (London, 1919), 27.

101. "Science and Modern Warfare," *SA*, 14, 39, 4 June 1859, 325.

102. Scott, *Fifty Years in the Royal Navy* (1919), 26; Lyon and Winfield, *The Sail & Steam Navy List* (2004), 209.

103. Luraghi, *A History of the Confederate Navy* (1996), 141; Scharf, *The Confederate States Navy* (1996), 159; Gibbons, *Warships and Naval Battles of the Civil War* (1989), 161.

104. Chester Hearn, *Naval Battles of the Civil War* (San Diego, 2000), 124, 127; Scharf, *The Confederate States Navy* (1996), 316.

105. Scharf, *The Confederate States Navy* (1996), 314.

106. Michael Embree, *Bismarck's First War: The Campaign of Schleswig and Jutland 1864* (Solihull, 2006), 119, 196, *Hansard*, 19 July 1864, 176, cc1766.

107. "The Rolf Krake," *Glasgow Herald*, 12 August 1864, 6.

108. "The Rolf Krake at Alsen," *Glasgow Herald*, 16 July 1864, 3.

109. Douglas H. Maynard, "The Forbes-Aspinwall Mission." *The Mississippi Valley Historical Review* 45 (June 1958), 68.

110. *Ibid.*, 71–72.

111. "Letter from "Manhattan," *London Evening Standard*, 8 May 1863, 5.

112. "Southern Views of American Affairs," *Liverpool Mercury* 18 April 1863, 5.

113. Maynard, "The Forbes-Aspinwall Mission." *The Mississippi Valley Historical Review* 45 (June 1958), 69, 75, 77.
114. *Ibid.*, 73.
115. "News from Jackson," *Dallas Herald*, 10 June 1863, 1.
116. Maynard, "The Forbes-Aspinwall Mission." *The Mississippi Valley Historical Review* 45 (June 1958), 81.
117. *The Diary of Gideon Welles*, I (1911), 322.
118. "'Times' Telegram," *Liverpool Mercury*, 15 June 1863, 5.
119. Bulloch, *The Secret Service of the Confederate States in Europe*. I (2012), 101
120. Richard Roberts, *Schroders Merchants & Bankers* (London, 1992), 64.
121. *ORN*, II, 2 (1921), 265.
122. Amos E. Taylor, "The Role of Washington in the National Economy during the Civil War," *Records of the Columbia Historical Society*, 53/56 (Washington, 1953/1956), 147–149.
123. *Ibid.*, 151–153.
124. Judith Fenner Gentry, "A Confederate Success in Europe: The Erlanger Loan," *The Journal of Southern History* 36 (May 1970), 157, 160.
125. Roberts, *Schroders* (1992), 62, 66.
126. Henry Blumenthal, "Confederate Diplomacy: Popular Notions and International Realities," *The Journal of Southern History* 32 (May 1966), 158; Gentry, "A Confederate Success in Europe: The Erlanger Loan," *The Journal of Southern History* 36 (May 1970), 177, 178.
127. Edwin DeLeon, *Secret History of Confederate Diplomacy Abroad*. Edited by William C. Davis (Lawrence, 2005), 173.
128. Roberts, *Schroders* (1992), 65.
129. *Ibid.*, 65, 68, Charles S. Davis, *Colin J. McRae: Confederate Financial Agent* (College Station, 2008), 36, 37, 39.
130. Blumenthal, "Confederate Diplomacy: Popular Notions and International Realities," *The Journal of Southern History* 32 (May 1966), 158, 161.
131. Stanley Lebergott, "Why the South Lost: Commercial Purpose in the Confederacy, 1861–1865," *The Journal of American History* 70 (June 1983), 61, 66, 67.
132. Roberts, *Schroders* (1992), 66. Maynard, "The Forbes-Aspinwall Mission." *The Mississippi Valley Historical Review* 45 (June 1958), 76.
133. Roberts, *Schroders* (1992), 66.
134. DeLeon, *Secret History of Confederate Diplomacy Abroad*. Edited by William C. Davis (2005), xx, 171.
135. *Ibid.*, 173.
136. *ORN*, II, 2 (1921), 372–373.
137. *Ibid.*, 567–569.
138. William Garrott Brown, "The Resources of the Confederacy," *The Atlantic Monthly* 88 (December 1901), 831.
139. Bulloch, *The Secret Service of the Confederate States in Europe*. I (2012), 65–66. Bulloch regarded Hull to be "a conscientious adviser…a watchful and safe mentor."
140. *Ibid.*, 66, "Royal Proclamation," *Reynold's Newspaper*, 19 May 1861, 10.
141. Bulloch, *The Secret Service of the Confederate States in Europe*. I (2012), 66.
142. Putnam, "The Building of Numbers 294 & 295: The Laird Rams." *Warship 1999–2000*. Edited by Antony Preston (London, 1999), 11.
143. *ORN*, II, 2 (1921), 445–446.
144. *Ibid.*, 445
145. *Ibid.*, 446.
146. Bulloch, *The Secret Service of the Confederate States in Europe*. I (2012), 398; Baxter, *The Introduction of the Ironclad Warship* (2001), 385.
147. *ORN*, II, 2 (1921), 445.
148. *Ibid.*, 445; Bulloch, *The Secret Service of the Confederate States in Europe*. I (2012), 400.
149. *ORN*, II, 2 (1921), 445.
150. *Ibid.*, 445.
151. *ORN*, II, 2 (1921), 654,709, "Ismail Pacha of Egypt," *Harper's New Monthly Magazine* 39 (October 1869), 740, TNA, FO 412/11 "Correspondence Respecting the Two-Ironclad Vessels Building at Messrs. Laird's Yard, Birkenhead," No. 70, dated 5 September 1863.
152. "The Lucky Shoemaker," *Belfast News-Letter*, 5 December 1863, 4.
153. *Ibid.*, 4, "More Electoral Defeats of the French Government," *Herts, Guardian, Agricultural Journal, and General Advertiser*, 23 January 1864, 2; Davis, *Colin J. McRae* (2008), 36.
154. "France," *London Daily News*, 2 June 1864, 5, "The Vote by Ballot," *Manchester Courier and Lancashire General Advertiser*, 22 January 1864, 3.
155. Edwin De Leon, "Ismail Pacha of Egypt," *Harper's New Monthly Magazine* 39 (October 1869), 740, 742.
156. Bulloch, *The Secret Service of the Confederate States in Europe*. I (2012), 404–405.
157. *Ibid.*, 404.
158. *Ibid.*, 406.
159. *ORN*, II, 2 (1921), 286–287.
160. Putnam, "The Building of Numbers 294 & 295: The Laird Rams." *Warship 1999–2000*. Edited by Antony Preston (London, 1999), 11.
161. Scharf, *The Confederate States Navy* (1996), 804.
162. Bulloch, *The Secret Service of the Confederate States in Europe*. I (2012), 413.
163. *ORN*, II, 2 (1921), 193; Luraghi, *A History of the Confederate Navy* (1996), 202–203.
164. *ORN*, II, 2 (1921), 197. This was a two bladed propeller.
165. "Who Cast the Screws for the Italian Frigate?," *SA* 11 (3 September 1864), 150.
166. *Ibid.*, 150.
167. *The War of the Rebellion: A Compilation of the Official Records of the Union and Confederate Armies* (ORA). Series 1, 6 (Washington, 1882), 626
168. "Arrival of the Russian Frigate General Admiral, and trial of the Russian Battery Pervenetz," *London Evening Standard*, 7 August 1863, 3; Parkes, *British Battleships* (1966), 16, 24.

169. "Naval Intelligence," *Liverpool Daily Post*, 1 October 1862, 5.
170. "The Navy," *Dublin Evening Mail*, 20 January 1863, 2; Anonymous, *The International Exhibition of 1862*, 2 (Cambridge, 2014), 37.
171. "Naval and Military Intelligence," *Morning Post*, 19 January 1863, 3.
172. Anonymous, *The International Exhibition of 1862* (Cambridge, 2014), 37.
173. *Ibid.*, 37.
174. *The Advent of Steam*, Editor Robert Gardiner, Consultant (London, 1992), 17.
175. Penn, "*Up Funnel, Down Screw!*" (1955), 26.
176. *Ibid.*, 26.
177. *Ibid.*, 26.
178. J. H. Ward, Commander, U.S. N. *Steam for the Million: A Popular Treatise on Steam and its Application to the Useful Arts Especially to Navigation* (New York, 1864), 118.
179. *Ibid.*, 118.
180. Anonymous, *The International Exhibition of 1862* (Cambridge, 2014), 37.
181. Bulloch, *The Secret Service of the Confederate States in Europe*. I (2012), 412–413.
182. *Ibid.*, 413.
183. "The Steam Rams Seized at Birkenhead," *Liverpool Mercury*, 10 March 1864, 6.
184. *Ibid.*, 6.
185. Bulloch, *The Secret Service of the Confederate States in Europe*. I (2012), 385–386.
186. Milton, *Lincoln's Spymaster* (2003), 119.
187. *Ibid.*, 80.
188. *Ibid.*, 80, 85.
189. *ORN*, II, 2 (1921), 384.
190. *Ibid.*, 384.
191. *ORN*, I, 13 (Washington, 1901), 331.
192. Milton, *Lincoln's Spymaster* (2003), 79, 80.
193. "Manufacture of Armour Plates, *Exeter Flying Post*, 15 April 1863, 6.
194. *Ibid.*, 6.
195. *ORN*, Series I, 9 (Washington, 1899), 127, 128.
196. *Ibid.*, 128–129.
197. *Ibid.*, 129.
198. Steven Roberts, "Captain Alexander Blakely, RA, "Original Inventor of Improvements in Cannon and the Greatest Artillerist of the Age" (London, 2012), 34.
199. *Ibid.*, 16.
200. "Liverpool News," *Glasgow Herald*, 13 April 1863, 4.
201. "Yankee Espionage in England," *London Evening Standard*, 23 April 1863, 5.
202. *Ibid.*, 5.
203. "Outlines of the Week," *Kentish Chronicle*, 25 April 1863, 5.
204. "The Spy System in Liverpool," *Liverpool Daily Post*, 17 April 1863, 4.
205. "Miscellaneous," *Leamington Spa Courier*, 23 May 1863, 5.
206. "Haymarket, Theatre Royal," *Era*, 7 June 1863, 8.
207. Bulloch, *The Secret Service of the Confederate States in Europe*. I (2012), 425.
208. Owsley, "Henry Shelton Sanford and Federal Surveillance Abroad, 1861–1865." *Mississippi Valley Historical Review* 48 (September 1961), 212.
209. *Ibid.*, 212.
210. *Ibid.*, 213.
211. "Mysterious Murder in Rhenish-Prussia, District of Coblenz, On the Rhine," *Cork Examiner*, 10 June 1861, 4; "'Insolvent Debtors' Court," *Morning Chronicle*, 8 April 1861, 8.
212. "Marriages" *London Evening Standard*, 5 June 1861, 7.
213. "Central Criminal Court," *Morning Post*, 9 May 1861, 7.
214. Owsley, "Henry Shelton Sanford and Federal Surveillance Abroad, 1861–1865." *Mississippi Valley Historical Review*. 48 (September 1961), 213.
215. *Ibid.*, 218.
216. "London Sketches," *Northampton Mercury*, 15 February 1862, 4, "Central Criminal Court" *Morning Post*, 9 May 1861, 7.
217. Milton, *Lincoln's Spymaster* (2003), 30.
218. Owsley, "Henry Shelton Sanford and Federal Surveillance Abroad, 1861–1865." *Mississippi Valley Historical Review*. 48 (September 1961), 227. Adams' secretary, Benjamin Moran, derisively referred to the energetic Sanford as "that Legation on Wheels."
219. *Ibid.*, 218–219. By the beginning of 1862, the intelligence system Sanford established was either disbanded or absorbed by the two networks run by Morse in London, and Dudley in Liverpool.
220. Stern, *The Confederate Navy* (1962), 166.
221. Milton, *Lincoln's Spymaster* (2003), 33–35, 79, 81.
222. *Ibid.*, 44, 82. Merli, *The Alabama* (2004), 67.
223. Stern, *The Confederate Navy* (1962), 166.
224. *Ibid.*, 166.
225. "The Steam Rams Seized at Birkenhead," *Liverpool Mercury*, 10 March 1864, 6.
226. *Ibid.*, 6.
227. TNA, FO 412/11 "Correspondence Respecting the Two-Ironclad Vessels Building at Messrs. Laird's Yard, Birkenhead," February to October 1863, 20.
228. Milton, *Lincoln's Spymaster* (2003), 32–33.
229. "Confederate Cruisers," *Liverpool Mercury*, 2 December 1863, 3.
230. *Hansard*, 27 March 1863, 170, cc 71.
231. Bulloch, *The Secret Service of the Confederate States in Europe*. I (2012), 418.
232. Milton, *Lincoln's Spymaster* (2003), 107.
233. "The Rebel Rams A Fit Case for Aid," *NYT*, 17 October 1864, 2.
234. *Ibid.*, 2, "The Steam Rams Seized at Birkenhead," *Liverpool Mercury*, 10 March 1864, 6.
235. "The Rebel Rams A Fit Case for Aid," *NYT*, 17 October 1864, 2.

Notes—Chapter Two

236. *Ibid.*, 2.
237. "Visit to Messrs Laird's Shipbuilding Yard," *Dundee Courier*, 19 September 1863, 2.
238. *Ibid.*, 2.
239. WA 5/195/39 &40 "Terms of Contract with Messrs A. Bravay & Co. 6 Rue de Londres Paris/for completing 2 Iron Screw Steamers," dated 16 June 1863.
240. *Ibid.*
241. "The Steam Ram Mystery," *Dundee, Perth, and Cupar Advertiser*, 8 September 1863, 3.
242. TNA, FO 412/11, "Correspondence Respecting the Two-Ironclad Vessels Building at Messrs. Laird's Yard, Birkenhead," No. 101, dated 18 June 1863.
243. *ORN*, II, 2 (1921), 509.
244. Gibbons, *Warships and Naval Battles of the Civil War* (1989), 66.
245. *Ibid.*, 66, *The Confederate Navy; The Ships, Men and Organization, 1861–65*. Edited by Dr. William N. Still, Jr. (1997), 26, 204–205.
246. Luraghi, *A History of the Confederate Navy* (1996), 287.
247. Barry, *The Dockyards, Shipyards, and Marine of France* (1864), 230.
248. "The Last Rebel Ram," *SA* XII (27 May 1865), 335.
249. "Trial Trip of One of the Mersey Steam Rams," *Liverpool Mercury*, 31 August 1864, 6, Philip Van Doren Stern, *The Confederate Navy* (New York, 1962), 222–223.
250. *Ibid.*, 247. "Naval and Military Intelligence," *London Evening Standard*, 14 August 1862, 6.
251. Barry, *The Dockyards, Shipyards, and Marine of France* (1864), 230.
252. Captain Thomas J. Page, C.S.N, "The Career of the Confederate Cruiser 'Stonewall.'" *Southern Historical Society Papers* 12 (Richmond, 1879), 263.
253. *Ibid.*, 263.
254. Gibbons, *Warships and Naval Battles of the Civil War* (1989), 66.
255. *ORN*, II, 2 (1921), 509.
256. *Ibid.*, 369.
257. *Ibid.*, 485–487.
258. *Ibid.*, 407.
259. Bulloch, *The Secret Service of the Confederate States in Europe.* II (2009). 233.
260. "Ship Launches on Saturday," *Liverpool Daily Post*, 6 July 1863, 5.
261. *Ibid.*, 5.
262. "Launch of Iron Steam 'Rams' at Birkenhead," *Sheffield Independent*, 31 August 1863, 3.
263. "The New Iron-clads in England," *SA*, 1009, 14, 3 October 1863, 214.
264. "Ship Launches on Saturday," *Liverpool Daily Post*, 6 July 1863, 5.
265. John Keegan, *The American Civil War: A Military History* (New York, 2009), 219.
266. *Ibid.*, 196, 201.
267. Bulloch, *The Secret Service of the Confederate States in Europe.* I (2012), 408, 410, 411.
268. *ORN*, II, 2 (1921), 456.
269. *Ibid.*, 456.
270. Bern Anderson, "The Naval Strategy of the Civil War," *Military Affairs* 26 (spring 1962), 14
271. Dan Blair, "One Good Port: Beaufort Harbor, North Carolina, 1863–1864," *The North Carolina Historical Review* 79 (July 2002), 302.
272. *Ibid.*, 310–311, 320.
273. *Ibid.*, 310, 314, 316, 317, 320.
274. James M. Barker, Henry W. Haynes, Samuel A. Green and Charles Francis Adams, "October Meeting. 1899 Tribute to Chief Justice Field; Tribute to Mr. W.W. Greenought; The Laird Rams; Memoir of Charles Francis Adams," *Proceeding of the Massachusetts Historical Society*, Second Series, 13 (1899–1900), 181, 182.
275. Gentry, "A Confederate Success in Europe: The Erlanger Loan," *The Journal of Southern History* 36 (May 1970), 173, 185.
276. *The Diary of Gideon Welles*, I (1911), 407.
277. *Ibid.*, 407.
278. Fuller, *Clad in Iron* (2008), n7, 340.
279. Bulloch, *The Secret Service of the Confederate States in Europe.* I (2012), 445.
280. Barker, Haynes, Green and Adams, "October Meeting. 1899 Tribute to Chief Justice Field; Tribute to Mr. W.W. Greenought; The Laird Rams; Memoir of Charles Francis Adams," *Proceeding of the Massachusetts Historical Society*, Second Series, 13 (1899–1900), 180.
281. "The American Navy in the Late War," *The Living Age* 90 (8 September 1866), 597, Henry Baldwin, "Farragut in Mobile Bay," *Scribner's Monthly* 13 (February 1877), 542.
282. Paul H. Silverstone, *Civil War Navies, 1855–1883* (New York, 2006), xx, xxi.
283. *Ibid.*, xxi, Ross, *Cities and Camps of the Confederate States* (1997), 151, "The Late Naval Engagement," *Dublin Evening Mail*, 30 June 1864, 4. This newspaper account compared the *Alabama*'s 100-pounder Blakely RML with the *Kearsarge*'s two 11-inch Dahlgren smoothbores, where Captain Blakely asserted that had the *Alabama* steel shot or shell ammunition for that gun, it could have fired from a distance "a full mile further than the smoothbores" of the *Kearsarge*.
284. "Mr. Whitworth and the 'Ironsides,'" *Aldershot Military Gazette*, 4 October 1862, 4; "Experiments at Shoeburyness," *Sheffield Daily Telegraph*, 2 August 1864, 7.
285. "English and American Ironclads," *Greenock Advertiser*, 5 May 1863, 4.
286. TNA, ADM 1/6083, *Director Naval Ordnance, In-Letters and Papers, 1860–1869*, 2.
287. *Ibid.*, no page.
288. Baldwin, "Farragut in Mobile Bay," *Scribner's Monthly* 13 (February 1877), 542.
289. Gibbons, *Warships and Naval Battles of the Civil War* (1989), 31, 33, 57, 58, 69, WA ZCL/005/0195/039/040, Description of Laird Rams, likely for Bravay of Paris, dated July 1863.

290. Anne Kelly Knowles, "Labor, Race, and Technology in the Confederate Iron Industry," *Technology and Culture* 42 (January 2001), 15.
291. *Ibid.*, 13–14.
292. David G. Surdam, "Northern Naval Superiority and the Economics of the American Civil War," *The Journal of Economic History* 56 (June 1996), 475.
293. Library of Congress, *The Abraham Lincoln Papers*, Letter from Assistant Secretary of the U.S. Navy Gustavus V. Fox, 8 September 1863.
294. No Subject, *Ashtabula Weekly Telegraph*, 26 September 1863, 2.
295. *ORN*. I, 14 (Washington 1902), 419.
296. *Ibid.*, 419.
297. Bulloch, *The Secret Service of the Confederate States in Europe*. I (2012), 445.
298. Marshall J. Bastable, *Arms and the State: Sir William Armstrong and the Remaking of British Naval Power 1854–1914* (Aldershot, 2004), 126.
299. *Ibid.*, 126, 127.
300. "The Last Phase of the Armstrong Gun," *SA* 6 (10 May 1862), 297.
301. "W," "The Alleged Failure of the Armstrong Gun," *Living Age* 80 (20 February 1864), 384.
302. *Ibid.*, 384.
303. Bastable, *Arms and the State* (2004), 127.
304. *Ibid.*, 127.
305. *Ibid.*, 127–128.
306. "Built for the Confederacy," *The Sun*, 28 June 1903, 2.
307. Various Authors, *The Nautical Magazine and Naval Chronicle for 1864* (Cambridge 2013), 101.
308. Spencer, *The Confederate Navy in Europe* (1983), 85.
309. "Royal Proclamation," *Reynold's Newspaper*, 19 May 1861, 10.
310. William H. Roberts, *Civil War Ironclads: The U.S. Navy and Industrial Mobilization* (Baltimore, 2002), 62, 133.
311. *ORN*. II, 1 (1921), 133, 228.
312. *ORN*. II, 2 (1921), 683, 694–695.
313. *Ibid.*, 683.
314. "The Federal Government and England's Neutral Rights," *Westmorland Gazette*, 26 September 1863, 2.
315. *Confidential Correspondence of Gustavus Vasa Fox*, II (1918), 331–332.
316. *Ibid.*, 331–332, 345.
317. *Ibid.*, 345.
318. Admiral C.C. Penrose Fitzgerald, *Memories of the Sea* (1913), 181.
319. Milledge Louis Bonham, *The British Consuls in the Confederacy* (New York, 1911), 91, 93–94.
320. *Ibid.*, 174–176.
321. William Watson, *Life in the Confederate Army, Being the Observations and Experiences of an Alien in the South during the American Civil War* (1887, reprinted New York, 1983), 123.
322. LOC, "Report of Trials in England of Various Parties for Violation of the Foreign Enlistment Act, in Recruiting for the Rebel Vessels, Case of Jones and Highatt." *United States Serial Set*, Number 1397, Appendix No. XIV (Washington, 1869), 553, 554.
323. LOC, "Proceedings Before the Crown Court at Cork in the Case of the Men received on Board the United States Steamer Kearsarge at Queenstown." *United States Serial Set*, Number 1397, Appendix No. XIII (Washington, 1869), 547, 548.
324. *Ibid.*, 548.
325. TNA, FO 881/2011 "Florida." No. 70, dated 23 September 1863; No. 71, dated 1 October 1863; No. 73, dated 22 September 1863. Printed November 1871.
326. "Visit to Messrs Laird's Shipbuilding Yard," *Dundee Courier*, 19 September 1863, 2.
327. *Ibid.*, 2.
328. "Another 'Ram' for a 'French' House," *Liverpool Daily Post*, 31 August 1863, 5.
329. *Ibid.*, 5.
330. "Launch of Iron Steam 'Rams' at Birkenhead," *Sheffield Independent*, 31 August 1863, 3.
331. TNA, TS 25/1274, Letter from Thomas Dudley, United States Consulate, Liverpool, 7 August 1863.
332. *Ibid.*
333. WA 005/0195, "Dimensions and Particulars of Vessels Vol. 2," "Green Book No. 2," (No Date), 039–040.
334. *Ibid.*
335. "News of the Day," *Liverpool Daily Post*, 29 August 1863, 4.
336. *Ibid.*, 4.
337. "British Neutrality," *The Living Age*, 77, 985, 18 April 1863, 138.
338. "American Slavery and its Abettors," *Dundee, Perth, and Cupar Advertiser*, 28 April 1863, 2.
339. No Title, *Devizes and Wiltshire Gazette*, 22 October 1863, 3.
340. LOC, "Correspondence Between Her Majesty's Government and Messr. Laird Brothers Relative to the Iron-Clad Rams." *United States Serial Set*, Number 1397, Senate Executive Department No. 11, Volume 4, 41st Congress Appendix No. XIII (Washington, 1869), 260.
341. *Ibid.*, 260.
342. *Ibid.*, 261.
343. "Correspondence between England and America about British Neutrality," *Daily Dispatch*, 1 February 1864, 1.
344. "Miscellaneous," *NYT*, 28 June 1855, 1.
345. *Hansard*, 27 March 1863, 170, cc 69, 70.
346. "Mr. J. Laird, M. P., and the United States Government," *Cheshire Observer*, 29 August 1863, 7.
347. *Ibid.*, 7. See TNA, ADM 231/5, Admiralty: *Foreign Intelligence Committee*, Report No. 43, "Eastern Siberian Ports and Anchorages" dated

January 1885, 61. The *America*, built by New York shipbuilder William H. Webb and completed in 1856, was 166 feet long, had a 28.4-foot beam, and a draft of 10 feet aft, 8 feet forward. Her engines produced 140 nominal horsepower and she displaced 554.67 tons. This steamer remained on service with the local defense force known as the "Siberian Flotilla" at Vladivostok until summer 1884, when she was reportedly sold at auction.

348. Bulloch, *The Secret Service of the Confederate States in Europe*. I (2012), 83.
349. "Mechanics for Russia," *SA* 10 (25 August 1855), 395.
350. "War News," *SA* 10 (21 July 1855), 355.
351. Various authors, *The Nautical Magazine and Naval Chronicle for 1864* (Cambridge 2013), 100.
352. "Value of Plain Talk," *Omaha Daily Bee*, 1 March 1898, 4.
353. TNA, FO 412/11, "Correspondence Respecting the Two-Ironclad Vessels Building at Messrs. Laird's Yard, Birkenhead," No. 101, dated 22 September 1863.
354. *Ibid.*
355. Foreman, *A World on Fire* (2010), 521.
356. Fuller, *Clad in Iron* (2008), 232.
357. "The Fleet and the Rams," *Liverpool Daily Post*, 15 September 1863, 5.
358. *Ibid.*, 5.
359. TNA, FO 412/11, "Correspondence Respecting the Two-Ironclad Vessels Building at Messrs. Laird's Yard, Birkenhead," No. 112, dated 28 September 1863, 76; Parkes, *British Battleships* (1966), 82.
360. TNA, FO 412/11, "Correspondence Respecting the Two-Ironclad Vessels Building at Messrs. Laird's Yard, Birkenhead," No. 112, dated 28 September 1863, 76.
361. *Ibid.*, 76.
362. *Ibid.*, 76–77.
363. *Hansard*, 27 February 1863, 169, cc 887, 888.
364. *Hansard*, 26 February 1863, 169, cc 798–802.
365. *Ibid.*, cc 834.
366. *Hansard*, 23 February 1863, 169, cc 669, 700.
367. TNA, FO 412/11, "Correspondence Respecting the Two-Ironclad Vessels Building at Messrs. Laird's Yard, Birkenhead," No. 112, dated 28 September 1863, 77.
368. *Ibid.*, 77.
369. TNA, ADM 1/5842, *Admiralty Correspondence*, "Steam Rams on the Mersey," letter written by James Reed, 17 September 1863, 4–5.
370. *Ibid.*, 8–9.
371. *Ibid.*, 10–13.
372. TNA, PRO 30/22, "Private Correspondence. Lord Palmerston (P) Prime Minister to Lord Russell (JR) Foreign Secretary," Volume 22, letter dated 4 September 1863, 243.
373. *Ibid.*, letter dated 21 September 1863, 258–259.
374. *Ibid.*, letters dated, 23 August 1863, 239–240, 4 September 1863, 243.
375. *Ibid.*, letter dated 21 September 1863, 258, 259.
376. TNA, F.O. 881/1200, "United States: Corres. Iron-Clad Vessels Building at Messrs. Laird's Yard Birkenhead," Part 1. Feb.–Oct 1863, 100–101, LOC, "Correspondence Between Her Majesty's Government and Messr. Laird Brothers Relative to the Iron-Clad Rams," *United States Serial Set*, Number 1397, Senate Executive Department No. 11, Volume 4, 41st Congress Appendix No. XIII (Washington, 1869), 264.
377. TNA, F.O. 881/1200, "United States: Corres. Iron-Clad Vessels Building at Messrs. Laird's Yard Birkenhead," Part 1. Feb.–Oct 1863, 100–101.
378. LOC, "Correspondence Between Her Majesty's Government and Messr. Laird Brothers Relative to the Iron-Clad Rams." *United States Serial Set*, Number 1397, Senate Executive Department No. 11, Volume 4, 41st Congress Appendix No. XIII (Washington, 1869), 264.
379. TNA, F.O. 881/2006, "Foreign Office Confidential Print, United States: Corres. Iron-Clad Vessels Building at Messrs. Laird's Yard Birkenhead," 1863–1864, 89, 119.
380. "The Confederate Rams in England," *SA* 9 (28 November 1863), 343.
381. "Capture of Mr. Laird's Iron Rams," *Dundee, Perth, and Cupar Advertiser*, 3 November 1863, 8.
382. "The Ram of Liverpool," *Living Age*, 79, 1019, 12 December 1863, 528.
383. "The Confederate Rams in England," *SA* 9 (28 November 1863), 343.
384. Ballard, *The Black Battlefleet* (1980), 121.
385. *Ibid.*, 121, Lyon and Winfield, *The Sail & Steam Navy List* (2004), 237, "The Disaster to the Prince Consort," *Dublin Evening Mail*, 31 October 1863, 2.
386. Ballard, *The Black Battlefleet* (1980), 121.
387. *Ibid.*, 122.
388. "Departure of the Prince Consort for Devonport," *Dublin Evening Mail*, 5 November 1863, 2.
389. LOC, "Correspondence Between Her Majesty's Government and Messr. Laird Brothers Relative to the Iron-Clad Rams." *United States Serial Set*, Number 1397, Senate Executive Department No. 11, Volume 4, 41st Congress Appendix No. XIII (Washington, 1869), 264.
390. *Ibid.*, 266.
391. TNA, TS 25/1285, "IRON CLAD SHIPS: Vessels under seizure: To Determine their Destination and Ownership," letter dated 29 October 1863.
392. *Ibid.*
393. LOC, "Correspondence Between Her Majesty's Government and Messr. Laird Brothers Relative to the Iron-Clad Rams." *United States Serial Set*, Number 1397, Senate Executive

Department No. 11, Volume 4, 41st Congress Appendix No. XIII (Washington, 1869), 270.
394. *Ibid.*, 270
395. *Ibid.*, 271.
396. TNA, F.O. 881/2006, "Foreign Office Confidential Print, United States: Corres. Iron-Clad Vessels Building at Messrs. Laird's yard Birkenhead," 1863–1864, 171.
397. *Ibid.*, 171.
398. Archibald, *The Fighting Ships in the Royal Navy AD 897–1984* (1984), 111.
399. "The use of armour in the Royal Navy," *Hampshire Telegraph*, 30 January 1886, 2.
400. TNA, ADM 1/5842, *Admiralty Correspondence*, "Steam Rams on the Mersey," letter written by James Reed, 17 September 1863, 10–13.
401. Archibald, *The Fighting Ships in the Royal Navy AD 897–1984* (1984), 111.

Chapter Three

1. Lautenschlager, "Technology and the Evolution of Naval Warfare," *International Security*, 8 (Fall, 1983), 7.
2. "A Naval Revolution," *Reynolds's Newspaper*, 9 November 1873, 2; William Ashworth, "Aspects of Late Victorian Naval Administration," *The Economic History Review*, 22 (December 1969), 494.
3. Baxter, *The Introduction of the Ironclad Warship* (2001), 319.
4. Sandler, *The Emergence of the Modern Capital Ship* (1979), 188, 294. Palmerston wrote this in a letter to the First Lord of the Admiralty, the Duke of Somerset, in mid-September 1863, before the rams were seized.
5. TNA, ADM 1/5842, *Admiralty Correspondence,* "Steam Rams on the Mersey," letter written by James Reed, 17 September 1863, 14.
6. Reed, *Our Iron-clad Ships* (2011), 96.
7. Parkes, *British Battleships* (1966), 78.
8. *Conway's All the World's Fighting Ships 1860–1945.* Editor Roger Chesneau (London, 1979), 19–20.
9. Baxter, *The Introduction of the Ironclad Warship* (2001), 320–321.
10. "Trial of Her Majesty's Turret Ram Scorpion," *Manchester Courier and Lancashire General Advertiser.* 31 August 1864, 3.
11. *Ibid.*, 3. "H.M.S. Scorpion," *Hampshire Advertiser*, 25 March 1865, 8; Reed, *Our Iron-clad Ships* (2011), 96.
12. "Trial Trip of H.M.S. Wivern," *Manchester Courier and Lancashire General Advertiser.* 10 June 1865, 11. She would require further work on her engines after she left Birkenhead on her first commission. See ADM 135/512, Office of the Controller of the Navy Ship's Book Series I, "*Wivern.*"
13. Reed, *Our Iron-clad Ships* (2011), 96.
14. Parkes, British *Battleships* (1966), 80, "H.M.S. Wivern, Double-Turreted Iron-Clad [sic] Steam-Ram," *ILN*, 16 December 1865, 594.
15. "H. M. Turret-Ships Wivern and Scorpion," *Illustrated Times*, 4 November 1865, 282.
16. "The Collison with the Scorpion," *Cheshire Observer*, 1 April 1865, 7, "Collison with the Scorpion," *Manchester Courier and Lancashire General Advertiser.* 30 March 1865, 2.
17. "The Collison with the Scorpion," *Cheshire Observer*, 1 April 1865, 7; *Sheffield Daily Telegraph*, 31 March 1865, 2; "Collison with Her Majesty's Ship 'Scorpion,'" *Hampshire Telegraph*, 1 April 1865, 4.
18. "Accident to the Screw-Steamer Balaclava," *Belfast News-Letter*, 25 February 1865, 3.
19. *Ibid.*, 3, "Miscellaneous," *North Wales Chronicle*, 25 March 1865, 2; Lyon and Winfield, *The Sail & Steam Navy List* (2004), 189.
20. "Departure from the Mersey of the Ram Scorpion," *Liverpool Mercury*, 20 March 1865, 7.
21. "Turret Ships," *London Evening Standard*, 11 November 1865, 5.
22. TNA, WO 55/2182, Records of Ordnance Office, Portsmouth, "*No. 7 Minute Book" May to November 1865,*" 477.
23. "Turret Ships," *London Evening Standard*, 11 November 1865, 5, "Naval and Military News," *Hampshire Telegraph*, 16 October 1869, 4.
24. *Hansard*, 13 June 1867, 187, 1790, 1811–1812.
25. TNA, WO 55/2182, Records of Ordnance Office, Portsmouth, "*No. 7 Minute Book, May to November. 1865.*" 110, 326.
26. *Ibid.*, 142, 152, 269.
27. *Ibid.*, 384, 544.
28. "Trial Trip of Her Majesty's Ship Wivern," *London Evening Standard*, 6 October 1865, 3; *Hampshire Advertiser*, 30 December 1865, 12.
29. "Naval Armaments," *Liverpool Daily Post*, 25 September 1867, 10.
30. "Trial Trip of H.M.S. Wivern," *Manchester Courier and Lancashire General Advertiser.* 10 June 1865, 11.
31. "The Birkenhead Rams, Scorpion and Wyvern [sic]," *Manchester Courier and Lancashire General Advertiser.* 12 September 1865, 4.
32. *Ibid.*, 4; David K. Brown, *Warrior to Dreadnought: Warships Design and Development 1860–1905* (Barnsley, 1997), 68.
33. "The Birkenhead Rams, Scorpion and Wyvern [sic]," *Manchester Courier and Lancashire General Advertiser.* 12 September 1865, 4.
34. TNA, ADM 135/512, Office of the Controller of the Navy Ship's Book Series I, "*Wivern.*"
35. "H. M. S. Wyvern [sic]," *Liverpool Daily Post*, 10 October 1865, 10. Of course the forecastle and poop decks would also require removal to permit all-around fire.
36. "The Laird Rams," *SA*, 10, 1 October 1864, 224.
37. *Ibid.*, 224.
38. "The Birkenhead Rams, Scorpion and Wyvern [sic]," *Manchester Courier and Lancashire General Advertiser.* 12 September 1865, 4.
39. *Ibid.*, 4.

40. Ballard, *The Black Battlefleet* (1980), 21, USNHC Photo #NH 52526, "H.M.S. Wivern At anchor in the Hamoaze River, off Plymouth, England, in 1865"; "Armour-Plated Iron Turret Ship, The Scorpion," *Illustrated London Almanack for 1869*, 34.
41. C. I. Hamilton, "The Victorian Navy," *The Historical Journal*, 25 (June 1982), 479.
42. Adrian Jarvis, "Protection and Decoration: A Tentative Investigation into Painting Ships Before the Great War," *The Great Circle*, 22 (2000), 24, 25, 27.
43. *Ibid.*, 27, 32, 36.
44. *Ibid.*, 26, 33.
45. Ballard, *The Black Battlefleet* (1980), 215, 217.
46. *Ibid.*, 215.
47. NMM, Ship Plans, "Devonport Yard, "Wivern," Curator 14142, Box 101. Each stanchion resembled an elongated capital letter "A" placed on end.
48. *Ibid.*, "The Royal Sovereign," *Western Daily Press*, 11 November 1864; 3, "The Volunteer Review at Dover: View of Dover from the Sea—The Naval Squadron Attacking the Forts," *ILN*, 10 April 1869, 356, 357.
49. "The Laird Rams," *SA*, 10, 1 October 1864, 224.
50. TNA, ADM 53/9512, *Ship's Log* H.M.S. *Scorpion*, 2 December 1868–31 December 1869.
51. Ward, *Steam for the Million* (1860), 117.
52. "H. M. S. Wyvern [sic]," *Liverpool Daily Post*, 10 October 1865, 10.
53. R. F. Scheltema de Heere, "The Prins Hendrik der Nederlanden," *The Mariner's Mirror*. 17 (Cambridge, 1931), 51.
54. Andrew Lambert, *Battleships in Transition: The Creations of the Steam Battlefleet 1815–1860* (London, 1984), 55, 58.
55. *Ibid.*, 63; Lyon and Winfield, *The Sail & Steam Navy List* (2004), 182, 184, 187; *The Advent of Steam*, Editor Robert Gardiner, Consultant Editor Dr. Basil Greenhill (London, 1992), 183.
56. TNA, ADM 1/5842, *Admiralty Correspondence*, "Steam Rams on the Mersey," letter written by James Reed, 17 September 1863, 13. Reed did not specifically mention which ship he was referring to regarding rigging and masts, but the *294* had masts and yards nearly ready by that time, whereas the *295* was a recently launched hull, devoid of masts and most topside fittings.
57. TNA, ADM 53/9512, *Ship's Log* H.M.S. *Scorpion*, 2 December 1868–31 December 1869.
58. *Ibid.*
59. TNA, ADM 135/417, Office of the Controller of the Navy Ship's Book Series 1, "H.M.S. *Scorpion*." See TNA, ADM 1/5842, *Admiralty Correspondence*, "Steam Rams on the Mersey," letter written by James Reed, 17 September 1863, 13. Reed remarked the engines of the Laird rams were well-designed, well-made, and were "in no way inferior, in my opinion, to the engines of like power in the Royal Navy."

60. TNA, ADM 135/417, Office of the Controller of the Navy Ship's Book Series 1, "H.M.S. *Scorpion*."
61. ADM 135/512, Office of the Controller of the Navy Ship's Book Series I, "Wivern."
62. *Ibid.*, "H.M. Turret-Ships Wivern and Scorpion," *Illustrated Times*, 4 November 1865, 282.
63. ADM 135/512, Office of the Controller of the Navy Ship's Book Series I, "Wivern."
64. *Ibid.*
65. "H. M. S. Wyvern [sic]," *Liverpool Daily Post*, 10 October 1865, 10, TNA, ADM 135/417, Office of the Controller of the Navy Ship's Book Series 1, "H.M.S. *Scorpion*."
66. *Exeter Flying Post*, 8 November 1865, 5.
67. "The French Fleet at Portsmouth," *Reading Mercury*, 2 September 1865, 2.
68. "The French Fleet at Portsmouth," *Cork Examiner*, 2 September 1865, 4.
69. "The French Fleet at Portsmouth," *Leeds Mercury*, 1 September 1865, 4.
70. *Ibid.*, 4.
71. "H.M. Turret-Ships Wivern and Scorpion," *Liverpool Daily Post*, 10 October 1865, 10.
72. *Ibid.*, 10, WA, 005/0030, "Dimensions and Particulars of Vessels Vol. 2, "Green Book No. 2," 67.
73. E. J. Reed, *Shipbuilding in Iron and Steel* (London, 1869), 13, 518.
74. "The Birkenhead Rams, Scorpion and Wyvern [sic]," *Manchester Courier and Lancashire General Advertiser*, 12 September 1865, 4.
75. "Naval and Military," *Bath Chronicle and Weekly Gazette*, 17 August 1865, 7.
76. "The Fleet at Cherbourg," *Times*, 15 August 1865, 7.
77. "H.M. Turret-Ships Wivern and Scorpion," *Illustrated Times*, 4 November 1865, 282.
78. *Ibid.*, 282; Parkes, *British Battleships* (1966), 78.
79. "Sea-Going Turret Ships-III," *London Daily News*, 18 October 1870, 2.
80. Ballard, *The Black Battlefleet* (1980), 105.
81. *Ibid.*, 105, TNA, ADM 1/5842, *Admiralty Correspondence*, "Specification of Cowper Phipps Coles Masts," 10 April 1862, 2. The mast was stepped to the "kelson" and attached at the main deck, while the two side tubes were fitted to the "bilge" and also attached or "keyed" to the deck. They were joined to the mast at their upper edges, and a separate tube was fitted above the main mast to form the top mast.
82. TNA, ADM 135/417, Office of the Controller of the Navy Ship's Book Series 1, "H.M.S. *Scorpion*."
83. *Ibid.*
84. "H. M. S. Wyvern [sic]," *Liverpool Daily Post*, 10 October 1865, 10, TNA ADM 135/417; Office of the Controller of the Navy Ship's Book Series 1, "H.M.S. *Scorpion*."
85. Arthur J. Marder, *The Anatomy of British Sea Power* (New York, 1976), 135.
86. "The Invasion of England," *Cheshire Observer*, 26 August 1865, 8.

87. *Ibid.*, 8.
88. "The Launch of H.M.S. Monarch," *London Daily News,* 26 May 1868; 5, Theodore Ropp, *The Development of a Modern Navy: French Naval Policy 1871–1904.* Edited by Stephen S. Roberts (Annapolis, 1987), 13, 16–17; Sandler, *The Emergence of the Modern Capital Ship* (1979), 70–71; TNA, ADM 231/3, *Admiralty: Foreign Intelligence Committee,* "France Effective Armourclads," dated 1 January 1884, 3. The former Union double-turreted monitor *Onondaga,* purchased by France after the Civil War, was referred to as coastal defense ironclad or a "Garde-Côtes Cuirassés," and was assigned to local defense duties at Brest.
89. NMM HND/101/3, Journal of Sub-Lieutenant Swinton C. Holland, *H.M.S Wivern,* September–December 1865
90. "Trial of Her Majesty's Turret Ram Scorpion," *Manchester Courier and Lancashire General Advertiser.* 31 August 1864, 3.
91. TNA, ADM 1/5842, *Admiralty Correspondence,* letter by Controller of the Navy, Rear Admiral Robert Spencer Robinson, dated 6 October 1863. Robinson also noted Coles wanted to fit tripod masts to the *Royal Sovereign,* but Robinson wrote both this ironclad and the *Prince Albert* were "not intended to be masted."
92. "Naval and Military," *London Daily News,* 30 October 1865, 2.
93. *Ibid.,* 2.
94. "Who's to Blame?" *Hampshire Telegraph,* 18 December 1869, 4. This source reported that while other warships sheltered in harbor, the steam ship-of-the-line *Donegal* was damaged during the same storm as she struggled down the Channel. She consumed at least 40 tons of coal for very limited headway against the heavy sea.
95. Captain Thomas J. Page, C.S.N., "The Career of the Confederate Cruiser 'Stonewall.'" *Southern Historical Society Papers,* Volume 7, No. 6 (Richmond, 1879), 263.
96. Scheltema de Heere, "The Prins Hendrik der Nederlanden." *The Mariner's Mirror.* Volume 17 (Cambridge, 1931), 49.
97. *Ibid.,* 46, 49, 50. Jensen performed his test during a storm that sank other vessels; the conclusion was that, if handled with caution, the low-hulled turret ship was adequately safe at sea. Once her heavy rig (including tripod fore and main masts) were removed and replaced with two slender signal poles, the Dutch turret ship shed 66 tons of weight aloft and her performance as a seaboat improved.
98. *Hansard,* 5 June 1866, 183, cc 1940, 1941.
99. "Turret Ships," *London Evening Standard,* 10 January 1866, 3.
100. *Ibid.,* 3.
101. *Ibid.,* 3.
102. *Hansard,* 8 March 1869, 194, cc 887.
103. Richard Millman, *British Foreign Policy and the Coming of the Franco-Prussian War* (Oxford, 1965), 152 n3.
104. *Hansard,* 8 March 1869, 194, cc 889, 890.
105. Millman, *British Foreign Policy and the Coming of the Franco-Prussian War* (1965), 150–151.
106. "The Channel Fleet," *Manchester Courier and Lancashire General Advertiser.* 9 October 1866, 3.
107. "Squandering the Taxes," *Liverpool Daily Post,* 13 October 1866, 7.
108. Brown, *Warrior to Dreadnought* (1997), 14.
109. "H.M.S. Wyvern [*sic*] in a swell of the Atlantic," *ILN,* 27 October 1866, 413.
110. *Ibid.,* 413.
111. "H.M.S. Wyvern [*sic*] in a Heavy Sea in the Channel," *Ibid.,* 413.
112. Fitzgerald, *Memories of the Sea* (1913), 309. Fitzgerald stated the funnels were heavy and the process by which the stokers winched up each section was both laborious and time-consuming.
113. *Ibid.,* 310; *Hampshire Advertiser,* 8 June 1872, 8.
114. Fitzgerald, *Memories of the Sea* (1913), 310.
115. "Squandering the Taxes," *Liverpool Daily Post,* 13 October 1866, 7.
116. "The Channel Fleet," *Manchester Courier and Lancashire General Advertiser.* 9 October 1866, 3.
117. *Hansard,* 2 April 1869, 195, cc 110.
118. *Ibid.,* cc 110, 111.
119. "Squandering the Taxes," *Liverpool Daily Post,* 13 October 1866, 7.
120. "The Cruise of the Channel Squadron," *Dublin Evening Mail,* 20 October 1866, 4,
121. "The Channel Fleet," *Sherborne Mercury,* 9 October 1866, 5.
122. *Ibid.,* 5.
123. Matthew Allen, "The Deployment of Untried Technology: British Naval Tactics in the Ironclad Era," *War in History,* 15 (01 July 2008), 269.
124. *Hansard,* 15 March 1866, 182, cc 345.
125. NMM, HND/101/3, Journal of Sub-Lieutenant Swinton C. Holland, H.M.S *Wivern,* September–December 1865.
126. *Ibid.*
127. TNA, ADM 53/8418, *Ship's Log* H.M.S. *Scorpion,* 10 July 1865 to 1 January 1866.
128. Lambert, *Battleships in Transition* (1984), 62–63. Political considerations during these years forced the Royal Navy to use "Baxter's Mixture," a blend of two-thirds Welsh, and one-third North Country coal. This was due to pressure from a Secretary to the Admiralty (and M.P. from Dundee), William Edward Baxter. Clouds of smoke from the poorer quality coal hindered safe navigation during fleet maneuvers and evolutions, and continued use of this coal was denounced by leading naval leaders, who pushed successfully for the switch to the cleaner Welsh coal. See Fleet Engineer R. C. Oldknow, R.N, "Trial Trips: Ancient

and Modern," *The Navy and Army Illustrated*, 20 March 1896, 146.
129. Lambert, *Battleships in Transition* (1984), 62.
130. *Ibid.* 63.
131. *Hansard*, 31 May 1894, 25, cc 11; *Hansard*, 18 July 1898, 62, cc 77–78.
132. *Hansard*, 15 March 1866, 182, cc 345.
133. *Ibid.*, cc 331.
134. *Hansard*, 2 April 1869, 195, cc 119.
135. *Ibid.*, cc. 118.
136. *Hansard*, 15 March 1866, 182, cc 331.
137. *Ibid.*, cc 342. The *Monadnock* was fitted with a square sail and jib during her voyage, and added 1.5 knots to her speed on average. See Commander John D. Alden, U.S.N. (Ret.), "The Old Navy: Monitors "Round Cape Horn," *Proceedings Magazine*, 100 (September 1974), 79.
138. *Hansard,* 15 March 1866, 182, 342, 343. Also see Howard J. Fuller, "Chilean Standoff," *Naval History*, 25 (June 2011), 1–3. This voyage also demonstrated the ironclad power of the United States, as Fuller holds, the American monitor fleet "spelled doom for the presence of France in Mexico" and the *Monadnock* was an uncomfortable surprise to the Spanish squadron at anchor in Valparaiso harbor in March 1866 (which included their flagship, the armored frigate *Numancia*) when Spain was at war with her former colonies of Bolivia, Chile, Ecuador, and Peru.
139. *Hansard*, 1 March 1866, 181, cc 1345.
140. *Hansard*, 15 March 1866, 182, cc 331.
141. "Imperial Parliament," *London Evening Standard*, 21 July 1866, 3.
142. "The American Monitor Miantonomoh," *Hull Packet*, 22 June 1866, 7.
143. *Ibid.*, 7.
144. Fuller, *Clad in Iron* (2008), 274–275.
145. *Ibid.*, 272–273
146. *Ibid.*, 273, 275.
147. "The American Monitor Miantonomoh," *Hull Packet*, 22 June 1866, 7.
148. *London Daily News*, 19 April 1867, 4.
149. "Naval and Military Intelligence," *London Evening Standard*, 24 August 1867, 3.
150. "Naval and Military News," *Hampshire Telegraph*, 26 June 1867, 2.
151. "A New Trade in Birmingham, Wire Rope Making," *Birmingham Daily Post*, 2 April 1866, 5.
152. "New Steel Wire," *SA*, 14, 12 March 1859, 221. This source reports the Admiralty standards for steel rope led to changes in rigging, and the steel version was over three times the strength of a similar gauge of iron rope.
153. "Rope Trade," *Aberdeen Journal*, 8 January 1868, 7.
154. "New Steel Wire," *SA*, 14, 12 March 1859, 221.
155. "Steel Ropes," *SA*, 13 (23 December 1865), 405; "A New Trade in Birmingham, Wire Rope Making," *Birmingham Daily Post*, 2 April 1866, 5; "The Science of Iron and Steel," *SA*, 8, 14 February 1863, 105.

156. "Naval and Military News," *Hampshire Telegraph*, 13 November 1867, 2; Lyon and Winfield, *The Sail & Steam Navy List* (2004), 293.
157. "The Sultan in England," *Exeter and Plymouth Gazette*, 17 July 1867, 9.
158. "The Review of 1867," *Hampshire Telegraph*, 20 July 1867, 4.
159. *Hampshire Telegraph*, 21 August 1867, 1.
160. "Magistrates Office-Tuesday," *Surrey Advertiser*, 27 January 1866, 2.
161. "Courts Martial on board the *Duke of Wellington*," *Hampshire Telegraph*, 12 January 1870, 2.
162. *Cork Examiner*, 23 September 1867, 2.
163. "Stations of the British Navy," *Bath Chronicle and Weekly Gazette*, 29 August 1867, 2; "Preparations of the Admiralty," *Dublin Evening Mail*, 21 September 1867, 3.
164. "Ireland," *Morning Post*, 23 September 1867, 8.
165. *Ibid.*, 8.
166. "Kelly and Deasey-Searching a Greek Vessel," *Dublin Evening Mail*, 2 October 1867, 4.
167. "Escape of Colonel Kelly and Capt. Deasey," *Dublin Evening Mail*, 20 September 1867, 3; "Colonel Kelly the Fenian Leader, in Manchester," *Manchester Courier and Lancashire General Advertiser*, 18 September 1867, 3.
168. Padraig O Concubhair, *The Fenians Were Dreadful Men: The 1867 Rising* (Cork, 2011), 146–147.
169. *Ibid.*, 149.
170. Oliver P. Rafferty, *The Church, the State and the Fenian Threat, 1861–75 (*London, 1999), 89, 93, 169 n 99.
171. "Intended Rescue at Holyhead," *Cork Examiner*, 15 November 1867, 3.
172. *Ibid.*, 3.
173. "Explosion on Board H.M.S. Wivern," *Liverpool Mercury*, 21 November 1867, 5.
174. *Ibid.*, 5, *Morning Post*, 18 November 1867, 3.
175. "Naval and Military Intelligence," *Morning Post*, 18 November 1867, 3.
176. "A Novel Armament," *Dublin Evening Mail*, 18 February 1868, 4.
177. "Heavy Guns for the Navy," *Newcastle Journal*, 22 November 1867, 4.
178. *Ibid.*, 4; Marshall J. Bastable, *Arms and the State: Sir William Armstrong and the Remaking of British Naval Power 1854–1914* (Aldershot, 2004), 97.
179. "H.M. Turret-Ships Wivern and Scorpion," *Illustrated Times*, 4 November 1865, 282.
180. Bastable, *Arms and the State* (2004), 97–98; "Compound Ordnance," *Dublin Evening Mail*, 10 October 1863, 4.
181. Henrietta Heald, *William Armstrong: Magician of the North* (Newcastle, 2010), 112.
182. "The Accident on the Thunderer," *Times*, 13 January 1879, 10.
183. "Heavy Guns for the Navy," *Newcastle Journal*, 22 November 1867, 4.
184. TNA, ADM 186/869, *Manual of Gun-*

nery for Her Majesty's Fleet 1885 (London, 1886), 39.

185. *Ibid.*, 39.

186. TNA, ADM 1/6083, "Diagram Shewing Construction of the Experimental 9 Inch 12 ton Guns" (Gun Nos. 298, 332 & 333), *Letters, Director of Naval Ordnance* 1868.

187. Sandler, *The Emergence of the Modern Capital Ship* (1979), 103.

188. Fitzgerald, *Memories of the Sea* (London, 1913), 298.

189. TNA, ADM 53/8623, *Ship's Log* H.M.S. *Royal Sovereign,* 15 October 1864 to 10 October 1866.

190. Lyon and Winfield, *The Sail & Steam Navy List* (2004), 139.

191. TNA, ADM 268/97, *Report of a Committee of Naval Officers, Appointed to Examine the Design of a Sea-Going Turret-Ship, submitted by Captain C.P. Coles, R.N* (1865), 17.

192. *Ibid.*, 17.

193. TNA, ADM 135/417, "Office of the Controller of the Navy Ship's Book Series 1, H.M.S. *Scorpion.*"

194. "The Royal Marine Artillery," *Portsmouth Evening News,* 10 October 1879, 2; "The Royal Marine Artillery," *Dundee Evening Telegraph,* 4 December 1879, 3.

195. "The Royal Marine Artillery," *Dundee Evening Telegraph,* 4 December 1879, 3.

196. *Ibid.*, 3; Fitzgerald, *Memories of the Sea* (1913), 187.

197. *ORN*, II, 2 (1921), 454; TNA, ADM 268/97; Coles, *Design of a Sea-Going Turret-Ship* (1865), 17.

198. Parkes, *British Battleships* (1966), 78.

199. *Ibid.*, 79; Lyon and Winfield, *The Sail & Steam Navy List* (2004), 139.

200. "Shoeburyness," *Aldershot Military Gazette,* 20 June 1868, 3.

201. Sandler, *The Emergence of the Modern Capital Ship* (1979), 100; "The Armstrong Guns," *London Evening Standard,* 2 November 1863, 2.

202. Marder, *The Anatomy of British Sea Power* (1976), 138.

203. "The Launch of the Monarch," *Reynold's Newspaper,* 31 May 1868, 2.

204. "Naval and Military Intelligence," *London Evening Standard,* 5 August 1868, 6.

205. "Naval and Military News," *Hampshire Telegraph,* 12 August 1868, 2.

206. Reed, *Our Iron-clad Ships* (2011), 32.

207. "Turrets v. Broadsides," *London Evening Standard,* 2 February 1870, 1.

208. Reed, *Our Iron-clad Ships* (2011), 96.

209. *Ibid.*, 138, 139.

210. "Turret Ships," *London Evening Standard,* 10 January 1866, 5.

211. "Turret Ships," *London Evening Standard,* 11 November 1865, 5.

212. "The Birkenhead Rams, Scorpion and Wyvern [sic]," *Manchester Courier and Lancashire General Advertiser.* 12 September 1865, 4.

213. TNA, ADM 135/417, "Office of the Controller of the Navy Ship's Book Series 1, H.M.S. *Scorpion.*"

214. *Ibid.*

215. "The Shoeburyness Experiments on Plymouth Fort Shield," *Illustrated Times,* 27 June 1868, 14–15; Ballard, *The Black Battlefleet* (1980), 231.

216. Ballard, *The Black Battlefleet* (1980), 231.

217. "Plymouth Breakwater Fort," *London Daily News,* 23 June 1868, 5; "Iron Cased Forts," *Sheffield Independent,* 17 June 1868, 2; *Hansard,* 18 July 1868, 193, cc 1430.

218. "Important Gunnery Experiments," *Morning Post,* 30 November 1872, 2; "Gunnery Trials of the Devastation," *London Evening Standard,* 17 July 1873, 3.

219. TNA, ADM 268/97, Coles, *Design of a Sea-Going Turret-Ship (*1865), 21.

220. "From our Naval Correspondent," *London Evening Standard,* 30 March 1869, 2.

221. *Ibid.*, 2, "From our Naval Correspondent," *London Evening Standard,* 29 March 1869, 6.

222. "The Easter Review at Dover," *Hampshire Advertiser,* 31 March 1869, 4. This newspaper also reported that during the storm, a merchant vessel went ashore under the nearby cliffs and soon sank with only her masts visible above the waves.

223. *Ibid.*, 4.

224. Parkes, *British Battleships* (1966), 80.

225. "From our Naval Correspondent," *London Evening Standard,* 30 March 1869, 2.

226. "The Dover Volunteer Review," *Sheffield Independent,* 29 March 1869, 2.

227. Lyon and Winfield, *The Sail & Steam Navy List* (2004), 139–140; "From our Naval Correspondent," *London Evening Standard,* 30 March 1869, 2.

228. "From our Naval Correspondent," *London Evening Standard,* 30 March 1869, 2.

229. "The Volunteer Review at Dover: View of Dover from the Sea-The Naval Squadron Attacking the Forts," *ILN,* 10 April 1869, 356–357.

230. *Ibid.*, 356–357. The Laird ram was depicted as rolling more than the *Royal Sovereign* as the *Scorpion* retained her earlier mast configuration with the heavy yards.

231. "From our Naval Correspondent," *London Evening Standard,* 29 March 1869, 6; "From our Naval Correspondent," *London Evening Standard,* 30 March 1869, 2.

232. "The Easter Review at Dover," *South London Press,* 3 April 1869, 11.

233. "The Volunteer Review," *Dover Express,* 2 April 1869, 4. The wind cleared away the smoke from the turrets of the ironclads almost immediately after the guns fired. Nevertheless, the naval gunfire was likely restricted in duration, as the bombardment produced "a roar that shook the houses in the town." "The Great Volunteer Review at Dover," *Dundee Courier,* 31 March 1869, 3.

234. TNA, ADM 53/9512, *Ship's Log* H.M.S. *Scorpion,* 2 December 1868–31 December 1869.

235. *Hansard*, 16 April 1869, 195, cc 991–992.
236. *Ibid.*, cc 991.
237. John Beeler, *British Naval Policy in the Gladstone-Disraeli Era 1866–1880* (Stanford, 1997), 222.
238. *Ibid.*, 222.
239. *Hansard*, 4 August 1866, 184, cc 2053.
240. "The Portsmouth Review," *Manchester Courier and Lancashire General Advertiser*, 27 April 1869, 5; "The Hampshire Volunteer Review," *Berkshire Chronicle*, 1 May 1869, 7.
241. "The Review at Portsmouth," *London Standard*, 27 April 1869, 6; "Playing at Warfare," *Lake's Falmouth Packet and Cornwall Advertiser*, 1 May 1869, 2.
242. "The Review at Portsmouth," *London Standard*, 27 April 1869, 6.
243. "The Hampshire Volunteer Review," *Berkshire Chronicle*, 1 May 1869, 7.
244. *Ibid.*, 7.
245. "The Review at Portsmouth," *London Standard*, 27 April 1869, 6–7. The *Scorpion* did not fire, but the gunboats reduced Southsea Castle in a "marvelously brief period." This account claims the commanders of the warships were in a hurry to end the maneuver in order to return to their moorings. Also see "The Portsmouth Volunteer Review," *Portsmouth Times and Naval Gazette*, 1 May 1869, 7. This account criticized the training of the volunteer troop formations, which were not armed with the Snider breechloading rifle, whereas the Continental powers were changing drill methods to take advantage of the new breechloading infantry weapons.
246. "Shipping Intelligence," *Belfast Morning News*, 3 May 1869, 2.
247. *Hampshire Advertiser*, 19 May 1869, 3.
248. "The Guard Ship at Queenstown," *Cork Examiner*, 4 May 1869, 3. The *Scorpion* was to relieve the frigate H.M.S. *Mersey* as the local flagship on 8 May as the *Mersey* was ordered to Falmouth.
249. "Queenstown Intelligence," *Cork Examiner*, 27 July 1869, 2.
250. *Hampshire Advertiser*, 23 October 1869, 8.
251. *Ibid.*, 8, "H.M.S. Scorpion," *Cork Examiner*, 20 September 1869, 2.
252. "The Loss of H.M.S. Captain," *London Evening Standard*, 29 September 1870, 3.
253. TNA, ADM 135/417, "Office of the Controller of the Navy Ship's Book Series 1, H.M.S. *Scorpion*."
254. "The Loss of H.M.S. Captain," *London Evening Standard*, 29 September 1870, 3.
255. "Shipping Intelligence," *Belfast Morning News*, 2 August 1869, 4.
256. TNA, ADM 268/97, Coles, *Design of a Sea-Going Turret-Ship (*1865), 299; Lyon and Winfield, *The Sail & Steam Navy List* (2004), 262–263.
257. "The 'Captain' Turret Ship," *Graphic*, 19 March 1870, 381.
258. "Her Majesty's Ship Scorpion," *Hampshire Advertiser*, 21 August 1869, 8.
259. "Miscellaneous Naval," *Portsmouth Times and Naval Gazette*, 7 August 1869, 4; TNA, ADM 53/9512, *Ship's Log* H.M.S. *Scorpion*, 2 December 1868–31 December 1869.
260. "An Ex-Confederate Ship of War," *London Evening Standard*, 6 August 1869, 3; "The Loss of H.M.S. Captain," *London Evening Standard*, 29 September 1870, 3.
261. Ballard, *The Black Battlefleet* (1980), 18, 133.
262. "Cork Drawings-Number One," *Cork Examiner*, 18 June 1869, 2.
263. *Ibid.*, 2.
264. "An Ex-Confederate Ship of War," *London Evening Standard*, 6 August 1869, 3.
265. *Royal Gazette*, 19 October 1869, 2.
266. TNA, ADM 53/9512, *Ship's Log* H.M.S. *Scorpion*, 2 December 1868–31 December 1869.
267. "The Turret Ship Scorpion," *London Evening Standard*, 24 September 1869, 3.
268. "The Cruise of the Lords of the Admiralty," *Star*, 5 October 1869, 2.
269. Andrew Lambert, "Economic Power, Technological Advantage, and Imperial Strength: Britain as a Unique Global Power, 1860–1890." *IJNH*, 5 (August 2006), 12, 19.
270. *Ibid.*, 17. Also see TNA, WO 28/348, *Defences of Bermuda*, "Misc Correspondence and Reports," letter dated 16 October 1869. This report (written before the *Scorpion* arrived on station) proposed in time of war to consider blocking the main channel by "sinking hulls laden with stone."
271. "Like a Big Mosquito Menacing Our Coast," *Morning Times*, 17 May 1896, 18.
272. *Ibid.*, 18.
273. Jarvis, "Protection and Decoration: A Tentative Investigation into Painting Ships Before the Great War," *The Great Circle*, 22 (2000), 29.
274. "The Great Floating Dock for Bermuda," *SA*, 1 January 1869, 20, 7.
275. Captain John Wells, RN, *The Immortal Warrior: Britain's First and Last Battleship* (Hampshire, 1987), 144.
276. *Ibid.*, 7.
277. *Ibid.*, 144, 148.
278. Thomas Brassey, *The British Navy: Its Strength, Resources, and Administration*, 2 (Cambridge, 2010), 227, 228.
279. Brassey, *The British Navy*, 4 (Cambridge, 2010), 116.
280. "The Scorpion," *Cork Examiner*, 14 October 1869, 2; "Naval and Military Intelligence," *Morning Post*, 7 September 1869, 2.
281. "Naval and Military News," *Hampshire Telegraph*, 29 September 1869, 2.
282. "Naval and Military News," *Hampshire Telegraph*, 20 October 1869, 2.
283. TNA, ADM 135/417, "Office of the Controller of the Navy Ship's Book Series 1, H.M.S. *Scorpion*."

284. *Ibid.*
285. *Ibid.*
286. "Military and Naval," *Reading Mercury*, 16 October 1869, 7.
287. *Hansard*, 11 May 1868, 192, cc 24, 25.
288. *Ibid.*, cc 24.
289. *Ibid.*, cc 24, 25.
290. Marder, *The Anatomy of British Sea Power* (1976), 8–9.
291. "Naval and Military Intelligence," *Morning Post*, 11 November 1869, 3.
292. "The Loss of H.M.S. Captain," *London Evening Standard*, 29 September 1870, 3; TNA, ADM 53/9512, Ship's Log H.M.S. Scorpion, 2 December 1868–31 December 1869.
293. "Naval and Military News," *Hampshire Telegraph*, 15 December 1869, 2.
294. TNA, ADM 268/97, Coles, *Design of a Sea-Going Turret-Ship* (1865), 6.
295. *Hampshire Advertiser*, 1 January 1870, 8; "Naval and Military Intelligence," *London Evening Standard*, 12 October, 1869, 6.
296. *Hampshire Advertiser*, 1 May 1869, 8.
297. "Naval and Military Intelligence," *London Standard*, 20 December 1869, 3; Lyon and Winfield, *The Sail & Steam Navy List* (2004), 197–198, 225, 228.
298. "Naval and Military Intelligence," *London Evening Standard*, 21 December 1869, 3.
299. "The Disastrous Fire at Hull," *Manchester Evening News*, 5 May 1870, 4.
300. "Great Fire in Hull," *Hull Packet*, 6 May 1870, 5–6.
301. "Great Fire at Hull," *York Herald*, 7 May 1870, 3.
302. *Ibid.*, 3.
303. *Ibid.*, 3, *Hull Packet*, 6 May 1870, 5; "War Notes," *Western Times*, 25 August 1870, 4.
304. "Great Fire in Hull," *Hull Packet*, 6 May 1870, 5; "Great Fire at Hull," *York Herald*, 7 May 1870, 3.
305. "England and the War," *Derby Mercury*, 10 August 1870, 3.
306. *Ibid.*, 3.
307. "*War Notes*," *Western Times*, 25 August 1870, 4.
308. Allen, "The Deployment of Untried Technology: British Naval Tactics in the Ironclad Era," *War in History*, 15 (01 July 2008), 269, 275–276; Jack Greene and Alessandro Massignani, *Ironclads at War: The Origin and Development of the Armored [sic] Warship 1854–1891* (Boston, 1998), 230.
309. TNA, ADM 135/512, Office of the Controller of the Navy Ship's Book Series I, "Wivern."
310. *Ibid.*
311. *Ibid.*
312. *Ibid.*
313. *Ibid.*
314. *The Advent of Steam*, Editor Robert Gardiner, Consultant Editor Dr. Basil Greenhill (1992), 184.
315. TNA, ADM 135/512, Office of the Controller of the Navy Ship's Book Series I, "Wivern."
316. *Ibid.*
317. "Naval and Military News," *Hampshire Telegraph*, 15 October 1870, 4; Lyon and Winfield, *The Sail & Steam Navy List* (2004), 250.
318. TNA, ADM 135/512, Office of the Controller of the Navy Ship's Book Series I, "Wivern."
319. *Ibid.*
320. John Beeler, *Birth of the Battleship: British Capital Ship Design 1870–1881* (London, 2001), 32.
321. TNA, ADM 135/417, Office of the Controller of the Navy Ship's Book Series 1, "H.M.S. Scorpion."
322. *Ibid.*
323. *Ibid.*
324. *Hansard*, 15 August 1867, 189, cc 1559–1560.
325. *Hansard*, 13 June 1867, 187, cc 1846.
326. Brown, *Warrior to Dreadnought* (1997), 158.
327. *Ibid.*, 158.
328. "H.M.S. Warrior," *West Middlesex Advertiser and Family Journal*, 11 July 1863, 3.
329. *Ibid.*, 57.
330. *Ibid.*, 13, 68.
331. TNA, ADM 135/417, Office of the Controller of the Navy Ship's Book Series 1, "H.M.S. Scorpion."
332. *Ibid.* The refit of the *Scorpion* was estimated to cost the Admiralty £620, but the value of the scrap brass tubes was assessed at £700.
333. Brown, *Warrior to Dreadnought* (1997), 75.
334. *Ibid.*, 75.
335. "Naval Notes and News," *Hampshire Telegraph*, 23 March 1878, 4–5.
336. "Naval and Military Intelligence," *Morning Post*, 23 March 1878, 6; Lyon and Winfield, *The Sail & Steam Navy List* (2004), 155, 300.
337. Timothy Collins, "HMS 'Valorous': Her Contribution to Galway Maritime History," *Journal of the Galway Archaeological and Historical Society*, 49 (1997), 122.
338. *Ibid.*, 124–125.
339. *Ibid.*, 125–126, "The Great Naval Review," *Dublin Evening Mail*, 16 July 1867, 2.
340. "Naval Notes and News," *Hampshire Telegraph*, 23 March 1878, 5.
341. WA ZCL/005/0270/004, letter from Admiralty, dated 24 June 1878.
342. "Shipbuilding on the Mersey during 1878," *Aberdeen Journal*, 25 December 1878, 7.
343. "Naval and Military Intelligence," *London Evening Standard*, 12 January 1880, 3.
344. "Naval and Military Intelligence," *Times*, 14 February 1880, 8.
345. *Ibid.*, 8.
346. "H.M.S. Wivern," *Times*, 20 February 1880, 12.
347. *Hansard*, 23 February 1880, 250, cc 1196.
348. "Naval and Military Intelligence," *Times*, 14 February 1880, 8.
349. *Ibid.*, 8.

350. "Naval and Military Intelligence," *Times*, 12 February 1880, 10.
351. *Ibid.*, 10.
352. *Hansard*, 8 May 1884, 287, cc 1762.
353. TNA, WO 28/348, *Defences of Bermuda*, "Misc Correspondence and Reports," letter dated 16 October 1869.
354. *Hansard*, 20 March 1884, 286, cc 339.
355. *Ibid.*, cc 347.
356. "Naval Notes & News," *Hampshire Telegraph*, 19 December 1891, 8.

Chapter Four

1. "Very Latest," *Royal Gazette*, 23 April 1878, 5.
2. Lt. Cdr. H. G. Middleton, "H.M.S. Scorpion," *Bermuda Historical Quarterly*, XXXVII (Spring 1980), 12–13; Stranack, *The Andrew and the Onions* (1990), 114.
3. TNA, ADM 135/417, Office of the Controller of the Navy Ship's Book Series I, "H.M.S. Scorpion."
4. *Ibid.*
5. *Ibid.*, "British Coal and Coaling Stations," *Pall Mall Gazette*, 3 January 1877, 2–3.
6. *Hansard*, 31 May 1894, 25, cc 11.
7. Stranack, *The Andrew and the Onions* (1990), 54; "Furious Hurricane at Bermuda," *NYT*, 9 September 1878, 8.
8. "The Recent Hurricane," *Royal Gazette*, 7 September 1880, 5.
9. "The Romance of the Sea," *Dundee Courier*, 22 October 1878, 7.
10. Stranack, *The Andrew and the Onions* (1990), 59.
11. TNA, ADM 195/5, Bermuda Dockyard. Includes 73 photographs depicting Royal Navy dockyard and naval base, Bermuda. Dated 1868–1899, 2.
12. "Cable between Halifax and Bermuda," *Hampshire Advertiser*, 29 September 1886, 3; "Dry Dock at Halifax, Nova Scotia," *Hampshire Advertiser*, 21 August 1886, 2.
13. "Our Power by Sea," *Liverpool Mercury*, 4 February 1876, 7; *London Evening Standard*, 14 May 1878, 5.
14. *Hansard*, 6 April 1865, 178, cc 846.
15. "Our Power by Sea," *Liverpool Mercury*, 4 February 1876, 7.
16. Charles L. Bristol, "Notes on the Bermudas," *Bulletin of the American Geographical Society* 33 (1901), 243.
17. Richard A. Gould. "The Archaeology of HMS *Vixen*, an early ironclad ram in Bermuda." *The International Journal of Nautical Archaeology* 20 (1991), 153.
18. Leonid I. Strakhovsky, "Russia's Privateering Projects of 1878," *Journal of Modern History*, 7 (March 1935), 23–24, 29–30, 35.
19. *Ibid.*, 23, 26–28.
20. "British Men-of-War," *NYT*, 26 May 1878, 9.
21. "The Russian Volunteer Fleet," *NYT*, 17 May 1878, 1.
22. "Naval and Military Intelligence," *London Evening Standard*, 2 April 1878, 3.
23. "Torpedoes," *Edinburgh Evening News*, 2 June 1876, 4.
24. "Naval and Military Preparations," *Hampshire Telegraph*, 1 May 1878, 2.
25. Martin Gilbert, *Routledge Atlas of Russian History* (New York, 2010), 40, 59; "Russia and China," *London Evening Standard*, 5 May 1879, 5; "The Kuldja Frontier," *Morning Post*, 1 April 1880 5.
26. "Summary," *York Herald*, 8 July 1880, 4; "Russia and China," *Bath Chronicle and Weekly Gazette*, 22 July 1880, 6; "Projected Increase to the Russian Pacific Fleet," *Manchester Courier and Lancashire General Advertiser*, 14 February 1880, 11.
27. "A Coming Event," *Sheffield Daily Telegraph*, 3 November 1880, 5.
28. *Manchester Courier and Lancashire General Advertiser*, 6 November 1880, 6.
29. "Russian Naval Activity," *Derby Daily Telegraph*, 27 August 1879, 3; "Russia in the Pacific," *Edinburgh Evening News*, 20 May 1880, 2.
30. "The Baltic Fleet," *Portsmouth Evening News*, 13 May 1878, 3; "The Russian Torpedo Fleet," *Portsmouth Evening News*, 4 November 1878, 3.
31. "H.M.S. Wivern," *Times*, 20 February 1880, 12.
32. *Hampshire Advertiser*, 21 February 1880, 8.
33. TNA, ADM 53/11329, *Ship's Log* H.M.S. *Wivern*, 14 January 1880–14 June 1880. Cutlass drills in the Royal Navy during this era were usually held aboard ship for an hour on Wednesday afternoon after dinner. See "Cutlass Drill on Board the 'Resolution,'" *The Navy and Army Illustrated*, 29 May, 1896, 262.
34. USNHC Photo #NH 65901, "H.M.S. Wivern, probably during the 1870s or 1880s."
35. *Ibid.*, USNHC Photo #NH 71211, "HMS Wivern off Plymouth, England" (1865).
36. USNHC Photo #NH 65901, "H.M.S. Wivern, probably during the 1870s or 1880s."
37. NMM Image N5260, "Devonport Yard, 'Wivern'" Curator 14142, Box 101, *Hansard*, 23 February 1880, 250, cc 1196; "News of the Day," *Portsmouth Evening News*, 17 February 1880, 2.
38. "Naval Notes and News, *Hampshire Telegraph*, 18 February 1880, 2.
39. NMM Image N5260, "Devonport Yard, 'Wivern'" Curator 14142, Box 101; TNA, ADM 53/11329, *Ship's Log* H.M.S. *Wivern*, 14 January 1880–14 June 1880.
40. "Naval Notes and News," *Hampshire Telegraph*, 25, February 1880, 2.
41. *Hampshire Advertiser*, 28 February 1880, 8; "Movements of Queen's Ships," *Portsmouth Evening News*, 20 March 1880, 2.
42. TNA, ADM 53/11329, *Ship's Log* H.M.S. *Wivern*, 14 January 1880–14 June 1880.

43. NMM Image N5260, "Devonport Yard, 'Wivern'" Curator 14142, Box 101.
44. *The Gatling Gun Notebook*, compiled by James B. Hughes (Lincoln, RI, 2000), 28, 29, 127, 129.
45. Graham Connah and David Pearson, "Artifact of Empire: The Tale of a Gun," *Historical Archaeology*, 36 (2002), 60–64.
46. Thorsten Nordenfelt, *The Nordenfelt Machine Guns* (Uckfield, Reprint of 1884 edition), 25.
47. *Ibid.*, 105.
48. Lieutenant C. Sleeman, R.N, "The Development of Machine Guns," *North American Review*, 139 (October 1884), 367.
49. L.T.C. Rolt, *Victorian Engineering* (London 1970), 95.
50. Ballard, *The Black Battlefleet* (1980), 43, 44.
51. "The New Steamship Adriatic," *London Evening Standard*, 3 April 1872, 3; "H.M.S. Dreadnought," *Portsmouth Evening News*, 15 June 1878, 2; "Launch of H.M.S. Phaeton," *Glasgow Herald*, 28 February 1883, 10.
52. NMM Image N5260, "Devonport Yard, 'Wivern'" Curator 14142, Box 101
53. "Shipping," *Liverpool Mercury*, 20 March 1880, 7.
54. TNA, ADM 53/11329, *Ship's Log* H.M.S. *Wivern*, 14 January 1880–14 June 1880.
55. Frank H. Winter, *The First Golden Age of Rocketry* (Washington, 1990), 26, 42.
56. *Ibid.*, 199–200, 207–208.
57. *Ibid.*, 210, "The 'Captain' Turret Ship," *Graphic*, 19 March 1870, 381.
58. "War Rockets," *London Evening Standard*, 27 September 1883, 2.
59. Winter, *The First Golden Age of Rocketry* (1990), 211, 214, 220–223.
60. *Ibid.*, 202, 224; "Naval Notes and News," *Hampshire Telegraph*, 25 February 1880, 2; "War Rockets," *London Evening Standard*, 27 September 1883, 2.
61. "Naval and Military Intelligence," *Morning Post*, 24 March 1880, 5.
62. TNA, ADM 53/11329, *Ship's Log* H.M.S. *Wivern*, 14 January 1880–14 June 1880; "Naval and Military Intelligence," *Morning Post*, 29 March 1880, 6.
63. "Movements of Queen's Ships," *Portsmouth Evening News*, 8 April 1880, 2; TNA, ADM 53/11329, *Ship's Log* H.M.S. *Wivern*, 14 January 1880–14 June 1880.
64. "The State of the Navy," *Bristol Mercury*, 8 April 1880, 3.
65. TNA, ADM 53/11329, *Ship's Log* H.M.S. *Wivern*, 14 January 1880–14 June 1880; *Hampshire Advertiser*, 21 February 1880, 8.
66. TNA, ADM 53/11329, *Ship's Log* H.M.S. *Wivern*, 14 January 1880–14 June 1880.
67. A. E. Ekoko, "The Theory and Practice of Imperial Garrisons: The British Experiment in the South Atlantic 1881–1914," *Journal of Historical Society of Nigeria* 12 (Dec. 1983–Jun 1984), 134.

68. Ballard, *The Black Battlefleet* (1980), 17, 56.
69. Brown, *Warrior to Dreadnought* (1997), 173.
70. TNA, ADM 53/11329, *Ship's Log* H.M.S. *Wivern*, 14 January 1880–14 June 1880; "Movements of Queen's Ships," *Portsmouth Evening News*, 22 May 1880, 2.
71. TNA, ADM 53/11329, *Ship's Log* H.M.S. *Wivern*, 14 January 1880–14 June 1880.
72. "London Correspondence," *Aberdeen Journal*, 19 February 1880, 5.
73. Lambert, "Economic Power, Technological Advantage, and Imperial Strength: Britain as a Unique Global Power, 1860–1890," *International Journal of Naval History (*August 2006), 21.
74. Ian Nish, "Politics, Trade and Communications in East Asia: Thoughts on Anglo-Russian Relations, 1861–1907," *Modern Asian Studies*, 21 (1987), 667; "From Our London Correspondent," *Derby Daily Telegraph*, 28 May 1880, 2.
75. "Another Ironclad for the China Squadron," *Hong Kong Daily Press*, 20 January 1880, 2.
76. "News from the China Station," *Hampshire Telegraph*, 6 November 1880, 5. Also see Bodleian Library, Oxford, "Papers of Sir John Pope-Hennessy, GB 0162 MSS.Brit.Emp.s.409, Box 8/2." Letter dated 4 November 1880. In this letter, the Colonial Secretary (Kimberley), replied to Hennessey's complaint (dated 30 August of that year) that British naval forces on the China Station were inferior. Kimberley assured Hennessy the Admiralty could send an ironclad from the Pacific during an emergency to reinforce the station. Kimberley concluded his letter by writing, "In the present state of our foreign relations I think you need not feel any anxiety."
77. "News from the China Station," *Hampshire Telegraph*, 6 November 1880, 5; *Navy List 1880* (London, 1880), 253.
78. "Another Ironclad for the China Squadron," *Hong Kong Daily Press*, 20 January 1880, 2.
79. TNA, ADM 125/83, *China Station Records: Correspondence: Naval Establishments, Bases and Stores, Steam Reserve, Ordnance and Torpedoes*. 1880–1883.
80. *Ibid.*
81. *Hong Kong Telegraph*, 20 December 1881, 2.
82. TNA, ADM 50/299, *Vice-Admiral George O. Willes, C. B., Commander-in-Chief on the China Station*, 1 January 1882–31 March 1882.
83. TNA, ADM 53/11744, *Ship's Log* H.M.S. *Albatross*, 11 August 1882–23 February 1883.
84. *Ibid.*
85. *Ibid.*
86. "Comic and Gossip Papers," *Bucks Herald*, 30 May 1885, 3.
87. "Modern Navies," *Dundee Courier*, 30 August 1865, 3.
88. NMM, MIL/1, Vice Admiral Charles Blois Miller, Log Book, H.M.S. *Audacious*, 1883–1884.
89. Author's collection. The photograph of a Royal Navy 2nd Class Petty Officer with a patch depicting crossed torpedo and rifled breechloading gun under a six-pointed star on his right sleeve

circa 1885, taken by A. King, Hong Kong. King may have been an Anglicized pseudonym for a Mr. Afong, the "well-known photographer of Queen's-road" [sic], *Hong Kong Telegraph*, 18 July 1881, 2.

90. TNA, ADM 125/83, *China Station Records*. 1880–1883. Form S-321, originated in December 1880.

91. "London Gossip," *Hampshire Advertiser*, 6 August 1881, 3.

92. TNA, ADM 125/83, *China Station Records*. 1880–1883.

93. *Ibid.*, "Torpedo Nets" *Sheffield Independent*, 12 May 1885, 2; "Goodbye to the Canada" *The Sun*, 16 May 1885, 2.

94. "Prolonged Patents," *Birmingham Daily Post*, 24 June 1881, 6; "Marine Engines and Engineering," *Shields Daily Gazette*, 6 September 1882, 5; "The Fisheries Exhibition," *Morning Post*, 22 June 1883, 3.

95. "The War Preparations," *London Evening Standard*, 4 May 1885, 2; "The Corvette Canada Keeps a Look Out for Dynamite," *The Sun*, 10 May 1885, 1.

96. Buford Rowland, "Revolution in Nets: An Unglamorous but Essential Phase of Naval Warfare," *Military Affairs*, 11 (1947), 149.

97. Bodleian Library, Oxford, "Papers of Sir John Pope-Hennessy, GB 0162 MSS.Brit.Emp.s.409, Box 8/2." Letter dated 23 April 1880. Hennessy had proposed that a larger ironclad be utilized to defend Hong Kong. Although the name or type of warship was not mentioned, the *Wivern* was en route to the Far East when the letter was written. Also see letter (same source) dated 22 April 1881; Kimberley had written to Hennessy informing him the Admiralty had turned down the Governor's "Wyvern" plan, *Hansard*, 19 February 1880, 250, cc 940.

98. Thomas Brassey, M.P., "On a Colonial Naval Volunteer Force," *RUSI Journal*, 22, 17 May 1878, 9.

99. *Hansard*, 1 August 1882, 273, cc 435.

100. "The Navy that is Needed," *National Republican*, 31 January 1885, 1.

101. *Ibid.*, 1. This article claimed that British ironclads were not designed for "our traditions" (American) and were too deep for U.S. harbors. They obviously forgot about the *Scorpion* and *Wivern*.

102. "Britain's War-Ships [sic]," *Salt Lake Herald*, 17 April 1885, 1.

103. Sergeev, *The Great Game, 1856–1907* (2014), 166.

104. "The Fortifications of Hong Kong," *Times*, 28 October 1884, 3.

105. "China's Concern in the Fate of Afghanistan," *China Mail*, 7 May 1885, 3.

106. "News from the China Station," *Hampshire Telegraph*, 22 November 1884, 8.

107. "England's Peril in Case of War," *Morning Post*, 6 December 1884, 3.

108. *Ibid.*, 3.

109. Peter Morris, "The Russians in Central Asia 1870–1887," *The Slavonic and Eastern European Review*, 53 (October 1975), 528.

110. *Ibid.*, 522.

111. *Ibid.*, 528, 529. Also see Evgeny Sergeev, *The Great Game, 1856–1907: Russo-British Relations in Central and East Asia* (Baltimore, 2014), 208. A Russian diplomat later remarked on the Anglo-Russian tensions of 1885, "One sometimes wonders how peace could have been maintained."

112. "Russia's Naval Strength," *Dundee Evening Telegraph*, 13 June 1885, 3.

113. "Naval News from the China Station," *Hampshire Telegraph*, 4 April 1885, 8; also see "The China Station," *Portsmouth Evening News*, 7 January 1885, 4. This account describes the *Wivern* being fitted with her tops, and with her two TBs aboard, "presents a formidable appearance, quite in contrast to the comical-looking Frenchmen, half-funnel, half-cork ram."

114. "Arrival of the Agamemnon," *China Mail*, 25 March 1885, 3.

115. "The Man in the Military Mast Fills a Post of Deadly Peril," *Salt Lake Herald*, 1 May 1898, 20. (From an undated article in the *New York Daily Tribune*. An article in a Dodge City, Kansas, newspaper referred to the French versions of the military mast as "Growths." See "The Evolution of the Fighting Top," *Globe-Republican*, 7 July 1898, 2.)

116. "Naval News from the China Station," *Hampshire Telegraph*, 25 April 1885, 8.

117. David Wilmshurst, "Hong Kong during the Sino-French War (1884–1885): Impressions of a French Naval Officer," *Journal of the Royal Asiatic Society Hong Kong Branch*. 50 (2010), 158. Regrettably, the French officer made no mention of the *Wivern* or her torpedo boats, but did write, "The residents of Hong Kong were worried about the possibility that the Russians, who have quite powerful forces in the vicinity, might bombard the town."

118. "Is Our Navy Ready for War?," *China Mail*, 24 April, 1885, 3.

119. "Naval News from the China Station," *Hampshire Telegraph*, 4 April 1885, 8.

120. Wilmshurst, "Hong Kong during the Sino-French War (1884–1885): Impressions of a French Naval Officer," *Journal of the Royal Asiatic Society Hong Kong Branch*. 50 (2010), 141, 157, TNA, MPI 1/492, *A Plan of Gun Boats [sic] Moorings at Kowloon laid down May 1881*.

121. Wilmshurst, "Hong Kong during the Sino-French War (1884–1885): Impressions of a French Naval Officer," *Journal of the Royal Asiatic Society Hong Kong Branch*. 50 (2010), 158–159. On 28 March 1885, Rollet de l'Isle observed the "great commotion" aboard the recently arrived *Agamemnon* as she hoisted her two torpedo boats aboard and weighed anchor. He noted that the loading was "delicate enough in a harbour, would have been impossible at sea."

122. TNA, ADM 125/83, *China Station Records: Correspondence: Naval Establishments, Bases and Stores, Steam Reserve, Ordnance and Torpedoes*. 1880–1883. Enclosure No. 3, "Suggestions Concerning Torpedo Service at Hong Kong," 3 January 1884.

123. "Naval News from the China Station,"

Portsmouth Evening News, 31 January 1885, 4. A British correspondent aboard the *Audacious* remarked that the allegations against the China Station were "so absurdly false that it deserves only to be laughed at."

124. *China Mail,* 21 April 1885, 2.

125. "The Defence of Hong Kong," *Portsmouth Evening News*, 23 May 1885, 4; "Naval and Military," *London Daily News*, 28 July 1885, 6. In 1884–5, the combined force of the Royal Navy and Royal Marines was slightly under 57,000 personnel on active duty, down from a total of 84,000 in 1860–1. The number (from 1884–5) would double over the next sixteen years. See William Ashworth, "Economic Aspects of Late Victorian Naval Administration," *The Economic History Review*, 22 (December 1969), 500.

126. TNA, ADM 53/12239, *Ship's Log* H.M.S. *Wivern*, 19 March 1885–22 July 1885; "Naval News from the China Station," *Hampshire Telegraph*, 29 August 1885, 8.

127. Terry Bennett, *Korea: Caught in Time* (Reading, 2009), xii, 4, 40, 41. Also see TNA, ADM 231/2, *Admiralty: Foreign Intelligence Committee*, "Port Hamilton," 1883–1884, 82. The anchorage of Port Hamilton was formed by the small islands of Tunodo, Observatory Island, and Sodo. British warships had visited the anchorage before, and in 1882 reported no cattle on the islands (which varied from 500 to 700 feet in height above sea level) and other food supplies were "not plentiful."

128. John Berryman, "British Imperial Defence Strategy and Russia: The Role of the Royal Navy in the Far East, 1878–1898," *IJNH*, 1 (April 2002), 4. Britain would occupy Port Hamilton until February 1887 as a precaution against Russia utilizing the port or another anchorage (Port Lazarev) on the Korean peninsula.

129. "Naval News from the China Station," *Portsmouth Evening News*, 29 August 1885, 8.

130. TNA, ADM 53/12239, *Ship's Log* H.M.S. *Wivern*, 19 March 1885–22 July 1885; "Naval and Military Intelligence," *Morning Post*, 28 July 1885, 5; "British Cruisers in Eastern Seas," *Dundee Evening Telegraph*, 6 August 1885, 3.

131. "Asking a Vote of Credit," *NYT*, 22 April 1885, 1; "England and Russia," *Derby Daily Telegraph*, 22 April 1885, 4.

132. "R.B.Y. Club Cruising Race," *Royal Gazette*, 12 July 1887, 2.

133. "Naval Ball at Ireland," *Royal Gazette*, 2 April 1895, 5.

134. "The Jubilee Celebrations at Bermuda," *The Navy and Army Illustrated*, 3 September 1897, 237–238.

135. *Particulars of the War Ships of the World.* Lloyd's Register of British and Foreign Shipping (London, 1893), 5.

136. "The Jubilee Celebrations at Bermuda," *The Navy and Army Illustrated*, 3 September 1897, 237–238.

137. *Ibid.,* 238, "Ireland Island," *Royal Gazette*, 6 July 1897, 5.

138. Captain H. T. R. Lloyd, RMLI, "Diary of a Young Marine," *Bermuda Historical Quarterly*, 24 (spring 1967), 13. The crisis was due to the Russian occupation of Port Arthur upon the withdrawal of the Chinese garrison (see "Russia's Easy Victory," *Edinburgh Evening News*, 28 March 1898, 4).

139. Lloyd, RMLI, "Diary of a Young Marine," *Bermuda Historical Quarterly*, 24 (spring 1967), 16, 29, 37.

140. *Ibid.,* 44, 45.

141. Robert K. Massie, *Dreadnought* (New York, 1991), 428, 434.

142. "The North American Station," *The Navy and Army Illustrated*, 9 December 1899, 291.

143. TNA, ADM 53/13179, Log, H.M.S. *Crescent*, 20 April 1900–14 April 1901.

144. NMM, ALB 1267, "The Career of Admiral G H Bedford, February 1901 to July 1902," Images 45, 46; "Old Warship for a Target," *New York Daily Tribune*, 5 May 1901, 2.

145. TNA, ADM 53/25083, H.M.S. *Quail*, 7 March 1901–31 December 1901.

146. TNA, ADM 53/13180, Log, H.M.S. *Crescent*, 15 April 1901–24 March 1902; "Another Belleisle," *Portsmouth Evening News*, 16 May 1901, 3. H.M.S. *Belleisle* was an 1870s vintage coastal defense ironclad used as a target in the English Channel by the battleship H.M.S *Majestic* the previous year. See Lyon and Winfield, *The Sail & Steam Navy List* (2004), 252.

147. NMM, ALB 1267, "The Career of Admiral G H Bedford, February 1901 to July 1902," Image 43.

148. "Another Belleisle," *Portsmouth Evening News*, 16 May 1901, 3; TNA, ADM 53/13180; Log, H.M.S. *Crescent*, 15 April 1901–24 March 1902.

149. "The Old Powder and the New," *The Navy and Army Illustrated*, 4 November 1899, 172.

150. "British Naval Gunnery," *Sheffield Daily Telegraph*, 28 May 1901, 5. The 6-inch was the largest caliber quick-firer in service with the Royal Navy (1896). See "At Drill with A 6-inch Quick-Firing Gun on Board the 'Resolution,'" *The Navy and Army Illustrated*, 15 May, 1896, 244.

151. Brown, *Warrior to Dreadnought* (1997), 136; Anthony Preston, *The World's Worst Warships*. Conway Maritime Press, London (2002), 46.

152. Stranack, *The Andrew and the Onions* (1990), 114; Wirral Archives, ZCL/005/0195/039/040, *Description of Laird Rams*, dated July 1863.

153. "H.M.S. Scorpion," *Royal Gazette*, 20 December 1902, 1; "Sale of H.M.S. Scorpion," *Royal Gazette*, 31 January 1903, 2.

154. "General Notes," *NYT*, 14 June 1903, 6; "Last of the Confederate Navy," *Confederate Veteran*, XI (Nashville, 1903), 352.

155. "Custom House-St. George's," *Royal Gazette*, 13 June 1903, 2; "The Scorpion Foundered," *Royal Gazette*, 20 June 1903, 2; "Sinking of the Scorpion," *Royal Gazette*, 30 June 1903, 1; "British Monitor Founders," *New York Daily Tribune*, 18 June 1903, 3.

156. *The Sailor's Magazine, and Naval Journal,*

9, American Seamen's Friend Society (New York, 1838), 15.

157. "Sinking of the Scorpion," *Royal Gazette*, 30 June 1903, 1, *The Sailor's Magazine, and Naval Journal, Volume* 9 (New York, 1837), 217.

158. "Local and General," *Hong Kong Telegraph*, 10 May 1888, 3.

159. *Particulars of the War Ships of the World.* Lloyd's Register of British and Foreign Shipping (London, 1893), 5.

160. TNA, ADM 53/16609, Log, H.M.S. *Wivern*, 11 September 1889–7 March 1901.

161. "Portsmouth Branch," *Hampshire Advertiser*, 19 April 1890, 8.

162. "Naval and Military Intelligence," *Times*, 14 February 1880, 8.

163. TNA, ADM 53/16609, Log, H.M.S. *Wivern*, 11 September 1889–7 March 1901.

164. *Ibid.*

165. "Movement of H. M. Ships," *Hampshire Telegraph*, 1 December 1894, 8; "Movement of H. M. Ships," *Portsmouth Evening News*, 11 December 1894, 2.

166. Thomas Allnutt Brassey, *The Naval Annual, 1895* (New York, 2006), 169.

167. Sir Edward Reed, "The British Navy," *Harper's New Monthly Magazine* 72 (February 1886), 354; Ballard, *The Black Battlefleet* (1980), 218–219.

168. TNA, ADM 53/16608, Log, H.M.S. *Wivern*, 1 January 1895–15 December 1895.

169. TNA, ADM 53/16609, Log, H.M.S. *Wivern*, 11 September 1889–7 March 1901.

170. "The Fleets in the Far East," *London Evening Standard*, 4 January 1898, 2.

171. "'The Back door': A Sketch of What Might Happen." *China Mail* (Hong Kong, 1897), 3, 10–14, 34, 36.

172. TNA, ADM 53/32184, Log, H.M.S. *Wivern*, 11–30 September 1899.

173. "Brigandage and Piracy in China," *London Standard*, 31 July 1899, 3.

174. "Piracy in Chinese Waters," *Liverpool Mercury*, 12 May 1899, 1-2.

175. "Chinese Pirates," *Freeman's Journal*, 29 August 1899, 6.

176. "Naval & Military," *Portsmouth Evening News* 16 November 1899, 2, Diana Preston, *The Boxer Rebellion* (New York, 2000), 14, 345–346.

177. TNA, ADM 53/32184, Log, H.M.S. *Wivern*, 11–30 September 1899.

178. "The Ineffective '*Wivern*,'" *China Mail*, 12 January 1901, 4; "Our China Squadron," *Lichfield Mercury*, 27 July 1900, 7.

179. TNA, ADM 53/16609, Log, H.M.S. *Wivern*, 11 September 1899–7 March 1901.

180. "Maritime Notes," *Shields Daily Gazette*, 6 December 1901, 4.

181. "H.M.S. Wivern," *China Mail*, 29 May 1902, 4; "Local and General," *Hong Kong Telegraph*, 19 December 1903, 4.

182. "Passing of the "Wivern,"" *Hong Kong Telegraph*, 13 March 1923, 7.

Conclusion

1. *Hansard*, 18 July 1887, 317, cc 1266.

2. *Hansard*, 6 May 1886, 305, cc 372. Comment made in the Commons by Secretary to the Admiralty, Sir John Hibbert.

3. Bernard Brodie, *Sea Power in the Machine Age* (Princeton, 1941), 212.

4. Fuller, "John Ericsson, the Monitors and Union Naval Strategy," *IJNH*, 2 (December 2004), 17.

5. Howard J. Fuller, *Empire, Technology and Seapower: Royal Navy Crisis in the Age of Palmerston* (New York, 2013), 63, n7. Here Fuller quotes from Lambert, who had held that "coastal defence vessels were 'really' for attack."

6. TNA, ADM 231/5, *Admiralty: Foreign Intelligence Committee*, Report No. 51, Captain W. H. Hall, R.N., "Remarks on a Naval Campaign," 24 September 1884, 25. Captain Hall also stated that five coastal defense ironclads in Britain "*might* (italics in original) be employed in some operations" against the northern coast of France, including on blockade against Cherbourg.

7. *Ibid.*, 36–37. The China squadron was to attack French warships, and patrol key straits, but was only to "watch" Saigon. On the North American and West Indies Station, the Royal Navy would seek to engage French warships and attack Fort de France (Martinique), Guadeloupe, and nearby Les Saintes.

8. Fuller, "John Ericsson, the Monitors and Union Naval Strategy," *IJNH*, 2 (December 2004), 17.

9. G. W. Steevens, *Naval Policy: With Some Account of the Warships of the Principal Powers* (London, 1896), 120.

10. H. W. Wilson, *Ironclads in Action; A Sketch of Naval Warfare from 1855–1895, With Some Account of the Development of the Battleship in England.* Volume II (London, 1896), 168, 241.

11. *Ibid.*, 214, "Is Our Navy Ready for War?," *China Mail*, 24 April, 1885, 3.

12. NMM, Ship Plans, "Devonport Yard, 'Wivern,'" Curator 14142, Box 101.

13. Ian Buxton, *Big Gun Monitors: The History of the Design, Construction and Operations of the Royal Navy's Monitors* (Annapolis, 1980), 11, TNA, ADM 231/5, *Admiralty: Foreign Intelligence Committee*, Report No. 51, Captain W. H. Hall, R.N., "Remarks on a Naval Campaign," 24 September 1884, 25.

14. Fuller, "The *Warrior*'s Influence Abroad: The American Civil War," *IJNH*, 10 (October 2013), 1, 6. Here the author also notes that the "*Monitor*, like all early ironclads, was expected to fulfill a variety of frequently 'urgent' yet conflicting roles." The same can be said for the Laird rams.

Bibliography

Primary Sources

Archival and Official Records

Bodleian Library, Oxford, "Papers of Sir John Pope-Hennessy," GB 0162 MSS.Brit.Emp.s.409, Box 8/2.

Library of Congress (LOC), *The Abraham Lincoln Papers*, Letter from Assistant Secretary of the U.S. Navy Gustavus V. Fox, 8 September 1863.

LOC, "Correspondence Between Her Majesty's Government and Messr. Laird Brothers Relative to the Iron-Clad Rams." *United States Serial Set*, Number 1397, Senate Executive Department No. 11, Volume 4, 41st Congress Appendix No. XIII (Washington, 1869).

LOC, "Proceedings Before the Crown Court at Cork in the Case of the Men received on Board the United States Steamer Kearsarge at Queenstown." *United States Serial Set*, Number 1397, Appendix No. XIII (Washington, 1869).

LOC, "Report of Trials in England of Various Parties for Violation of the Foreign Enlistment Act, in Recruiting for the Rebel Vessels, Case of Jones and Highatt." *United States Serial Set*, Number 1397, Appendix No. XIV (Washington, 1869).

National Maritime Museum (NMM), MLN/114/9, 1st Bt., Sir Alexander Milne, Admiral of the Fleet. "Additional Instructions for the guidance of Cruizers (sic) employed in the Protection of British Commerce on the East Coast of America."

NMM, Ship Plans, "Devonport Yard, '"Wivern,'" Curator 14142, Box 101.

NMM, HND/101/3, Journal of Sub-Lieutenant Swinton C. Holland, H.M.S. *Wivern*, September-December 1865.

NMM, *Navy List 1880*, (London, 1880).

NMM, MIL/1, Vice Admiral Charles Blois Miller, Log Book, H.M.S. *Audacious*, 1883–1884.

NMM, ALB 1267, "The Career of Admiral G. H. Bedford, February 1901 to July 1902."

The War of the Rebellion: A Compilation of the Official Records of the Union and Confederate Armies (ORA). Series 1, Volume 6 (Washington, 1882).

The Official Records of the Union and Confederate Navies in the War of the Rebellion (ORN). Series I, Volume 9 (Washington, 1899).

ORN, Series I, Volume 12 (Washington, 1901).

ORN, Series I, Volume 13 (Washington, 1901).

ORN, Series I, Volume 14 (Washington, 1902).

ORN, Series II, Volume 1 (Washington, 1921).

ORN, Series II, Volume 2 (Washington, 1921).

The National Archives, Kew (TNA), ADM 1/5842, *Admiralty Correspondence*, "Steam Rams on the Mersey," letter written by James Reed, 17 September 1863.

TNA, ADM 1/5842, *Admiralty Correspondence*, "Specification of Cowper Phipps Coles Masts," 10 April 1862, Patent No. 1027.

TNA, ADM 1/5842, *Admiralty Correspondence*, Letter by Controller of the Navy Rear Admiral Robert Spencer Robinson, dated 6 October 1863.

TNA, ADM 1/6083, *Director Naval Ordnance, In-Letters and Papers, 1860–1869*.

TNA, ADM 1/6083, "Diagram Shewing Construction of the Experimental 9 Inch 12 ton Guns" (Gun Nos. 298, 332 & 333) *Letters, Director of Naval Ordnance* 1868.

TNA, ADM 50/299, *Vice-Admiral George O. Willes, C. B., Commander-in-Chief on the China Station*, 1 January 1882–31 March 1882.

TNA, ADM 53/8205, *Ship's Log* H.M.S. *Terror*, 16 December 1861–31 December 1862.

TNA, ADM 53/8623, *Ship's Log* H.M.S. *Royal Sovereign*, 15 October 1864 to 10 October 1866.

TNA, ADM 53/8418, *Ship's Log* H.M.S. *Scorpion*, 10 July 1865 to 1 January 1866.

TNA, ADM 53/9512, *Ship's Log* H.M.S. *Scorpion*, 2 December 1868 to 31 December 1869.

TNA, ADM 53/11329, *Ship's Log* H.M.S. *Wivern*, 14 January 1880–14 June 1880.

TNA, ADM 53/11744, *Ship's Log* H.M.S. *Albatross*, 11 August 1882–23 February 1883.

TNA, ADM 53/12239, *Ship's Log* H.M.S. *Wivern*, 19 March 1885–22 July 1885.

TNA, ADM 53/16608, Log, H.M.S. *Wivern*, 1 January 1895–15 December 1895.

TNA, ADM 53/32184, Log, H.M.S. *Wivern*, 11–30 September 1899.

TNA, ADM 53/16609, Log, H.M.S. *Wivern*, 11 September 1899–7 March 1901.

TNA, ADM 53/13179, Log, H.M.S. *Crescent*, 20 April 1900–14 April 1901.

TNA, ADM 53/25083, Log, H.M.S. *Quail*, 7 March 1901–31 December 1901.
TNA, ADM 53/13180, Log, H.M.S. *Crescent*, 15 April 1901–24 March 1902.
TNA, ADM 125/83, *China Station Records: Correspondence: Naval Establishments, Bases and Stores, Steam Reserve, Ordnance and Torpedoes*. 1880–1883.
TNA, ADM 125/83, *China Station Records: Correspondence: Naval Establishments, Bases and Stores, Steam Reserve, Ordnance and Torpedoes*.1880–1883. Enclosure No. 3, "Suggestions Concerning Torpedo Service at Hong Kong," 3 January 1884.
TNA, ADM 135/417, Office of the Controller of the Navy Ship's Book Series 1, H.M.S. *Scorpion*.
TNA, ADM 135/512, Office of the Controller of the Navy Ship's Book Series I, "*Wivern.*"
TNA, ADM 186/869, *Manual of Gunnery for Her Majesty's Fleet 1885* (London, 1886).
TNA, ADM 195/5, *Bermuda Dockyard*. Includes 73 photographs depicting Royal Navy dockyard and naval base, Bermuda. Dated 1868–1899.
TNA, ADM 231/2, *Admiralty: Foreign Intelligence Committee*, "Port Hamilton," 1883–1884.
TNA, ADM 231/3, *Admiralty: Foreign Intelligence Committee*, "France Effective Armourclads," dated 1 January 1884.
TNA, ADM 231/5, *Admiralty: Foreign Intelligence Committee*, Report No. 51, Captain W. H. Hall, R.N., "Remarks on a Naval Campaign," 24 September 1884.
TNA, ADM 231/5, *Admiralty: Foreign Intelligence Committee*, Report No. 43, "Eastern Siberian Ports and Anchorages," dated January 1885.
TNA, ADM 268/97, *Report of a Committee of Naval Officers, Appointed to Examine the Design of a Sea-Going Turret-Ship, submitted by Captain C. P. Coles, R.N.* (1865).
TNA, F.O. 412/11 "Correspondence Respecting Two Iron-Clad Vessels Building at Messr. Laird's Yard, Birkenhead, February to October 1863," dated 11 July 1863; No. 70, dated 5 September 1863; No. 101, dated 22 September 1863, dated 28 September 1863.
TNA, F.O. 881/1200, "United States: Corres. Iron-Clad Vessels Building at Messrs. Laird's yard Birkenhead," Part 1. February–October 1863.
TNA, F.O. 881/2006, "Foreign Office Confidential Print, United States: Corres. Iron-Clad Vessels Building at Messrs. Laird's yard Birkenhead," 1863–1864.
TNA, F.O. 881/2011 "Florida." No. 70, dated 23 September 1863; No. 71, dated 1 October 1863; and No. 73, dated 22 September 1863. Printed November 1871.
TNA, MPI 1/492, *A Plan of Gun Boats [sic] Moorings at Kowloon laid down May 1881*.
TNA, PRO 30/22 "Private Correspondence. Lord Palmerston (P) Prime Minister to Lord Russell (JR) Foreign Secretary," Volume 22, letter dated 23 August 1863, letter dated 4 September 1863, letter dated 21 September 1863.
TNA, TS 25/1274, letter from Thomas Dudley, United States Consulate, Liverpool, 7 August 1863.
TNA, TS 25/1285, "Treasury Solicitor and HM Procurator General: Law Officers" and "Counsel's Opinion. Steam rams, Birkenhead Seizure of iron clad ship, from Messrs Laird." Letter dated 29 October 1863.
TNA, TS 25/1285, "IRON CLAD SHIPS: Vessels under seizure: To Determine their Destination and Ownership," letter dated 29 October 1863.
TNA, WO 55/2182, Records of Ordnance Office, Portsmouth, "No. 7 Minute Book May to November 1865."
TNA, WO 28/348, *Defences of Bermuda*, "Misc Correspondence and Reports," letter dated 16 October 1869.
Wirral Archives (WA), Birkenhead, WA, Z/CL2/9/0000/005 "Records of Cammell Laird and Co. H.M.S. Wivern, Engines No. 81, copy of plans."
WA, 5/195/39 & 40, "Captain Coles License for ships 294 and 295," 10 December 1862.
WA, 005/0195, "Dimensions and Particulars of Vessels Vol. 2, 'Green Book No. 2,'" 039–040.
WA, 5/195/39 & 40, "Terms of Contract with Messrs A. Bravay & Co. 6 Rue de Londres Paris/ for completing 2 Iron Screw Steamers," dated 16 June 1863.
WA, ZCL/005/0195/039/040, Description of Laird Rams, dated July 1863.
WA, Birkenhead Map, Ordnance Survey Office, Southampton (1875).
WA, ZCL/005/0270/004, letter from Admiralty, dated 24 June 1878.

Parliamentary Debates

Hansard, 26 July 1861, 164, cc 1633.
Hansard, 10 July 1862, 168, cc 163.
Hansard, 23 February 1863, 169, cc 669–700.
Hansard, 26 February 1863, 169, cc 798–802, 834.
Hansard, 27 February 1863, 169, cc 887, 888.
Hansard, 12 March 1863, 169, cc 1361.
Hansard, 27 March 1863, 170, cc 33, 38, 69, 70, 71, 72.
Hansard, 23 July 1863, 172, cc 1271.
Hansard, 19 July 1864, 176, cc 1766.
Hansard, 6 April 1865, 178, cc 846.
Hansard, 1 March 1866, 181, cc 1345.
Hansard, 15 March 1866, 182, cc 331, 342, 343, 345.
Hansard, 5 June 1866, 183, cc 1940, 1941.
Hansard, 4 August 1866, 184, cc 2053.
Hansard, 13 June 1867, 187, cc 1790, 1811–1812, 1846.
Hansard, 15 August 1867, 189, cc 1559–1560.
Hansard, 11 May 1868, 192, cc 24, 25.
Hansard, 18 July 1868, 193, cc 1430.
Hansard, 8 March 1869, 194, cc 887, 889, 890.
Hansard, 2 April 1869, 195, cc 110, 111, 118, 119.
Hansard, 16 April 1869, 195, cc 991–992.

Hansard, 19 February 1880, 250, cc 940.
Hansard, 23 February 1880, 250, cc 1196.
Hansard, 1 August 1882, 273, cc 435.
Hansard, 20 March 1884, 286, cc 339.
Hansard, 8 May 1884, 287, cc 1762.
Hansard, 15 July 1890, 346, cc 1725.
Hansard, 6 May 1886, 305, cc 372.
Hansard, 31 May 1894, 25, cc 11.
Hansard, 18 July 1898, 62, cc 77, 78.
Hansard, 8 November 1916, 87, cc 165–167.

Magazines and Newspapers

"The Accident on the Thunderer," *Times*, 13 January 1879, 10.
"Accident to the Screw-Steamer Balaclava," *Belfast News-Letter*, 25 February 1865, 3.
"Admiralty Order for Nordenfelt Guns," *Aberdeen Journal*, 23 October 1880, 6.
"America," *Morning Post*, 27 July 1863, 5.
"The American Monitor Miantonomoh," *Hull Packet*, 22 June 1866, 7.
"American Slavery and its Abettors," *Dundee, Perth, and Cupar Advertiser*, 28 April 1863, 2.
"Another 'Ram' for a 'French' House," *Liverpool Daily Post*, 31 August 1863, 5.
"Another Belleisle," *Portsmouth Evening News*, 16 May 1901, 3.
"Another Ironclad for the China Squadron," *Hong Kong Daily Press*, 20 January 1880, 2.
"The Armstrong Gun," *Dublin Evening Mail*, 10 October 1861, 1.
"The Armstrong Guns," *London Evening Standard*, 2 November 1863, 2.
"Arrival of Mason and Slidell," *Berkshire Chronicle*, 1 February 1862, 6.
"Arrival of the Agamemnon," *China Mail*, 25 March 1885, 3.
"Arrival of the Russian Frigate General Admiral, and trial of the Russian Battery Pervenetz," *Ashtabula Weekly Telegraph*, 26 September 1863, 2.
"Asking a Vote of Credit," *NYT*, 22 April 1885, 1.
"Assize Intelligence," *Morning Post*, 23 August 1870, 7.
"At Drill with A 6-inch Quick-Firing Gun on Board the 'Resolution,'" *The Navy and Army Illustrated*, 15 May 1896, 244.
"'The Back Door': A Sketch of What Might Happen," *China Mail* (Hong Kong, 1897), 3, 10–14, 34, 36.
"The Baltic Fleet," *Portsmouth Evening News*, 13 May 1878, 3.
"The Birkenhead Rams, Scorpion and Wyvern [sic]," *Manchester Courier and Lancashire General Advertiser*. 12 September 1865, 4.
"Brigandage and Piracy in China," *London Standard*, 31 July 1899, 3.
"Britain's War-Ships," *Salt Lake Herald*, 17 April 1885, 1.
"British Coal and Coaling Stations," *Pall Mall Gazette*, 3 January 1877, 2–3.
"British Cruisers in Eastern Seas," *Dundee Evening Telegraph*, 6 August 1885, 3.
"The British Forces on the North American & West India Station," *Yorkshire Gazette*, 7 December 1861, 11.
"British Men-of-War," *NYT*, 26 May 1878, 9.
"British Monitor Founders," *New York Daily Tribune*, 18 June 1903, 3.
"British Naval Gunnery," *Sheffield Daily Telegraph*, 28 May 1901, 5.
"Built for the Confederacy," *The Sun*, 28 June 1903, 2
"Cable between Halifax and Bermuda," *Hampshire Advertiser*, 29 September 1886, 3.
"The 'Captain' Turret Ship," *Graphic*, 19 March 1870, 381.
"Capture of Mr. Laird's Iron Rams," *Dundee, Perth, and Cupar Advertiser*, 3 November 1863, 8.
"Central Criminal Court," *Morning Post*, 9 May 1861, 7.
"The Change of Ministry," *Times*, 29 June 1885, 5.
"The Channel Fleet," *Manchester Courier and Lancashire General Advertiser*, 9 October 1866, 3.
"The Channel Fleet," *Sherborne Mercury*, 9 October 1866, 5.
China Mail, 21 April 1885, 2.
"The China Station," *Portsmouth Evening News*, 7 January 1885, 4.
"Chinese Pirates," *Freeman's Journal*, 29 August 1899, 6.
"Collison with Her Majesty's Ship 'Scorpion,'" *Hampshire Telegraph*, 1 April 1865, 4.
"The Collison with the Scorpion," *Cheshire Observer*, 1 April 1865, 7.
"Collison with the Scorpion," *Manchester Courier and Lancashire General Advertiser*. 30 March, 1865, 2.
"Colonel Kelly the Fenian Leader, in Manchester," *Manchester Courier and Lancashire General Advertiser*, 18 September 1867, 3.
"Comic and Gossip Papers," *Bucks Herald*, 30 May 1885, 3.
"A Coming Event," *Sheffield Daily Telegraph*, 3 November 1880, 5.
"Commodore Wilkes in Bermuda," *Carlisle Journal*, 24 October 1862, 11.
"Compound Ordnance," *Dublin Evening Mail*, 10 October 1863, 4.
"Confederate Cruisers," *Liverpool Mercury*, 2 December 1863, 3.
"The Confederate Rams in England," *SA*, 9 (New Series), 28 November 1863, 343.
"The Confederates iron-clad navy-Yankee information on the subject-What England is Doing about it." *Daily Dispatch*, 22 November 1862, 1.
"Cork Drawings-Number One," *Cork Examiner*, 18 June 1869, 2.
Cork Examiner, 23 September 1867, 2.
"Correspondence between England and America about British Neutrality," *Daily Dispatch*, 1 February 1864, 1.
"The Corvette Canada Keeps a Look Out for Dynamite," *The Sun*, 10 May 1885, 1.

"Courts Martial on board the *Duke of Wellington*," *Hampshire Telegraph*, 12 January 1870, 2.

"The Cruise of the Channel Squadron," *Dublin Evening Mail*, 20 October 1866, 4.

"The Cruise of the Lords of the Admiralty," *Star*, 5 October 1869, 2.

"Cunningham's Self-Reefing Topsails," *Hampshire Telegraph*, 23 May 1857, 5.

"Custom House-St. George's," *Royal Gazette*, 13 June 1903, 2.

"Cutlass Drill on Board the 'Resolution,'" *The Navy and Army Illustrated*, 29 May 1896, 262.

"Defects of the British Ironclads," *SA*, 10, 13 February 1864, 101.

"The Defence of Hong Kong," *Portsmouth Evening News*, 23 May 1885, 4.

"Departure from the Mersey of the Ram Scorpion," *Liverpool Mercury*, 20 March 1865, 7.

"Departure of the Prince Consort for Devonport," *Dublin Evening Mail*, 5 November 1863, 2.

Devizes and Wiltshire Gazette, 22 October 1863, 3.

"The Disaster to the Prince Consort," *Dublin Evening Mail*, 31 October 1863, 2.

"The Disastrous Fire at Hull," *Manchester Evening News*, 5 May 1870, 4.

"The Double-Turreted Ship Wyvern," *ILN*, 16 December 1865, 594.

"The Dover Volunteer Review," *Sheffield Independent*, 29 March 1869, 2.

"Dry Dock at Halifax, Nova Scotia," *Hampshire Advertiser*, 21 August 1886, 2.

"The 'Dunderberg,'" *SA*, 8, 14 March 1863, 162.

"The Easter Review at Dover," *Hampshire Advertiser*, 31 March 1869, 4.

"The Easter Review at Dover," *South London Press*, 3 April 1869, 11.

"England and Russia," *Derby Daily Telegraph*, 22 April 1885, 4.

"England and the War," *Derby Mercury*, 10 August 1870, 3.

"England's Peril in Case of War," *Morning Post*, 6 December 1884, 3.

"English and American Ironclads," *Greenock Advertiser*, 5 May 1863, 4.

"The Ericsson Battery," *SA*, 6, 1 February 1862, 73.

"Escape of Colonel Kelly and Capt. Deasey," *Dublin Evening Mail*, 20 September 1867, 3.

"The Evolution of the Fighting Top," *Globe-Republican*, 7 July 1898, 2.

"An Ex-Confederate Ship of War," *London Evening Standard*, 6 August 1869, 3.

Exeter Flying Post, 8 November 1865, 5.

"The Exhibition of Iron and Steel," *SA*, 16, 15 June 1867, 374.

"The Experimental Squadron," *Morning Chronicle*, 5 June 1846, 3.

"Experiments at Shoeburyness," *Sheffield Daily Telegraph*, 2 August 1864, 7.

"Experiments with Bessemer's Process" *SA*, 12, 1 November 1856, 64.

"Explosion on Board H.M.S. Wivern," *Liverpool Mercury*, 21 November 1867, 5.

"The Fastest Tug-Vessel on the Mersey," *Liverpool Daily Post*, 14 January 1863, 5.

"The Federal Government and England's Neutral Rights," *Westmorland Gazette*, 26 September 1863, 2.

"The Federal Government and Mr. Laird," *Dundee, Perth and Cupar Advertiser*, 25 August 1863, 8.

"The Fisheries Exhibition," *Morning Post*, 22 June 1883, 3.

"The Fleet and the Rams," *Liverpool Daily Post*, 15 September 1863, 5.

"The Fleet at Cherbourg," *Times*, 15 August 1865, 7.

"The Fleets in the Far East," *London Evening Standard*, 4 January 1898, 2.

"For Sale, The Fine Paddle Tug Steamer Lion," *Liverpool Daily Post*, 29 July 1863, 8.

"The Foreign Iron-Clads" *SA*, 9, 12 December 1863, 377.

"The Fortifications of Hong Kong," *Times*, 28 October 1884, 3.

"France," *London Daily News*, 2 June 1864, 5.

"French and Sardinian Preparations" *Western Daily Press*, 25 February 1859, 3.

"The French Fleet at Portsmouth," *Cork Examiner*, 2 September 1865, 4.

"The French Fleet at Portsmouth," *Leeds Mercury*, 1 September 1865, 4.

"The French Fleet at Portsmouth," *Reading Mercury*, 2 September 1865, 2.

"From Our London Correspondent," *Derby Daily Telegraph*, 28 May 1880, 2.

"From our Naval Correspondent," *London Evening Standard*, 30 March 1869, 2.

"From our Naval Correspondent," *London Standard*, 29 March 1869, 6.

"Furious Hurricane at Bermuda," *NYT*, 9 September 1878, 8.

"General Notes," *NYT*, 14 June 1903, 6.

"Goodbye to the Canada," *The Sun*, 16 May 1885, 2.

"The Great Exhibition," *Dundee Advertiser*, 10 May 1862, 3.

"Great Fire at Hull," *York Herald*, 7 May 1870, 3.

"Great Fire in Hull," *Hull Packet*, 6 May 1870, 5–6.

"The Great Floating Dock for Bermuda," *SA*, 1 January 1869, 20, 7.

"The Great Naval Review," *Dublin Evening Mail*, 16 July 1867, 2.

"The Great Volunteer Review at Dover," *Dundee Courier*, 31 March 1869, 3.

"The Guard Ship at Queenstown," *Cork Examiner*, 4 May 1869, 3.

"Gunboat Building on the Mersey," *Westmorland Gazette*, 22 November 1862, 8.

"Gunnery Trials of the Devastation," *London Evening Standard*, 17 July 1873, 3.

"H. M. S. Warrior," *West Middlesex Advertiser and Family Journal*, 11 July 1863, 3.

"H. M. S. Wyvern [sic]," *Liverpool Daily Post*, 10 October 1865, 10.

Hampshire Advertiser, 30 December 1865, 12.

Hampshire Advertiser, 1 May 1869, 8.

Hampshire Advertiser, 19 May 1869, 3.

Hampshire Advertiser, 23 October 1869, 8.
Hampshire Advertiser, 1 January 1870, 8.
Hampshire Advertiser, 8 June 1872, 8.
Hampshire Advertiser, 21 February 1880, 8.
Hampshire Advertiser, 28 February 1880, 8.
Hampshire Telegraph, 21 August 1867, 1.
"The Hampshire Volunteer Review," *Berkshire Chronicle*, 1 May 1869, 7.
"Haymarket, Theatre Royal," *Era*, 7 June 1863, 8.
"Heavy Guns for the Navy," *Newcastle Journal*, 22 November 1867, 4.
"Henry H. Laird," *Engineer*, 75, 2 June 1893, 467.
"Her Majesty's Ship Majestic Keeping Watch over the Steam-Rams in the Mersey," *ILN*, 28 November 1863, 552.
"Her Majesty's Ship Scorpion," *Hampshire Advertiser*, 21 August 1869, 8.
"H.M. Turret-Ships Wivern and Scorpion," *Illustrated Times*, 4 November 1865, 282.
"H.M.S. Dreadnought," *Portsmouth Evening News*, 15 June 1878, 2.
"H.M.S. Scorpion," *Cork Examiner*, 20 September 1869, 2.
"H.M.S. Scorpion," *Hampshire Advertiser*, 25 March 1865, 8.
"H.M.S. Scorpion," *Royal Gazette*, 20 December 1902, 1.
"H. M. S. Warrior," *West Middlesex Advertiser and Family Journal*, 11 July 1863, 3.
"H.M.S. Wivern," *China Mail*, 29 May 1902, 4.
"H.M.S. Wivern," *Times*, 20 February 1880, 12.
"H. M. S. Wyvern [sic]," *Liverpool Daily Post*, 10 October 1865, 10.
"H.M.S. Wyvern [sic] in a swell of the Atlantic," *ILN*, 27 October 1866, 413.
Hong Kong Telegraph, 18 July 1881, 2.
Hong Kong Telegraph, 20 December 1881, 2.
"Imperial Parliament," *London Evening Standard*, 21 July 1866, 3.
"An Important Confession," *Daily National Republican*, 3 November 1863, 1.
"The Ineffective 'Wivern,'" *China Mail*, 12 January 1901, 4.
"Insolvent Debtors' Court," *Morning Chronicle*, 8 April 1861, 8.
"Intended Rescue at Holyhead," *Cork Examiner*, 15 November 1867, 3.
"The International Exhibition," *Hampshire Chronicle*, 17 May 1862, 3.
"International Exhibition," *Kentish Chronicle*, 31 May 1862, 2.
"The Invasion of England," *Cheshire Observer*, 26 August 1865, 6.
"Ireland," *Morning Post*, 23 September 1867, 8.
"Ireland Island," *Royal Gazette*, 6 July 1897, 5.
"Iron Cased Forts," *Sheffield Independent*, 17 June 1868, 2.
"Iron Shipbuilding at Liverpool," *Illustrated London News (ILN)*, 25 October 1856, 417.
"Iron-Cased Shipbuilding," *London Evening Standard*, 10 February 1863, 3.
"Iron-clad Jack: A Sea-Song of the Future," *Punch*, 12 April 1862, 146.
"Iron-Plated Frigates," *Dublin Evening Packet and Correspondent*, 2 October 1860, 2.
"Is Our Navy Ready for War?" *China Mail*, 24 April 1885, 3.
"The Japanese Ambassadors in Liverpool," *Liverpool Daily Post*, 29 May 1862, 5.
"John Laird," *Engineer*, 85, 28 January 1898, 88.
"John Laird's Contract for the New Iron-Clad Frigate," *Cheshire Observer*, 14 September 1861, 5.
"The Jubilee Celebrations at Bermuda," *The Navy and Army Illustrated*, 3 September 1897, 237–238.
"Kelly and Deasey-Searching a Greek Vessel" *Dublin Evening Mail*, 2 October 1867, 4.
"The Kuldja Frontier," *Morning Post*, 1 April 1880, 5.
"The Laird Rams," *SA*, 11, 1 October 1864, 224.
"The Last Phase of the Armstrong Gun," *SA*, 6, 10 May 1862, 297.
"The Last Rebel Ram," *SA*, 12 (New Series), 27 May 1865, 335.
"The Late Naval Engagement," *Dublin Evening Mail*, 30 June 1864, 2.
"Later from the North," *Daily Dispatch*, 24 November 1862, 1.
"Launch of a Government Troopship at Birkenhead," *Liverpool Mercury*, 24 November 1862, 3.
"Launch of a Yacht at Birkenhead," *Liverpool Mercury*, 17 July 1858, 9.
"Launch of Her Majesty's Iron-Cased Screw Frigate Resistance," *Morning Post*, 12 April 1861, 5.
"Launch of Her Majesty's Ironclad Frigate Lord Warden," *Sheffield Daily Telegraph*, 30 May 1865, 3.
"The Launch of H.M.S. Monarch," *London Daily News*, 26 May 1868, 5.
"Launch of H.M.S. Phaeton," *Glasgow Herald*, 28 February 1883, 10.
"Launch of Iron Steam 'Rams' at Birkenhead," *Sheffield Independent*, 31 August 1863, 3.
"Launch of Iron Steam Rams at Birkenhead," *Birmingham Daily Post*, 31 August 1863, 4.
"Launch of the Agincourt," *London Evening Standard*, 28 March 1865, 6.
"Launch of the Ironcased [sic] Frigate 'Resistance,'" *Newcastle Journal*, 13 April 1861, 3.
"The Launch of the Monarch," *Reynold's Newspaper*, 31 May 1868, 2.
"Launch of the Resistance," *London Evening Standard*, 12 April 1861, 3.
"Launch of the Valiant," *Lloyd's Weekly Newspaper*, 18 October 1863, 1.
"Lectures on the American Crisis," *Liverpool Mercury*, 7 February 1863, 6.
"Letter from 'Manhattan,'" *London Evening Standard*, 8 May 1863, 5.
"Like a Big Mosquito Menacing Our Coast," *Morning Times*, 17 May 1896, 18.
"Liverpool News," *Glasgow Herald*, 13 April 1863, 4.
"Liverpool News," *Glasgow Herald*, 2 July 1864, 7.
"Liverpool News," *Glasgow Herald*, 30 September 1861, 5.

"Local and General," *Hong Kong Telegraph*, 10 May 1888, 3.
"Local and General," *Hong Kong Telegraph*, 19 December 1903, 4.
"London Correspondence," *Aberdeen Journal*, 19 February 1880, 5.
London Daily News, 19 April 1867, 4.
London Evening Standard, 7 August 1863, 3.
No Subject, *London Evening Standard*, 14 May 1878, 5.
"London Gossip," *Hampshire Advertiser*, 6 August 1881, 3.
"London Sketches," *Northampton Mercury*, 15 February 1862, 4.
"Lord Clarendon at Liverpool," *Dublin Evening Mail*, 16 October 1862, 4.
"The Loss of H.M.S. Captain," *Hampshire Telegraph*, 17 September 1870, 7.
"The Lucky Shoemaker," *Belfast News-Letter*, 5 December 1863, 4.
"Magistrates Office-Tuesday," *Surrey Advertiser*, 27 January 1866, 2.
"The Man in the Military Mast Fills a Post of Deadly Peril," *Salt Lake Herald*, 1 May 1898, 20.
Manchester Courier and Lancashire General Advertiser, 6 November 1880, 6.
"Manufacture of Armour Plates," *Exeter Flying Post*, 15 April 1863, 6.
"Marine Engines and Engineering," *Shields Daily Gazette*, 6 September 1882, 5.
"Maritime Notes," *Shields Daily Gazette*, 6 December 1901, 4.
"Marriages" *London Evening Standard*, 5 June 1861, 7.
"Mechanics for Russia," *SA*, 10, 25 August 1855, 395.
"The Mersey Steel and Iron Company, Limited," *Liverpool Daily Post*, 26 September 1865, 7.
"Military and Naval," *Reading Mercury*, 16 October 1869, 7.
"Miscellaneous," *Leamington Spa Courier*, 23 May 1863, 5.
"Miscellaneous," *New York Times (NYT)*, 28 June 1855, 1.
"Miscellaneous," *North Wales Chronicle*, 25 March 1865, 2.
"Miscellaneous Naval," *Portsmouth Times and Naval Gazette*, 7 August 1869, 4.
"Miscellaneous, Return of a Blockade-Runner, Departure of the Scorpion," *NYT*, 8 April 1865, 2.
"Modern Navies," *Dundee Courier*, 30 August 1865, 3.
"More Electoral Defeats of the French Government," *Herts, Guardian, Agricultural Journal, and General Advertiser*, 23 January 1864, 2.
"Movement of H. M. Ships," *Hampshire Telegraph*, 1 December 1894, 8.
"Movement of H. M. Ships," *Portsmouth Evening News*, 11 December 1894, 2.
"Movements of Queen's Ships," *Portsmouth Evening News*, 20 March 1880, 2.
"Movements of Queen's Ships," *Portsmouth Evening News*, 8 April 1880, 2.
"Movements of Queen's Ships," *Portsmouth Evening News*, 22 May 1880, 2.
"Mr. J. Laird, M. P., and the United States Government," *Cheshire Observer*, 29 August 1863, 7.
"Mr. John Laird, and the Birkenhead Ironworks and Docks," *ILN*, 27 July 1861, 74.
"Mr. John Laird. The Birkenhead Ironworks and Docks," *Liverpool Daily Post*, 29 July 1861, 3.
"Mr. Whitworth and the 'Ironsides,'" *Aldershot Military Gazette*, 4 October 1862, 4.
"Multum In Parvo," *Liverpool Mercury*, 7 October 1861, 7.
"Mysterious Murder in Rhenish-Prussia, District of Coblenz, On the Rhine," *Cork Examiner*, 10 June 1861, 4.
"Naval and Military," *Bath Chronicle and Weekly Gazette*, 17 August 1865, 7.
"Naval and Military," *London Daily News*, 28 July 1885, 6.
"Naval and Military," *London Daily News* 30 October 1865, 2.
"Naval and Military," *London Daily News*, 2 October 1861, 3.
"Naval and Military," *London Daily News*, 27 January 1862, 2.
"Naval & Military," *Portsmouth Evening News*, 16 November 1899, 2.
"Naval and Military Intelligence," *Essex Standard*, 27 September 1861, 4.
"Naval and Military Intelligence," *London Evening Standard*, 14 August 1862, 6.
"Naval and Military Intelligence," *London Evening Standard*, 24 August 1867, 3.
"Naval and Military Intelligence," *London Evening Standard*, 5 August 1868, 6.
"Naval and Military Intelligence," *London Evening Standard*, 12 October 1869, 6.
"Naval and Military Intelligence," *London Evening Standard*, 21 December 1869, 3.
"Naval and Military Intelligence," *London Evening Standard*, 2 April 1878, 3.
"Naval and Military Intelligence," *London Evening Standard*, 12 January 1880, 3.
"Naval and Military Intelligence," *London Standard*, 20 December 1869, 3.
"Naval and Military Intelligence," *Morning Post*, 21 March 1862, 2.
"Naval and Military Intelligence," *Morning Post*, 19 January 1863, 3.
"Naval and Military Intelligence," *Morning Post*, 18 November 1867, 3.
"Naval and Military Intelligence," *Morning Post*, 7 September 1869, 2.
"Naval and Military Intelligence," *Morning Post*, 11 November 1869, 3.
"Naval and Military Intelligence," *Morning Post*, 23 March 1878, 6.
"Naval and Military Intelligence," *Morning Post*, 24 March 1880, 5.
"Naval and Military Intelligence," *Morning Post*, 29 March 1880, 6.
"Naval and Military Intelligence," *Morning Post*, 28 July 1885, 5.

"Naval and Military Intelligence," *Morning Post*, 25 July 1888, 7.

"Naval and Military Intelligence," *Times*, 12 February 1880, 10.

"Naval and Military Intelligence," *Times*, 14 February 1880, 8.

"Naval and Military News," *Hampshire Telegraph*, 26 June 1867, 2.

"Naval and Military News," *Hampshire Telegraph*, 13 November 1867, 2.

"Naval and Military News," *Hampshire Telegraph*, 12 August 1868, 2.

"Naval and Military News," *Hampshire Telegraph*, 29 September 1869, 2.

"Naval and Military News," *Hampshire Telegraph*, 16 October 1869, 4.

"Naval and Military News," *Hampshire Telegraph*, 20 October 1869, 2

"Naval and Military News," *Hampshire Telegraph*, 15 December 1869, 2.

"Naval and Military News," *Hampshire Telegraph*, 15 October 1870, 4.

"Naval and Military Preparations," *Hampshire Telegraph*, 1 May 1878, 2.

"Naval Armaments," *Liverpool Daily Post*, 25 September 1867, 10.

"Naval Ball at Ireland," *Royal Gazette*, 2 April 1895, 5.

"Naval Intelligence," *Liverpool Daily Post*, 1 October 1862, 5.

"Naval News from the China Station," *Hampshire Telegraph*, 4 April 1885, 8

"Naval News from the China Station," *Hampshire Telegraph*, 25 April 1885, 8.

"Naval News from the China Station," *Hampshire Telegraph*, 29 August 1885, 8.

"Naval News from the China Station," *Portsmouth Evening News*, 29 August 1885, 8.

"Naval News from the China Station," *Portsmouth Evening News*, 31 January 1885, 4.

"Naval Notes and News," *Hampshire Telegraph*, 23 March 1878, 4–5.

"Naval Notes and News," *Hampshire Telegraph*, 18 February 1880, 2.

"Naval Notes and News," *Hampshire Telegraph*, 25 February 1880, 2.

"Naval Notes and News," *Hampshire Telegraph*, 14 August 1886, 8.

"Naval Notes and News," *Hampshire Telegraph*, 19 December 1891, 8.

"A Naval Revolution," *Reynolds's Newspaper*, 9 November 1873, 2.

"The Navy," *Dublin Evening Mail*, 15 July 1862, 1.

"The Navy," *Dublin Evening Mail*, 20 January 1863, 2.

"The Navy," "H.M. Gun-battery 'Terror,'" *Royal Gazette*, 20 October 1857, 2.

"The Navy that is Needed," *National Republican*, 31 January 1885, 1.

"The Neutrality Proclamation," *The Spectator*, 18 May 1861, 521.

"A New Confederate Iron-clad," *Sheffield Independent*, 18 August 1862, 4.

"A New French Gunboat," *Falkirk Herald*, 7 March 1861, 2.

"The New Iron-clads in England," *SA*, 9, 3 October 1863, 214.

"The New M.P.'s." *Morning Chronicle*, 25 December 1861, 6.

"The New Steamship Adriatic," *London Evening Standard*, 3 April 1872, 3.

"New Steel Wire," *SA*, 14, 12 March 1859, 221.

"A New Trade in Birmingham, Wire Rope Making," *Birmingham Daily Post*, 2 April 1866, 5.

"News from Jackson," *Dallas Herald*, 10 June 1863, 1.

"News from the China Station," *Hampshire Telegraph*, 6 November 1880, 5.

"News from the China Station," *Hampshire Telegraph*, 22 November 1884, 8.

"News of the Day," *Liverpool Daily Post*, 29 August 1863, 4.

"News of the Day," *Portsmouth Evening News*, 17 February 1880, 2.

"The North America and West India Station," *Exeter and Plymouth Gazette*, 6 December 1861, 10.

"The North American Station," *The Navy and Army Illustrated*, 9 December 1899, 291.

"Note on Naval Estimates," *Wrexham Advertiser*, 23 March 1861, 3.

"A Novel Armament," *Dublin Evening Mail*, 18 February 1868, 4.

"Obituary," *Manchester Courier and Lancashire General Advertiser*, 15 September 1894, 13.

"The Old Powder and the New," *The Navy and Army Illustrated*, 4 November 1899, 172.

"Old Warship for a Target," *New York Daily Tribune*, 5 May 1901, 2.

"Oldknow, Fleet Engineer R. C., R.N, "Trial Trips: Ancient and Modern," *The Navy and Army Illustrated*, 20 March 1896, 146.

"Ordnance in the London Exhibition," *SA*, 6, 21 June 1862, 391.

"Our China Squadron," *Lichfield Mercury*, 27 July 1900, 7.

"Our Naval Position in the Event of War," *Huddersfield Chronicle*, 7 December 1861, 6.

"Our Power by Sea," *Liverpool Mercury*, 4 February 1876, 7.

"Outlines of the Week," *Kentish Chronicle*, 25 April 1863, 5.

"Passengers Arrived," *NYT*, 22 May 1861, 8.

"Passing of the 'Wivern,'" *Hong Kong Telegraph*, 13 March 1923, 7.

"Patent Railway Axles-Interesting Chance in Extending a Patent" *Scientific American*, 4, 14 April 1849, 235.

"Piracy in Chinese Waters," *Liverpool Mercury*, 12 May 1899, 12.

"Playing at Warfare," *Lake's Falmouth Packet and Cornwall Advertiser*, 1 May 1869, 2.

"Plymouth Breakwater Fort," *London Daily News*, 23 June 1868, 5.

"Points," *Leeds Times*, 21 February 1880, 4.

"Portsmouth Branch," *Hampshire Advertiser*, 19 April 1890, 8.

"Portsmouth, June 6, 1846," *Hampshire Advertiser*, 6 June 1846, 5.

"Portsmouth, May 30, 1846," *Hampshire Advertiser*, 30 May 1846, 5.

"The Portsmouth Review," *Manchester Courier and Lancashire General Advertiser*, 27 April 1869, 5.

"The Portsmouth Volunteer Review," *Portsmouth Times and Naval Gazette*, 1 May 1869, 7.

"The Premier Gas," *Morning Chronicle*, 18 September 1858, 7.

"Preparations of the Admiralty," *Dublin Evening Mail*, 21 September 1867, 3.

"Prince Alfred in Liverpool," *Blackburn Standard*, 25 September 1861, 4.

"Progress of the New Railway into Liverpool," *Liverpool Daily Post*, 20 September 1862, 5.

"Projected Increase to the Russian Pacific Fleet," *Manchester Courier and Lancashire General Advertiser*, 14 February 1880, 11.

"Prolonged Patents," *Birmingham Daily Post*, 24 June 1881, 6.

"Queenstown Intelligence" *Cork Examiner*, 27 July 1869, 2.

"R.B.Y Club Cruising Race," *Royal Gazette*, 12 July 1887, 2.

"The Rebel Pirates. Ironclads on the Mersey. Description of the Vessels," *NYT*, 16 September 1863, 1, 2.

"The Rebel Rams A Fit Case for Aid," *NYT*, 17 October 1864, 2.

"The Recent Hurricane," *Royal Gazette*, 7 September 1880, 5.

"A Reclassification of Her Majesty's Ships," *Times*, 6 September 1892, 9.

"Reefing Topsails," *London Daily News*, 16 September 1861, 2.

"Return of Lord Lyons from Washington," *Caledonian Mercury*, 17 June 1862, 3.

"The Review at Portsmouth," *London Standard*, 27 April 1869, 6.

"The Review of 1867," *Hampshire Telegraph*, 20 July 1867, 4.

"The Rolf Krake," *Glasgow Herald*, 12 August 1864, 6.

"The Rolf Krake at Alsen," *Glasgow Herald*, 16 July 1864, 3.

"The Romance of the Sea," *Dundee Courier*, 22 October 1878, 7.

"Rope Trade," *Aberdeen Journal*, 8 January 1868, 7.

Royal Gazette, 19 October 1869, 2.

"The Royal Marine Artillery," *Dundee Evening Telegraph*, 4 December 1879, 3.

"The Royal Marine Artillery," *Portsmouth Evening News*, 10 October 1879, 2.

"The Royal Naval Reserve," *Carlisle Journal*, 6 December 1861, 8.

"Royal Proclamation," *Reynold's Newspaper*, 19 May 1861, 10.

"The Royal Sovereign," *Western Daily Press*, 11 November 1864, 3.

"Russia and China," *Bath Chronicle and Weekly Gazette*, 22 July 1880, 6.

"Russia and China," *London Evening Standard*, 5 May 1879, 5.

"Russia in the Pacific," *Edinburgh Evening News*, 20 May 1880, 2.

"Russian Naval Activity," *Derby Daily Telegraph*, 27 August 1879, 3.

"The Russian Torpedo Fleet," *Portsmouth Evening News*, 4 November 1878, 3.

"The Russian Volunteer Fleet," *NYT*, 17 May 1878, 1.

"Russia's Easy Victory," *Edinburgh Evening News*, 28 March 1898, 4.

"Russia's Naval Strength," *Dundee Evening Telegraph*, 13 June 1885, 3.

"Sale of H.M.S. Scorpion," *Royal Gazette*, 31 January 1903, 2.

"Science and Modern Warfare," *SA*, 14, 4 June 1859, 325.

"The Science of Iron and Steel," *SA*, 8 (New Series), 14 February 1863, 105.

"The Scorpion," *Cork Examiner*, 14 October 1869, 2.

"The Scorpion Foundered," *Royal Gazette*, 20 June 1903, 2.

"Sea-Going Turret Ships-III," *London Daily News*, 18 October 1870, 2.

"Secretary Welles and Mr. Laird," *New York Daily Tribune*, 10 August 1863, 4.

"Semi-Steel Locomotive Tires," *SA*, 4, 5 January 1861, 3.

Sheffield Daily Telegraph, 31 March 1865, 2.

"Ship Launch," *Sussex Advertiser*, 18 January 1859, 6.

"Ship Launches on Saturday," *Liverpool Daily Post*, 6 July 1863, 5.

"Shipbuilding on the Mersey," *Chester Chronicle*, 29 November 1862, 7.

"Shipbuilding on the Mersey during 1878," *Aberdeen Journal*, 25 December 1878, 7.

"Shipping," *Liverpool Mercury*, 20 March 1880, 7.

"Shipping Intelligence," *Belfast Morning News*, 3 May 1869, 2.

"Shipping Intelligence," *Belfast Morning News*, 2 August 1869, 4.

"Shoeburyness," *Aldershot Military Gazette*, 20 June 1868, 3.

"The Shoeburyness Experiments on Plymouth Fort Shield," *Illustrated Times*, 27 June 1868, 14–15.

"The Siege of Washington, N.C.," *Daily Dispatch*, 16 April 1863, 1.

"Sinking of the Scorpion," *Royal Gazette*, 30 June 1903, 1.

"Southern Views of American Affairs," *Liverpool Mercury* 18 April 1863, 5.

"The Spy System in Liverpool," *Liverpool Daily Post*, 17 April 1863, 4.

"Squandering the Taxes," *Liverpool Daily Post*, 13 October 1866, 7.

"The State of the Navy," *Bristol Mercury*, 8 April 1880, 3.

"Stations of the British Navy," *Bath Chronicle and Weekly Gazette*, 29 August 1867, 2.

"Stations of the Royal Navy in Commission," *Morning Post*, 5, December 1861, 6.
"The Steam Battery 'Monitor,'" *SA*, 6, 22 March 1862, 177.
"The Steam Ram Mystery," *Dundee, Perth, and Cupar Advertiser*, 8 September 1863, 3.
"The Steam Ram of Sartorius," *Hampshire Telegraph*, 18 September 1858, 4.
"The Steam Rams at Birkenhead," *Chester Chronicle*, 26 September 1863, 2.
"The Steam Rams Seized at Birkenhead," *Liverpool Mercury*, 10 March 1864, 6.
"Steel Ropes," *SA*, 13 (New Series), 23 December 1865, 405.
"The Sultan in England," *Exeter and Plymouth Gazette*, 17 July 1867, 9.
"Summary," *York Herald*, 8 July 1880, 4.
"Telegraphic," *Shreveport Weekly News*, 4 May 1863, 1.
"Times Telegram," *Liverpool Mercury*, 15 June 1863, 5.
"To Make Steel from Pig Iron," *SA*, 3, 20, 10 November 1860, 308.
"Torpedo Nets," *Sheffield Independent*, 12 May 1885, 2.
"Torpedoes," *Edinburgh Evening News*, 2 June 1876, 4.
"Trial of Her Majesty's Turret Ram Scorpion," *Manchester Courier and Lancashire General Advertiser*, 31 August 1864, 3.
"Trial of Mr. MacKay's New Gun," *Cheshire Chronicle*, 16 April 1864, 3.
"Trial Trip of Her Majesty's Ship Wivern," *London Evening Standard*, 6 October 1865, 3.
"Trial Trip of H.M.S. Wivern," *Manchester Courier and Lancashire General Advertiser*, 10 June 1865, 11.
"Trial Trip of One of the Mersey Steam Rams," *Liverpool Mercury*, 31 August 1864, 6.
"A Trifling Chronological Error," *Punch*, 26 April 1862, 163.
"The Turret Ship Scorpion," *London Evening Standard*, 24 September 1869, 3.
"Turret Ships," *London Evening Standard*, 11 November 1865, 5.
"Turret Ships," *London Evening Standard*, 10 January 1866, 3.
"Turrets v. Broadsides," *London Evening Standard*, 2 February 1870, 1.
"The '292,'" *Dublin Evening Mail*, 20 November 1862, 3.
"The use of armour in the Royal Navy," *Hampshire Telegraph*, 30 January 1886, 2.
"Value of Plain Talk," *Omaha Daily Bee*, 1 March 1898, 4.
"Very Latest," *Royal Gazette*, 23 April 1878, 5.
"Vessels Building for the Confederates," *Liverpool Mercury*, 13 February 1863, 6.
"Visit to Messrs Laird's Shipbuilding Yard," *Dundee Courier*, 19 September 1863, 2.
"The Volunteer Review," *Dover Express*, 2 April 1869, 4.
"The Vote by Ballot," *Manchester Courier and Lancashire General Advertiser*, 22 January 1864, 3.
"Vulcan Arming Neptune," *Punch*, 19 April 1862, 157.
"War News," *SA*, 10, 21 July 1855, 355.
"War Notes," *Western Times*, 25 August 1870, 4.
"The War Preparations," *London Evening Standard*, 4 May 1885, 2.
"War Rockets," *London Evening Standard*, 27 September 1883, 2.
"The Week's News," *Cheshire Observer*, 25 June 1864, 4.
"The Whitworth Gun," *Daily Dispatch*, 22 June 1861, 4.
"Who Cast the Screws for the Italian Frigate?", *SA*, 11, 3 September 1864, 150.
"Who's to Blame?" *Hampshire Telegraph*, 18 December 1869, 4.
"The Wonders of the Port of London," *SA*, 9, 5 December 1863, 357.
"The Yankee Blockade of Bermuda," *Newcastle Journal*, 30 October 1862, 3.
"Yankee Espionage in England," *London Evening Standard*, 23 April 1863, 5.

Secondary Sources

Articles

Alden, Commander John D. U.S.N. (Ret.), "The Old Navy: Monitors 'Round Cape Horn," *Proceedings Magazine*, 100 (September 1974).
Allen, Matthew, "The Deployment of Untried Technology: British Naval Tactics in the Ironclad Era," *War in History*, 15 (July 2008).
"The American Navy in the Late War," *The Living Age*, 90 (8 September 1866).
Anderson, Bern, "The Naval Strategy of the Civil War," *Military Affairs*, 26 (Spring 1962).
Ashworth, William, "Aspects of Late Victorian Naval Administration," *The Economic History Review*, 22 (December 1969).
Baldwin, Henry, "Farragut in Mobile Bay," *Scribner's Monthly*, 13 (February 1877).
Ballard, Admiral G. A. "The First Mastless Capital Ship H.M.S. Devastation," *The Mariner's Mirror*, XXII (1946).
Bastable, Marshall J., "From Breechloaders to Monster Guns: Sir William Armstrong and the Invention of Modern Artillery, 1854–1880," *Technology and Culture*, 33 (April 1992).
Baugh, Daniel A. *The Journal of Interdisciplinary History*, 27 (Summer 1996), review of C. I. Hamilton, *Anglo-French Naval Rivalry 1840–1870* (New York, 1993).
Baxter, Colin F., "Lord Palmerston: Panic Monger or Naval Pacemaker?" *Social Science*, 47 (Autumn, 1972)
Berryman, John, "British Imperial Defence Strategy and Russia: The Role of the Royal

Navy in the Far East, 1878–1898," *IJNH*, 1 (April 2002).
Berube, Lieutenant Commander (USNR) Claude G., "American Thunder Childs" *Naval History*, 24 (June 2010).
Bjerg, Hans Christian, "When the Monitors Came to Europe: The Danish Monitor Rolf Krake, 1863," *International Journal of Naval History (IJNH)*, 1 (October 2002).
Blair, Dan, "One Good Port: Beaufort Harbor, North Carolina, 1863–1864," *The North Carolina Historical Review*, 79 (July 2002).
Blumenthal, Henry, "Confederate Diplomacy: Popular Notions and International Realities," *The Journal of Southern History*, 32 (May 1966).
Brassey, Thomas, M. P., "On a Colonial Naval Volunteer Force," *RUSI Journal*, 22 (17 May 1878).
Bridge, Horatio, "Personal Recollections of Nathanial Hawthorne, *Harper's New Monthly Magazine*, 84 (March 1892).
Bristol, Charles L., "Notes on the Bermudas," *Bulletin of the American Geographical Society*, 33 (1901).
"British Neutrality," *The Living Age*, 77 (18 April 1863).
Brown, Alexander Crosby, "The John Randolph: America's First Commercially Successful Iron Steamboat," *The Georgia Historical Quarterly*, 36 (March 1952).
Brown, William Garrott, "The Resources of the Confederacy," *The Atlantic Monthly*, 88 (December 1901).
Brown, William O. Jr., and Burdekin, Richard C. K., "Turning Points in the U.S. Civil War: A British Perspective," *Journal of Economic History*, 60 (Mar. 2000).
Chere, Lewis M., "The Hong Kong Riots of October 1884: Evidence for Chinese Nationalism," *Royal Asiatic Society Hong Kong Branch*, 20 (1980).
Connah, Graham and Pearson, David, "Artifact of Empire: The Tale of a Gun," *Historical Archaeology*, 36 (2002).
De Heere, R. F. Scheltema, "The Prins Hendrik Der Nederlanden," *The Mariner's Mirror*, 17 (Cambridge, 1931).
De Leon, Edwin, "Ismail Pacha of Egypt," *Harpers New Monthly Magazine*, 39 (October 1869).
"Description of the Birkenhead Iron Works," *The Practical Magazine* (London, 1874).
Ekoko, A. E., "The Theory and Practice of Imperial Garrisons: The British Experiment in the South Atlantic 1881–1914," *Journal of Historical Society of Nigeria*, 12 (December 1983–June 1984).
Ferreiro, Larrie D., "The Social History of the Bulbous Bow," *Technology and Culture*, 52 (April 2011).
Fuller, Howard J., "Chilean Standoff," *Naval History*, 25 (June 2011).
Fuller, Howard J., "The *Warrior*'s Influence Abroad: The American Civil War," *IJNH*, 10 (October 2013).
Fuller, Howard J., "John Ericsson, the Monitors and Union Naval Strategy," *IJNH*, 2 (December 2004).
Gentry, Judith Fenner, "A Confederate Success in Europe: The Erlanger Loan," *The Journal of Southern History*, 36 (May 1970).
Gould, Richard A., "The Archaeology of HMS *Vixen*, an early ironclad ram in Bermuda," *The International Journal of Nautical Archaeology*, 20 (1991).
Guernsey, A. H., "Iron-Clad Vessels," *Harpers New Monthly Magazine*, 25 (September 1862).
Guernsey, A. H. "The Revolving Iron Tower and Its Inventor," *Harper's New Monthly Magazine*, 26 (January 1863).
Hamilton, C. I., "The Victorian Navy," *The Historical Journal*, 25 (June 1982).
Hernon, Joseph M., "British Sympathies in the American Civil War: A Reconsideration," *Journal of Southern History*, 33 (August 1967).
Holley, Alexander L., "Iron-Clad Ships and Heavy Ordnance" *Atlantic Monthly*, 1 (January 1863).
Horres, C. R.,. "Charleston's Civil War 'Monster Guns,' The Blakely Rifles," *The South Carolina Historical Magazine*, 97 (April 1996).
Jarvis, Adrian, "Protection and Decoration: A Tentative Investigation into Painting Ships Before the Great War," *The Great Circle*, 22 (2000).
Knowles, Anne Kelly, "Labor, Race, and Technology in the Confederate Iron Industry," *Technology and Culture*, 42 (January 2001).
Kubicek, Robert V. "The Design of Shallow-Draft Steamers for the British Empire, 1868–1906." *Technology and Culture*, 31 (July 1990).
Lambert, Andrew, "Economic Power, Technological Advantage, and Imperial Strength: Britain as a Unique Global Power, 1860–1890," *IJNH*, 5 (August 2006).
"Last of the Confederate Navy," *Confederate Veteran*, XI (Nashville, 1903).
Lautenschlager, Karl, "Technology and the Evolution of Naval Warfare," *International Security*, 8 (fall 1983).
Lebergott, Stanley, "Why the South Lost: Commercial Purpose in the Confederacy, 1861–1865," *The Journal of American History*, 70 (June 1983).
Lloyd, Captain H. T. R., RMLI, "Diary of a Young Marine," *Bermuda Historical Quarterly*, 24 (spring 1967).
Loy, Wesley, "10 Rumford Place: Doing Confederate Business in Liverpool," *The South Carolina Historical Magazine*, 98 (October 1997).
Maynard, Douglas H., "The Forbes-Aspinwall Mission," *The Mississippi Valley Historical Review*, 45 (June 1958).
"The Mechanics of Modern Naval Warfare," *The North American Review*, 103 (July 1866).
Middleton, Lt. Cdr. H. G., "H.M.S. Scorpion," *Bermuda Historical Quarterly*, XXXVII (Spring 1980).
Morris, Peter, "The Russians in Central Asia 1870–1887," *The Slavonic and Eastern European Review*, 53 (Oct. 1975).

Morus, Iwan Rhys, "'The Nervous System of Britain': Space, Time and the Electric Telegraph in the Victorian Age." *The British Journal for the History of Science*, 33 (December 2000).
Neblett, Thomas R. "Major Edward C. Anderson and the C.S.S. Fingal," *The Georgia Historical Quarterly*, 52 (June 1968).
Nish, Ian, "Politics, Trade and Communications in East Asia: Thoughts on Anglo-Russian Relations, 1861–1907," *Modern Asian Studies*, 21 (1987).
O'Dea, W. T., "A Century of British Engineering," *Journal of the Royal Society of Arts*, 99 (4 May 1951).
Owsley, Harriet Chappell, "Henry Shelton Sanford and Federal Surveillance Abroad, 1861–1865," *Mississippi Valley Historical Review*, 48 (September 1961).
Page, Captain Thomas J., C.S.N, "The Career of the Confederate Cruiser 'Stonewall,'" *Southern Historical Society Papers*, 7 (Richmond, 1879).
Pollard, S. "The "Decline of Shipbuilding on the Thames," *The Economic History Review*, 3 (1950).
Pollard, S., "Lassez-Faire and Shipbuilding," *The Economic History Review*. 5, 1 (1952).
Preston, Antony, "Creating an Inshore Navy: Royal Navy Littoral Warfare Forces in the Russian War 1854–56," *Warship 1999–2000*, edited by Antony Preston (London, 1999).
Putnam, Arnold A., "The Building of Numbers 294 & 295: The Laird Rams," *Warship 1999–2000*, edited by Antony Preston (London, 1999).
"The Ram of Liverpool," *Living Age*, 79 (12 December 1863).
Reed, Sir Edward, "The British Navy," *Harper's New Monthly Magazine*, 72 (February 1886).
Roberts, Steven, "Captain Alexander Blakely, RA, 'Original Inventor of Improvements in Cannon and the Greatest Artillerist of the Age.'" (London, 2012).
Roberts, William P., "James Dunwoody Bulloch and the Confederate Navy." *The North Carolina Historical Review*, 24 (July 1947).
Rowland, Buford, "Revolution in Nets: An Unglamorous but Essential Phase of Naval Warfare" *Military Affairs*, 11 (autumn, 1947).
The Sailor's Magazine, and Naval Journal, 9, American Seamen's Friend Society (New York, 1838).
Sandler, Stanley L. "The Day of the Ram," *Military Affairs*, 40 (December 1976).
Saul, S. B., "The Market and Development of the Mechanical Engineering Industries in Britain 1860–1914," *The Economic History Review*, New Series, 20, 1 (April 1967).
Sleeman, C. Lieutenant, R.N, "The Development of Machine Guns," *North American Review*, 139 (October 1884), 367.
Strakhovsky, Leonid I., "Russia's Privateering Projects of 1878," *Journal of Modern History*, 7 (March 1935).
Surdam, David G., "Northern Naval Superiority and he Economics of the American Civil War," *The Journal of Economic History*, 56 (June 1996).
Taylor, Amos E., "The Role of Washington in the National Economy during the Civil War," *Records of the Columbia Historical Society*, Washington D. C., 53/56 (1953/1956).
"Visit to Birkenhead" *Living Age*, 6 (5 July 1845).
"W," "The Alleged Failure of the Armstrong Gun," *Living Age*, 80 (20 February, 1864).
Wilmshurst, David, "Hong Kong during the Sino-French War (1884–1885): Impressions of a French Naval Officer," *Journal of the Royal Asiatic Society Hong Kong Branch*, 50 (2010).

Illustrations and Photographs

"The Anglo-Rebel Pirates-One of Laird's Steam-Rams," *Harpers Weekly*, 17 October 1863, 661.
"Armour-Plated Iron Turret Ship, The Scorpion," *Illustrated London Almanack for 1869*, 34.
"Her Majesty's Ship Majestic Keeping Watch over the Steam-Rams in the Mersey," *ILN*, 28 November 1863.
"H.M.S. Wivern, Double-Turreted Iron-Clad [sic] Steam-Ram," *ILN*, 16 December 1865.
"H.M.S. Wyvern [sic] in a Heavy Sea in the Channel," *ILN*, 27 October 1866, 413.
"One of the Steam-Rams in Course of Construction in Messrs. Laird's [sic] Ship-Building Yard, Birkenhead," *ILN*, 26 September 1863.
U.S. Naval Historical Center, Washington (USNHC), photo #NH 61923, "*U.S.S. Monitor (1862.)*"
USNHC Photo #NH 48145, "Engraving of Confederate ironclad built by John Laird during the Civil War."
USNHC Photo #NH 52526, "H.M.S. Wivern At anchor in the Hamoaze River, off Plymouth, England, in 1865."
USNHC Photo #NH 71211, "HMS Wivern off Plymouth, England" (1865).
USNHC Photo #NH 65901, "H.M.S. Wivern, probably during the 1870s or 1880s."
"The Volunteer Review at Dover: View of Dover from the Sea-The Naval Squadron Attacking the Forts," *ILN* 10 April,1869, 356–357.

Books

Archibald, E. H. H. *The Fighting Ships in the Royal Navy AD 897–1984*. Poole: Blandford, 1984.
Ballard, Admiral G. A. *The Black Battlefleet*. Greenwich: Society for Nautical Research, 1980..
Barry, Patrick. *Dockyard Economy and Naval Power*. London: S. Low, 1863, reprinted 2005.
Bastable, Marshall J., *Arms and the State: Sir*

William Armstrong and the Remaking of British Naval Power 1854–1914. Aldershot: Routledge, 2004.

Baxter III, James Phinney. *The Introduction of the Ironclad Warship*. Originally published Cambridge, MA: Harvard University Press, 1933; Annapolis: Naval Institute Press, 2001.

Beeler, John, *Birth of the Battleship: British Capital Ship Design 1870–1881*. London: Caxton, 2001.

Beeler, John, *British Naval Policy in the Gladstone-Disraeli Era 1866–1880*. Stanford: Stanford University Press, 1997.

Bennett, Terry, *Korea: Caught in Time*. Reading: Garnet, 2009.

Bonham, Milledge Louis, *The British Consuls in the Confederacy*. New York: Columbia University Press, 1911.

Bowcock, Andrew, *CSS Alabama: Anatomy of a Confederate Raider*. London: Chatham, 2002.

Brassey, Thomas, *The British Navy: Its Strength, Resources, and Administration*. Volumes 2, 4 Cambridge: Cambridge University Press, 2010.

Brassey, Thomas Allnutt, *The Naval Annual, 1895*. New York: Arco, 2006.

Brodie, Bernard, *Sea Power in the Machine Age*. Princeton: Princeton University Press, 1941.

Brooke, George M. *John M. Brooke; Naval Scientist and Educator*. Charlottesville: University of Virginia Press, 1980.

Brown, David K., *Warrior to Dreadnought: Warships Design and Development 1860–1905*. Barnsley: Seaforth, 1997.

Bulloch, James Dunwoody, *The Secret Service of the Confederate States in Europe; or, How the Confederate Cruisers were Equipped*. Vol. I. London: Bentley, 1883, reprinted 2012.

Bulloch, James Dunwoody, *The Secret Service of the Confederate States in Europe; or, How the Confederate Cruisers were Equipped*. Vol. II. London: Bentley 1883, reprinted 2009.

Buxton, Ian, *Big Gun Monitors: The History of the Design, Construction and Operations of the Royal Navy's Monitors*. Annapolis: Naval Institute Press, 1980.

Chesneau, Roger (ed.), *Conway's All the World's Fighting Ships 1860–1945*. London: Conway, 1979.

Church, Roy (ed.), *The Dynamics of Victorian Business: The Problems and Perspectives to the 1870s*. New York: Routledge, 2006.

Concubhair, Padraig O, *The Fenians Were Dreadful Men: The 1867 Rising*. Cork: Mercier, 2011.

Confidential Correspondence of Gustavus Vasa Fox, Volumes I, II. New York: Naval Historical Society, 1918.

Davis, Charles S., *Colin J. McRae: Confederate Financial Agent*. College Station: Texas A&M Universtiy Press, 2008.

Davis, Lance E., and Engerman, Stanley L., *Naval Blockades in Peace and War*. Cambridge: Harvard University Press, 2006.

De Leon, Edwin, *Secret History of Confederate Diplomacy Abroad*. Edited by William C. Davis. Lawrence: University Press of Kansas, 2005.

Dufour, Charles L. *The Night the War Was Lost*. Lincoln: University of Nebraska Press, 1994.

Eardley-Wilmot, Captain S, RN. *Our Fleet To-Day and Its Development during the Last Half-Century*. London: N.p., 1900.

Embree, Michael, *Bismarck's First War: The Campaign of Schleswig and Jutland 1864*. Solihull: Helion, 2006.

Evans, David, *Building the Steam Navy. Dockyards, Technology and the Creation of the Victorian Battlefleet 1830–1906*. London: Conway, 2004.

Fitzgerald, Admiral C. C. Penrose, *Memories of the Sea*. London: Penrose, 1913.

Foreman, Amanda, *A World on Fire. Britain's Crucial Role in the American Civil War*. New York: Random House, 2010.

Fowler, Will, and Sweeney, Patrick, *The Illustrated Encyclopedia of Rifles and Machine Guns*. London: Lorenz, 2007.

Fuller, Howard J. *Clad in Iron: The American Civil War and the Challenge of British Naval Power*. Annapolis: Naval Institute Press, 2008.

Fuller, Howard J. *Empire, Technology and Seapower: Royal Navy crisis in the age of Palmerston*. New York: Routledge, 2013.

Gardiner, Robert (ed.) *The Advent of Steam: The Merchant Steamship before 1900*. Edison: Conway, 2000.

Gardiner, Robert (ed.) *Conway's All the World's Fighting Ships 1860–1905*. Greenwich: Conway, 1979.

Gardiner, Robert (ed.) *Steam, Steel & Shellfire. The Steam Warship 1815–1905*. Consultant Editor Dr. Andrew Lambert. London: Conway, 1992.

Gibbons, Tony, *Warships and Naval Battles of the Civil War*. New York: Gallery, 1989.

Gilbert, Martin, *Routledge Atlas of Russian History*. New York: Routledge, 2010.

Goodwin, Doris Kearns, *Team of Rivals, The Political Genius of Abraham Lincoln*. New York: Simon and Schuster, 2005.

Greene, Jack and Massignani, Alessandro, *Ironclads at War: The Origin and Development of the Armored Warship 1854–1891*. Boston: Combined Publishing, 1998.

Greenhill, Basil and Gifford, Ann, *Steam, Politics and Patronage: The Transformation of the Royal Navy, 1815–1854*. London: Conway, 1994.

Hattaway, Herman, and Beringer, Richard, *Jefferson Davis, Confederate President*. Lawrence: University Press of Kansas, 2002.

Heald, Henrietta, *William Armstrong: Magician of the North*. Newcastle: Northumbria, 2010.

Hearn, Chester G., *Naval Battles of the Civil War* San Diego: Thunder Bay Press, 2000.

Hoogenboom, Ari, *Gustavus Vasa Fox of the Union Navy*. Baltimore: Johns Hopkins University Press, 2008.

Hughes, James B. (Compiler), *The Gatling Gun Notebook* Lincoln, RI: Mowbray, 2000.

Hunter, Alvah Folsom Hunter, *A Year on a Monitor and the Destruction of Fort Sumter.* Edited by Craig L. Symonds Columbia: University of South Carolina Press, 1987.

Keegan, John, *The American Civil War: A Military History.* New York: Vintage, 2009.

Kennedy, Paul. *The Rise and Fall of the Great Powers.* New York: Vintage, 1989.

Kinnaman, Stephen Chapin, *The Most Perfect Cruiser.* Indianapolis: Dog Ear, 2009.

Lambert, Andrew, *Battleships in Transition: The Creations of the Steam Battlefleet 1815–1860.* London: Conway, 1984.

Luraghi, Ramondo. *A History of the Confederate Navy.* Annapolis: Naval Institute Press, 1996.

Lyon, David, and Winfield, Rif. *The Sail & Steam Navy List: All the Ships of the Royal Navy 1815–1889.* London: Conway, 2004.

Marder, Arthur J. *The Anatomy of British Sea Power.* New York: Octagon, 1976.

Massie, Robert K. *Dreadnought.* New York: Random House, 1991.

Merli, Frank J. *The Alabama, British Neutrality, and the American Civil War.* Edited by David M. Fahey. Bloomington: Indiana State University Press, 2004.

Millman, Richard, *British Foreign Policy and the Coming of the Franco-Prussian War.* Oxford: Oxford University Press, 1965.

Milton, David Hepburn, *Lincoln's Spymaster: Thomas Haines Dudley and the Liverpool Network.* Mechanicsburg, PA: Stackpole, 2003.

Murray, William M. *The Age of Titans: The Rise and Fall of the Great Hellenistic Navies.* Oxford: Oxford University Press, 2012.

Niven, John, *Gideon Welles: Lincoln's Secretary of the Navy.* Baton Rouge: Louisiana State University Press, 1994.

Nordenfelt, Thorsten, *The Nordenfelt Machine Guns* Uckfield, Reprint of 1884 edition.

Parkes, Oscar, *British Battleships "Warrior" 1860 to "Vanguard" 1960 A History of Design Construction and Armament.* London: Conway, 1966.

Parkinson, J. R. *The Economics of Shipbuilding in the United Kingdom.* Cambridge: Cambridge University Press, 2011.

Particulars of the War Ships of the World. Lloyd's Register of British and Foreign Shipping. London: Lloyd's, 1893.

Penn, Commander Geoffrey, R.N. *"Up Funnel, Down Screw!" The Story of the Naval Engineer.* London: Hollis and Carter, 1955.

Philbrick, Nathaniel, *In the Heart of the Sea: The Tragedy of the Whaleship Essex.* New York: Random House, 2000.

Preston, Anthony, *The World's Worst Warships.* London: Conway Maritime Press, 2002.

Preston, Diana, *The Boxer Rebellion.* New York: Berkley, 2000.

Rafferty, Oliver P., *The Church, the State and the Fenian Threat, 1861–75* London: Palgrave Macmillan, 1999.

Reed, E. J., *Shipbuilding in Iron and Steel.* London: N.p., 1869.

Reed, Edward James, *Our Iron-clad Ships. Their Qualities, Performances, and Costs.* London: N.p., 1869, reprinted Cambridge, 2011.

Roberts, Richard, *Schroders: Merchants & Bankers.* London: Palgrave Macmillan, 1992.

Roberts, William H., *Civil War Ironclads: The U.S. Navy and Industrial Mobilization.* Baltimore: Johns Hopkins University Press, 2002.

Rolt, L.T.C., *Victorian Engineering.* London: Penguin, 1970.

Ropp, Theodore, *The Development of a Modern Navy: French Naval Policy 1871–1904.* Edited by Stephen S. Roberts. Annapolis: Naval Institute Press, 1987.

Ross, FitzGerald, *Cities and Camps of the Confederate States.* Urbana: Illinois State University Press, 1997.

Sandler, Stanley, *The Emergence of the Modern Capital Ship.* Newark: Delaware State University Press, 1979.

Scharf, J. Thomas, *History of the Confederate States Navy.* New York: Gramercy, 1996.

Scott, Admiral Sir Percy, *Fifty Years in the Royal Navy.* London: Murray, 1919.

Sennett, Richard and Oram, Henry J. *The Marine Steam Engine: A Treatise for Engineering Students, Young Engineers, and officers of the Royal Navy and Merchant Marine.* Reprint of London: Longmans, 1898 version, Bremen, 2012.

Sergeev, Evgeny, *The Great Game, 1856–1907: Russo-British Relations in Central and East Asia.* Baltimore: Johns Hopkins University Press, 2014.

Silverstone, Paul H., *Civil War Navies, 1855–1883.* New York: Routledge, 2006.

Smith, Edgar C., *A Short History of Naval and Marine Engineering.* Cambridge: Harvard University Press, 1938 reprinted 2013.

Spencer, Warren F., *The Confederate Navy in Europe.* Tuscaloosa: Alabama University Press, 1983.

Steevens, G. W., *Naval Policy: With Some Account of the Warships of the Principal Powers.* London: Methuen, 1896.

Still, William N. *Iron Afloat: The Story of the Confederate Armorclads.* Columbia: South Carolina University Press, 1971.

Still, William N. (ed.) *The Confederate Navy: The Ships, Men and Organization.* London: Conway, 1997.

Stranack, Ian, Lt. Cdr. RN (Ret.) *The Andrew and the Onions. The Story of the Royal Navy in Bermuda 1795–1975.* Bermuda: Bermuda Maritime Press, 1990.

Tunstall, Brian, *The Realities of Naval History.* London: Allen and Unwin, 1936.

Van Doren Stern, Philip. *The Confederate Navy.* New York: Doubleday, 1962.

Verne, Jules, *Paris in the Twentieth Century.* New York: Hachette, 1996.

Verne, Jules, *20,000 Leagues Under the Sea*. New York: Random House, 1966.

Ward, J. H. Commander, U.S.N. *Steam for the Million: A Popular Treatise on Steam and its Application to the Useful Arts Especially to Navigation*. New York: N.p., 1860.

Warren, Kenneth, *Steel, Ships and Men: Cammell Laird, 1824–1993*. Liverpool: Liverpool University Press, 1998.

Watson, William, *Life in the Confederate Army, Being the Observations and Experiences of an Alien in the South during the American Civil War*. New York: Scribner, 1887, reprinted, New York, 1983.

Wells, Captain John, R.N., *The Immortal "Warrior": Britain's First and Last Battleship*. Hampshire: Mason, 1987.

Welles, Gideon. *The Diary of Gideon Welles*, Volume I. 1861–30 March 1864. Boston: Norton, 1911.

Williams, Hamilton, *Britain's Naval Power: A Short History of the Growth of the British Navy*. 2. New York: Nabu Press, 2009.

Wilson, H. W. *Ironclads in Action; A Sketch of Naval Warfare from 1855–1895, With Some Account of the Development of the Battleship in England*. Volumes I, II. London: N.p., 1896.

Wilson, Walter E. and McKay, Gary L., *James D. Bulloch: Secret Agent and Mastermind*. Jefferson, NC: McFarland, 2012.

Winter, Frank H., *The First Golden Age of Rocketry*. Washington, D.C.: Smithsonian Institution Press, 1990.

Wise, Stephen R. *Lifeline of the Confederacy: Blockade Running During the Civil War*. Columbia: South Carolina University Press, 1988.

Index

Abernethy, James 13
Abyssinia, H.M.S., armored turret ship 141, 157
Achilles, H.M.S., armored steam frigate 31, 35, 98, 100, 102
Adams, Charles Francis, U.S. Minister to the United Kingdom 5, 6, 43, 44, 67, 68, 74, 78, 81, 82
Aden, Yemen 134
A.E. Byrne & Co. (Liverpool) 17, 18
Agamemnon, H.M.S., armored turret ship 142
Agincourt, H.M.S., armored steam frigate 20, 32, 33, 47, 83, 96, 99, 102, 113, 114
Alabama, C.S.S., steam sloop 1, 6, 17–20, 32, 38, 44, 45, 47, 48, 63, 68, 71, 82, 88
Alacrity, H.M.S., gunboat 152
Albatross, H.M.S., steam sloop 137
Alexandra, H.M.S., armored central battery ship 118
Alexandra, S.S., intended Confederate cruiser 66, 67, 69
America, S.S., steam paddle sloop, Imperial Russian Navy 81
Amsterdam 57
Antigua 51, 114
Archimedes, S.S. 21
Ariadne, H.M.S., steam frigate 50, 78
Arkansas, C.S.S., casemate ironclad 54
Arman, Jean-Lucien 60, 70
Armstrong, Sir William 76, 131
Armstrong gun 18, 27, 39, 70, 107–108
Asia, R.M.S., Royal Mail Ship, paddle ocean liner, Cunard line 79
Aspinwall, William H. 55–57, 63
Atlanta, C.S.S., casemate ironclad 24, 74
Atlas Ironworks (Sheffield) 32
Audacious, H.M.S., armored (central battery) steam frigate 138, 141, 142
Australia 135, 141

Aziya, steam sloop, Imperial Russian Navy 135
Aziz, Abdul, Sultan of Turkey 104
Azores Islands, Portugal 114, 115

Balaklava, S.S., ordnance steamer 89
Ballard, Admiral George A., R.N. 154
Baltimore, Maryland 73, 81
Bantry Bay, Ireland 100, 117
Baring Brothers, London bankers 55, 58
Barker, Wharton 127
Barron, Captain James, U.S.N. 21
Barron, Captain Samuel S., C.S.N. 71
Barry, Patrick 33, 70
Baton Rouge, Louisiana 78
Battlecruiser 47
Beaufort, North Carolina 73
Beauregard, General P.T.G., C.S. Army 38
Bedford, Vice Admiral Sir Frederick, R.N. 145
Beijing (Peking) China 155
Bellerophon, H.M.S., armored steam frigate 99, 100, 114
Bermuda 7, 50, 70, 113–116, 122, 125, 126, 127, 135, 143–148, 151
Bermuda, floating dry dock 114, 122, 125, 135
Bermuda Dockyard 118–120, 122, 124, 125
Birkenhead, H.M.S., paddle troopship 13
Birkenhead, England 1, 6, 9, 10, 13, 14, 19, 21, 24, 32–35, 40, 42, 44, 45, 47–49, 52, 60, 65, 68–70, 74, 76, 77, 88, 89, 95, 119, 125
Birkenhead Ironworks 12, 15, 16, 18–20, 24, 34–36, 43, 44, 46, 60, 63, 68, 83, 97
Birmingham, England 33, 104
Black Prince, H.M.S. armored steam frigate 1, 22, 62, 104, 114, 135
Blair, Montgomery, U.S. Postmaster General 46

Blakely, Captain Alexander T., Royal Artillery 38, 39
Blakely Pattern Ordnance 38, 39, 63–65, 74, 76
Bombay (Mumbai) India, 13, 141
Booker, Captain George A.C., R.N. 105, 115
Bordeaux 60, 61, 70, 82
Boston, Massachusetts, 55, 76, 77, 150, 151
Brassey, Sir Thomas 122, 154
Bravay, Adrien 60, 61, 82
Bravay, François 60, 61
Bravey & Co. (Paris) 60, 61, 69, 82, 86
Breazley, James 20
Brest, France 79, 98
Bright, John 45
Britannia Ironworks (Birkenhead) 33, 125
Brooke, Commander John M., C.S.N. 38, 76
Brooke Pattern Ordnance 38
Brooklyn Navy Yard (New York) 24, 69
Brunel, Isambard Kingdom 28
Brussels, Belgium 66
Bull, John, as a symbol of Britain 4, 29, 56
Bullivant, William M. 140
Bulloch, Commander James Dunwoody, C.S.N. 4, 5, 7, 16–21, 26, 28, 30, 32–35, 37–40, 42, 44–48, 52, 56, 57, 59–63, 66–72, 74, 76, 79, 82, 107, 158
Bulwark, H.M.S., armored steam frigate 41
Burgoyne, Captain Hugh, R.N. 95, 100, 113
Byrne, Andrew 17
Byrne, Thomas 17

Cairo, Egypt 61
Canton (Guangzhou) China 137, 155
Cape Cod, Massachusetts 76, 151
Cape Horn (Argentina and Chile) 103
Cape of Good Hope, South Africa 13, 114

203

Index

Captain, H.M.S. armored turret ship 1, 88, 113
Cardiff, Wales 77, 79, 105
Carmichael, Charles 62
Carmichael, James 62
Carter, Lieuttenant R.R., C.S.N. 63
Cerberus, Her Majesty's Victorian Ship (H.M.V.S.) armored turret ship 157
Chang, Viceroy Li-Hung 155
Charleston, South Carolina 15, 16, 18, 39, 46, 65, 73, 76
Chatham, steamboat 17
Cheops, ironclad ram 70
Cherbourg, France 94, 96
Clay, William 32
Coastguard 105, 116
Coles, Captain Cowper Phipps, R.N. 26, 28–30, 98, 109
Coles turret 26–29, 83, 90
Columbus, S.S. 127
Columbus, steam paddle tug 20
Commerell, Admiral Sir John, R.N. 125, 157
Condor, H.M.S. steam sloop 135
Confederate veterans 150
Congreve rocket 133
Connecticut, U.S.S., steam paddle sloop 40
Constantinople (Istanbul, Turkey) 128
Continental Ironworks (New York) 34
Cordite (propellent) 148
Cork, Ireland 79, 100, 103, 112, 113
Courbet, Admiral Anatole Amede Prosper, French Navy 141
Crescent, H.M.S., cruiser 145–149
Cromwell, Oliver 82
Cruse, Henry 20
Cumberland, U.S.S., sailing sloop 2, 23, 54
Cunningham, H.D.P. 37
Curacoa, H.M.S., steam corvette 129
Cutlass 96

Dacres, Vice-Admiral Sir Sidney 113
Dahlgren, Rear Admiral John A. 74, 76
Dalrymple, Admiral Sir J.C., R.N. 141
Dauntless, H.M.S., steam frigate 116
Davis, Jefferson 57, 80, 84
Deasey, Captain Timothy, Union Army, Fenian 105
Deerhound, steam yacht 32
Defence, H.M.S., armored steam frigate 23, 37
Defiance, paddle river steamer 20

Deleon, Edwin 58, 59
Deptford dockyard 83
Desertion (and Leave Breaking) 78, 104–105, 152
Devastation, H.M.S., steam paddle sloop 50
Dictator, U.S.S., monitor 76
Disraeli, Benjamin, Prime Minister 98
Donegal, H.M.S., steam ship-of-the-line 89
Dover, S.S., paddle mail packet 12
Dover, England 109, 110
Dreadnought, H.M.S., battleship 28
Dudley, Thomas H., U.S. Consul at Liverpool 30, 31, 52, 55, 56, 63, 65, 67–69
Duke of Somerset, First Lord of the Admiralty 83
Dundee, Scotland 62
Dunderberg, casemate ironclad 24
Du Pont, Rear Admiral Samuel F., U.S. Navy 46, 47, 74

Eardley-Wilmot, Captain S., R.N. 7
Echo, H.M.S., steam paddle tug 53, 54
El Monassir, Egyptian (intended) armored turret ship 5, 61, 79, 84, 158
El Tousson, Egyptian (intended) armored turret ship 5, 6, 61, 71, 79, 81, 84, 85, 86, 158
Elk, H.M.S. gunboat, 140
Elliot, Admiral C.W., R.N. 117
Elpinstone, Sir James 111
Elswick Ordnance Works (Newcastle) 77
Emile Erlanger & Co., Paris bankers 57, 58
Emperor Napoleon III 60, 96
Engine room telegraph 62, 63, 131
Enrica, S.S., later C.S.S. *Alabama* 20
Enterprise, H.M.S., armored steam sloop 83, 98, 109
Erebus, H.M.S., armored steam floating battery 50
Ericsson, John 26, 30, 31, 74
Ericsson turret 26–29
Erlanger, Emile 58
Erlanger loan 57–59, 69
Essex, whaler 21
Excellent, H.M.S., gunnery training ship 110

Fawcett, Preston & Company (Liverpool) 12, 39, 64–67
Faxon, C.H., Chief Clerk, U.S Navy Department 46
Fenian 7, 105
Ferret, H.M.S. 109
Fingal, S.S. 17, 18

Fisher, Sir John (First Sea Lord) R.N. 133, 145
Florida, C.S.S., steam sloop 1, 6, 38, 39, 48, 67, 71, 79, 88
Forbes, John Murray 55–57, 63
Foreign Enlistment Act of 1819 5, 50, 59, 60, 77, 78, 81, 84
Forrester & Company (Vauxhall Foundry, Liverpool) 132
Fort Sumter, South Carolina 64
Fox, Gustavus Vasa, U.S. Assistant Secretary of the Navy 15, 16, 46–48, 55, 74, 76, 78
Fraser, Trenholm & Co. (Liverpool) 57, 59
Freemantle, Admiral Sir E.R., R.N. 152

Galena, Illinois 64, 65
Gamble, Lieutenant Douglas, R.N. 139, 140, 142
Gatling gun 131, 134, 152, 154–155
General Admiral, armored steam frigate, Imperial Russian Navy 128, 142
George IV, steam ferry 62
Georges Shoal 150–151
Georgia, C.S.S., steam sloop 78
Gettysburg, Pennsylvania 43, 72
Gibraltar 114, 129, 132, 134
Gibraltar, S.S. 65, 66
Gladiator, S.S. 67
Gladstone, William, Prime Minister 141
Glasgow, Scotland 25, 26, 62
Glassbrook Frank (Frank Rimmers) 78
Glatton, H.M.S. 112
La Glorie, armored steam frigate, French Navy 22, 40, 41, 52, 94
Graham, Commander J.E.D., R.N. 156
Grant, General Ulysses, S., U.S. Army 72
Gray, John McFarlane 131, 132
Great Eastern, S.S. 22, 131
Greenock, Scotland 17
Griffiths propeller 62, 115
Guadalupe, paddle frigate, Mexican Navy 13

Hale rocket 80, 133, 134
Halifax, Nova Scotia 51, 79, 114, 125, 127
Hamburg, Germany 57
Hamilton, Bermuda 144
Hamilton, George A., H.M. Treasury official 84
Hampton Roads, Virginia 2, 18, 23, 24, 28, 54
Hand, Austin Joseph 68, 69
Hay, Sir John (First Lord of the Admiralty) 140
Hay's Protective Varnish 118, 119
Hazard, hulk 27

Hecla, H.M.S., torpedo boat carrier 121
Hercules Steam Tug Company (Liverpool) 20
Hicks-Beach, Sir Michael E. 140
Holland, Sub-Lieutenant Swinton, R.N. 101
Holyhead, Wales 7, 89, 105
Hong Kong 7, 120, 128, 129, 135, 136, 137, 138, 140–143, 151, 152, 154–156
Hope, Captain Charles W., R.N. 117
Hopkins, Captain John R.N. 99
Hore, Captain E., R.N., British Naval Attaché to France 82
Hotchkiss machine gun 131
Hotspur, H.M.S., armored ram 120
Howard, John T. 15, 16, 46
Hudson, Captain William H., U.S.N. 81
Hull, F.S. 59
Hull, England 116, 117
Hull number "61" 25, 61
Hull number "290" 20, 33
Hull number "291" 20
Hull number "292" 20
Hull number "293" 20
Hull number "294" 20, 23, 26, 33–37, 60, 61, 68, 72, 74, 79, 80, 84, 85
Hull number "295" 5, 20, 23, 33–37, 61, 68, 74, 79, 83, 85
Hurricane Deck 103, 110, 112, 113, 115, 116, 118
Hutton, Captain F., R.N. 50

Inglefield, Captain Edward A., R.N. 84
Invincible, H.M.S., armored (central battery) steam frigate 118
Iron Duke, H.M.S., armored (central battery) steam frigate 120, 128, 136
Ismail, Pasha of Egypt 61

J. Henry Schroder & Co., London bankers 58
Jamacia 114
James Taylor & Co. (Birkenhead) 125
Jansen, Captain M.H., Royal Netherlands Navy 98
John Brown & Company (Sheffield) 32, 83
John Randolph, steamboat 12
Jones, Commander T.G., R.N. 134

Kearsarge, U.S.S., steam sloop 32, 79
Kelly, Colonel Thomas, Union Army, Fenian 105
Kestrel, H.M.S., gunboat 136
Kimberley, Earl (John Wodehouse) 136

Kuldja (also known as Kuldzha), China 128

La Ciotat, France 19
Labrousse lieutenant Nicolas-Hippolyte, French Navy 21, 23
Lady Tredegar, S.S. 127
Laird, Henry 14, 19
Laird, John (The Younger) 14, 19
Laird, Sir John 14–16, 20, 22, 44–46, 48, 68, 82, 83, 97, 103
Laird, William 14, 16, 18, 19, 82
Laird, William (grandfather) 12
Lairds, shipbuilders 1, 4, 6, 9, 10, 12–21, 26, 30, 32, 33, 35–37, 42, 46–49, 52, 61, 63, 68, 69, 71, 79–86, 96, 116, 119, 120
Lake Ontario 126
Lamar, G.B. 12
Lapwing, H.M.S., gunboat 114
Lay, Horatio Nelson 48
"Leard," misidentification of Lairds shipbuilders by Jules Verne 4
Lee, General Robert E., C.S. Army 72, 73
Lee, Rear Admiral S.P., U.S.N. 48, 65, 66
Lennox, Lord Henry 122
Lincoln, Abraham 46, 51, 76, 82
Liverpool, England 13, 16–18, 20, 30, 33, 39, 44, 52, 55–57, 59, 60, 63, 65–71, 76, 78, 79, 81, 82, 85, 96, 105, 132
Livingston, Dr. David 32
Lloyd, Lieutenant H.T.R., R.M.L.I. 144
London 10–13, 44, 51, 55–57, 63, 66, 67, 77, 87, 101, 112, 140, 142, 143, 154
Lord Panmure, S.S., ordnance steamer 89, 90
Lorient, France 21
Low Moor Iron Works (Yorkshire) 32, 78
Ludlam, Thomas 78
Lyons, Lord Richard, British ambassador to the U.S. 51, 56

Ma Roberts, steamboat 32
Macao, China 137
Madeira Island, Portugal 114, 116
Magdala, H.M.S. armored turret ship 141, 157
Maguire, Matthew, detective 63, 66
Majestic, H.M.S., steam ship-of-the-line 84
Mallory, Stephen R., Confederate Secretary of the Navy 5, 10, 11, 18, 20, 37, 44, 48, 52, 57, 59, 60, 70–72, 76
Malta 130, 134
Manassas, C.S.S. armored ram 23, 47
Manchester, England 33, 39, 44, 57, 105

"Manchester Martyrs" 105
Marseilles, France 19
Martini-Henry rifle 134
Mary, S.S., former S.S. *Alexandra* (intended Confederate cruiser), blockade runner 67
Maudslay, Sons and Field, marine steam engine manufacturer (London) 36, 39
May, J.W.S., Dutch Consul in Liverpool 18
Medina, H.M.S., armored gunboat 145
Medway, H.M.S., armored gunboat 145
Melbourne, Australia 37, 157
Melville, Herman 21
Memel (Klaipeda) Lithuania 81
Mersey Steel & Iron Company (Liverpool) 30–32, 63, 65
Merv, Turkmenistan 128
Messagerie Maritimes, shipbuilders (La Ciotat, France) 19
Meteor, H.M.S., armored steam floating battery 37
Miantonomoh, U.S.S., monitor 103
Milne, Vice Admiral Sir Alexander 51
Minin, armored steam frigate, Imperial Russian Navy 128, 142
Minotaur, H.M.S., armored steam frigate 20, 36, 94, 98, 104
Mississippi, C.S.S. Confederate (intended) armored turret ship 5, 61
Mississippi, U.S.S. steam paddle frigate 47
Mobile Bay, Alabama 75
Monadnock, U.S.S., monitor 103
Monarch, H.M.S., armored turret ship 97
Monitor, U.S.S. armored turret ship 3, 26–29, 31, 54
Montgomery, Alabama 18
Montreal, Quebec 126
Moore, Thomas, Governor of Louisiana 78
Morse, Freeman H., U.S. Consul in London 56, 66, 67
Murray's anchorage (Bermuda) 147

Nahant, U.S.S. armored turret ship 42
Nantes, France 61
Napier and Sons, shipbuilders (Glasgow) 26
Nasmyth, James 32, 36
Nautilus, Jules Verne's fictional submarine in *20,000 Leagues Under the Sea* 4
Nemesis, S.S., steam paddle sloop, East India Company 12–14

New Ironsides, U.S.S., armored steam frigate 41
New Orleans, Louisiana 5, 23, 47, 70, 72, 150
New York 15–17, 24, 34, 41, 43, 48, 55, 62, 77, 78
Newcastle, England 101, 131
Niagara, U.S.S., steam frigate 76
Nile, H.M.S., steam ship-of-the-line 51
Nordenfelt machine gun 130, 131, 132, 134, 142, 152, 154–156
Nore anchorage 117
North, Commander James, C.S.N. 25, 61, 62
North Carolina, C.S.S. Confederate (intended) armored turret ship 5, 61
Northumberland, H.M.S., armored steam frigate 31, 52, 114

Osborn, Captain Sherard 48

Page, Captain Thomas J., C.S.N. 70
Paget, Lord Clarence, Secretary to the Admiralty 40, 101–103
Pallas, H.M.S., armored steam corvette 89, 99
Palliser, William 106
Palmerston, Lord, Henry, Prime Minister 6, 43, 82, 83, 87
Paris 57, 58, 60, 66, 67, 72, 97
Passaic, U.S.S., monitor 41
Pegasus, H.M.S. steam sloop 137
Peking (Beijing) China 128, 155
Pelorus, H.M.S., steam corvette 54
Pembroke Castle, S.S., auxiliary cruiser 142
Penjdeh, Turkmenistan 141
Penn, John 36
Penn Trunk Engine, 36
Persia, R.M.S., Royal Mail Ship, steam paddle ocean liner, Cunard line 16
Petropavlovsk, Russia 81
Philadelphia, Pennsylvania 127
Philadelphia Navy Yard 21
Plover, H.M.S., gunboat 104
Plymouth, England, naval base and Royal Dockyard (Devonport) 84, 89, 94, 96, 128
Pollaky, Ignatius 66, 67
Pope-Hennessy, Sir John 135, 136, 140
Port Hamilton (Komundo), Korea 143
Port Royal, South Carolina 72, 76
Port Said, Egypt 134
Portland Rolling Mill, St. John, New Brunswick 150
Portsmouth, England, naval base and Royal Dockyard 13, 28,
62, 89, 93, 97, 98, 104, 108, 111, 112, 113, 116, 118, 119, 121
Portsmouth, New Hampshire, Navy Yard 5, 72, 73
Powerful, steam tug 150–151
Powhatan, U.S.S., steam paddle frigate 46, 47
Price, S. Edward, Collector of Customs at Liverpool 81
Primauguet, cruiser, French Navy 142
Prince Albert, H.M.S., armored turret ship 28, 87, 88, 97
Prince Consort, H.M.S., armored steam frigate 84, 85, 89
Princess Royal, S.S., blockade runner 75
Princeton, U.S.S., steam frigate 31
Prins Hendrik der Netherlanden, armored turret ship, Royal Netherlands Navy 18, 35, 98
Punch, magazine 2, 4
Puritan, U.S.S., monitor 76

Quail, H.M.S., torpedo boat 147
Quebec, Canada 114
Queen Victoria 49, 85, 144
Queenstown (Cobh), Ireland, 112, 113
Quick Firing guns (QF) 154; 3-pounder 147; 6-inch 147–149; 6-pounder 147

Rainbow, H.M.S., gunboat 116
Raleigh, H.M.S. steam frigate 129
Ram 2, 3, 21–25, 70
Rattler, H.M.S., gunboat 152
Reed, Sir Edward J. 7, 10, 82, 83, 86, 87, 89, 92, 98, 99, 103, 108, 109, 112, 115, 118, 121, 134, 143, 154
Research, H.M.S., armored steam sloop 89, 98, 99, 103, 109
Resistance, H.M.S., armored steam frigate 22, 23, 37, 52
Richmond, Virginia 5, 16, 28, 39, 44, 47, 48, 57, 60, 70, 72
Richmond, U.S.S., steam sloop 23
Rifled Breechloader (RBL) 18, 40; 4-inch 138; 40-pounder 27; 100-pounder 27
Rifled Muzzleloader (RML) 18, 30, 39, 40, 106, 156; 7-pounder 131, 133, 134; 9-inch 38, 66, 70, 74, 75, 89, 90, 106, 108, 110, 111, 117, 134, 137, 147, 151, 154–155; 9-pounder 131; 10½-inch 106, 110; 12-pounder 64; 64-pounder 118; 70-pounder 39, 54, 70, 74, 75; 300-pounder 98, 105–106, 108; 600-pounder 39
Ritchie, Colonel Harrison, U.S. Army 76, 77

Roanoke, U.S.S., steam frigate/armored turret ship 24
Rodgers, Captain John, U.S.N. 87
Rolf Krake, armored turret ship, Royal Danish Navy 26, 54, 55
Rollet de l'Isle, Charles Dominique Maurice, French Navy 142
Ross, Captain Edward FitzGerald, British Army 39
Royal Artillery 38, 107
Royal Horse Artillery 131
Royal Marines 84, 105, 107, 129, 143, 145; Royal Marine Artillery (R.M.A) 107, 136; Royal Marine Light Infantry (R.M.L.I.) 107, 144
Royal Sovereign, H.M.S. armored turret ship 28, 29, 83, 89, 107, 109, 110, 112, 138
Ruby, H.M.S., steam paddle tender 13
Russell, Earl John, British Foreign Secretary 5, 6, 51, 68, 81, 83, 84
Russell, John Scott 22, 77

Saad, Pasha of Egypt 60, 61
St. Georges, Bermuda 147, 150
St. Petersburg, Russia 141
Salt Lake City, Utah 140
Samuda Brothers, shipbuilders (London) 28
San Francisco, California 37, 103
San Jacinto, U.S.S., steam sloop 50, 56
Sanford, Henry Shelton, U.S. Consul to Belgium 66, 67
Saratoga, S.S. 127
Sartorius, Vice Admiral G.R., R.N. 21
Savannah, Georgia 12, 17, 18, 73
Scorpion, H.M.S. armored turret ship 7, 88–95, 97, 98, 101, 103, 104, 106–113, 115, 116, 118–120, 122, 123, 125, 127, 143–151, 157, 158
Scotia, H.M.S., steam paddle tug 119
Scott, Admiral Sir Percy, R.N. 54
Searchlight 151–152, 156
Semetschkin, Captain Leonid Pavlovich, Imperial Russian Navy 127
Sevastopol (Russian occupied) Ukraine 81
Seward, William, U.S. Secretary of State 30, 46, 51, 52, 63, 67, 68, 74, 82
Shanghai, China 154
Sheffield, England 32, 65, 83
Shoeburyness, England 27, 29, 39, 108
Singapore 135, 141
Slidell, John 60
Smith, Frederic 25
Smoothbore muzzleloader

(SBML): 8-inch 13; 9-inch 54; 10-inch 54; 11-inch 15, 24; 12-inch 31; 12-pounder 54; 15-inch 24, 74, 75, 77; 24-pounder 54; 32-pounder 13, 23; 68-pounder 27, 50, 110; 300-pounder 77
Snowden & Mason (Pittsburgh, Pennsylvania) 78
Southsea, England 111
Speaking tube 118, 131
Sphinx (later *Stonewall*), ironclad ram 70
Spithead anchorage (England) 7, 54, 97, 121
Squarely, A.F. 67
Stanton, Edwin, U.S. Secretary of War 46
State of California, S.S. 127
Stonewall, C.S.S., ironclad ram 70, 97
Suez Canal 127, 134
Sumner, Charles, U.S. Senator 46
Sumter, C.S.S., steam sloop 65
Swift, H.M.S., gunboat 137

Tamar, H.M.S., receiving ship 155, 156
Tattnall, Commodore Josiah, C.S.N. 11
Taylor, James 33, 125
Telescopic funnel 53, 55, 99, 101, 110, 128
Tennessee, C.S.S., casemate ironclad , 74, 75
Terrible, H.M.S., steam paddle frigate 114–116, 119
Terror, H.M.S., armored steam floating battery 50, 51
Theresa Titiens, merchant ship 89
Thomas Butler & Company (Boston) 150

Thomson, George 25
Thomson, James 25
Thomsons, shipbuilders 25
Torpedo Boats (TBs) 131, 138, 139, 142, 147, 151, 152, 154–156; 1st Class 129, 138; 2nd Class 121, 128, 129, 135, 137, 138, 142, 152; Russian 128, 154
Torpedo nets 140
Toulon, France 19
Trenholm, George 16, 17, 56
Trent, S.S. 50, 56
Trent Affair 5, 50, 51
Tripod masts 5, 90, 94, 95, 99, 128
Trusty, H.M.S., armored steam floating battery 27, 29
Tweed, H.M.S., gunboat 140, 152, 154, 155

Undaunted, H.M.S., cruiser 153

Valorous, H.M.S., steam paddle frigate 119
Vancouver, British Columbia 135
Vauxhall Foundry (Liverpool) 125
Verne, Jules 1
Vicksburg, Mississippi 43, 54, 72
Victor Emmanuel, H.M.S., ship-of-the-line, receiving ship 136, 139
Viper, H.M.S., armored corvette 115, 122, 124–127
Virginia, C.S.S., casemate ironclad 2, 23, 28, 54
Vixen, H.M.S. armored corvette 115, 122, 124–127
Vladimir Monomakh, armored steam frigate, Imperial Russian Navy 142
Vladivostok 128, 142
"Volunteer cruisers" 135
Voruz, J. 61

Walker, Robert J. 57
Warrior, H.M.S. armored steam frigate 1, 22, 35, 39–42, 47, 50, 88, 94,104, 114, 119, 125, 135, 138, 158
Washington, D.C. 10, 16, 27, 51, 56, 74, 77, 80, 82, 140
Washington Navy Yard 73, 75
Waterwitch, H.M.S., armored corvette 115
Webb, William H. 24
Webster & Horsfall (Birmingham) 104
Wei-Hai-Wei, China 156
Welles, Gideon, U.S. Secretary of the Navy 10, 16, 45, 46, 56, 65, 74
Westwood & Baillie (London) 22
Whitehead torpedo 130, 137, 138, 149, 152
Whitworth, Joseph 39
Whitworth rifled ordnance 39, 40, 74–76
Wilkes, Rear Admiral Charles, U.S.N. 56
Willes, Admiral G. O, R.N. 113, 136, 138
William Miller & Sons (Liverpool) 67
Wilmington, North Carolina 40, 72, 73
Winchester, England 105
Wivern, H.M.S., armored turret ship 7, 53, 88–91, 93–106, 108, 111, 112, 115–124, 127, 128, 129, 131, 132, 134–143, 151–158
Woolwich Arsenal 1, 89, 90, 106, 108, 111, 131
Woolwich dockyard 62

Yelverton, Admiral Hastings R., R.N. 100

www.ingramcontent.com/pod-product-compliance
Lightning Source LLC
Chambersburg PA
CBHW080805300426
44114CB00020B/2837